Ancient Maya Pottery

MAYA STUDIES

UNIVERSITY PRESS OF FLORIDA

Florida A&M University, Tallahassee
Florida Atlantic University, Boca Raton
Florida Gulf Coast University, Ft. Myers
Florida International University, Miami
Florida State University, Tallahassee
New College of Florida, Sarasota
University of Central Florida, Orlando
University of Florida, Gainesville
University of North Florida, Jacksonville
University of South Florida, Tampa
University of West Florida, Pensacola

Ancient Maya Pottery

Classification, Analysis, and Interpretation

Edited by James John Aimers

Foreword by Diane Z. Chase and Arlen F. Chase

University Press of Florida

Gainesville/Tallahassee/Tampa/Boca Raton

Pensacola/Orlando/Miami/Jacksonville/Ft. Myers/Sarasota

This publication is made possible in part with support from
The Research Foundation of the State University of New York.

Printed in the United States of America on acid-free paper

This book may be available in an electronic edition.

First cloth printing, 2013
First paperback printing, 2014

Ancient Maya pottery : classification, analysis, and interpretation / edited by James John Aimers ; foreword by Diane Z. Chase and Arlen F. Chase.
p. cm. -- (Maya studies)
Includes bibliographical references and index.
ISBN 978-0-8130-4236-7 (cloth: alk. paper)
ISBN 978-0-8130-6092-7 (pbk.)
1. Maya pottery--Classification. 2. Mayas--Antiquities. I. Aimers, James J. II. Chase, Diane Z. III. Chase, Arlen F. (Arlen Frank), 1953- IV. Series: Maya studies.
F1435.3.P8A64 2012
972.81--dc23
2012031675

The University Press of Florida is the scholarly publishing agency for the State University System of Florida, comprising Florida A&M University, Florida Atlantic University, Florida Gulf Coast University, Florida International University, Florida State University, New College of Florida, University of Central Florida, University of Florida, University of North Florida, University of South Florida, and University of West Florida.

University Press of Florida
15 Northwest 15th Street
Gainesville, FL 32611-2079
http://www.upf.com

Contents

Figures

Tables

Foreword

A decade ago, when we decided to start the Maya Studies series with the University Press of Florida, we did so with two specific targeted books in mind. The first of these was a volume that synthesized all of the results of the various archaeological projects that were then taking place in central Belize; that volume was published by the press in 2004 as *The Ancient Maya of the Belize Valley: Half a Century of Archaeological Research*, edited by James Garber. The second book that we solicited was one that dealt with new approaches to and issues in Maya ceramic analysis. While this second book took a bit longer to come to fruition, it was worth the wait. *Ancient Maya Pottery: Classification, Analysis, and Interpretation*, edited by James John Aimers, is an excellent contribution to understanding Maya pottery and how it is analyzed and interpreted.

For a Maya archaeologist, ceramics are crucial to interpreting the archaeological record. Large numbers of pottery sherds are found at all Maya sites. To some extent, they are both a bane and a blessing for archaeologists. They are a blessing because they can be dated and used to interpret past societies—provided that their stratigraphic and contextual situations are understood; they are a bane because their quantity and often poor preservation make them difficult and time-consuming to analyze. Pottery is plastic and malleable, changing to reflect cultural mores and preferences. In a society that did not use metal objects until very late in their history, this meant that most containers were made of pottery and that these containers morphed into different forms and styles as time passed. Thus, ceramics are a keystone in Maya archaeology for relative dating, for interpreting social differences within past groups at any one point in time, and for determining contextual functions.

Spectacular examples of Classic period Maya polychrome ceramics (A.D. 250–A.D. 900) are rightly prized by the countries in which they have been found, and many examples are professionally displayed in the world's museums. However, the vast majority of Maya pottery does not meet this artistic standard, and most of the materials with which archaeologists work would never be placed on exhibit. Yet all pottery—whether beautiful or mundane, partial or whole—is of great significance to archaeological interpretation, and methodology relating to its classification and interpretation is important for an understanding of past civilizations.

Ceramics first appeared sometime after 1200 B.C. in the Maya area; exactly what constitutes the earliest Maya pottery is still under discussion. The earliest ceramic complexes (Swasey, Cunil, Eb, Xe, Ox, and Ek), distributed throughout the Maya region, are among the least well known because of how difficult they are to locate archaeologically. Cunil pottery, described in detail in this volume, is one of the earliest known ceramic complexes from the Maya area, but whether it is in fact Maya is contested. Transitional ceramic complexes, occurring at times of change in the Maya past, are similarly difficult to identify, define, and interpret—whether they are the orange wares and polychromes that appeared between the Preclassic and Classic periods or the modeled wares, fine wares, and red wares relating to the transition between the Classic and Postclassic periods. Attempts at better defining and interpreting these enigmatic materials—as is undertaken by almost half the chapters in this volume—provide great benefit to all students of Maya archaeology.

Pottery will always be of critical importance to the archaeological interpretation of ancient Maya society. This book provides a needed background to the serious issues involved in the classification and interpretation of Maya ceramics and also addresses the significance of ceramic analysis for defining transitions that occur within the archaeological record. The chapters in this volume will have lasting value for researchers engaged in both Maya studies and ceramic analysis in other parts of the world.

Diane Z. Chase and Arlen F. Chase
Series Editors

Preface

Most of the chapters in this volume originated as papers presented at two electronic symposia held at the Society for American Archaeology (SAA) meetings in 2005 and 2007, and all deal in one way or another with type: variety-mode method and theory.[1] I organized the 2005 symposium because I was struggling with the classification of Postclassic period pottery from Lamanai in northern Belize.[2] Having worked previously in the upper Belize River valley, I was accustomed to using Gifford's (1976) Barton Ramie study as the basis of my work, which mainly amounted to the identification of wares, groups, types, and varieties established by Gifford and the other contributors to the 1976 volume. There are problems with *Prehistoric Pottery Analysis and the Ceramics of Barton Ramie in the Belize Valley* (Gifford 1976), some of which I address in the conclusion of this volume, but that classic work is still the backbone of most studies in the Belize Valley.

When I got to Lamanai in northern Belize, I was faced with a large collection of well-preserved pottery that had not been previously classified using the type-variety system. Because the Lamanai collection is, in my opinion, one of the most important ceramic collections in the Maya lowlands, and because its original excavator, David Pendergast, has been a critic of the type-variety approach (see, for example, Pendergast 1979:33), I was hesitant to assign type-variety names immediately, based on my more-or-less intuitive recognition of stylistic groupings. As a first step I set out to identify the standard methods of type-variety. This brought me back to an issue I had noticed in the Belize Valley, which has been discussed by Rice (1976): problems with the ware concept. Even if one ignores the original concept, which includes both paste and surface characteristics (as Willey and colleagues [1994] did for Copán), in a type-variety classification one must decide where to place paste variation.[3] Does it belong at the top of the hierarchy to define wares or some similar category (such as Rice's paste wares), at the bottom to define varieties, or as a modal quality associated with any of the hierarchical levels of type-variety?

When I walked into the symposium in April 2005 this was the main issue on my mind, but there was much more in store. In an electronic symposium, papers are posted in advance on a Web site and the two hours of the meeting are devoted to discussion of them, so I was expecting a fairly placid conversation about archaeological method. What I experienced was one of the most impassioned discussions I have seen at the SAA meetings since I began attending in 1991. There seemed to be disagreements at every turn, not just about the ware concept but about what type-variety actually is, what it can (or should) do, and especially about how to use it. By the time I left the room two hours later it was abundantly clear to me that there are many versions of type-variety and very little agreement about its goals and methods. This prompted a second symposium in 2007 where the discussion was more subdued but no less useful, and thus this volume came into being.

Compiling and editing this volume has taught me a great deal about Maya pottery generally and type: variety-mode classification specifically, but I am now only more aware of the complexity of many of the issues and how much I have to learn. It is surreal to edit a volume with scholars who have been so influential in the study of Maya pottery. As I put together these chapters I continually drew upon their expertise, as well as that of others not directly involved in the volume, such as Carol Gifford, and I am grateful to them all for their patience and intellectual generosity. I hope that this volume is useful to others who, like me, continue to grapple with the issues raised by ancient Maya pottery classification, analysis, and interpretation.

Notes

1. The term *type-variety* was coined soon after the concepts of types and varieties were established (as in Smith, Willey, and Gifford's classic 1960 *American Antiquity* article). Later, the term was expanded to *type: variety-mode* (e.g., Gifford 1976: 41–42) to indicate that modal attributes were not consistently presented in type and variety descriptions and more explicit ways of dealing with modes were desirable (see, e.g., the various tables in Sabloff 1975: ch. 4, and Forsyth's 1983 use of paste and other modes). Independent modal classification has only inconsistently been part of published type-variety reports, however, so I do not think it is accurate to use the term *type: variety-mode* in all cases. There is also variation in the terminology used by different writers. Compare, for example, Culbert and Rands's (2007) general use of the term *type-variety* in an article that mentions type: variety-mode classification (but hyphenates the three terms as *Type-Variety-Mode*) and Adams's (2008) consistent use of the term *Type: Variety-Mode*. There is probably a good argument to be made to use *type: variety* and *type: variety-mode*, because the colon between the first two terms reflects the intimate connection between types and their varieties and is also used in notation (e.g., San Felipe Brown: San Felipe Variety), whereas the

hyphen nicely indicates the less consistent and potentially separable inclusion of modal data in type variety. In this volume I have chosen to use the general term that seems most appropriate (uncapitalized) for the study or topic at hand (sometimes *type: variety-mode* but more commonly *type-variety*) and to allow the individual authors to decide which term to use.

2. The terms *pottery* and *ceramics* are used interchangeably in this volume, as they normally are in Maya archaeology, but the term *ceramics* is sometimes used to refer only to high-fired or vitrified cooking and serving utensils and art objects (for a discussion, see Rice 1987c: 3–6).

3. I use the term *paste* to refer to the composition of fired pottery excluding surface treatment, but the term *fabric* for the fired product is more accurate. *Paste* should refer to the clay or clay mixture used to produce the pottery before firing (see definitions in Rice 1987c). This distinction is more consistently made in Old World archaeology than in New World studies (see comments in Howie 2005).

1

Introduction

JAMES JOHN AIMERS

The ancient Maya produced a broad range of pottery, which has attracted concerted scholarly attention for nearly a century. The authors of the chapters in this volume address a range of issues around the classification, interpretation, and analysis of ancient Maya pottery linked in one way or another to the type: variety-mode approach. Given the many years of research devoted to Maya pottery, one might expect that there would be agreement over the goals and methods of the type: variety-mode approach, but as I note in the preface, this is not the case. In fact, it seems that every Maya archaeologist has an opinion on type-variety, including (and perhaps especially) those who know little about it. The authors of the chapters here also do not agree on a number of issues, and no doubt readers will have plenty to say. In this chapter, I present a brief review of each of the chapters. In the concluding chapter, I address some of the issues that have been raised about type: variety-mode more generally.

In the chapter that follows this one, Prudence Rice provides a concise historical and theoretical introduction to type-variety and discusses important aspects of classification in general. She highlights the difference between a positivist view of classification, in which types are defined in any number of ways depending on the questions one is asking, and what Hill and Evans (1972) have characterized as an empirical view in which types are seen to be inherently meaningful (for example, as expressions of individual and group values and norms, as in the work of Gifford and others). She links the empirical view to the "revisionist history" of Gifford's (1976: 6) claim that type-variety is conceptually based on whole vessels and argues that type-variety was in fact intended to help manage large amounts of sherds, a task to which it is well suited.

Rice also returns to the issues she raised in her important article on the ware concept (Rice 1976). She reiterates and further explains her argument that paste and surface should be treated separately and the value of the category of "paste ware" for paste alone. She follows this point with an example from her research in the Petén Lakes region (in this volume, see also chapters by Cecil and by Urban and colleagues). Rice also discusses ceramic systems, a somewhat neglected concept that I find very useful (see Henderson and Agurcia 1987; Urban and Schortman 1987; Wheat et al. 1958; in this volume, see also chapters by Aimers and Graham and by Bill). Systems lump stylistically analogous types (that is, ceramics that look basically the same and are from the same period but have been given different type names for various reasons). Rice is a leader in the study of archaeological ceramics, and her contribution to this volume provides an excellent starting point for the chapters that follow.

In her contribution, Cassandra Bill addresses some of the integrative categories of type-variety, including ones that are commonly used (types and spheres) and others that are rarely used (such as horizons and systems). Appropriately (or perhaps ironically), Bill creates a classification of systems and spheres. Bill identifies two types of systems (which we might call regular and long-lived) and three types of spheres.

Because systems as originally defined lump together types, which are typically associated with a particular time period (phase), they are not normally conceived as long-lived. Following observations by archaeologists working in Honduras, where the systems concept has been used most extensively, Bill reminds us that styles often continue through time (that is, across phases identified as ceramic complexes) and that the concept of system can thus be used to lump analogous types that continue through time (that is, stylistically similar ceramics that span multiple phases/complexes). She notes that these long-lived systems are rather like ceramic traditions without the spatial restriction characteristic of traditions, and because systems are ideally relatively circumscribed in time she suggests calling these long-lived systems "macro-traditions."

Bill looks closely at the concept of spheres, which group together entire ceramic complexes when they share a majority of their most common types (See Ball 1976 for a good discussion). Bill makes distinctions between at least three kinds of spheres. First, there are spheres in which pottery vessels themselves are produced and exchanged across a region, indicating a relatively high level of economic integration in that area. I think of these as "economic" or "production and distribution" spheres. Types in these kinds of spheres would be identical down to the varietal level. Second, there are spheres in which pottery *styles* are produced and exchanged across a region, indicating shared ceramic production practices and social interaction of some sort but not necessarily a high level of economic integration in that area. I think of these as "social" or perhaps "stylistic" spheres in which types are shared but are expressed locally through varieties designated (as varieties normally are) based on differences in technological attributes, minor formal attributes, or both. Third, there are spheres in which the same *conventions* are found at different sites but are manifest in ceramics that are different enough to be considered different types. Nevertheless, the similarities of the types in such a sphere would be close enough so that they could be lumped into a ceramic system, so I think of these as "systems spheres." This third type of sphere is intriguing because it resolves a problem raised by the fact that some archaeologists use existing type names when analyzing a new sample, whereas others prefer to assign new type names. As Bill notes, using the same type names may suggest closer similarities than there are between samples; assigning new types does the opposite. Henderson and Agurcia (1987: 433) have also suggested creating sphere-like entities based on systems, and I agree since it resolves this methodological bind and allows us to efficiently use ceramics to address questions of interaction (Aimers 2007a, 2007b). Bill's different types of spheres are concepts through which we may refine our approaches to different kinds of interaction (for example, vessel exchange versus stylistic emulation).

The complexity of Bill's ideas here will hopefully stimulate reflection on our varied and often uncritical (or worse, simplistic) use of some of the categories she discusses, and perhaps further refinement of them. One of the gratifying elements of her chapter is that it squarely addresses a common criticism of type-variety: the idea that type-variety classifications tell us little about ancient Maya ideas and practices (or Maya "culture" more generally). As Bill shows with a number of specific examples, each of the concepts she discusses can be used as a starting point for inferences about ancient Maya life, especially the relationships among groups of potters (or potentially even individual potters) and the communities of which they were a part. Type-variety need not be used as anything other than a common language—that alone is of great benefit—but the idea that type-variety *cannot* usefully be used as a basis for cultural inferences is discredited by the array of observations Bill derives from just a few of the concepts of type-variety.

Arlen Chase and Diane Chase's chapter serves as a counterpoint to Bill's because they highlight the inadequacies of type-variety. They argue for context-based approaches to Maya pottery with an emphasis on the associations of whole vessels and refitting of sherds because full or reconstructable vessels from good primary deposits are the ideal material from which to derive information about ancient Maya behaviors and beliefs. Unfortunately, this is not always possible, for any number of reasons (for example, when excavations are limited due to funding or as part of early investigations at a site). I suspect that fewer and fewer projects will have the resources to engage in the sort of intensive sampling the Chases quite reasonably advocate. The reality is that we are often forced to deal with poor samples of sherds (sometimes eroded ones) from secondary or poorly understood contexts. If the resources of the two major projects at Tikal could not solve some of these issues, one wonders how small projects could hope to do so.

Despite beginning the chapter with a provocative quotation from Thompson (1970),[1] the Chases end on a more conciliatory note with comments similar to those made by Culbert and Rands (2007): we can derive the most information from Maya pottery when we use multiple approaches. This is a theme that runs through this volume as a whole, and I return to it in the concluding chapter.

In his contribution, Robert Fry interrogates assumptions about pottery production and exchange with case studies from two regions using monochrome slipped bowls and unslipped jars—the more ordinary pottery of the Maya, which has not been given as much attention in regard to these issues. Because of issues of sample size, Fry (unlike the authors of other chapters in the volume) does not use type-variety, but this would be easy to do with significant samples. Instead, Fry uses multidimensional scaling (MDS) to conduct what is essentially a complex modal analysis. Importantly, due to the relatively homogenous geology of the region, stylistic variables were more revealing of regional patterning than were technological attributes.

In my contribution with Elizabeth Graham, we describe how ceramics have been approached at Lamanai, Belize. Several people are conducting multiple independent analyses of the ceramics using contextual associations of vessels, type: variety-mode classification, material science approaches, and iconographic analysis. We emphasize type-variety in the chapter, particularly the usefulness of ceramic system assignments as a preliminary stage of analysis or for sherds that lack important features diagnostic of specific types, as well as poorly preserved sherds. We also briefly indicate some of the results of combining various approaches to pottery at Lamanai.

At this point the focus of the volume shifts slightly from chapters oriented to method and theory to chapters that deal more directly with specific sites and samples, although each of these also has much to say about pottery classification and analysis generally.

Lauren Sullivan and Jaime Awe discuss the pottery of the earliest-known ceramic complex in the Maya region, Cunil, which they date from 1100 to 900 B.C. As the authors note, because these dates are so early, the Cunil ceramics have been assessed very cautiously. For those outside the debates around the

Preclassic period and its pottery, this chapter may appear straightforward, but it represents nearly two decades of work on the definition of the Cunil complex, especially its dating, and the result of years of discussion among archaeologists.

Sullivan and Awe's chapter makes a fitting starting point to this section of the volume not only because the Cunil complex is the earliest currently known pottery complex in the Maya lowlands but also for the attention they draw to one of the most basic functions of type-variety analysis: stylistic comparison for chronological assessment. The capabilities of radiocarbon dating still do not match the precision of date estimates that can be gained by close stylistic analysis of Maya pottery (especially for later and better-known periods like the Late Classic, where archaeologists now discuss chronology in hundred- or even fifty-year segments with some confidence). Overconfidence in ^{14}C dates can lead to serious misunderstandings, as in the confusion and controversy caused by the misdating of the Swasey complex at Cuello based on ^{14}C dates (see, for example, Andrews and Hammond 1990; Hammond et al. 1979; Kosakowski 1998). Sullivan and Awe note that it was "gratifying" to see the level of agreement among different archaeologists when samples of Cunil pottery were laid out stratigraphically at the Belize Ceramic Workshop in 2007 and compared directly with those of Swasey and other complexes by archaeologists intimately familiar with these materials. This reinforces Ball and Taschek's observation in this volume that hands-on visual inspection of pottery is not just desirable but essential for reliable comparisons, a fundamental point that is too often overlooked.

Sullivan and Awe present here their preliminary typology of the wares, groups, types, and varieties of the Cunil complex. These provide a succinct language for further discussion of Cunil across the Maya lowlands; as they note, this discussion has already begun. But, as they caution, types are always open to further revision. Although I have only been on the margins of the protracted discussions about Cunil, I suspect this revision will continue, as it should for this early and very important pottery and, in fact, any Maya pottery.

In their chapter, Michael Callaghan, Francisco Estrada-Belli, and Nina Neivens investigate the idea that the glossy orange-slipped polychrome pottery produced in the late Terminal Prelassic to early Early Classic period in the Holmul region was a form of "social currency" linked to the emergence of formal elite power signified in various ways (for example, the appropriation of sacred space for elite burials). They note, however, that these fancy serving vessels are found not only in elite contexts but also in ritual contexts of various sorts, including *chultuns* and caves. Reporting on some of the findings in Callaghan's

(2008b) dissertation, the authors combine manufacture-related evidence with distributional and stylistic data to suggest that the change from glossy red-slipped pottery to glossy orange-slipped vessels reflects more general changes in worldview that may be linked to changes in social structure. They discuss technological attributes (including paste recipes, firing technology, and surface finish), possible number of production groups, and distribution within the region and beyond. Overall, it seems that the number of production groups expanded through time, or at least that manufacturing technologies became more varied. Specifically, Preclassic period monochrome Sierra Red vessels showed less technological variation than later orange-slipped types (both monochrome and polychrome).

The usefulness of type-variety here as a descriptive language is clear, but the complexity indicated by the technological analyses is much greater than that conveyed by stylistic or formal classification alone. Notably, paste recipes crosscut stylistic types, suggesting that a single production group made multiple stylistic types with essentially the same technology (for similar examples from Lamanai, Belize, see Howie 2005). Another important finding in terms of the themes of this volume is that orange-slipped ceramics were not introduced to the Holmul region from elsewhere in the Terminal Preclassic but derived from local production traditions (see, for example, Brady et al. 1998).

The authors conclude with some speculative but provocative suggestions about possible links between changes in technological style (as defined by Lechtman 1977) and social structure and worldview, including the idea that crushed sherd (grog) temper in new vessels represents an attempt to connect with the past. Milbrath and Peraza (this volume) note a similar idea in reference to ethnohistorical evidence that temper made from ground Chen Mul Modeled censers was used in the manufacture of new ones as a means to transfer the power of the deity image (Chuchiak 2009). Callaghan and colleagues suggest, conversely, that the abandonment of grog temper may reflect an attempt to break with the past. Overall, this chapter is well suited to this volume since it demonstrates how productive the use of multiple analytical techniques can be in the study of ancient Maya pottery. The combination of stylistic analysis and technological analysis provides a window into ancient Maya behavior (and, as they suggest, perhaps worldview as well) that neither could provide alone.

In a chapter rich with culture-historical interpretations as well as methodological commentary, Joseph Ball and Jennifer Taschek begin with the useful reminder (via Robert Sonin) that type-variety classification is not analysis but merely a step toward analysis (see also quotes from Dunnell in Rice's chapter). Too often in Maya archaeology there is a sense that type-variety classification is standard operating procedure for pottery and if one simply "does" type-variety, then any number of interpretations on a variety of topics can then be extracted from the classification. I believe this is a part of a usually unexamined assumption that all type-variety classifications are essentially equivalent and easily comparable. On the contrary, the questions one is posing will shape how the classification proceeds (as Rice notes at the beginning of her chapter, the corollary is that classifications also limit the research questions one can address), so research questions should be defined *before* the classification begins. Once the questions and methods of classification are defined, classification occurs and the analysis flows from there (see also Aimers 2009).

Similarly, Ball and Taschek conclude their chapter by forcefully emphasizing the need for hands-on examination of sherds and vessels in type-variety identifications/classifications and the related inadequacy of publications for this task. Their distinctions between *identities* (ceramics that are stylistically and technologically indistinguishable) and *homologies* (ceramics that share stylistic elements but are technologically distinguishable) are essential to their interpretations yet usually impossible based on photographs or illustrations alone. The need for firsthand observation may seem obvious in a discipline as empirical as archaeology, yet it is astonishing—even scandalous—how often people make assessments based on written descriptions and/or black-and-white illustrations alone, and the problems this procedure causes are disconcerting. Erroneous equivalencies between ceramics at different sites and the opposite (a proliferation of identical types with different names) are just two of the problems this procedure causes.

This chapter also contains examples of how ceramic phases may overlap in time and space. Ceramic phases are not always sequential: they can overlap or be separated by a hiatus, or they can be partially overlapping and partially sequential (see also comments by Urban and colleagues, this volume). This complexity is not easy to diagram or describe but fits better with the reality of stylistic change. Even today where stylistic change is rapid in many areas (for example, in fashion or interior design), new styles do not immediately and totally replace old ones, yet in archaeological ceramic chronology the battleship curves that were the basis of the earliest stylistic seriations are often ignored in the presentation of data. Foias (2004) and Forsyth (1983) have discussed this; Gifford (1976: 5) explains the logic behind it. Thus, even the slanted and dotted lines and the nested Xcocom *a* phase in Ball and Taschek's chronological chart make important methodological points.

In substance, Ball and Taschek's chapter is a reevaluation of their older ideas about the significance of the Xcocom phase ceramics at Becán using the strengths of type-variety: intersite comparison and chronology. Ball and Taschek both redate and reinterpret the meaning of these deposits, arguing that Xcocom comprises two subcomplexes (Xcocom *a* and Xcocom *b*), representing a Gulf Coast/Puuc-associated occupation and a Caribbean-associated one, respectively. This highlights another often-overlooked characteristic of type-variety: classifications are not meant to fossilize after publication but should always remain open to reassessment and refinement as data accumulate. The fact that many archaeologists acknowledge this (for example, Gifford 1976: 20; Forsyth 1989: 7) has not prevented fossilization from occurring. Continual revision is, of course, the nature of science as well.

I suspect, as Ball and Taschek indicate, that their specific culture-historical interpretations (for example, about Itza invasion at Acanmul) may be questioned and, as usual, more excavation would be useful, as they acknowledge. Still, their chapter is unusually clear in revealing the processes through which ceramic data (including contexts and associations), type-variety methods, and culture-historical interpretation are linked.

Patricia Urban, Edward Schortman, and Marne Ausec examine their use of type-variety classification to identify the Early Postclassic in three areas of Honduras. Like Sullivan and Awe, these authors stress the flexibility of type: variety-mode, which they continue to modify as new types of data are recognized and new questions are asked. While recognizing some shortcomings (particularly that type-variety alone tells us little about vessel function), they argue that type: variety-mode has been useful for the identification of spatial and temporal variation and has allowed them to deal efficiently with sherd samples that sometimes number in the millions (a prospect that makes me shudder) in a relatively small area with striking pottery diversity.

They make these points with discussions of the three areas. In the middle Ulua–Santa Barbara area, the identification of the Early Postclassic was relatively straightforward due to the emergence of new types—including a new type within an existing group—and some reliable nonlocal markers such as Las Vegas Polychrome. They caution, however, against reliance on nonlocal markers, because such markers were not present at all loci known to have Early Postclassic occupation based on shifts in the presence or absence of local types.

For the Naco Valley area, they note that in the absence of ceramic markers of the Early Postclassic they relied on negative evidence (the absence of common Early Postclassic types) and shifts in the frequencies of types. In the Middle Chamelecon-Cacaulapa zone, they note first the great variety of paste formulas in use with the same surface treatments (for a similar case see Rice, this volume) and the fact that increasing coarseness in paste composition has been a useful temporal diagnostic. Thus, they have used paste as an important distinguishing feature in their classifications, as do Rice and others. Shape-based modes are also important to their work, but new vessel forms do not appear and disappear neatly—their relative frequency changes.

Leslie Cecil's chapter, like the contribution by Callaghan and colleagues, demonstrates the advantages of combining information gleaned from technological and stylistic analysis. In this case, the focus is predominantly on slips, although research on pastes is included, and Cecil is able to incorporate another valuable type of information: ethnohistorical accounts of the Petén Lakes groups, especially the Kowoj and Itza. By marshalling these disparate sources, Cecil is able to make suggestions about links between style, technology, and sociopolitical identity and even trading patterns that would remain speculative using archaeological data alone.

One of the exciting aspects of Cecil's research is her ability to link patterns in the pottery data with these ethnohistorically and historically known groups. Thus, her work contributes to a substantial literature in ceramic studies on the contested links between style (technological and otherwise) and identity, particularly the problematic concept of "ethnic" identity (for an entire volume on the concept of ethnicity in Maya studies, see Sachse 2006). Debates over the presence or definition of ethnicity among the ancient Maya aside, Cecil concludes that the multiple known sociopolitical groups in the Petén Lakes region shared some of their manufacturing traditions and that trade among these groups was relatively unrestricted. Again, the productivity of bringing multiple sources of data and interpretive frameworks to bear on Maya ceramics is evident.

In their chapter, Susan Milbrath and Carlos Peraza discuss the famous Chen Mul Modeled full-figure effigy censers of Mayapán. Variants of these are found across the Maya area in the Late Postclassic; in an article we wrote with Lynda Folan (Milbrath et al. 2008), we argued that archaeologists should be more cautious in using the Chen Mul Modeled type name for effigy censers with significant stylistic variation from the Mayapán censers. We suggested that many people are using the Chen Mul Modeled type name like a system name, to identify broad stylistic similarity that nevertheless encompasses significant local variation that may be of use in mapping intersite and interregional interaction.

Milbrath and Peraza provide the most comprehensive summary to date of the possible origins of Chen Mul and conclude that the origins of this ceramic system in all likelihood lie to the west of the Maya heartland in the Late and Terminal Classic, possibly as part of the famous Mixteca-Puebla tradition at sites like Cacaxtla and Cholula, or perhaps on the Gulf Coast. In any case, the most current data suggest that the style is first found at Mayapán near the beginning of the thirteenth century.

The authors also provide a concise and well-illustrated stylistic description of the Chen Mul Modeled censers from Mayapán, an analysis that brings together formal, iconographic, ethnohistorical, and even linguistic evidence and will be of great value to Maya scholars given the widespread distribution of the Chen Mul Modeled system. Near the end of the chapter, they point out that the central Mexican deities depicted on Chen Mul Modeled censers at Mayapán suggest trade contacts between the site and the central highlands (for example, the Aztec empire) at the end of the fourteenth century and into the fifteenth. They note that Mayapán's most famous export, Maya blue pigment, was one of the Maya elements that went west; this may help explain why Mayapán shows such strong iconographic connections to the central highlands of Mexico.

Along with Petén polychromes, the Mayapán Chen Mul Modeled censers are icons of Maya pottery in general because of the visual richness of their style and iconography. The widespread distribution of the Chen Mul Modeled ceramic system makes it an excellent resource for understanding ceramic exchange and stylistic interaction. Milbrath and Peraza's chapter provides a wealth of insights of value to those of us trying to reconstruct Postclassic patterns of interaction across the Yucatán Peninsula and beyond.

As a whole, the chapters in this volume raise a host of issues about type: variety-mode specifically and the study of Maya pottery more generally. Given what I saw at the symposia from which most of the chapters are derived, there will no doubt be disagreement among archaeologists about some of the opinions expressed and the various conclusions reached. I address some of the broader issues in the concluding chapter to the volume.

Note

1. In response, I am tempted to create a type called Abracadabra Black, although placenames are more typically used in type names.

2

Type-Variety

What Works and What Doesn't

PRUDENCE M. RICE

> Because classifications organize and structure data, they inevitably also organize and structure the formulation of research problems. However, classifications are only tools: they are a means to an end, not ends themselves. Thus it is necessary to ask continually if the goals and the procedures of ceramic research are existing in optimal relationships, or if classificatory systems, which are always conservative and resistant to innovation, may be impeding rather than enhancing ceramic research.
>
> Rice 1982: 48

The type-variety system has been used for pottery classification in the Maya area for nearly half a century, surviving—or "doomed to success" (Adams 2008)—despite recurrent attacks. The type-variety approach works well at what it was originally intended to do—structure descriptions of archaeological pottery for spatiotemporal comparisons—but its detractors complain when it fails to accomplish things far beyond this goal. Different units of the type-variety system can have different kinds and degrees of utility, depending on the goals of any particular analysis, but type-variety is, first and foremost, simply a hierarchical framework for organizing descriptive data about pottery.

Pottery Systematics: An Overview of Classification

Study of a collection of archaeological pottery generally proceeds in three stages or levels: classification, analysis, and interpretation or explanation (Hill and Evans 1972: 234; Rice 1982: 48–49). My focus in the following discussion is on the first and lowest level, classification and its constituent procedures. *Analysis* (Greek, "break up, loosen, separate") involves collapsing a collection (of pottery) into some set of constituent attributes to determine their nature, proportions, and/or relations; thus, pottery analysis may be stylistic, compositional, modal, morphological, and so forth. The highest level of study is *interpretive* or explanatory, in which the pottery of interest is situated into some broader context (theoretical, spatial, chronological, social, economic) to contribute to the resolution of a theoretical issue, answer a question, or solve a problem.

Classification (also known as taxonomy or systematics) refers to the most general scientific process of ordering objects, be they potsherds, plants, or animals. The process involves organizing the objects into "similarity groups" based on one or more characteristics of interest. Members of similarity groups are more similar to each other than they are to members of other groups. This "high within-group homogeneity" is the goal of all scientific systematics and informatics operations (Rice 1987c: 274–76). Classificatory activities may be pursued in two ways, through categorization or identification.

Categorization is the creation of groups of previously unclassified or ungrouped materials. An example would be a ceramic assemblage from a relatively unknown site in a relatively unexplored area or time period. Few such assemblages emerge from the heavily explored Maya lowlands in the twenty-first century, but my work at Spanish-colonial wineries in Moquegua, southern Peru, provides a case in point. Excavations produced mixtures of locally made, hand-built, pre-Hispanic pottery, plus Spanish-influenced wheel-made, tin-enameled, lead-glazed, and unglazed pottery. Initial categorization of this material was based on two variables: surface treatment (presence/absence of enamel/glazing) and technique of manufacture (wheel-thrown versus hand-built).

Categorization often results in the creation of new, provisional ceramic types: for Maya pottery, see, for example, the procedures of early classification of the pottery of Altar de Sacrificios (Adams 1971: 8–9) and Barton Ramie (Smith, Willey, and Gifford 1960: 333; Gifford 1963, 1976). Procedures of ceramic taxonomy can be contrasted with those of other archaeological materials: for example, classification of human, deer, or chicken bones does not—indeed, cannot—involve the process of categorization or naming of new types, because all such bones are already known and named.

Identification is the process of assigning individual objects to previously established classes. In the case of human bone, classification is always a process of identification: a specimen can only be identified as one of the 206 long-known and long-named bones in the human body, the variability of which is further constrained by left-side/right-side distinctions. With pottery, identification consists of evaluating objects with respect to already-established categories that set out the parameters of variability that we can expect in our collections. In the case of the Moquegua material, I compared my hand-built, unglazed sherds to numerous published reports on pre-Hispanic southern Peruvian pottery to *identify* them as examples of those materials. However, very little systematic description of early colonial Peruvian wheel-made and/or tin-enameled/glazed pottery existed. Thus, for these colonial materials I began with simple categorization and used type-variety structuring principles to create a typology (Rice 1997).

The distinction between categorization and identification seems obscurantist, but it is important. It is based on—and also illuminates the history of—what is already known or has been accomplished in Maya pottery analyses, as compared to what has not. It is important to remember that categorization and identification are empirical processes: both refer to the assignment of *actual, physical objects*, such as the Moquegua sherds, to organizing units.

This distinction between categorization and identification has been expanded and effectively diagrammed by Robert Dunnell (1971b: 94). He distinguishes between the phenomenological or empirical (objectively "real") versus the ideational ("conceptual") realms in the general activity of ordering objects, such as pottery. Dunnell also makes the distinction between "grouping" procedures and procedures of "classification proper" or paradigmatic classification sensu stricto (table 2.1).

Grouping occurs in the phenomenological (that is, materially "real") realm. It refers to the *physical* sorting (or categorization) of *actual objects*, such as sherds excavated from the Moquegua Valley, into similarity *groups* created

Table 2.1. Schematic of classificatory principles and characteristics of resultant units

REALM		
	PHENOMENOLOGICAL	**IDEATIONAL**
PROCEDURE	**GROUPING**	**CLASSIFICATION**
	(categorization)	(identification)
Creates:	Groups of objects	Conceptual classes
Based on:	Objects, single attributes	Attribute clusters, ideas
Interpretation:	Actual, historical, finite	Potential, historical, infinite
UNIT RELATIONS		
EQUIVALENT (unordered)	Statistical clustering, most modal analysis	Some modal analysis
HIERARCHICAL	Numerical taxonomy, cluster analysis	Typology, classification (e.g., Linnean; type-variety)

Source: After Dunnell 1971a: fig. 9.

for convenience. Groups are thus historical or contingent by virtue of being bounded by that finite set of objects being grouped.

Classification proper (or paradigmatic classification) is based in the ideational realm and is a *conceptual structure* for ordering *attributes or features* (not actual objects!) into *classes* that are proposed on the basis of some *criterion or theory*. The features or variables of pottery being ordered may be size, form, color, iconography, technology, composition, and so on. Criteria for their selection may be overarching social, political, economic, or other theoretical issues, concepts, or problems encompassing power, status, production, trade, feasting, ideology, mortuary ritual, and so on. In the case of the colonial Moquegua pottery, subsequent sorting criteria included glazing versus enamel, and color of the enamel.

The outcome of classification proper is the creation of a *typology*: "a theoretically oriented classification that is directed toward the solution of some problem or problems" (Gifford 1960: 346, quoting Kluckhohn) and broadly useful comparatively. The units in a typology are based on *ideas* about attributes or features—method of manufacture, kind of surface treatment, color, form—and their relations as criteria for membership. Thus typologies are, in principle, ahistorical and infinite in their spatiotemporal applicability, rather than being limited to a finite set of excavated objects on the sorting table.[1] These ideational classes also organize the phenomenological ("grouping") realm for later ordering operations—which permits the process of identification.

The advantage of paradigmatic classification systems (as opposed to groupings) lies in their replicability and testability. Groupings (statistical clusters and numerical taxonomy) are created on the basis of a *specific data set,* and their utility cannot be tested on the same set or even, technically, on a different one. An important contribution of groupings is to generate hypotheses about the formation of classes and then, subsequently, to test them with other data sets (Spaulding 1974: 515).

In summary, classification is a general term that refers to several procedures for organizing objects into units having high within-group similarity.

> *Grouping* refers to procedures of *physically sorting actual objects* to create groups of similar things, a process that may be accomplished in two ways:
>
> 1. Categorization: creation of *new* groups of objects
> 2. Identification: assigning objects to *existing* groups or categories
>
> *Classification proper*, or paradigmatic classification, refers to procedures based on, and formalized into, a typology: a conceptual structure of attributes relating to theoretical needs.

Dunnell (1971b) further distinguishes between attributes that are equivalent and of equal weight in the sorting versus those that are nonequivalent, ordered, or weighted. An example of the former is classes based on form: bowl, jar, plate, and cup are equivalent, unordered dimensions of the attribute "form," and we need not have these categories physically present to conceive of their existence. Type-variety, by contrast, is a scheme of units ordered by quasi-theoretical concepts (or objectives) in which the various pottery attributes of interest are nonequivalent and ordered in different levels. Thus, the resulting classificatory units or levels are nested: varieties are organized into types, types into ceramic groups, and ceramic groups into wares. Most simply stated, the type-variety system is a hierarchically organized typology.

The important point is that the theoretical basis of a typology is manifest in the selection of, and relations among, the attributes that underlie its ideational structure and operations. Throughout most of the twentieth century, the research problem(s) addressed by classifications of archaeological ceramics were those of comparative chronology and dating of sites. In the twenty-first century, other issues are of greater interest and may or may not be addressed by the type-variety system. Regardless, it is these underlying theoretical goals that move us beyond simple systematics and into the realms of analysis and interpretation of pottery.

Historical Development of the Type-Variety System

Methods of classification in general and type-variety in particular are a uniquely Americanist concern of the past two centuries (see Willey and Sabloff 1980), particularly with respect to determining the origins—ethno-culturally and temporally—of the indigenous inhabitants of North America and the earthen mounds in the eastern United States. Absent reliable dating methods, the study of archaeological remains was largely confined to description and development of chronologies. Advances occurred primarily in the southwestern United States in the 1930s, where vigorous and systematic efforts to create pottery types bearing chronological or historical significance, rather than simply descriptive clarity, were led by a handful of archaeologists (Gladwin and Gladwin 1930; Hargrave and Colton 1935; Colton and Hargrave 1937).

These efforts resulted in a hierarchical classificatory system built on the earlier binomial nomenclature adopted at the 1927 Pecos Convention (Kidder 1927; Willey and Sabloff 1980: 102, 128n18). For pottery, this was a variant of biological taxonomy in which the ceramic equivalent of a "genus" name refers to the surface treatment and the "species" name is taken from local geography.[2] Descriptions of types were to be presented in a set format of name, shape, decoration, "type site," cultural affiliations, and temporal data (Willey and Sabloff 1980: 102). This system was adopted in the southeastern United States (for example, Phillips 1958). At the same time, a crosscutting analytical or modal system of descriptive organization (technically, phenomenological "grouping"), based on modes/attributes rather than on sherds, was introduced by Irving Rouse (1939).

The apparent agreement on the conceptual structuring of pottery classifications in the American Southwest and Southeast was followed by two decades of disputes about practice and interpretation (see Hill and Evans 1972). The debate is typically framed in terms of two polarized positions. On the one side was James Ford (1952) and his adherents (see, for example, Brew 1946; Dunnell 1971a, 1971b), who believed types were arbitrary constructs or concepts imposed over a collection of artifacts by the archaeologist. On the other was Alfred C. Spaulding (1953), who saw types as meaningful, statistically verifiable associations of attributes discovered by archaeologists; like-minded archaeologists (see, for example, Gifford 1960; Rouse 1939) claimed that pottery types are inherent in a collection and represent the ideas ("mental templates") of the producers and users.

The contentious atmosphere was influenced by the 1948 publication of Walter W. Taylor's 1943 Harvard University dissertation, "A Study of Archaeology." In it, Taylor inveighed against archaeologists' practice of mere "comparative chronicle" and the vacuity of Maya pottery studies as practiced to date, quipping famously that "the road to Hell and the field of Maya archaeology are paved with good intentions" (Taylor 1983: 58). Taylor's dissertation was influenced by an earlier diatribe against Middle American archaeology penned by his advisor, Clyde Kluckhohn (1977 [1940]).[3] Kluckhohn, an ethnologist of the culture and personality school, promoted an emic approach: ethnographers must seek to understand the minds of their subjects, their attitudes, values, ideas, and feelings. Both publications excoriated the Carnegie Institution of Washington (CIW) and particularly Alfred Vincent Kidder for focusing on elite architecture instead of trying to understand "the culture," and both derided Carnegie's lack of rigor and theory and its emphasis on (allegedly badly written) culture history. Both advocated a more robust, "scientific" approach to archaeology, which Taylor termed "conjunctive."

Type-Variety in the Maya Lowlands

In 1960, the classificatory procedures of North American archaeology entered the realm of Maya lowland pottery studies. The main proponents were Harvard University archaeologists and students Richard E. W. Adams, Jeremy A. Sabloff, Gordon R. Willey, and particularly James C. Gifford, who had cut his teeth in Southwest archaeology and pottery classification (Gifford 1957). Earlier Maya pottery studies had followed procedures of modal or attribute analysis and description, typically segregating pottery into generic "wares" on the basis of slip color and form as at Uaxactún (Smith 1955) and San José, Belize (Thompson 1939).

In an important article in *American Antiquity*, Robert E. Smith (of the Carnegie Institution), Willey, and Gifford (1960: 332; hereafter cited as SWG 1960) announced the merger of the refined variety concept (from Wheat, Gifford, and Wasley 1958; hereafter abbreviated as WGW 1958), with the type, as modified for application in the Southeast (Phillips 1958), into what they referred to as the "type-variety concept." In the same issue, Gifford (1960) published his ideas about this method "as an indicator of cultural phenomena." The newly named type-variety "system" was adopted into the Maya area because an "explosion" of archaeological fieldwork had produced massive amounts of pottery fragments that introduced "complications . . . into the culture-historical picture," requiring a new classificatory structure to facilitate data sharing (Willey, Culbert, and Adams 1967: 290; hereafter abbreviated as WCA 1967).

Smith, Willey, and Gifford (1960: 330–31) begin their exposition of type-variety with what could be read as a tacit apologia for the Carnegie Institution's procedures, so heavily criticized by Taylor.[4] These authors claimed that the Carnegie's inadequacies resulted because "no two people followed the same definition or concept of ware and type" and because, except for some of Anna Shepard's work, compositional analyses were "largely neglected." Their solution was the type-variety concept, and they redefined various concepts, discussed methods of sorting and rules of nomenclature, and advocated integrating modal studies. They identified the variety as the "basic unit" of analysis (following WGW 1958: 35–38), suggesting that classification should begin with varieties; types and larger, more inclusive units should be distinguished later in the process (SWG 1960: 330; contra Sabloff and Smith 1969: 278).[5]

The Mayanists argued that types and varieties were "realities within the cultural configuration of their origin and it is our job as analysts to recognize" them; they were "mental templates," not merely analytical constructs imposed on a collection (SWG 1960: 332; Gifford 1960: 343). Gifford (1960: 343, 1976: 3–4) expanded the interpretation of these "realities" beyond the spatiotemporal to include societal values and "innate human tendencies." Within traditional societies, he writes, there is an acceptable range of variation in ideas, standards, and preferences about the quality of any good, such as pottery, and producers and consumers conform to these norms. Thus, varieties "closely approximate actual material ceramic manifestations of individual and small social group variation in a society" (Gifford 1960: 342). It follows, then, that types are summations of individual and small social group variation and represent the "crystallization of conscious or unconscious ceramic esthetic images conditioned by values" (Gifford 1960: 343).

I find it difficult to believe that this line of thought is anything other than a response, whether direct or indirect, to Kluckhohn's and Taylor's fierce critiques that Maya archaeology was oriented toward accumulating facts rather than driven by (cultural anthropological) theory and synthesis. Gifford (1976: 346) thanks Kluckhohn in his acknowledgments and cites two of his papers on the study of values (Kluckhohn 1951, 1958).

The introduction of type-variety to Mayanists, particularly the endlessly disputed esoterica of nomenclature (Gifford 1961), did not sail smoothly, prompting the organization of the "Conference on the Prehistoric Ceramics of the Maya Lowlands" in Guatemala City in 1965. As reported in *American Antiquity* (WCA 1967), this conference of only ten participants, all North American, included discussions of theoretical concepts and units, particularly spheres, and hands-on comparisons of actual sherds. In hindsight, the conference summary, while chronicling participants' disagreements, may convey more solidarity and acceptance than actually existed, because arguments about type-variety continued to rage throughout the 1960s and 1970s.

In 1969, Sabloff and Smith updated and critiqued current practices, including a comparison of procedures used in the Mayapán and Seibal reports. They reiterated the earlier (for example, SWG 1960) call to combine typological and analytical/modal analysis, if only by listing the principal identifying modes, and detailed the criteria for and significance of ceramic groups and wares. In a sharp counterpoint, Robert Dunnell (1971a, 1971b) assailed the type-variety system from the point of view of general systematics and positivism: "If classifications of any kind are to be devices useful in constructing explanations, . . . they must be *hypotheses about the ordering of data for a specific problem. . . . Only with specifically defined problems is it possible to evaluate the utility, parsimony, elegance, and sufficiency of a given classification*" (Dunnell 1971b: 117–18, emphasis added; also Hill and Evans 1972). Opposed to a basic premise of type-variety, Dunnell (1971b: 118) concludes that "[c]lassifications are logical constructs whose justification lies in their utility. They are not inherent, nor do they explain. They are imposed constructs that function to order data so that explanation is possible."

On Wares and Pastes and Paste Wares

I am particularly interested in the "ware" unit of type-variety classification. As defined and used by Southwestern archaeologists, a ware is "a large grouping of pottery types which has little temporal or spatial implication but consists of stylistically varied types that are similar technologically and in method of manufacture" (WGW 1958: 34–35, citing Hargrave and Colton 1935: 49–51; Colton and Hargrave 1937: 1–2). In the introduction of type-variety to Mayanists, wares were characterized as displaying "consistency in such technological attributes as paste or surface finish" (SWG 1960: 330). The report of the 1965 Maya ceramic conference described a ware as "a number of ceramic types sharing a cluster of technological attributes" (WCA 1967: 304). Later, this was elaborated such that "a defined ware is a ceramic assemblage in which all attributes of paste composition (with the possible exception of temper) and of surface finish remain constant" (Sabloff and Smith 1969: 278). Paste composition variables were those of texture, temper material, hardness, porosity, and color, whereas surface finish attributes included presence/absence of a slip, smoothness, luster/matte finish, and color.

The 1965 Maya ceramic conference reported some disagreement about where ware belonged in the hierarchical arrangement of taxonomic units: Smith felt it was a higher-order unit, "making the separation of wares the first procedural step in ceramic analysis," whereas others thought wares were more integrative and "abstracted from completed type definitions" (WCA 1967: 304). Thus, wares organized the Mayapán and Barton Ramie type-variety classifications but not the Copán analysis (Willey et al. 1994).

This ambivalence bespeaks a continuing fundamental problem with the ware unit. Note that as originally presented (SWG 1960: 330), the attributes of ware were paste *or* surface finish, echoing the Southwesternists' concern with technology. Later, wares were defined by paste *and* surface finish (Sabloff and Smith 1969: 278). More than thirty years ago, I published a commentary on type-variety, laying out my views of what "ware" should be and mean (Rice 1976). I believed then, and still believe, that identifying wares by both paste composition and surface treatment is illogical and confusing. In my view, for Maya pottery, at least, wares should be reconceived specifically as "paste wares" that refer specifically to paste characteristics alone, rather than a combination of paste and surface.

One reason is that I always have been suspicious of a too-heavy reliance on slip characteristics, particularly color variations. Slip colors can vary enormously on individual vessels fired using bonfire-type techniques, as well as by conditions of use and depositional environment (which may completely remove slips), so that it is difficult to know whether different colors were intentionally achieved or accidental.

Paste, however, is a characteristic of all sherds and pots, slipped and unslipped, no matter their size or degree of preservation. Paste composition also represents choices of clay and temper resources, primarily locally available, that allow insights into areas of manufacture and patterns of distribution. Adams (2008: 222) seems to turn this into a detriment in noting that surface treatment is "most culturally defined and influenced," whereas paste (ostensibly by negative contrast) is "greatly dependent on the clay and trace elements available locally and therefore is partially a product of natural elements that often were unknown or controlled in prehistory." But that is precisely the point, albeit garbled: clay and temper resources *are* locally available, and they *can* be characterized in the recovered pottery, thereby providing a basis for insights into manufacturing areas as well as potters' behavior.

Adams (2008: 222) goes on to complain that "paste analysis is also time consuming and therefore the sample sizes are miniscule." To the contrary, the attributes used for identifying paste wares in a field lab are those visible to the naked eye or with a 10X hand lens, including color; texture; fracture characteristics; general kinds, quantities, sizes, and shapes of inclusions; and tactile qualities (for example, the sandpapery feel of volcanic ash-tempered wares and the silty/clayey texture of Postclassic Snail-Inclusion Paste Ware). These rough field sorts can later be tested and refined by mineralogical and then chemical analyses, which permit insight into potters' decisions (Cecil 2001b, 2007, 2009). Potters make a cascade of decisions, or "technological choices," in selecting and manipulating resources on the basis of the desirability of their properties in forming, drying, decorating, firing, and using the final products (see Rice 1987c: 113–66). The decisions may be the result of experimentation or dictated by custom, but they can be revealed by rigorous research designs. For example, Leslie Cecil (1997, 2001a, 2001b, 2004, 2007, 2009; Cecil and Neff 2006) used a combination of basic classificatory and stylistic observations plus petrography, x-ray diffraction, SEM, ED-XRS, INAA, and LA-ICP-MS to characterize the pastes and pigments of Postclassic slipped and decorated pottery from sites in the Petén Lakes region (see also Cecil, this volume).

True, these latter studies are time-consuming and expensive and therefore are performed on only small samples, which must be judiciously selected to answer specific questions about the meaning of detected variability. They are properly carried out as the *final* step of analysis: basic field lab identifications of paste wares are not only useful in and of themselves but also are essential preliminaries to interpretively sound compositional studies.

Case Study: A Petén Postclassic Slipped Pottery "System"

Postclassic slipped and decorated pottery at sites in the Petén Lakes region was manufactured of three distinctive paste wares: coarse red-orange carbonate (Vitzil Orange-red Ware; A. Chase 1983), silty gray-to-brown with snail inclusions (Snail-Inclusion Paste Ware; Cowgill 1963), and marly "white" or cream (Clemencia Cream Paste Ware; Rice 1979). These indicate minimally three production nodes of Petén Postclassic pottery, at least one for each paste. We do not know exactly where those production nodes were, although it is fairly certain that Clemencia Cream Paste Ware pottery was manufactured from clays in the vicinity of the Topoxté Islands and Lake Yaxhá (Cecil 1997). Snail-Inclusion Paste Ware pottery incorporates a variety of freshwater aquatic snails and hematite lumps, apparently naturally present in these lacustrine clays (Rice 1987b: 105), and it exhibits sufficient variability in both pastes and pigments that there were probably multiple centers of manufacture in the lakes region (Cecil 2001a, 2001b; Cecil and Neff 2006).[6] These paste wares were used to manufacture the three most common red-slipped ceramic groups of the Postclassic: Augustine (Vitzil), Paxcamán (Snail-Inclusion), and Topoxté (Clemencia Cream). Besides these common red-slipped groups, we recovered small quantities of pottery with other slip colors—"pink," black, brown, and purplish red.

There is a striking coherence in the "design structure" (Friedrich 1970) of this pottery, evident in its layout: whether painted or incised, decoration appeared in circumferential bands on the interior walls of tripod dishes (Rice 1983, 1985, 1989). The bands are defined above and below by multiple lines and divided into two or four panels by vertical lines or placement of simple motifs, which also may appear inside the panels (see Rice and Cecil 2009). This decorative coherence structures the classificatory coherence of types and varieties in the slipped ceramic groups across the three paste wares: monochrome, black-painted, red-painted, and incised (table 2.2). In other words, potters across the Petén Lakes area had a fairly uniform and widely shared set of ideas about what constituted proper pottery decoration regardless of their different clay and temper resources.

By the Late Postclassic period, some significant variations in this scheme are noted: the basic structure continued at the ware and group level, but innovations occurred at the type and variety level. For example, instead of red *or* black painted decoration, there began to be red-*and*-black painted decoration. In addition, elaborate decoration began to be placed over the entire interior of tripod dishes, rather than restricted to encircling bands. By the very Late Postclassic period, still more decorative freedom can be noted

Table 2.2. Parallel distributions of decorative types and varieties within Postclassic Petén paste wares

	Snail-inclusion				Cream	Red	Uapake
Group:	Paxcamán (Red)	Fulano (Black)	Trapeche (Pink)	Macchiato (Brown)	Topoxté (Red)	Augustine (Red)	Chipotle
Types							
Monochrome	X	X	X	X	X	X (2)	X
Polychrome							
Black paint	X	X	X	X	X	X	
Red paint							
Banded		X	X		X		X
Curvilinear	X				X		
Geometric	X				X		
Red + black	X (2)				X	X	X
Incised	X	X	X		X	X	
Fine	X	X	X		X	X	
Groove	X	X	X (2)		X	X	
Incised + paint	X						
Censer	X				X		X

as greater variation and combinations of possible choices came into use: for example, some vessels exhibit both painting *and* incising, or interior *and* exterior decoration, and so on.

This pattern conforms well to what was called in Southwestern pottery analysis a "ceramic system" (WGW 1958: 39–44; see also Colton's [1943] "principle of analogous pottery types") and was introduced to lowland Maya type-variety practice by Gifford (1976) in discussing the classification of pottery from Barton Ramie. Gifford described it as having relatively little time depth: "an essentially horizontal or very shallow diagonal arrangement of roughly contemporaneous pottery types that range over a wide area and that are related to one another in particular from the standpoint of decorative treatment, design styles, and surface manipulation" and that crosscut wares (1976: 12). Gifford's examples included a possible Usulután system (Gifford 1976: 42) and an Aguacate system (Gifford 1976: 128, 322), but he did not actually apply the concept to the Barton Ramie collection. The ceramic system concept has been little used in Petén, although it was incorporated into Honduran classification schemes (Henderson and Agurcia 1987; see also Bill, this volume).

What does a ceramic system "mean"? Most obviously, it means that Postclassic Petén potters recognized and adhered to a decorative canon—a set of rules—for design structure, layout, and colors. Vessel forms and proportions varied from ware to ware and settlement to settlement, but the principles that structured what kinds of decoration were to be applied, and where and how, were strictly adhered to in at least three production resource-groups (minimally defined by paste compositions) throughout the lakes area (approximately seventy-five kilometers east–west) over three hundred years. In addition, we were eventually able to successfully *predict* the decorative types we would find (which would otherwise be a process of categorization) in each ceramic group. This is the difference between a classification structured by conceptual categories, as opposed to phenomenological groupings or modal analysis.

This Petén Postclassic ceramic system—based on the traditional rules for slipped pottery decoration—appears to have broken down in the very Late Postclassic period, with a surge in decorative variability, and a new paste ware appeared that was used not just for slipped pottery but also for unslipped vessels and censers. Significantly, the Late Postclassic in the lowlands was a time of population movements, in-migration of new groups, and general cultural disruptions. Some of the pottery appears to have declined in certain technological variables (quality of finishing, and incomplete oxidation), as is commonly noted in times of societal stress. The increase in decorative variety and freedom, plus some new forms, in Petén Postclassic pottery also coincided with an increase in hostilities among the Petén populations and vis-à-vis the immigrants, accompanied by what we believe was the assertion of distinct ethno-linguistic or social identities, Kowoj versus Itza, in this regional context (Rice and Cecil 2009).

Type-Variety: What Works and What Doesn't Work?

The type-variety system establishes a series of concepts and principles for ordering attributes and attribute clusters, and this means it can be universally applicable for purposes of organizing descriptions. Proponents of type-variety, of which I am one, highlight its advantages for quickly and efficiently handling large quantities of pottery fragments (Adams 1971: 6) and its usefulness in intersite comparisons, especially with the growth of regional and settlement pattern studies since the 1960s (Sabloff and Smith 1969: 283–84). Many users have noted the flexibility and versatility of its hierarchical structure, which allows comparative analyses at different levels of variability. Sabloff (1975: 3) noted its strengths in both categorization and identification: "[I]t is easy to work with in analyzing ceramics from a previously unstudied site."[7]

Mayanists' dissatisfactions with the type-variety system have abounded (for example, Ball 1977b, 1979b; Culbert and Rands 2007; Hammond 1972; Smith 1979), and several criticisms recur: it leaves a lot of variability unaccounted for, it should be accompanied by modal analysis, and it has limited use with whole vessels. For my part, I have long been concerned about the legacy of Gifford's mapping mentalistic meanings and values onto what are simply descriptive classes. For example, he (Gifford 1976: 32, emphasis in original) interprets

> the ceramic variety as a reflection of *overt individual* and small group behavior (Gifford 1960), the pottery type as reflecting the interplay of both *covert individualness* and *covert culturalness*, and the ceramic group as reflecting *overt culture* . . . [such] that the ceramic group is telling us of the everyday *ceramic activities* of a culture; that the pottery type is telling us of the subconscious ceramic value orientations of both the *culture* and the *individual*; and that the ceramic variety is an expression through pottery of individual or small social group ceramic preferences.

Before addressing these critiques, let us remember that the type-variety system of pottery classification used by Mayanists today had its ultimate origins in the southwestern United States in the 1930s to meet the needs of the emerging discipline of Americanist archaeology for improvements in description, nomenclature, chronology, regional integration, and culture change. Its concepts and procedures were adopted into the southeastern United States and from there into Maya archaeology in the 1960s. These beginnings are important because they help explain the how and why of type-variety practice and some of the problems perceived by Mayanists.

For example, in both the Southwest and the Southeast, the early emphasis was on surface finish. Similarly, in the Maya area, variables of surface finish and decoration were deemed most important and therefore prescribed as the basis for the first sorting, because surface finish was held to be the "most susceptible of ceramic attributes to culturally determined change" (Adams 1971: 7, 2008: 222). Regardless of the veracity of this assertion, mitigating preservation issues must be remembered: Southwestern pottery enjoys excellent preservation of its complex polychrome decoration because of the region's dry environment, and in the humid Southeast the surface finish is usually plastic manipulation, which also preserves well. However pottery from the tropical forests of the southern Maya lowlands often has eroded surfaces, making it difficult to sort reliably by surface treatment.

In addition, type-variety was developed in the Southwest to sort, classify, and organize descriptions of large volumes of pottery fragments. Many Maya archaeologists who work with whole vessels, especially complex Classic pictorial polychromes, from burials or other contexts find the type-variety system unworkable and therefore dismiss its usefulness (Ball 1994; D. Chase and A. Chase 1994: 158–60; Pendergast 1979: 28, 33). But in its original formulation, type-variety analysis was not intended for whole pots. Only with the "new archaeology" and other developments did the logical inconsistencies between studying sherds as proxies for pots come to be addressed. As Willey and Sabloff (1980: 102) commented about the Southwest, potsherds were a convenient "statistical unit highly adapted for counting and manipulation," but classifications had "grown steadily farther away from the whole pot." Concerns about "the Indian behind the artifact," as it was sometimes crudely put, prompted Gifford (1976: 6) to assert that "in conceptual substance 'type-variety' is based on whole vessels as opposed to broken pieces (sherds). Theoretical implications adduced from varieties and types are founded on the realization that the production of whole vessels was the intent of the prehistoric potters." But this is revisionist history. Today, except for comparative exercises, there is generally little need for or value added by classifying whole vessels through type-variety's formulaic organizational principles designed to create condensed descriptions.

The most recent critique of the type-variety system has come from Culbert and Robert L. Rands, whose focal complaint is that the resultant classifications do not take into consideration many variables, resulting in "the loss of important information" (2007: 181). But *all* classifications result in loss of information: it is theoretically and practically impossible for any classification to take into consideration all possible attribute states of an entity (see Dunnell 1971b: 115, 117). The fundamental issue is to specify initially what information is "important," that importance dictated by the underlying goal or purpose of the classificatory exercise.

According to the basic precepts of systematics, classes of whatever object of interest are supposed to represent something "inherently significant" in the objects as indicated by the goal of high within-group similarity. It is generally agreed that classifications structure inquiry by furnishing a system for describing and naming the objects of study, fostering communication through shared terminology and nomenclature, permitting predictions about the relation of the classified items to other objects studied, and serving as extensions of and empirical justification for concepts used within the body of theory (Rice 1982: 48, 1987c: 275, citing Blashfield and Draguns 1976: 574). How does the type-variety system stack up against these expectations for scientific taxonomies?

1. By solving a problem: Type-variety was established to aid the dating of archaeological sites through comparison of ceramic complexes. This it has done well.
2. By describing and naming objects: The type-variety system uses binomial nomenclature to name objects, the second term being a descriptor of color, decoration, and so forth. This too has worked fairly well. Color descriptions are now nearly universally supplemented with Munsell measurements (contra Sabloff 1975) as opposed to the quaint Ridgway bird-color system that gave us "Vinaceous Tawny."
3. By fostering communication: In general, when someone says Tinaja Red, Mayanists know that this is a Late Classic red-slipped type in the southern lowlands; the type name is not used for other pottery elsewhere in the lowlands, and the type is not confused with a ware or a variety.
4. By permitting predictions: This capability is illustrated above with Petén Postclassic pottery, allowing us to predict decorative variants.
5. By extending theoretical concepts: Here is where we get into trouble. In Maya ceramic studies we need to ask, Do we actually *have* any theoretical concepts that we want to extend? What are the goals of classification today? Are there problems that classifications can best handle, or are they better handled with modal analyses, as many archaeologists have asserted? To date, none of the critics of type-variety have proposed alternative, new *theory-based* goals in connection with their discontent.

As I remark in the epigram, classifications are tools and a means to an end, but for classifications to be useful we need to know what those ends *are.* Absent different and clearer (non-chronologically comparative) goals for ceramic analyses, type-variety will always come up short. If analysts are unable to equate types and varieties with meaningful social units, as Gifford hyperbolically claimed they could, we should not be surprised: given type-variety's history and the procedural sequence of classification, analysis, and interpretation, that final interpretive level today is clearly not what type-variety was originally intended to achieve.

I conclude with another pitch for wares and for keeping them in the type-variety system of pottery classification (Rice 1976; contra Culbert and Rands 2007: 185). The paste ware concept "works" both in practice and in structuring useful inferences about behavior and change. It allows us to describe objects in meaningful and comparative ways. It meets the expectations of scientific taxonomies: problem-solving, describing, and permitting predictions. It enables us to move beyond the time-space comparisons at the core of type-variety analysis and address broader social and behavioral issues, questions, and processes in ways that wares defined by slip colors cannot. It has the potential to be one of the most interpretively useful components of the type-variety system because it allows us to integrate our classificatory analyses with socioeconomic models, theories, and processes such as production (including resource procurement) and trade, all increasingly salient given the growing incorporation of physicochemical compositional studies.

The dating of sites and structures and deposits is only the first step—a very important step, but at this point only a preliminary one—in situating archaeological findings within the existing narratives of Maya culture history and change. What is more intellectually satisfying and of greater lasting interest to all of us are questions that go beyond dating to address social and/or economic activities, which in turn can and should be driven by theoretical concerns guiding the excavation of the site in the first place. Clearly, as others have argued for decades, we need to systematically address a broad range of attributes of the pottery, whether by modal analysis or other procedures. I have discussed here two of these kinds of attributes—paste wares and decorative structures (systems)—with examples drawn from Postclassic Petén pottery, not just to show how they can illuminate areas of Postclassic behavior but also to demonstrate that such analyses can be easily accommodated *within* the type-variety structure, rather than only outside of it.

Acknowledgments

I am grateful to Jim Aimers for inviting me to contribute a chapter to this volume. I thank Jerry Sabloff and Mike Smith for generously taking the time to read a longer version of this manuscript and sharing their thoughts with me about pottery classification in general and type-variety analysis and this contribution in particular. Nonetheless, any errors in presentation or interpretation herein are entirely my own.

Notes

1. I say these are ahistorical "in principle" because the type-variety system was intended to create categories that are explicitly historical as chronological indicators.

2. In this vein, Gifford (1976: 1) asserted that "ideas, mental images, are the 'genes' of culture."

3. I am grateful to Jerry Sabloff for reminding me about this earlier publication as well as his own (2004) that discuss this issue. The reason for these vicious personal attacks is unclear. Kluckhohn is said to have had "various political problems in the Department of Anthropology" at Harvard and as a consequence was in the Department of Social Relations (Vogt 1994: 47).

4. Jerry Sabloff informed me via e-mail (July 5, 2008) that he recalled "no explicit

discussion with Bob Smith, Jim Gifford, or Dick Adams about Taylor's criticisms of CIW pottery studies" during his time at Harvard.

5. Practically speaking, they seem to be describing "categorization" of a previously unanalyzed collection. But I cannot comprehend the frustration of trying to analyze a bag of sherds by first separating varieties and using them to create types, then groups, and so on in an "agglomerative" procedure. Instead, I use a divisive procedure, first segregating unslipped from slipped wares, then red- from black-slipped groups, for example, and so on.

6. Paxcamán Red pottery at Barton Ramie exhibits several paste variants: (1) gray with snail shell; (2) white (not Clemencia Cream); (3) black (usually for jars); (4) brown-tan to orange lacking snail shell; and (5) ash (Sharer and Chase 1976: 289, 295). Three of these (2, 3, and 4) are likely firing variants, rather than variations in "paste"; snail inclusions are present in varying amounts in Paxcamán pottery everywhere. At Macanché Island, Paxcamán paste variants included yellowish ash and a coarse gray, which I believe represent early (transitional Terminal Classic–Early Postclassic) experimentation with new (clay) and old (volcanic ash) resources, possibly by potters new to the lakes area (Rice 1987b: 107–9). In contrast, Augustine group pottery "may in fact be the indigenous product of Barton Ramie potters" in the Belize Valley (Sharer and Chase 1976: 289, 293; see also Willey, Bullard, Gifford, and Glass 1965: 388).

7. I have not only applied type-variety analysis to Spanish Colonial pottery from Moquegua, Peru, but also briefly demonstrated the system with a basket of Chinese pottery during a workshop in Shangdong, China.

3

Types and Traditions, Spheres and Systems

A Consideration of Analytic Constructs and Concepts in the Classification and Interpretation of Maya Ceramics

CASSANDRA R. BILL

Types and spheres have been some of the most, if not *the* most, common constructs employed in the analysis and interpretation of ceramic complexes from the Maya lowlands, and they have served well both as a means for categorizing the contents of individual site assemblages and for exploring and expressing the degree of similarity between assemblages from different sites. While not denying their utility, this chapter examines the additional contributions of some less commonly utilized concepts—including technological styles and ceramic systems—to the establishment of a more comprehensive perspective on the development of, and relationships between, regional ceramic complexes.

Technological Style

The features that characterize a particular vessel—that is, its paste, form, and surface treatment—derive from the raw materials and procedures utilized by the potter in its manufacture. If pottery making around the world and across time is taken into consideration, an almost infinite number of choices could theoretically exist with regard to how to make a pot. The individual potters living in a given region or community, however, are, in fact, often sharply limited in their choices by a number of factors over which they have little or no control, including features of the local resource environment, which will determine what kinds of clays and tempers a potter can use. Local customs in diet and food preparation, as well as other activities involving the use of ceramic vessels, will also determine the particular classes and even specific forms of vessels that a potter produces. The precise behaviors practiced by a potter in the making of a pot are also "conditioned by learning patterns and processes of personal interaction among potters within communities" (Dietler and Herbich 1989: 150).

Potters (typically women) are usually taught the craft by family members (such as their mothers or mothers-in-law, depending on local marriage and residence rules) who received their instruction from their mothers or mothers-in-law, and so forth. Each potter in a given community thereby learns that community's particular practices (or "rules") for making pottery, including which clays to use, how to prepare them, how to shape a pot, how to finish it, and so on. Thus, although all ceramic production involves the same basic stages—consisting of raw material collection and paste preparation, forming, finishing, and firing—there can be a considerable degree of variability in the specific raw materials and techniques utilized by local potters during each of these stages. As originally phrased by Lechtman (1977: 7), the term *technological style* refers to "that which arises from the formal integration of these behavioral events."

These technological styles will be different from region to region, as well as among different pottery-making communities within the same region, as a function of different patterns of learning in each community. Learning patterns are structured by specific learning environments and local traditions concerning "the way things are always done" (Stark 1999: 27) with regard to the specific technical choices made from available options at each stage in the operational sequence, or *chaîne de opératoire*, involved in making a pot (Lechtman 1977; Lemonnier 1986; Gosselain 1992; Dobres and Hoffman 1994). Style thus "reside[s] in the material results of patterns of choices made at all stages in the operational sequence of production" (Dietler and Herbich 1989: 156–57) and includes, but is not limited to, decoration (Chilton 1999: 50).

The focus of traditional typological schemes on general surface treatment or decorative programs (a focus indicated by the inclusion of definitive surface treatment characteristics in type names such as Pantano Impressed, Encanto Striated, and Triunfo Striated) may reveal correspondences in general finishing practices or decorative conventions that persist over time and/or are widespread across a large area. But because decoration and surface treatment are the most salient aspects of finished products, they are often more readily copied and may, as a result, become widely distributed across a region or even among regions (Gosselain 2000). Such a focus can, therefore, obscure variation in specific practices that characterize the products of local pottery-making communities—the kinds of differences that less visible technological attributes often express (see also Culbert and Rands 2007).

Ethnographic and ethnoarchaeological research suggest that technical choices made at other stages of the operational sequence—including forming techniques (Gosselain 2000), as well as the selection and processing of locally available raw materials (Stark et al. 2000)—may be more constrained by certain factors, including conditioned motor habits (Gosselain 2000; Dietler and Herbich 1989) and/or local environmental features (Stark et al. 2000; Reina and Hill 1978), and thus may be more conservative and resistant to change or innovation.

The features of finished products directly affected by these choices—including specific forms or form attributes and paste characteristics, as well as localized variations in the execution of regional decorative programs (Stark 1999; Graves 1991; Dietler and Herbich 1989; Longacre 1981; Reina and Hill 1978)—may therefore constitute socially meaningful markers of local technological styles in pottery-making practices. Thus, a detailed comparative modal analysis of regional assemblages (including form and decorative modes, as well as paste composition) can potentially reveal the products of different pottery-making groups and their local technological styles and traditions (Stark 1999: 38; Stark et al. 2000: 303). As such, their distribution may not only indicate the economic boundaries of ceramic production and distribution systems (see, for example, Stark 1999) but also reflect, or even more actively mark, the social boundaries of different communities (see various articles in Stark 1998).[1]

Patterns of Material Culture Affiliation

Various terms such as *ceramic horizons*, *spheres*, and *systems* are used to describe certain kinds of similarities or patterns of affiliation between the ceramic complexes of archaeological sites. These patterns are thought to characterize certain types of relationships or interactions between the communities that once occupied those sites.

Ceramic Horizons

The most extensive patterns of ceramic affiliation are represented by ceramic horizons, which typically encompass a large geographic area and are relatively short-lived, compared to other patterns. Specifically,

> [c]eramic horizons are ceramic complexes linked by a set of horizon markers . . . [which are] distinctive and chronologically significant modes shared by two or more ceramic complexes. . . . Ceramic horizons are based upon the presence of shared [and temporally specific] habits of ceramic production [or customs of pottery making] but do not involve a consideration of the relative degrees of cultural connections between complexes. Thus, a single horizon may include some very closely related complexes and others that are quite distinct except for a few markers. (Willey, Culbert, and Adams 1967: 305–6)

Ceramic horizons thus represent extensive, but not necessarily intensive, networks of interaction or communication between different communities, or even different societies, over a broad geographic region. The specific types or modes (that is, horizon markers) that define horizons do not typically become a part of local pottery-making customs, although they may (see, for example, Gosselain 2000: 200), but appear more often as temporarily adopted practices. In some cases, the adoption of horizon markers (such as Teotihuacan-style pottery modes and other features) may make a statement of affiliation or identification with, through emulation of, what is perceived as a more powerful society or prestigious social entity. In other cases, the status connotations of adopted styles are seemingly absent (or perhaps just less transparent), and certain decorative practices (for example, Usulután-style resist) or form modes (such as mammiform supports) have the appearance of short-lived "fads."

While these types of ceramic affiliation may represent relatively temporary or superficial kinds of associations between different communities or regions, the periodic appearance of material culture horizons is nonetheless significant. The size of the area they encompass and the relative speed with which they spread would appear to signal a vibrant period of increased interaction and the sharing of information (if only in a "down-the-line" fashion) over a vast geographic region for a relatively brief period of time and, in the case of some horizons, the sharing of a status-related identity among the leaders of otherwise unrelated societies.

Ceramic Systems

A ceramic system—which similarly represents a pattern of ceramic affiliation over a large (although typically not as large) geographic region—represents a closer relationship between and, in some cases, a much greater endurance in shared pottery-making practices. A ceramic system consists of a number of "roughly contemporaneous types that range over a wide [geographically continuous] area and that are related to one another in particular from the standpoint of decorative treatment, design style, and surface manipulation" (Gifford 1976: 12; see also Ball 1993: 259–60n15).

Although Gifford (1976: 12) stipulated that a ceramic system should ideally be limited in time, a more recently "refined ceramic system concept recognizes the likelihood that many ceramic systems will have considerable time depth" (Henderson and Agurcia 1987: 432; see also Urban and Schortman 1987). In this revised formulation, at least some ceramic systems (that is, those with "considerable time depth") constitute a geographically broad counterpart to certain local ceramic traditions (that is, long-standing practices with regard to the making of certain kinds of vessels), the latter representing specific renditions of generic area-wide conventions, and both reflecting a continuity in certain widely shared ideas and practices with regard to making and, especially it seems, decorating a pot.

While not characteristic of all such long-lived ceramic systems, a significant feature of some is the stability of their geographic boundaries. That is, while the boundaries of ceramic spheres can shift over time (meaning that the geographic area encompassed by the ceramic sphere of one phase may not be isomorphic with those of the ceramic spheres of other phases), the distribution pattern for certain long-lived ceramic systems remains constant, as presumably does the meaning of the relationship(s) they reflect.

The term *macro-tradition* is suggested here to refer to these specific types of long-lived and widely shared ceramic systems that (1) continue over very long periods of time, indeed, often over the entire occupational history of a region (that is, even with changes within them, they remain recognizable, distinctive and consistent, as such); (2) maintain the same geographic boundaries over time (that is, their boundaries do not shift during different phases, as can occur with successive ceramic spheres); and (3) the ceramics (that is, pottery types and modes) associated with these long-lived systems are not generally found outside of those boundaries except as occasional imports or with rare, and explainable, exceptions (as with the introduction of the Maya-area polished black/brown tradition at Copán at the onset of the dynastic period [see below]).

A case in point from the Maya area consists of a distinctive class of fine wares that are characterized by a highly polished black or brown surface (achieved through specific kinds of firing practices) and by decorative treatments involving various kinds of displacement and penetration techniques (see Rice 1987c: 144–47), such as incising and carving. Vessels with these characteristics are found at sites throughout both the highlands and the lowlands of the Maya area in Preclassic through Classic period contexts (including, for example, the Preclassic Chunhinta and Polvero groups and the Classic period Balanza, Infierno, and Achote groups in the lowlands). Although there are clear regional differences in certain technological attributes (such as paste characteristics) and chronological differences in specific design conventions and forms, from start to finish, this is the same pottery in the sense of representing local versions of, and gradual developments within, a single, ongoing, widespread pottery-making tradition.[2] Regardless of what other ceramic affiliations might exist at different points in time within and between different regions of the Maya area, the presence of polished black/brown pottery in virtually every regional assemblage during successive phases of occupation represents an enduring pattern of material culture affiliation that suggests an equally enduring sociocultural affiliation or shared historical connection.

That this is quintessentially "Maya pottery" can also be seen, for example, in the southeastern periphery of Mesoamerica, where the distribution of polished black/brown fine wares does not permeate the putative boundary with non-Maya societies, such as those in western Honduras.[3] Thus, although (and perhaps paradoxically) these types of long-lived and widespread systems can represent some of the loosest kinds of affiliations from a technological perspective, they also arguably represent the strongest or at least most enduring affiliations in terms of social, or even truly cultural, identities.

Ceramic Spheres

Within the larger geographic areas encompassed by systems and horizons are typically more circumscribed distributions of material culture affiliations defined as ceramic spheres. "A ceramic sphere exists when two or more complexes share a majority of their most common types" (Willey, Culbert, and Adams 1967: 306). According to Ball (1993: 256–57), ceramic spheres "are the products of common cultural traditions. Their content is the result of shared values and information among a populace of both producers and consumers, and the unobstructed flow of both goods and ideas among this population."

Although shared ideas and practices with regard to what kinds of pottery to make and how to make it are, of course, part of "common cultural traditions," the close similarity between ceramic complexes in a region, which "share a majority of their most common types," potentially reflects stronger social and economic relationships rather than (or in addition to) strictly cultural ones per se. That is, given that other kinds of material culture affiliations (similarly reflecting "common cultural traditions") can exist between material culture assemblages that would not technically be included in the same ceramic sphere (based on a high degree of commonality in overall ceramic complexes), the last part of Ball's definition ("an unobstructed flow of both goods and ideas among this population") is arguably the most significant feature of ceramic spheres because the close sharing of a majority of common ceramic types in member complexes suggests regular contact being sustained between pottery producers and consumers within a particular region during a given period of time. The fact that sphere boundaries can shift over time, however (that is, sites included in the same sphere in one phase may not be included in the same sphere in another phase), suggests that this kind of contact, and the relationships associated with it, can be relatively temporary. Thus, spheres are not strictly patterns of cultural affiliation (which should be more lasting) but represent additional, potentially more immediate and sometimes impermanent kinds of relationships as well.

Different Kinds of Ceramic Spheres or Sphere Affiliations

In defining ceramic spheres and evaluating their significance, an initial consideration involves determining whether the content similarity observed between ceramic complexes derives from shared *products* versus shared *practices* or *conventions*.

The simplest and most obvious reason that different sites might share the same ceramic types is that they participated in the same pottery production and distribution system as part of a local or regional economic network. Ethnographic data indicate that such systems can exist at a range of spatial scales, from relatively circumscribed networks that serve a small number of communities within a day's walk of each other (see, for example, Stark 1999: 38), a pattern most commonly associated with the door-to-door peddling or purchase of vessels by potters or consumers, to broader regional networks through which the goods of individual pottery-making communities can circulate over a much larger area, a pattern often associated with institutions such as a centralized marketplace or annual ceremonial gatherings (see for example, Mohr-Chavez 1992: 89) where the goods of numerous pottery-making communities may be represented.

In the latter case especially, there is often, or even usually, a certain degree of product specialization among the participating communities, in which different villages specialize in the manufacture of different kinds of vessels (Arnold 1978; Mohr-Chavez 1992; Reina and Hill 1978; Rice 1991: 262–63; Smith 1976; Fry 1981; Rands and Bishop 1980). The result is that a mixture of technological properties (such as paste characteristics and surface treatments) may be represented in the various types of vessel that make up the pottery assemblages from individual sites within the network. Because each location acquires its pottery from the same source(s), however, content similarity between assemblages should be high.[4] For example, if one production group manufactures all of the *comales* for the community or region while another makes all of the water jars, then the same technological styles of water jars and comales should be found in the domestic inventories of each participating site.[5]

The existence and extent of such localized ceramic production and distribution spheres would theoretically be possible to determine on the basis of detailed comparative technological analyses to identify consistent patterns of covariation in small details of form (for example, particular rim treatments), paste characteristics (including chemical composition, where required), and particular surface treatment features or decorative attributes that can represent the specific characteristics associated with the technological styles of individual workshops and even potters (Dietler and Herbich 1989; Stark 1999).[6] In fact, for experienced ceramicists, such detailed modal analyses are often not necessary to recognize differences in local versions of the same type (see, for example, Culbert 1991: 338).

The recognition of content similarity in terms of shared products could potentially add much to the reconstruction of local economic networks for domestic goods as well as the opportunity to trace out possible changes in such over time. The shifting boundaries of these kinds of ceramic spheres, for example, may represent changes in (at least one aspect of) domestic or regional economies that, in some cases, could be attendant upon changing sociopolitical conditions (see for example, Graves 1991: 121), including the possible expansion or contraction of territorial realms.

For example, during the Late Preclassic and Early Classic periods, the ceramics in use in the El Paraíso Valley of western Honduras consisted almost entirely of pottery belonging to a number of long-standing local technological traditions (Bill 2005b). Then, near the beginning of the Late Classic period, there was a dramatic influx into the El Paraíso region of both utilitarian and fine ware pottery produced in the Copán Valley. This arrival of Copán ceramics coincided with the construction of the site of El Paraíso—a center characterized by sculpted building facades and other architectural features found on the structures at Copán—which appears to have been established as an outpost of, and by, the Copán polity in a region strategically located at a crossroads between a number of heavily populated areas, including those of Copán and its rival Quirigua (see Canuto and Bell 2005).

A second, more geographically extensive, kind of ceramic sphere (that encompasses the first) can also be defined in terms of complexes, which share many or most of the same ceramic *types* but not the same ceramic *products*. That the pottery assemblages from sites at some distance from each other can include vessels produced in different locations but belonging to the same ceramic types suggests a different kind of sphere membership (or, perhaps, membership in a different kind of sphere) than that represented by close economic connections between communities. The similarities in ceramic complexes included in this second kind of sphere derive from shared practices and ideas with regard to making pottery and, depending on the degree of sphere membership (full, peripheral, and so forth), likely reflect greater or lesser degrees of social interaction between the member communities. This kind of ceramic affiliation, represented by shared practices but not shared products, can exist at different geographic scales.

The closest similarities—both at the overall complex level as well as in terms of the attributes of individual vessel types (including specific forms and form modes, the execution of design programs, and so forth)—are found among the sites in localized regions (Ball 1993: 255). This suggests a close social connection among the potters of these centers that might be associated with well-integrated regional territories (Graves 1994: 14–19) forming cohesive social entities, or "communities" (Ball 1993: 255). Within these communities some degree of pottery exchange may also have been carried out (Foias and Bishop 1997: 283).

Increasing differences between local versions of individual vessel types can begin to be observed in the comparison of complexes over an increasingly larger geographic area that may still technically be encompassed by the same "ceramic sphere" (as defined by the "sharing of a majority of the most common types"). Late Classic ceramic complexes at sites in southern Belize, for example, are dominated by the same types of pottery that characterize Tepeu sphere centers in other parts of the lowlands, including large striated utilitarian jars, orange-based polychromes, modeled-appliquéd censers, and red-slipped bowls and jars, some of which are decorated with stamped or impressed designs (see Bill 2003, 2005a for a description of the Late Classic ceramic assemblage from the site of Pusilhá).

Certain form and decorative modes associated with local versions of some of these types, however, are distinctive to southern Belize. For example, red-slipped jars with stamped decoration along the shoulder (belonging to the Pantano Impressed Stamped Variety established by Adams [1971: 23, 47–48]) are found at sites in the Pasión and northern Petén regions of Guatemala during the Late Classic period; similar kinds of jars also occur at sites in southern Belize, including Lubaantun (Hammond 1975) and Uxbenka (Prufer, personal communication 2008). The typical stamp motifs on the vessels from southern Belize, however, consisting of birds and particularly monkeys, are not found on the stamped jars from other regions (see also Hammond 1975: 304–5); nor are motifs on stamped jars from other regions found on those in southern Belize. Thus, while sharing in a widespread decorative convention of stamped decoration along the shoulder of red-slipped jars, the specific motifs on the stamped jars from Lubaantun and Uxbenka represent the kinds of local practices, or "twists" on shared conventions, that may be distinctive of the vessels from different regions.

The fact that the geographic distributions of individual ceramic systems may not be isomorphic with each other and that the complexes encompassed by a given system or systems may not, on the basis of overall complex content, belong to the same ceramic sphere (at least in terms of "full sphere membership") raises questions about the kinds of relationships that might have potentially existed between the communities sharing in a particular ceramic system.[7] At the very least, however, the marked deviations in specific practices that can characterize the local renditions of (that is, types belonging to) such systems suggest more distant social relationships than those between communities where such practices are more closely shared.

Thus, at least three different levels of sphere affiliation (or, perhaps, three different kinds of spheres) can theoretically exist—all of which could be interpreted, or defined, as a "sharing of a majority of most common types." At one level (the most geographically limited), shared types may be represented by shared *products*, recognizable as an identity in all technological attributes of form, paste, surface treatment, and decoration within each vessel class. With regard to current terminology, we would say that these vessels belong to the same type and variety.

At a second level of inclusiveness, shared types may represent shared *practices*, reflecting closely shared ideas about specific pottery-making techniques (with regard, for example, to shaping a vessel, forming the rim, finishing the surfaces, and executing decorative treatments) that result in very similar but not identical ceramic vessels. Although these vessels would all clearly belong to the same type, they could be given different variety names from each other to indicate the fact that they represent slightly different versions of that type, as a function of having been produced by potters from different communities utilizing local raw materials and their own specific ways of making pottery—that is, their own technological styles.

A third type of "ceramic sphere" (although one that may not, in all cases, be technically equivalent with the traditional definition of the term) can be defined on the basis of shared pottery-making *conventions* (including, for example, general vessel forms, decorative programs, or surface treatments). These conventions are widespread across a large geographic area, but local versions (for example, in design program execution) can differ considerably between sites or regions within that area. Thus, different type names could arguably be assigned to these localized versions in some cases. For example, Hammond (1975) has done this with the stamped red-slipped jars from Lubaantun that are assigned to his Remate Red Type.

This is one of the occasions in which the archaeological practice of assigning type names has been problematic. Assigning the same type name to vessels from different sites may suggest closer similarities between the vessels than actually exist. Alternatively, when a different type name is used, similarities that do exist may be obscured. In these types of situations, the use of ceramic systems (of limited chronological duration, as proposed by Gifford [1976: 12]) would be a workable solution that would express the relationship between the pottery-making conventions being employed at different sites while at the same time denoting the variability in their application, in terms of specific practices, that characterizes the actual vessels being produced in different locations. Thus, for example, we could define a "Pantano Impressed System" that is characterized by the application of stamped decoration along the shoulder of red-slipped jars and that includes the types Pantano Impressed: Stamped Variety from the Lower Pasión region and Remate Red from southern Belize.

In sum, membership (even "full membership") in the same ceramic sphere can potentially reflect different kinds of affiliations (economic, social/sociopolitical, cultural/historical, and so on) between the sites and regions encompassed by it. Thus, in addition to defining sphere membership ("full," "peripheral," and so on) on the basis of the *degree* of content similarity, we can also evaluate the nature of sphere membership based on the *kind* of content similarity that exists between specific complexes. That is, we can determine whether the components that are shared between specific complexes represent the same products ("varieties"), practices ("types"), or conventions ("systems"). We can also assess which components are part of long-standing traditions characteristic of a particular area and which belong to short-lived horizons spanning several different areas, and so forth. Many other possibilities can surely be imagined as well.[8] Although more consideration is needed with regard to establishing the significance of particular kinds of components (and their combinations), it would nevertheless seem that examining more precisely how the diagnostic content of a ceramic sphere is represented in individual complexes could potentially contribute to our understanding of the different kinds of relationships that might have existed among different sites and regions of the Maya lowlands at various points in time.

The nondiagnostic content of a ceramic sphere—that is, those components that are not shared among member complexes—can be equally significant from the perspective of revealing patterns of affiliation additional to those represented by sphere membership. A case in point can be seen in certain aspects of the Late Classic ceramic complex from the site of Cancuén, located in the Upper Pasión region of the Maya lowlands near the foothills of the Alta Verapaz (see Bill 2001 for a description of the ceramics from Cancuén).

While certain components of the Late Classic assemblage at Cancuén incorporate some of the major pottery-making trends of this period throughout much of the lowlands (as represented, for example, in the presence of Saxche/Palmar Orange polychromes and various types of the Tinaja Group), other features characteristic of the Upper Pasión complex are virtually unique to this region of the lowlands. Most notable in this regard are the relatively large numbers of cream-slipped fine wares that occur at Cancuén, including vessels with incised and/or "Classic resist" decorative treatments (see Castellanos et al. 2003: figs. 9–11; see figure 3.1 for an example of a Classic resist vessel from Copán). In paste, form, and surface treatment, these vessels are very similar to pottery produced in the northern highlands of Guatemala (including the Alta Verapaz; see Smith 1952)[9] and occur only as very occasional imports in the Late Classic assemblages of sites in other lowland regions. This component of the Cancuén assemblage (as well as certain attributes associated with other

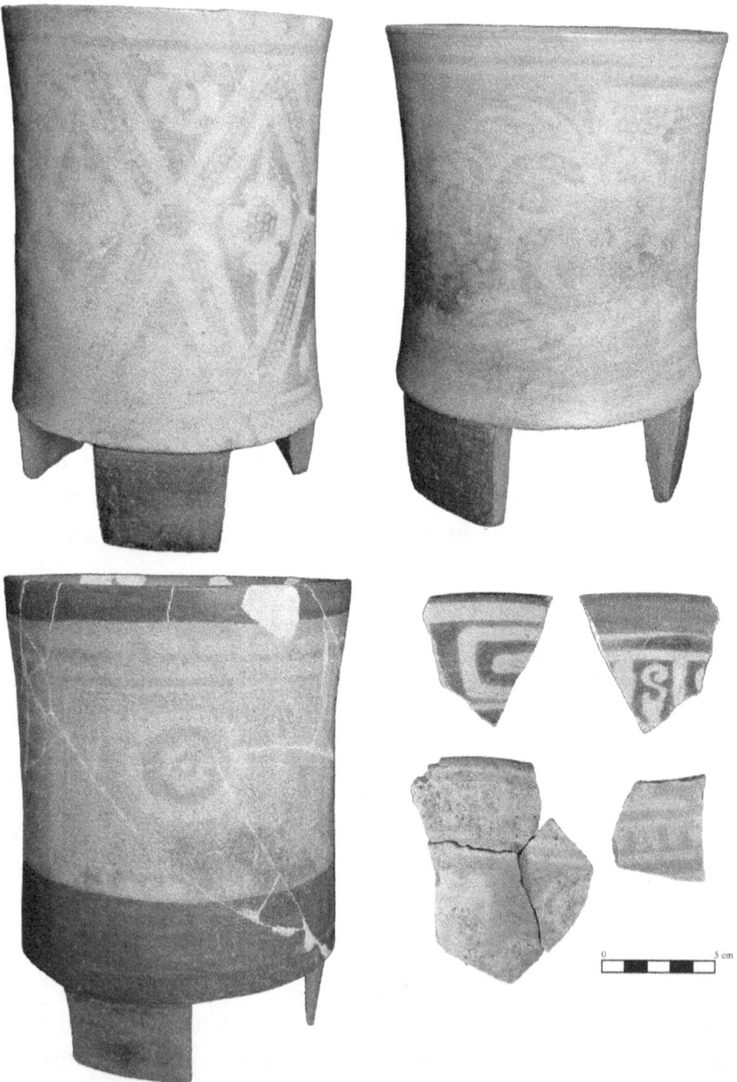

Figure 3.1. Sovedeso Negative-painted vessels and sherds from Copán. (Photo by author.)

types) reflects a degree of interaction, or even more meaningful sociocultural affiliations, with the northern highlands that was greater than at other lowland sites.

A more dramatic example pertains to the overall Late Classic ceramic complex from the site of Copán in western Honduras. Certain elements of the Classic period ceramic assemblage at Copán clearly reflect the site's connections with the Maya area, including the presence of finely made polished black/brown pottery that was decorated using a variety of techniques, including incising, fluting, and carving (figure 3.2). Alongside these "Maya-style" ceramics are other components of Classic period assemblages at Copán that are part of long-standing local ceramic traditions of the southeast periphery. Among these are vessels belonging to several Honduran ceramic systems (see Urban and Schortman 1987; Henderson and Agurcia 1993; Henderson and Beaudry-Corbett 1993), including distinctive forms of utilitarian jars that are decorated with painted and/or incised designs on the neck and body (figure 3.3). These

Figure 3.2. Polished black/brown pottery from Copán: *a–b*, Madrugada Modeled-carved; *c*, Tasu Fluted; *d*, Ardilla Incised and Excised. (Photos by author.)

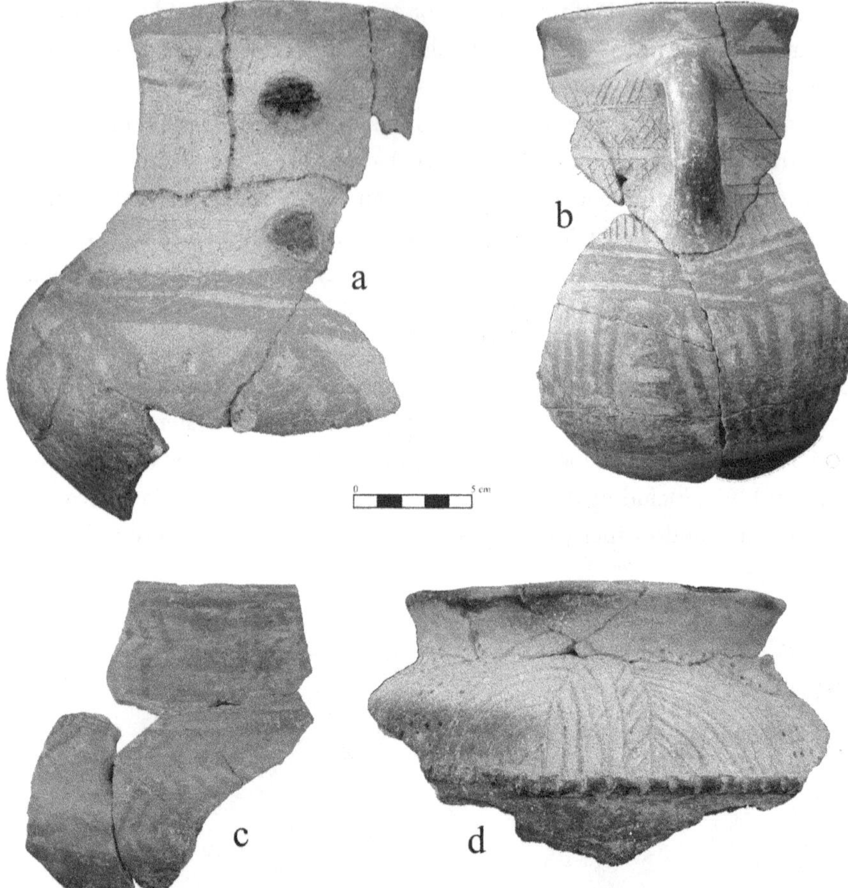

Figure 3.3. Painted and incised jars from Copán: *a*, Reina Incised; *b*, Juanita Incised; *c*, Favela Red-on-beige; *d*, Cementerio Incised. (Photos by author.)

and other material culture relationships between Copán and sites in the southeast periphery represent the maintenance of shared traditions with local regions (some of which extend back into the Preclassic period) that suggest both a common cultural heritage and continuing community interaction in addition to, and independent of, the elite connections and associations of Copán during the Classic period.

Conclusions

We have come to realize that Maya polities (as sociopolitical entities) had distinctive histories. These are detailed at some sites on inscribed monuments and are represented in the archaeological record of monumental construction programs at many more. We can also, however, view their underlying communities as being distinctive, in terms of both their histories and their social identities as individual communities. Furthermore, different kinds of relationships existed at the community level within and between the various regions encompassed by Classic Maya civilization. Although such differences may have become more pronounced toward the end of the Late Classic and into the Terminal Classic period (when we see, for example, the increasing regionalization of lowland ceramic complexes), they were doubtless always there beneath the unifying veneer of the elite culture that defines the Classic period.

While it is true, of course, that pots are not people, it is equally true that potters are and that they practice their craft according to canons and conventions that are part of sometimes long-standing technological traditions that are themselves embedded in the social systems of communities (Gosselain 1998). Thus, the analysis of the practices characteristic of such traditions can potentially reveal the social boundaries of those communities, as well as patterns of affiliation between and among communities (Stark 1999). That is, if all of the features of a finished product are recognized as representing the results of technical choices made at each stage in an operational sequence of specific pottery-making practices (see also Culbert and Rands 2007), then both the differences and the similarities in particular features at different sites become more socially meaningful. Differences potentially reflect or even actively mark certain kinds of boundaries between communities. Similarities resulting from the limited borrowing or widespread sharing of particular techniques potentially represent different kinds or levels of interaction between communities and regions. Taken together, these patterns may indicate different kinds or levels of social identity within Maya society.

Notes

1. To be fair (and historically accurate), I must note that some of the original concepts and reasoning behind the establishment of a type-variety classification scheme (e.g., Gifford 1960: 343) incorporate a careful consideration of these same kinds of cultural "values" and human behaviors (including the "tendency to form habits") that condition and influence the making of different pottery vessel "types" and "varieties." In the application of a type-variety scheme to the analysis of archaeological assemblages, however, there can be a tendency to reify types into static constructs with limited spatial and temporal validity that, within some existing schemes at least, "replace each other" over time. Although entirely new ceramic types (reflecting the introduction or innovation of new practices) can, of course, occur, what are sometimes represented as consecutive types within a ceramic sequence may often be ongoing developments within long-lived pottery-making traditions.

2. A more geographically circumscribed example is the production of striated utilitarian jars in the central and southern lowlands—a practice that similarly began in the Preclassic period and continued throughout the occupational history of most lowland centers.

3. A notable exception is Copán and its later affiliates. Although small numbers of polished black/brown vessels were imported to the site during the Late Preclassic period, the initiation of local production of this kind of pottery at Copán coincides with the onset of the dynastic period, circa A.D. 400, when we also begin to see other features of Classic Maya civilization at the site.

4. That is, the fact that the vessels circulating through a given regional distribution network were produced in the same pottery-making center(s) should give the assemblages of participating communities a high degree of comparability with regard to the technological properties (i.e., consistent patterns of covariations in paste, form, and surface treatment) of vessels within product classes. Depending on the range of variability present in product classes, however, the needs or preferences of consumers in individual communities may result in somewhat idiosyncratic assemblage profiles with regard to specific form or size attributes (e.g., Stark 1994: 180–82).

5. Distributional patterns may vary, however, in association with different modes of production or exchange (Graves 1991; Longacre and Stark 1992). There may be situations, for example, in which a production group specializes in the manufacture of water jars or comales for exchange but also produces all of its own pottery for household consumption. That is, product specialization may exist at the level of vessels produced *for exchange* but not necessarily at the level of vessels produced *in total* (Mohr Chávez 1992: 80). In such cases, one would expect to find some assemblages (those of the non-pottery-producing communities) having a wide variety of different products and for these assemblages to be similar in overall composition. At the same time, and within the same production and distribution system, there may also be a smaller number of assemblages (those of the pottery-producing communities) that are more internally homogeneous (Graves 1991: 136–37) in terms of certain technological attributes, such as paste (Mohr Chávez 1992: 85), and that contain types of vessels that do not occur elsewhere because they were made for the potters of that community for their own use.

6. In reality, however, a full reconstruction of localized or regional ceramic production and distribution systems may, in practice, be a relatively complicated undertaking. Among other things, for example, different kinds of vessels can "behave" differently in terms of how and to what spatial extent they are circulated (e.g., Beaudry 1984; Fry 1979, 1980, 1981; Rands and Bishop 1980). Pottery being a bulky and fragile commodity, large vessels in particular may not travel any great distance from where they were made, and their particular distribution pattern may define a geographically circumscribed supply zone mode of exchange. Smaller vessels, in contrast, particularly ones that are stackable or otherwise easier to transport, might be more widely circulated (through peddling or marketplace exchange), resulting in a different pattern of geographic distribution for these classes of vessels within what might technically be the same domestic or intraregional economic network.

7. Similar patterns involving intercommunity variations and regionally distinctive versions of shared decorative programs have been observed in various ethnographic studies. For example, Kalinga potters in the Philippines decorate the upper body and shoulder of their vessels with a series of impressed bands. Although they thus "share a similar conception for the location of design . . . and the arrangement of the two bands [etc.]" (Graves 1994: 47), variations can be seen in the execution of this decorative treatment as well as in design motifs (Graves 1991, 1994). Graves found that the distribution of decorative variants corresponded to the boundaries of recognized sociopolitical territories, or "regions," and further suggests that the distinctive pottery designs within each region "serve as subtle icons for individuals linked to a common polity" (Graves 1991: 118–19).

8. For example, although this discussion has focused on types, other classificatory components, including groups and wares, could and should also be included in these kinds of considerations. Late Classic ceramics from the southern Belize site of Pusilhá, for example, include local corollaries of some Tinaja Group types (including red-slipped jars, jars with impressed designs on the shoulder, and large bowls) but not others (such as the Stamped Variety of Pantano Impressed and Chaquiste Impressed). At the same time, the red-slipped pottery at Pusilha also includes comales, which are not common at sites in most other regions.

9. Some of the cream-slipped pottery at Cancuén may also have been of local manufacture. Vessels more common in later contexts at the site, for example, were made on a different paste, have a softer cream slip, and were decorated with more crudely executed incised designs.

4

Interpreting Form and Context

Ceramic Subcomplexes at Caracol, Nohmul, and Santa Rita Corozal, Belize

ARLEN F. CHASE AND DIANE Z. CHASE

> Archaeology is in mortal danger of losing itself on the bypaths of abracadabra. There is precious little difference between the Maya medicine man mystifying his patients with muttered incantations and the ceramicist awing his scant congregation with still more esoteric names.
>
> Thompson 1970: xvii

The vast majority of artifactual materials recovered at Maya sites are broken sherds recovered from the fills of stratigraphic excavations. While whole vessels are incorporated into ceramic analysis, they are generally less plentiful than pottery sherds and, thus, are less likely to be the primary unit of ceramic analysis. Jeremy Sabloff (1975: 4) distinguished between the type-variety study of sherds and the modal analysis of form, noting that in most Maya ceramic analyses "the study of individual modes is either forgotten or relegated to a minor role." James Gifford (1976: 6) pointed out that ceramic analyses were "obliged to cope with large quantities of sherds and adapt the type: variety-mode approach to the *limitations* of the sherd collections" (our emphasis) even though "our conceptual scheme is based on whole vessels and culturally meaningful segments of vessels." For half a century, it has been primarily broken sherds that have been the focus of Maya ceramic analysis. Many site chronologies are based on type: variety-mode analyses of sherds, and many cultural reconstructions of ancient Maya society are also premised on these fragmented materials. But are there other ways of approaching ancient Maya pottery? As both Sabloff (1975: 4) and Gifford (1976: 6, 8) have noted, the answer is "yes."

The goals of type: variety-mode analysis are to categorize and label Maya ceramics to promote intersite comparisons (Sabloff 1975: 4)—and the use of a common system of nomenclature and illustration does permit this. But much current research in Maya archaeology seeks to look at intrasite variability and to deal with questions involving social, economic, political, or ideological organization that are not easily studied using the type: variety-mode analysis, referred to hereafter as "t-v-m." Some analysts (for example, Gifford 1976: 5–6) have argued that emic units are discovered through t-v-m. In this view, the standards and practices of producers and consumers are manifest in the attributes of ceramic products, so the point of t-v-m analysis is not merely the creation of analytically useful classes (such as types) but also the discovery of patterned associations of attributes that inherently identify cultural ideas, practices, and even individuals or groups (see also Gifford 1960). In contrast, most ceramic analysts appear to agree that t-v-m does not discover actual cultural units (Adams 1971: 14) and that the analytic system was not designed to directly engage in social considerations (see Rice this volume). We also question the ability of t-v-m to identify emic stylistic units. The analyst's classifications of ancient pottery may or may not mirror ancient cultural considerations. While modern researchers may think that a major difference occurs between red-slipped and black-slipped pottery (even distinguishing this material at a higher-order "group" level), this may not have been of primary cultural importance to the ancient Maya consumer. While an analyst in the t-v-m system focuses on surface treatment and lumps together various forms based on surface characterization, creating separate types for incision, grooving, modeling, and other decorative techniques, the ancient Maya likely categorized these materials differently. We have no way of knowing what the ancient Maya considered to be important and should not assume that t-v-m automatically conveys any sort of ancient reality. Differences in categorization and inconsistencies in the use of t-v-m by analysts also mean that it may not always be "an efficient and effective medium for establishing spatiotemporal frameworks" (Ball 1979b: 830) and dealing with questions of chronology, one of its presumed strengths (as will be seen below).

In this chapter, we attempt to demonstrate the benefits of expanding Maya ceramic analysis to include alternatives to t-v-m analysis. We are specifically focused on the concept of ceramic subcomplexes—a culturally meaningful component of ceramic complexes (Willey et al. 1967)—as originally suggested by Joseph Ball (1977a) and subsequently modified by ourselves (A. Chase and D. Chase 1987a), particularly within the framework of the contextual review of ceramics as articulated by David Pendergast (1979). To better delineate the utility of ceramic subcomplexes within the study of Maya ceramics, we briefly review the advantages and constraints of t-v-m and then explore the utility of contextual ceramic analysis with materials from three sites in Belize—Nohmul, Santa Rita Corozal, and Caracol.

Stratigraphy and Ceramic Analysis

Not all stratigraphic sequences are equal; stated another way, multiple sequential floors do not necessarily a good ceramic sequence make. Sampling would be simple if archaeological remains were always evenly distributed throughout a site, but this, of course, is virtually never the case. Type: variety-mode analysis, like all analyses, is only as good as the archaeological data from which it was ultimately derived. If the sampling scheme was initially skewed or misinterpreted, so too may be any interpretations based on t-v-m. Complicated stratigraphic records may show evidence of continuous development but not necessarily what this development was or how and why it occurred. Detailed, constructed analytic sequences may not have much relevance to theoretical questions having to do with social process, change, or organization. While not the defined unit of t-v-m analysis, a complex stratigraphic sequence that contains multiple primary deposits in association with abundant ceramics is more easily ordered, analyzed, and seriated than a complex stratigraphic sequence consisting only of broken sherd material. Such primary deposits form the basis of our ceramic methodology.

The long-term excavations undertaken at Tikal, Guatemala, may be used to illustrate some of the problems involved in conjoining ceramic analysis and the archaeological record—particularly the impact of sampling, even at well-excavated sites. The University of Pennsylvania Tikal Project ran from 1956 through 1969 and constituted one of the longest-running projects in the Maya area (Coe and Haviland 1982; Sabloff 2003). However, in spite of the project's length and size—and even though complex architectural sequences relating to this era were excavated in the site epicenter (Coe 1990; Jones 1991)—the transition between the Late Preclassic and Early Classic period proved difficult to define in terms of ceramic subcomplexes (Culbert 1977, 1993; Culbert et al. 1990: 120; Fry 1990: 290, 297). The recovered sample included a series of Late Preclassic (Cauac) primary deposits, dating prior to A.D. 75, and a series of late Early Classic (Manik 3) primary deposits, dating to after A.D. 380 (Culbert 1993). In spite of 14 years of extensive excavation, no primary deposits were recovered with associated ceramics that could be dated to between A.D. 75 and A.D. 380. While sherds recovered from the secondary contexts could be used to flesh out a t-v-m analysis for this 300-year period (Culbert n.d.), the archaeological record had not provided a full ceramic inventory—making cultural interpretations relating to this transition difficult (Culbert 1977; Jones 1991).

A second Tikal Project carried out excavations at the site from 1980 through 1984 under the auspices of the Guatemalan government. This Proyecto Nacional Tikal concentrated both on Tikal's "Lost World" section of the site and on a series of residential groups immediately south of this imposing complex. The result was the recovery of a ceramic sample that largely filled the gap in ceramic data recovered by the earlier Tikal Project (Laporte and Fialko 1987, 1990, 1995; Laporte et al. 1992). These materials, mostly from primary deposits, fleshed out Tikal's prehistory between the years A.D. 200 and A.D. 380 and hinted at some even earlier transitional materials. But in spite of the intensive excavation programs carried out by these two projects over two decades, there are still no known primary deposits with associated ceramics from Tikal for the period of time between A.D. 75 and A.D. 200. It is evident from the many stratigraphic excavations that multiple construction episodes occurred during this time period, but the recovered ceramic sample (while defined in terms of t-v-m) does not contain ceramic materials from mortuary or cache subcomplexes and still remains incomplete. Thus, even after substantial excavation by multiple projects, the transition from the end of the Late Preclassic through the beginning of the Early Classic at Tikal—a time that witnessed major changes in ceramic content—is still not fully understood.

Subcomplexes

Ceramic analysis that is focused on material recovered from stratigraphic sequences by necessity most often uses sherd material from structure fills in mixed debris building cores rather than de facto use-related debris (Schiffer 1987). The analyst must sort and seriate materials that may be culturally mixed into categories with temporal and cultural meaning. A single fill context can include mixed ceramics of Preclassic to Late Classic date as well as a wide variety of fine wares and plain wares. Some archaeologists assume that a t-v-m sorting of sherd material from mixed contexts automatically gives you useful information about chronology and past Maya ideas, behaviors, and organization; this is emphatically not the case. David Pendergast (1979: 33) has noted that such practices "may in fact widen the gulf that separates us from the people whose culture we are studying"; he chose not to use t-v-m analysis but rather to focus on groupings of ceramics and artifacts left in the archaeological record by the Maya themselves. Our practice has been to use contextual analysis to identify archaeological situations from which meaningful artifactual associations may be derived (A. Chase 1994; A. Chase et al. 2007). Contexts suitable for such consideration include both purposefully placed and accidentally discarded materials. Unlike fill items, which are usually from secondary contexts divorced from their original cultural milieu, de facto vessel groups, which are recoverable archaeologically (and can be placed into the context of associated formation processes [Schiffer 1987: 286]), often permit insight into issues of both contemporaneity and function. From an analytical standpoint, these culturally significant groupings of vessels have been called "ceramic subcomplexes," following their original definition in t-v-m (Willey et al. 1967: 304).

Ideally, many ceramic subcomplexes exist. The most common ones recognized by archaeologists are mortuary subcomplexes consisting of vessel sets that are found buried with the dead (A. Chase and D. Chase 1987b). Cache and *incensario* subcomplexes are also ritual in nature (D. Chase 1988) but often show minimal overlap with mortuary subcomplexes. Still other ritual subcomplexes have been recovered in association with caves (Brady 1992). These various subcomplexes exhibit a wide variety of forms, groups, and types, ranging from entirely fine ware pottery to entirely plain ware vessels to entirely ritual containers. Ideally, domestic subcomplexes should also be common in the archaeological record; in practice, however, such materials are often not found in primary use-related contexts, either due to sampling problems or because they were more usually recycled into fills and other areas of mixed trash disposal. When ceramics do occur as de facto refuse on floors, however, they can provide important clues for interpreting the use of associated rooms and buildings (D. Chase and A. Chase 2000; Inomata 1997; Inomata and Triadan 2000; Pendergast 1979). The subcomplexes formed by these materials are quite variable from locus to locus, presumably because of the range of activities that were undertaken and because of differences in ancient status and role. Although some researchers feel that on-floor in situ materials are rare in the Maya archaeological record, they are in fact quite common and even occur in stratigraphically buried contexts.

The overlap of vessel types and forms between ceramic subcomplexes that can be defined at a given site is often not great (being dependent on the vagaries of archaeological sampling and research). When overlap does occur, it is not always common (even in sites that have seen intensive, long-term archaeological research). Compounding this overlap issue is the fact that mortuary vessels may often be different from sherds recovered in fill materials. This is due both to temporal factors, in which earlier ceramic materials constitute the fills that surround in situ deposits, and to curate behavior, in which certain vessels are purposefully removed from the archaeological record to accompany these deposits (meaning that their probability of occurrence as fill material is significantly lessened).

While mortuary subcomplexes are sometimes discussed in the archaeological literature (Haviland et al. 1985), other subcomplexes are rarely defined, for a variety of reasons. They are often hard to find contextually in the archaeological record, as they usually require broader areal excavations in contrast to the test pits so useful to t-v-m. When such deposits are located, they also involve more time and effort to reassemble sherds into complete vessels. Finally, earlier subcomplexes are especially hard to locate because subsequent rebuilding at any given site usually disturbs any in situ materials. However, in our estimation, such subcomplexes provide the primary way of gaining specific behavioral insights from the archaeological record relating to ceramics.

A broader question for the analyst is how to assemble the pottery contained within diverse archaeological contexts not only into a ceramic sequence but also into behaviorally meaningful units. While sherds can be temporally ordered with much work in a t-v-m analysis, this ordering does not reveal how they were used, what they were used with, what the relative frequency of an item really was, or if certain items were in fact restricted to certain levels or parts of a given society. Within a t-v-m analysis, sherds, and even reconstructable vessels, do not reveal what was behaviorally meaningful (Lyman et al. 1997: 117, 157); only the archaeological contexts—correctly interpolated—can do that. While inferences about production behavior may be made from a physical inspection of sherd materials and gross patterns of ceramic interaction may be made from a simple inspection of ceramics, t-v-m analysis by itself only organizes ceramics typologically. While conducive to facilitating interanalyst communication, the typological units that are produced are clearly divorced from any past behavioral contexts and considerations. The ceramic "complex" is difficult to relate to any functioning subcomplex or subassemblage of behaviorally meaningful vessels.

A case in point is the Floral Park complex of Barton Ramie (Gifford 1976: 51). While a "complex" by definition includes all of the existing ceramic materials during a given phase (Willey et al. 1965), the Floral Park ceramic complex includes only three groups (striated, unslipped, and orange-slipped); this combination seems rather unlikely given the group variety evident in the preceding Mount Hope ceramic complex and in the succeeding Hermitage ceramic complex. Thus, while defined as an analytical unit, the Floral Park ceramic complex is probably lacking both content and context. To a large extent, the interpretation of meaning is not only context dependent but also dependent on the analytical questions that are being asked and the kinds of archaeological samples that exist. Fill sherds can provide an idea of what is present in a sample and what the temporal parameters are but—in and of themselves—can only rarely be used to address other issues. Thus, while researchers have used fill materials to argue for various interpretations, from feasting (following arguments made by Hayden and Gargett 1990) to population numbers (following Millon 1973 for Teotihuacan) to status (following Ford 1991: 39–40), such interpretations are always problematic.

Schiffer (1987: 285–86, 359–60) has noted the "vast potential that ceramic reassembly holds for illuminating formation processes" while at the same time noting that "considerable caution" must be exercised when "using restored vessels as evidence of formation processes and past behaviors of interest," in case "other restorable pots were missed." In the cases presented below for the Belizean sites of Nohmul, Santa Rita Corozal, and Caracol, great care was taken in looking at and analyzing the total potential ceramic sample, both vertically (fill and humus overburden) and horizontally (entire sample for building and area excavated). Much time was spent looking for fits and reconstructable vessels through cross-mending and refitting to minimize the exact problems to which Schiffer refers. Related to these analyses was also a consideration of curate behavior (Binford 1979) to see what may have been missing from the given ceramic deposits. In light of the detailed refitting and cross-mending that was done, consideration of what was *not* present in a given deposit proved to be particularly informative.

Nohmul Structure 20

Investigations in Nohmul Structure 20 (figure 4.1) undertaken in 1978 provide an excellent example of the utility of conjoining contextual analysis with traditional t-v-m analysis. They also demonstrate the importance of analyzing nonsealed contexts within a broad spatial setting. Nohmul, Belize, is one of the largest sites known in northern Belize (Pyburn 1990: 183). Nohmul Structure 20 is located in the site's epicenter and is a "patio-quad" construction, a type of building most closely associated with Chichén Itzá, Mexico (D. Chase and A. Chase 1982), where it is thought to have functioned either as an elite residence (Freidel 1981) or as a men's house (Arnauld 2001). The structure measured approximately 15.6 meters square and was demarcated by base walls that defined a sunken interior court, which measured 3.2 by 4.2 meters. A single door exited the building to the west. Excavations demonstrated that the building was a late addition inserted into Nohmul's east-central plaza (D. Chase 1982b).

Investigations uncovered substantial ceramic remains (D. Chase 1982a, 1982b). Had the ceramics from this excavation been viewed solely from a t-v-m perspective, it is possible that the pottery—which included what were previously viewed as temporally distinct ceramics (southern lowland Late Classic and Terminal Classic types as well as northern lowland Early Postclassic types)—could have been segregated into more than one phase. Had this been the case, the resultant interpretations might well have suggested that the Structure 20 locus was in use for a substantial period of time. However, areal excavation, ceramic reconstruction, and subsequent contextual analysis indicated

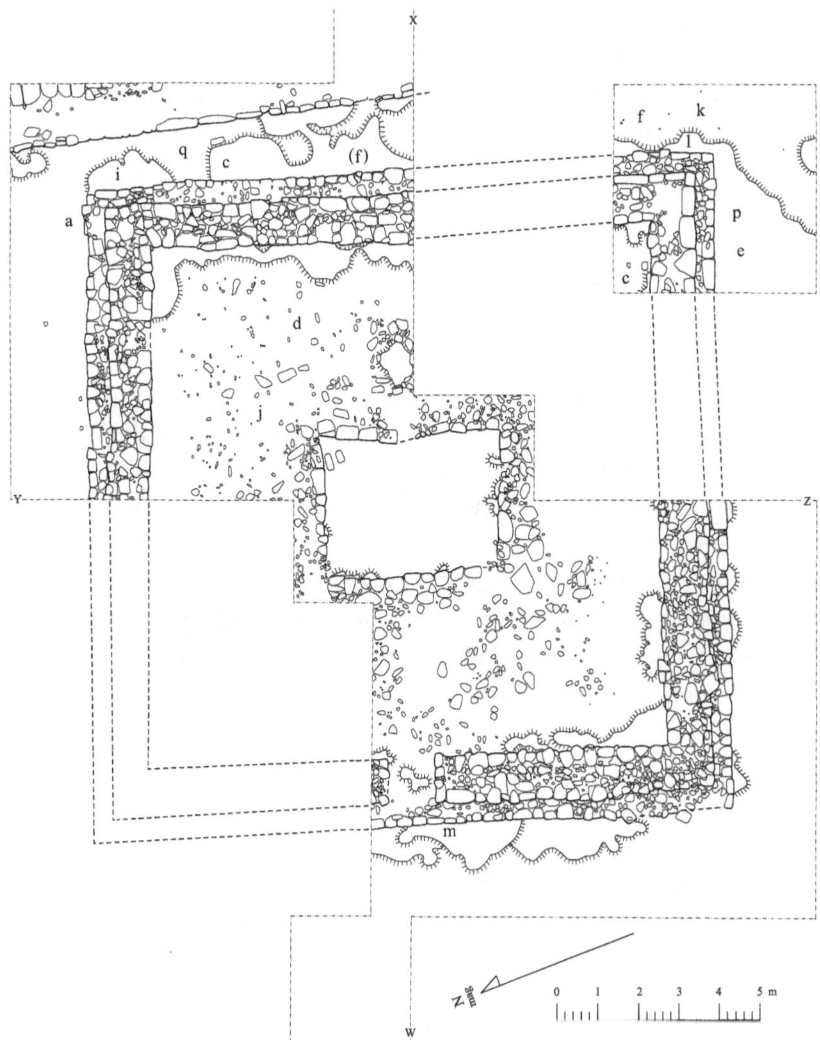

Figure 4.1. Plan of Nohmul Structure 20 showing location of recovered vessels. Letters on plan correlate with letters associated with vessels in figure 4.2. (Courtesy of D. Z. Chase and A. F. Chase, Corozal Postclassic Project.)

not only that all of the ceramics were contemporaneous but also that much of the garbage behind the structure was originally broken in the building's central courtyard. Analysis made it clear that artifacts were used within the building and, after breakage, were swept up and carried as refuse to the rear of the structure. There were sherd fits from a variety of locales about the building (on the floor within the structure, in the central patio, in front of and on the side of the structure) to the refuse at its rear, which appears to have accumulated relatively rapidly.

As a result of analyzing the refuse that was gathered from the floors both within and outside Nohmul Structure 20, it is possible to say something about the nature of an elite ceramic subcomplex of Terminal Classic date—or at least about the materials that were last broken and not removed from the building. The assemblage of pottery recovered in association with Nohmul Structure 20 included a wide range of slipped wares but also included some plain wares (figure 4.2). The majority of the pottery appears to have been oriented to the preparation, cooking, and serving of food and/or drink; however, the excavations also uncovered a ceramic musical instrument. Large vessels (Chambel Striated), presumably used for cooking, were recovered both inside the building and in the rear refuse deposit. A large striated serving vessel (Red-Neck Mother Striated), which probably held liquid, was recovered in the rear trash deposit, as were a variety of serving basins (Ohel Red; Campbells Red) and a large pedestaled dish or chalice (Kik Red). At least two large water jars (Sansomal Black-on-cream) were present. A smaller jar (Chacil Black-on-red) was also recovered. Three different kinds of small bowls (Kik Red, Savinal Cream, Metzabok Slate) came from the front and rear of the building; pieces of footed plates (Achote Black) were in evidence as well. A footed grater bowl (Xixilic Incised), or *molcajete*, also was part of this assemblage. Small double-mouthed striated jars (Buyuk Striated), which are quite common in northern Belize in the Terminal Classic (Sidrys and Krowne 1983), were present as well. Finally, over half of a very large drum (Chembeku Modeled) was recovered from the interior of the building.

The contextual analysis of the Nohmul ceramics not only permitted insight into the functional use of Structure 20 but also effectively showed the relationship between northern and southern lowland ceramic sequences (D. Chase and A. Chase 1982); this relationship was subsequently verified through reinterpretations of northern lowland ceramic sequences (Lincoln 1986). The Nohmul data supported a variant dating scheme for the alignment of these two sequences that was at one point controversial (Ball 1979a) but is now strongly supported by data from most northern lowland sites (Anderson 1998; Cobos 1999, 2004). The Nohmul data can be used to argue for total overlap in the Terminal Classic period (circa A.D. 800–900) with ceramic materials that were at one point placed substantially later in the Postclassic period in the northern lowlands. Again, these interpretive breakthroughs in aligning intersite chronologies come not so much from t-v-m but rather from a detailed contextual analysis of associated ceramics—and a focus on vessel reconstruction. As defined and championed by Gifford (1976: 21; see also 34–36) for Maya ceramic analysis, t-v-m methodology was not contextual but rather analytical: "[T]he chronology at Barton Ramie was derived

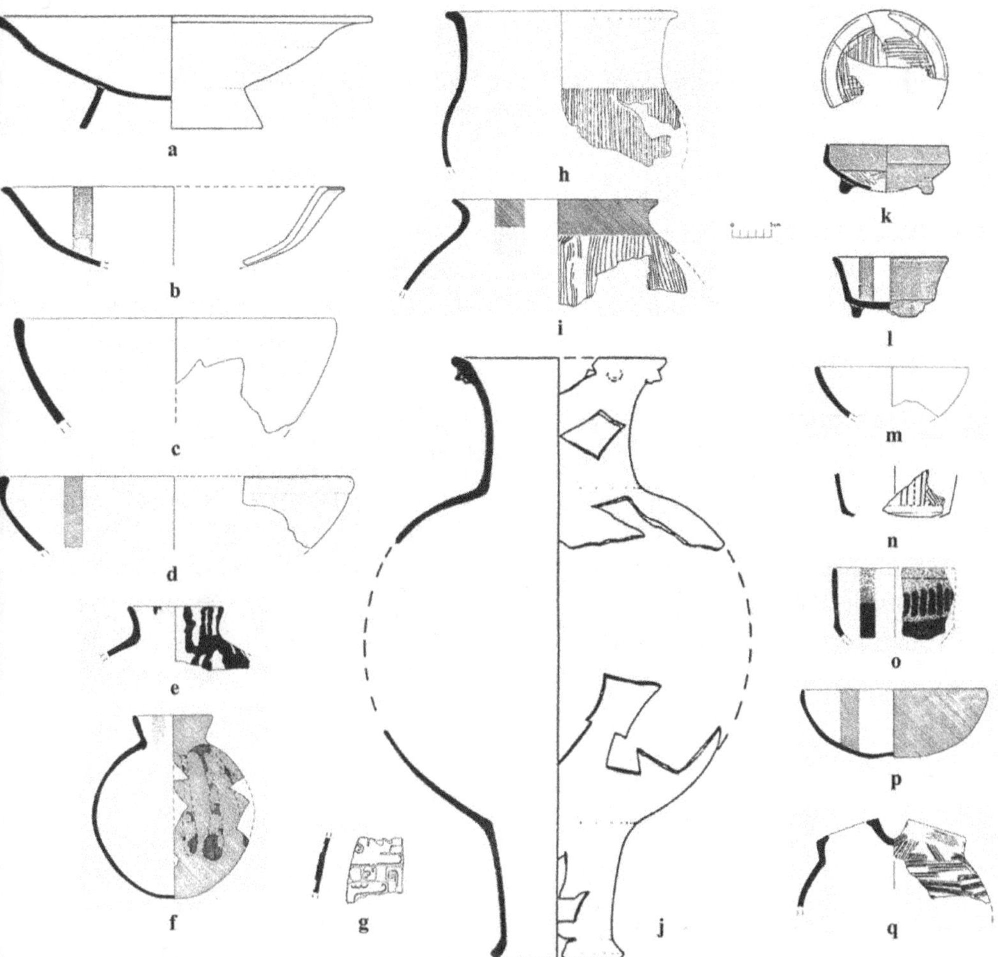

Figure 4.2. Vessels associated with Nohmul Structure 20: *a*, Kik Red; *b*, Taak Orange-red; *c*, Ohel Red; *d*, Campbells Red; *e*, Sansomal Black-on-cream; *f*, Chacil Black-on-red; *g*, Tzibana Gouged-incised; *h*, Chambel Striated; *i*, Red-Neck Mother Striated; *j*, Chembeku Modeled; *k*, Xixilic Incised; *l*, Metzabok Slate; *m*, Savinal Cream; *n*, Usukum Gouged-incised; *o*, Achote Black; *p*, Kik Red; *q*, Buyuk Striated. (Courtesy of D. Z. Chase and A. F. Chase, Corozal Postclassic Project.)

from ceramic analysis alone rather than from a consideration of 'constructional phases.'" Because t-v-m was explicitly operationalized as a taxonomic method for sequencing out-of-context fill materials at Barton Ramie, consideration of formation process (Schiffer 1987) has sometimes been neglected in the creation of ceramic complexes, meaning that temporal associations can be inappropriately established and inaccurate chronologies can be perpetuated.

Santa Rita Corozal Structure 81

The site of Santa Rita Corozal is located primarily on the bluff that overlooks Corozal Bay outside modern Corozal Town in northern Belize. It attracted early attention because of its extraordinary Postclassic remains (Gann 1900). The site is most likely the location of the Late Postclassic Maya capital of the Chetumal region (D. Chase 1986; D. Chase and A. Chase 1988: 65–68). Santa Rita Corozal Structure 81 was located in the northeastern limit of the site. It was the northern building of a formally arranged plaza group that was integrated with a raised acropolis area to its southwest (Platform 2; D. Chase and A. Chase 1988: 25–31).

Investigations were undertaken in Santa Rita Corozal Structure 81 during the summer of 1980. Excavations consisted of both areal clearing and axial penetration. Areal clearing revealed a multiroomed Late Postclassic construction that measured some 36 meters wide by 8.5 meters deep and was fronted by a formal terrace that extended for an additional 7.7 meters to the south of the building. Within Structure 81 were several interior rooms that were arranged around a central shrine room (figure 4.3). The shrine room contained a single

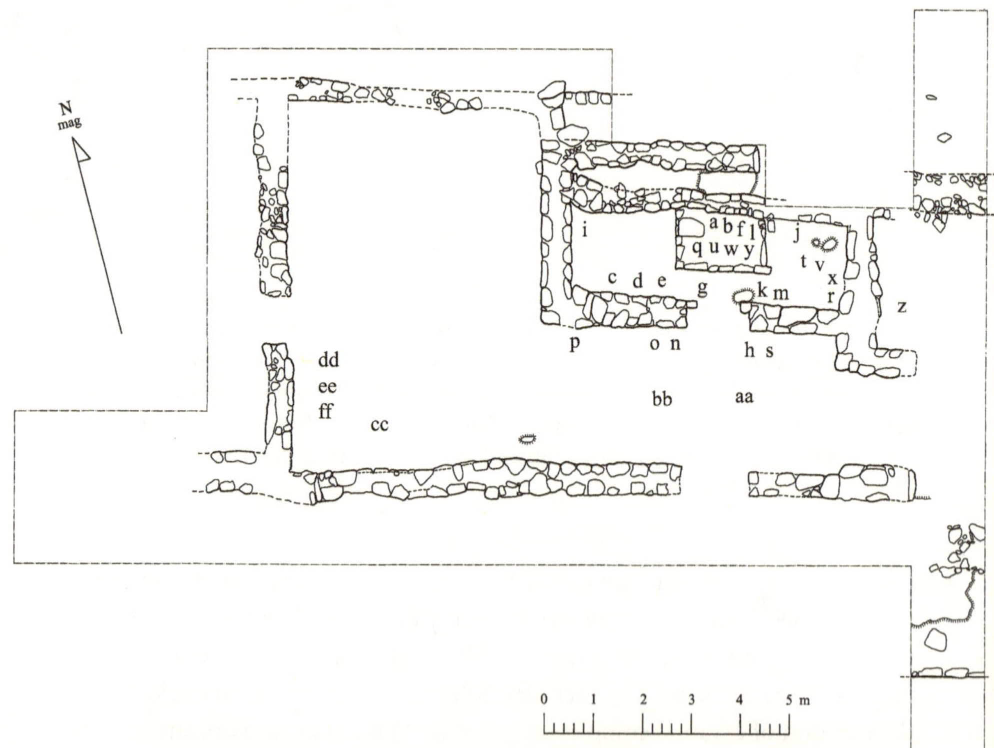

Figure 4.3. Plan of Santa Rita Corozal Structure 81 showing location of recovered vessels. Letters on plan correlate with letters associated with vessels in figure 4.4. (Courtesy of D. Z. Chase and A. F. Chase, Corozal Postclassic Project.)

formal door and had a constructed stone bench centered on its rear (north) wall. Contextual analysis of ceramics demonstrated that Structure 81 probably housed an oracle and that the narrow chamber or "alley" paralleling the northern wall of the shrine room was likely employed to provide cover for a hidden orator (D. Chase 1982b: 302–3); the form of the structure is, thus, similar to that of oracles noted ethnohistorically for Cozumel Island (Freidel 1975).

Substantial ceramic debris was located on the building's floors and within the construction core of the building. Although widely scattered, many of the ceramic materials located on the structure's floors could be reconstructed into almost whole pottery vessels (table 4.1; for distribution of the associated ceramics, see D. Chase 1982b: 259–88). It is only when t-v-m analysis is combined

Table 4.1. Sherds and vessels recovered from latest use of Santa Rita Corozal Structure 81

Ceramic group/type	No. of sherds	% of total	Non-vessel sherds	% of total	Vessel sherds	% of total	Total vessels	% of total	Sherds / vessel
Rita Group	1,418	36.54%	961	51.50%	457	22.68%	13	39.39%	35
Rita Red	1,262	32.52%	961	51.50%	301	14.94%	10	30.30%	30
Zanga Modeled	124	3.20%	0	0.00%	124	6.15%	1	3.03%	124
Kulel Modeled	32	0.82%	0	0.00%	32	1.59%	2	6.06%	16
Nucil Group	482	12.42%	0	0.00%	482	23.92%	3	9.09%	161
Nucil Modeled	93	2.40%	0	0.00%	93	4.61%	1	3.03%	93
Chontalli Red	247	6.36%	0	0.00%	247	12.26%	1	3.03%	247
Arroba Modeled	142	3.66%	0	0.00%	142	7.05%	1	3.03%	142
Cimatl Group	47	1.21%	18	0.97%	29	1.44%	1	3.03%	29
Cimatl Buff	47	1.21%	18	0.97%	29	1.44%	1	3.03%	29
Manta Group	37	0.95%	0	0.00%	37	1.84%	1	3.03%	37
Manta Buff	37	0.95%	0	0.00%	37	1.84%	1	3.03%	37
Cohokum Group	1,573	40.53%	683	36.60%	890	44.17%	14	42.43%	64
Kol Modeled	440	11.34%	307	16.45%	133	6.60%	2	6.06%	67
Santa Unslipped	1,078	27.77%	376	20.15%	702	34.84%	11	33.34%	64
Ayal Unslipped	55	1.42%	0	0.00%	55	2.73%	1	3.03%	55
Specials	120	3.09%	0	0.00%	120	5.95%	1	3.03%	120
Palmul Incised	120	3.09%	0	0.00	120	5.95%	1	3.03%	120
Other	204	5.26%	204	10.93%	0	0.00%	0	0.00%	0
Total	3,881	100.00%	1,866	100.00%	2,015	100.00%	33	100%	61

with the contextual analysis of the associated pottery that the activities in the Structure 81 locus may be reconstructed.

Type: variety-mode analysis of the pottery from the Structure 81 investigations appropriately reveals two different ceramic complexes. The fill materials sealed below the floor level of the Structure 81 supporting platform are mostly Terminal Classic–Early Postclassic in date (D. Chase 1982b: 252) and contain characteristic northern Belize types such as Buyuk Striated, Campbells Red, and Kik Red (D. Chase 1982a; Graham 1987); however, two caches purposefully placed in the building fill during construction establish the Postclassic dating for the building. The materials above the floor and intruded into the shrine room altar are Late Postclassic in date and include a majority of the Late Postclassic types identified for the Xabalxab ceramic complex (D. Chase 1982b, 1984).

If one were to make interpretations from t-v-m alone, the logical assumption would be the existence of two robust phases of activity, one dating to the Terminal Classic–Early Postclassic and the other to the Late Postclassic period. However, a contextual review of the ceramic deposition indicates a somewhat variant and far more detailed picture. First, contextual analysis makes it clear that the Terminal Classic–Early Postclassic materials—in spite of their abundance and the large size of the sherd pieces—were redeposited fill items in a Late Postclassic platform. They are not directly related to any earlier activity, as there was no earlier construction at the Structure 81 locus. In addition, while there is a dense concentration of large pottery sherds, few of these fit together as would be expected if the refuse was primary and use-related rather than redeposited. Second, contextual analysis makes it evident that the 33 reconstructable Late Postclassic vessels found in association with the use of Structure 81 do not represent a single abandonment event, but rather a protracted series of ritual activities (D. Chase 1982b; D. Chase and A. Chase 2000). In fact, ceramics were apparently left on the floor of the building even after initial breakage.

All of the sherd material that was excavated in the overlying humus, in the building collapse, on the floors of Structure 81, in between refurbished Late Postclassic building floors, and in pits cut through these floors—some 3,862 sherds—was processed according to t-v-m analysis. Analysis also considered the number of sherds in each reconstructable vessel. Thus, it is possible to examine the relationship between sherds and vessels (table 4.1; extrapolated from D. Chase 1982b: 624–39). These data reveal that almost half of the total sample of sherds recovered from Structure 81 could be refitted as vessels; other sherds recovered in excavation may have derived from some of these vessels but could not be securely fitted to them and thus were classified as "extraneous." An average of 61 sherds went into each of the 33 vessels that were cross-mended. As expected (P. Chase 1985: 217), the number of sherds per vessel was partially dependent on the size, thickness, and complexity of the resultant vessel. Smaller red ware bowls (Rita Group) averaged 30 sherds per vessel. The larger and thinner red wares (Nucil Group) broke into the most vessel pieces, averaging 161 sherds per vessel. Unslipped vessels, which included effigy incense burners and various-sized ollas, averaged a fairly standard 64 sherds per vessel. However, there were "outlier" ceramics as well; Kulel Modeled vessels had an average of 16 sherds per vessel, while a single Chontalli Red vessel was reconstructed from 247 pieces. One hundred and twenty sherds of a partial Palmul Incised vessel were also distributed throughout the excavations; at least twice this number of sherds would have been necessary to reconstruct the ceramic piece; they probably exist in the unexcavated eastern portion of Structure 81. Rita Red Group ceramics made up 36.54 percent of the sample by sherd count and 39.39 percent of the sample by vessel count. Nucil Group ceramics made up 12.42 percent of the sherd count and 9.09 percent of the vessel count. Cimatl Group ceramics made up 1.21 percent of the sherd count and 3.03 percent of the vessel count. Manta Group ceramics made up 0.95 percent of the sherd count and 3.03 percent of the vessel count. Cohukum Group ceramics made up 40.53 percent of the sample by sherd count and 42.43 percent of the sample by vessel count.

These data demonstrate that while overall ceramic group sherd frequency can be correlated broadly (within 2–3 percent) with the actual number of recovered reconstructable vessels, certain types are more prevalent as complete vessels than their relative sherd frequency would indicate (D. Chase 1982b: 617–19). The differences between sherd and vessel frequency become more striking when types are considered. For Structure 81, the most extreme case of this can be seen in Kulel Modeled, which makes up 0.82 percent of the sample by sherd count but 6.06 percent of the sample by vessel count. However, none of the relative sherd or gross vessel counts by type reflect the functional forms of the vessels that are present or are lacking in the sample. Most significantly, when the partial assemblage is reviewed in detail, it becomes evident that no water jars or sherds from water jars occur within this building (figure 4.4cc is a specialized vessel; see below), confirming the nondomestic ritual use of Structure 81. Thus, while attempts to quantify ceramics by simple counts or weights are better than nothing, such quantification may not be fully representative of the composition of the actual assemblage or subassemblage.

Detailed analysis and reassembly of the vessels in association within Structure 81 (figure 4.4) resulted in the definition of four distinct groupings of vessels and additional reconstruction of the behavioral events associated with these vessels (D. Chase 1982b). These four vessel groups were, to some extent, spatially segregated. The first vessel group (n=4) was located in the southwest corner of the main room. A set of three plain ware vessels that included two ollas and one shallow platter (thought to have functioned as a "roaster"; figure 4.4ee and 4.4ff [one not illustrated]) were stacked atop each other and had clearly been left in situ. In addition, most of a special-use large *tinajera* (Arroba Modeled; figure 4.4cc)—a tinajera is "a very large version of a *tinaja*, although the neck may be lower and wider" (Reina and Hill 1978: 26)—was located here; sherds from this vessel were also found in the shrine room. Together, these four vessels presumably formed an activity set, perhaps related to the preparation of an alcoholic drink (given the ritual function of this structure [as determined by the location of the interior shrine]). A second group of more elaborately decorated and larger vessels (n=9) appeared to have been part of a funerary ritual.

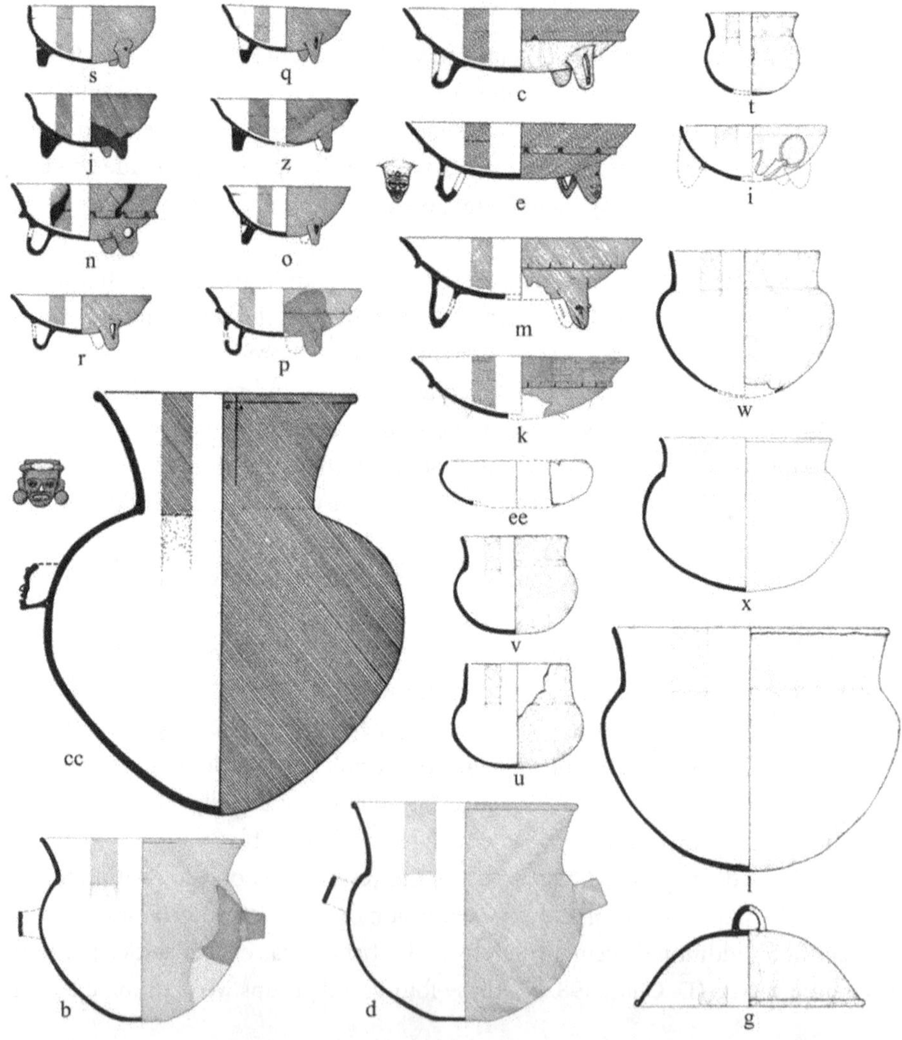

Some of these vessels (3 large red-slipped ollas [figure 4.4a, b, y], 1 red tripod bowl [figure 4.4q], and 1 unslipped olla [figure 4.4l]) were found only within a burial pit that had been intruded through the rear bench of the shrine room. However, other vessels that were included within this grave (1 red-slipped tripod jar [figure 4.4f], 2 unslipped ollas [figure 4.4u and 4.4w], and 1 red tripod bowl [figure 4.4j]) could also be refitted with sherd fragments from the floor of the shrine room; thus, they had been broken either intentionally or accidentally prior to their deposition in the grave.

By far the greatest number of vessels (*n*=18) made up a third grouping: these were found smashed, but scattered, within or immediately outside the shrine room and its doorway. While a large red-slipped olla (figure 4.4d) and a large unslipped lid (figure 4.4g) are included in this grouping, most were smaller

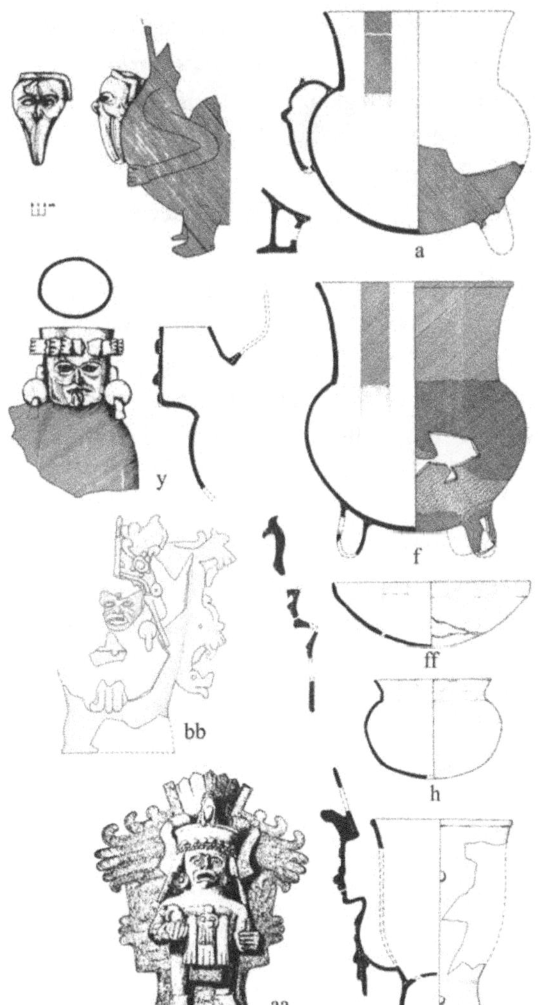

Figure 4.4. Vessels associated with Santa Rita Corozal Structure 81: *a*, Nucil Modeled; *b*, Rita Red; *c*, Manta Buff; *d*, Rita Red; *e*, Cimatl Buff; *f*, Chontalli Red; *g*, Ayal Unslipped; *h–i*, Santa Unslipped; *j*, Rita Red; *k*, Kulel Modeled; *l*, Santa Unslipped; *m*, Kulel Modeled; *n–s*, Rita Red; *t–x*, Santa Unslipped; *y*, Zanga Modeled; *z*, Rita Red; *aa–bb*, Kol Modeled; *cc*, Arroba Modeled; *dd*, Santa Unslipped (not shown); *ee–ff*, Santa Unslipped. (Courtesy of D. Z. Chase and A. F. Chase, Corozal Postclassic Project.)

vessels; six were tripod bowls (5 red-slipped [figure 4.4n, o, p, r, s] and 1 unslipped [figure 4.4i]), four were unslipped ollas (figure 4.4h, t, v, x), and four were red-slipped or buff-slipped tripod plates (figure 4.4c, e, k, m)—all presumably serving vessels suitable for holding offerings. One bowl (figure 4.4z) was located east of the shrine room. Virtually all of these ceramics were wholly or partially reconstructable, but again pieces of several nearly complete vessels in this group were found distributed in multiple locations and in more than one building room. Pieces of three of these vessels had been left smashed on the floor of the central shrine long enough to have been brushed, knocked, or otherwise located in the back "alley" of Structure 81 sealed below a plaster floor (*n*=2; figure 4.4j and 4.4p) and in the fill around a plaster-sealed cache pit (*n*=2; figure 4.4n and 4.4p). The fourth and final vessel grouping (*n*=2) consisted of a pair of effigy incense burners (figure 4.4aa and 4.4bb) that appear to have been placed in the main room in front of the rear shrine, possibly representing the latest activity at the Structure 81 locus. Elsewhere, similar *incensarios* have been related to calendric ritual and community organization thought to be correlated with *katun* ceremonies (D. Chase 1985b, 1985b; D. Chase and A. Chase 1988: 72, 2008). The effigy incense burners may also represent the physical idols that would have been associated with the postulated oracle that occupied the center of Structure 81.

The vessels and their pattern of archaeological occurrence are suggestive of accumulative ritual deposition rather than a single short-term abandonment event. The reassembly of this ritual subcomplex is also telling in what is present and in what is missing. Two effigy incensarios are present. Three large slipped collared ollas or jars, all with feet or handles, are present, and part of a fourth was also recovered. Nine tripod bowls (8 slipped red), four slipped and footed plates, and one large slipped tinajera are also present. Unslipped vessels include eight ollas of various sizes, one unslipped lid, and one roaster. Within this set of 33 vessels, however, several forms are lacking that would typically be expected in an elite domestic subcomplex. There were no water jars from Structure 81; there were no small jars; there were no grater bowls; and there were no drums or other musical instruments. These items were all included in the elite subcomplex from Terminal Classic Nohmul (see above), and all of these Postclassic forms are present in the ceramic materials recovered south of the adjoining Santa Rita Corozal Platform 2 (D. Chase 1982b: 318–50). From these data it is clear that the plentiful Structure 81 ceramic forms are quite specialized. Thus, contextual analysis provides functional information for the Structure 81 ceramics on long-term building use that could not have been determined through t-v-m analysis alone.

Caracol Epicentral Palaces and Structure A31

Caracol is one of the largest sites in the Maya lowlands. Located in western Belize high in the Maya Mountains, the city of Caracol integrated a settlement system that covered some 177 square kilometers (A. Chase and D. Chase 1994b, 1996). The site has been excavated by the Caracol Archaeological Project annually since 1985. These investigations have recovered detailed archaeological data from most of the epicentral temples and palaces as well as from over 120 outlying residential groups (A. Chase 1998; D. Chase 1998; field reports at www.caracol.org). A large amount of ceramic materials has been recovered from these investigations, and the outlines of the site's ceramic sequence have been presented (A. Chase 1994). Based on a consideration of these ceramic data, it is possible to tentatively identify palace and mortuary subcomplexes at Caracol as well as to examine spatial variation in the use of censer ware at the site (A. Chase and D. Chase 2004, 2005, 2007).

During the Caracol Archaeological Project excavations, on-floor debris has been recovered from many buildings at the site. At least for Caracol's palaces, these ceramics are remarkably consistent among the various contexts (A. Chase and D. Chase 2004, 2007), indicating that these materials were clearly coeval use-related assemblages and not a hodgepodge of various occupations (A. Chase and D. Chase 2008). That they are all Terminal Classic in date is clear both from the presence of recognized markers such as Tinaja Red tripod bowls and Sahcaba and Pabellon Molded-carved forms and from a consistent set of associated radiocarbon dates, all centering on approximately A.D. 895.

While both traditional and local Terminal Classic ceramic markers are easily recognized within t-v-m and are omnipresent in Caracol's epicentral palaces, they are relatively rare in outlying core area excavations. Although individual vessels, like those found in the epicentral palace ceramic subcomplex, have been found in many of Caracol's outlying residential groups, such vessels do not occur as part of a complete palace subcomplex in the outlying settlement (A. Chase and D. Chase 2005). While the relative absence of Terminal Classic markers in Caracol's residential settlement could be interpreted as a lack of Terminal Classic occupation in Caracol's core area, this would be incorrect. Areal clearing and substantial vessel reconstruction undertaken at the site make it evident that there are plain wares and censer wares that cross-tie the epicentral and core ceramic inventories but that the fine ware inventories are divergent. In fact, contextual analysis of Caracol's late ceramics suggests that traditional Terminal Classic ceramic markers form a status-linked ceramic subcomplex. This ceramic subcomplex, consisting of Terminal Classic fine wares (such as Sahcaba and Pabellon Molded-carved vases and Tinaja Red tripod bowls) that are recognizable throughout a broad region of the Maya lowlands, is strongly associated with the final elite occupants of the site's epicentral palaces (A. Chase and D. Chase 2004, 2005, 2007; D. Chase and A. Chase 2000). Again, this interpretation would not be apparent from simply undertaking traditional t-v-m analysis alone, as such an analysis would have minimized the Terminal Classic Period occupation at the site.

An interesting variant of the Terminal Classic period palace subcomplex was found in an epicentral building excavated during the 2006 field season at Caracol. Structure A31 is located in the middle of the Caracol epicenter between the A Plaza and the Central Acropolis. Situated immediately northeast of the A Group ballcourt, Structure A31 formed a western focus for what was apparently a late epicentral group placed in what had previously been an open epicentral space. The companion buildings for Structure A31 were both low-lying platforms placed to the north and east of Structure A31 to form an irregular plaza.

Structure A31 was raised approximately 1.5 meters above the surrounding plaza level. No traces of a formal structure were found atop the raised substructure. However, the stonework associated with the substructure was very high in quality, and the stone step on the eastern side of Structure A31 was in relatively good shape (see figure 4.5). A trench dug through the center of Structure A31 found the building to rest directly on an underlying plaza floor and to have been constructed as a single event. The four corner areas of the building substructure were all excavated. No artifactual materials were found to the rear of the building or on its sides, but some 21 reconstructable pottery vessels were recovered to either side and in front of Structure A31's stairway (figure 4.6).

The recovered ceramic materials from the Structure A31 stairway area provide some clues as to the building's use. The location of one larger and one smaller brazier to either side of the stairway hints that a symmetrical relationship was necessary for the rituals that were carried out at this locus. The braziers themselves are unusual. The taller brazier (figure 4.6d) may have been imported from northern Belize; similar vessels are common at Lamanai (Graham 1985: fig. 4.5a), where they are most common in the Buk phase, currently dated from A.D. 962 to 1200/1250 based on a preliminary assessment of a suite of radiocarbon dates (Graham 2008); this Lamanai dating is later than the dating assigned at Caracol (A. Chase and D. Chase 2007: 21, 2008) and elsewhere in central Belize (Awe and Helmke 2007: 37). The paste of this Buk-related Caracol brazier was analyzed in 2010; Aimers (personal communication 2012 and this volume) suggests that it can be placed in the Zalal Gouged-incised ceramic system based on its stylistic similarity to vessels from Cerros and Lama-

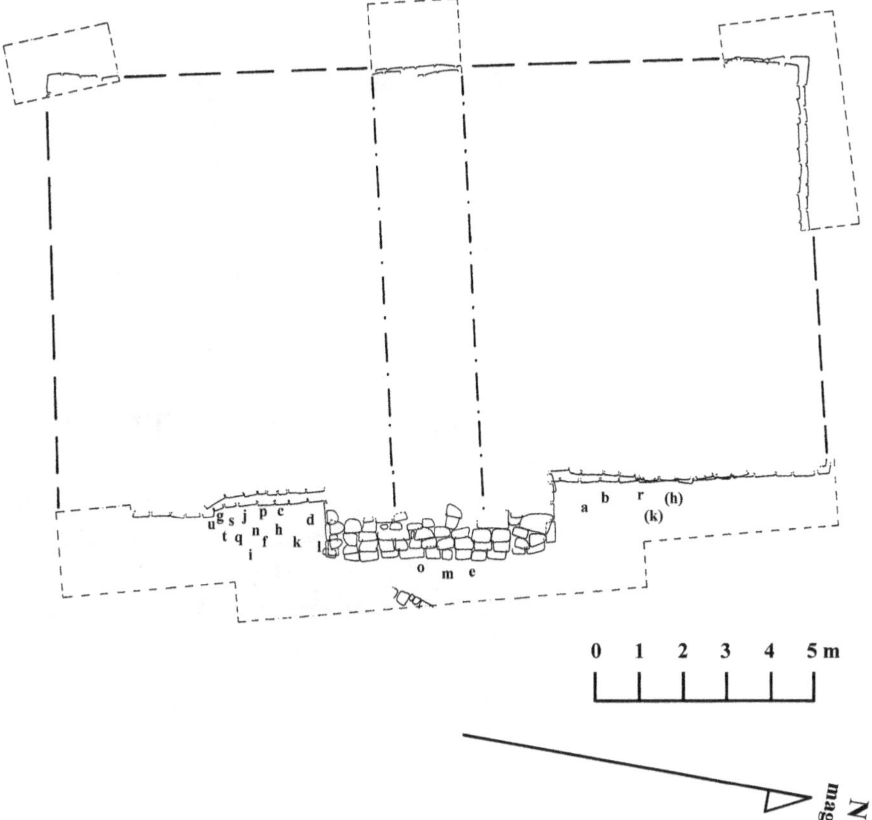

Figure 4.5. Plan of Caracol Structure A31. Letters on plan correlate with letters associated with vessels in figure 4.6. (Courtesy of A. F. Chase and D. Z. Chase, Caracol Archaeological Project.)

nai. However, the Terminal Classic context (with a late dating of approximately A.D. 900) of the Structure A31 vessel is clear (A. Chase and D. Chase 2007, 2008). The other globular brazier (figure 4.6a) is unique for Caracol but is related in size and concept to one recovered from the interior room of Structure A3 in 1985 (A. Chase and D. Chase 1987a: 14); similar braziers are reported as occurring at Isla Cerritos in the Yucatán (R. Cobos, personal communication, 2007). The smaller censers are also distinctive; one is a "fry-pan" type censer (figure 4.6c) of a kind found at Terminal Classic sites in the Petén region (Sabloff 1975) and at Chichén Itzá (Brainerd 1958); the other is a nonlocally made, fine-orange Mixtec incensario (figure 4.6b) that is widely dated to circa A.D. 900 throughout Mesoamerica (A. Chase and D. Chase 2007: 23). Thus, all four censers represent ritual items potentially manufactured outside the Caracol region.

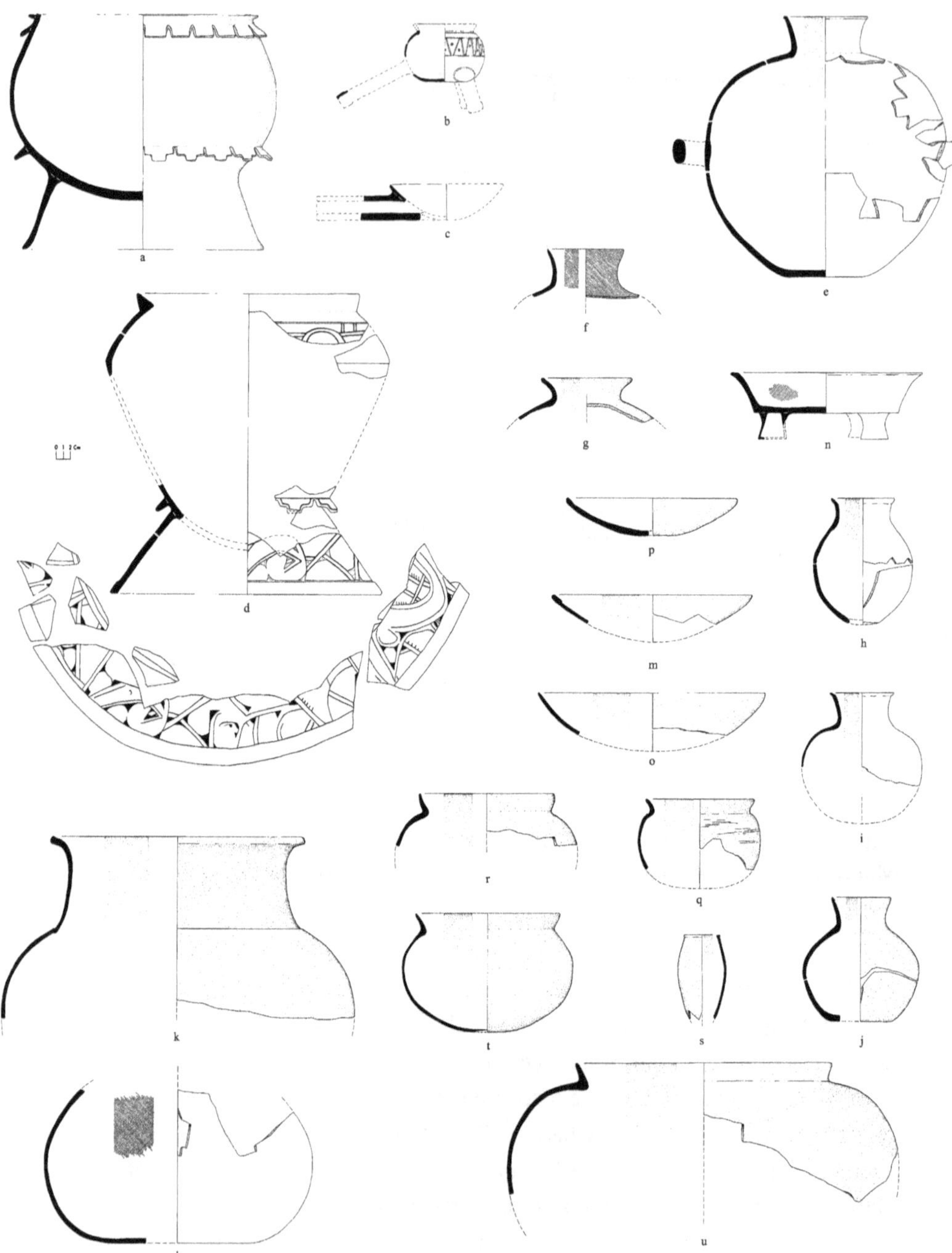

Figure 4.6. Vessels associated with Caracol Structure A31: *a*, undesignated; *b*, related to Altar Orange; *c*, possibly Miseria Appliqued; *d*, type possibly in the Zalal Gouged-incised ceramic system; *e*, undesignated; *f*, Tinaja Red; *g*, probably Valentin Unslipped; *h–j*, undesignated; *k*, Valentin Unslipped; *l*, possibly Infierno Black; *m*, undesignated; *n*, possibly copy of Altar Orange; *o–p*, undesignated; *q–u*, Valentin Unslipped. (Courtesy of A. F. Chase and D. Z. Chase, Caracol Archaeological Project.)

The other vessels from Structure A31 are also useful for interpreting function. Three larger water jars, one of which has handles on its sides, are represented in the collection, as are three smaller jars (possibly mugs). These six vessels indicate the use of a liquid in this vicinity. Four plain ware ollas, or cooking pots, are also included in the collections; these resemble later Postclassic ollas in form and rim treatment but are again of clear Terminal Classic period date (A. Chase and D. Chase 2007). One unslipped vessel may represent a small cup. Three round-bottomed dishes and one small plate with trumpet feet constitute the "serving" vessels. The tripod plate was once polychrome. Its diminutive size is appropriate for its Terminal Classic date. Its foot form and rim/lip treatment resemble examples from Chichén Itzá (Brainerd 1958: fig. 81). A rimless olla that was possibly burnt on its interior was also collected, as was a large storage jar that is modally similar to other Terminal Classic vessels recovered from excavations in the Northwest Acropolis (2006 field report at www.caracol.org).

Taken as a whole, the ceramics suggest that activities in the Structure A31 locus included both the preparation of food (that is, cooking) and the serving or offering of liquids. While some of these forms may derive from standard household goods, they are few in number and presumably represent containers used for ritual offerings in a nondomestic arena. The distinct assemblage suggests that this was a locus for specialized rituals that were not carried out elsewhere at the site.

The mix of ceramics found in sheet refuse associated with Structure A31 also points to the need to consider entire vessel units and not individual sherds in terms of dating (A. Chase and D. Chase 2008). Had the analysis been noncontextual and only analytically integrated (Gifford 1976: 21), these ceramics possibly could have been interpreted as indicative of a much longer use of the building. When combined with the problematic overlap among latest-use materials from palace floors in the site's epicenter and residential groups in the site's settlement that point to the existence of distinct but coeval ceramic subcomplexes, the importance of contextual analysis for determining contemporaneity of ceramics and estimating occupations during different timespans is abundantly evident.

Further Issues in Mortuary and Censer Ware Subcomplexes

Caracol Archaeological Project investigations have uncovered more than three hundred interments; almost 70 percent of these burials have ceramics associated with them. As with the Tikal, Guatemala, sample (Culbert 1993), it is possible to use these contextual ceramic groupings to seriate other pottery that has been gathered from fills. Because eight tombs at Caracol are associated both with ceramic offerings and with painted hieroglyphic dates, it is also possible to more securely date the internal Caracol seriation of the burial subcomplexes (A. Chase 1994). Such a seriation may be accomplished independently of any t-v-m analysis and helps to provide alternative datings for ceramic types as well as to suggest developmental origins for certain kinds of pottery. For instance, the ceramics grouped together as "Belize Red" (figure 4.7)—and first defined by Gifford (1976; Willey et al. 1965) for the Belize Valley—have a long history at Caracol.

Belize Red ceramics constitute an important part of burial offerings throughout the Late Classic era and may even have originated within the extended Caracol polity. Mend holes, or "crack-lacing," is a common occurrence within Belize Red vessels and sherds at Barton Ramie—"noticeably more in evidence than in connection with any other type ever represented at Barton Ramie" (Willey et al. 1965: 380). This could indicate that once these vessels were broken, it was difficult to replace them in the Belize Valley. The lack of mend holes in the Caracol ceramic sample (of both vessels and sherds) may indicate that the Belize Red vessels were more easily accessed in the Vaca Plateau than in parts of the Belize Valley. Even if not local in origin (A. Chase and D. Chase 2012), Belize Red vessels were available to most, if not all, households at Caracol throughout the Late Classic period, indicating easy access to, if not actual control over, at least one group of producers of this kind of pottery. While Belize Red sherds and partial vessels do appear regularly in construction fills at Caracol, the widespread occurrence of whole vessels of this type in burials and on floors of buildings also permits temporal faceting of its various form changes, something that would not be possible without contextual analysis. Thus, within the Caracol sample it is possible to demonstrate that the highly formalized concave-rim, sag-bottom plate is late Late Classic in date and that shallow vessels with thicker rims and nubbin feet are generally earlier in the sequence (A. Chase and D. Chase 2012).

Another example of the utility of contextual analysis can be found in the dating of vases as a form class at Caracol. Traditionally, polychrome cylinder vases were used as late Late Classic markers in the Petén (for example, Coggins 1975), but this form spans the entire Late Classic period at Caracol and can be faceted into earlier and later versions (like the Belize Red vessels). Earlier versions are consistently much shorter in height, broader in diameter,

Figure 4.7 (*facing page*). Sample of Belize Red vessels recovered from Caracol, Belize, illustrating possible standardization within different forms. (Courtesy of A. F. Chase and D. Z. Chase, Caracol Archaeological Project.)

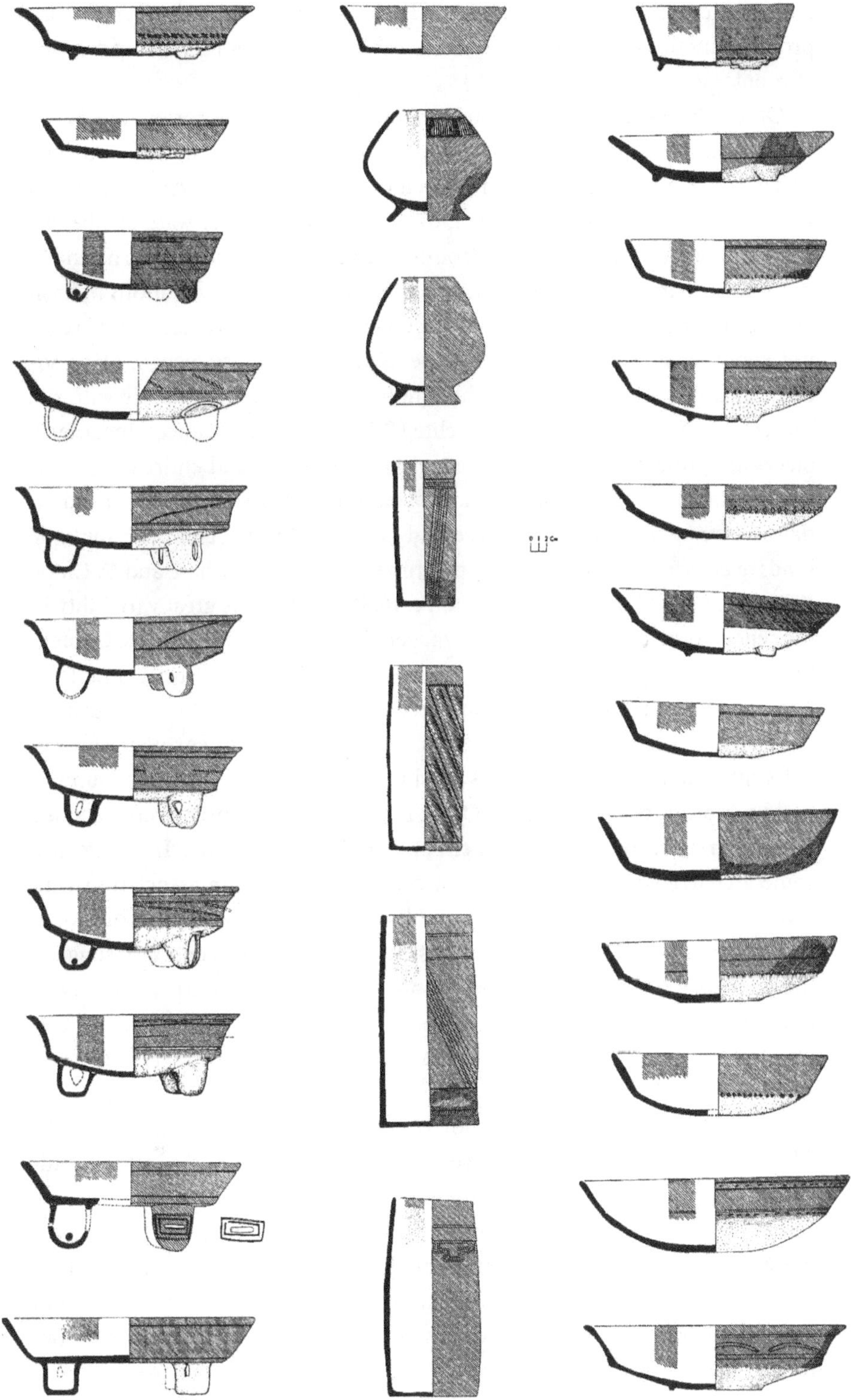

and more cuplike than the later vases. Thus, contextual analysis not only may provide functional information but also can be used to refine existing ceramic chronology.

Other classes of ceramics also may provide useful interpretations when considered contextually. Censer ware is sometimes included in t-v-m analysis (Adams 1971; Sabloff 1975; Smith 1971), and sometimes it is excluded (Gifford 1976; Culbert 1993 [but see Ferree 1967]). Regardless, censer ware can be difficult to analyze. Most of it is encountered in very fragmented form and is notoriously hard to piece together, which makes identifying variations in form and decoration difficult. In spite of presumed ideological connotations, we do not know exactly how incensarios were used within Classic period Maya society. In general, incensarios are thought to correlate predominantly with site centers, large architecture, and the elite (P. Rice 1999). At Caracol, incensario pieces are present in many non-epicentral excavations, and entire effigy censers are sometimes found on the stairs of buildings in "less-than-elite" residential housemound groups (A. Chase and D. Chase 1994b). However, multiple kinds of censers also existed at any one time at Caracol (A. Chase and D. Chase 1987a: fig. 9; 2004: figs. 16.4a, 16.5, 16.7c, 16.8), and there is great variability in the censer form, even though some imagery is repeated among forms. Contextual analysis suggests that Caracol's censers served several distinct functions. The majority of the censers that are reconstructable appear to have been associated with the latest use of buildings, having been left either singularly or in pairs either at the base of stairways for shrines or temples or within the summit buildings prior to abandonment. Other reconstructable censers were included within burials as offerings, again either singularly or in pairs. There are also some archaeological indications that censers were used in association with some household or domestic subcomplexes. And because of the contextual focus and the emphasis on vessel reconstruction, the Caracol data also suggests that some of the materials that are traditionally called "incensarios" within t-v-m or other analyses may actually be more mundane decorated "burners" that were used for general cooking purposes within residential groups (see also Ball and Taschek 2007b).

A similar contextual consideration of censer ware at Santa Rita Corozal (D. Chase 1988; D. Chase and A. Chase 1998, 2008) also demonstrates that multiple kinds of censers were used simultaneously (figure 4.8) and, as at Caracol, sometimes preserved in situ as remnants of the latest preabandonment activity at a given locus. Additionally, Late Postclassic effigy hourglass incensarios found at Santa Rita Corozal (for example, figure 4.4aa and 4.4bb) did not merely represent the willy-nilly deposition of a plethora of Maya deities but rather were idols that were purposely created and purposefully deposited in

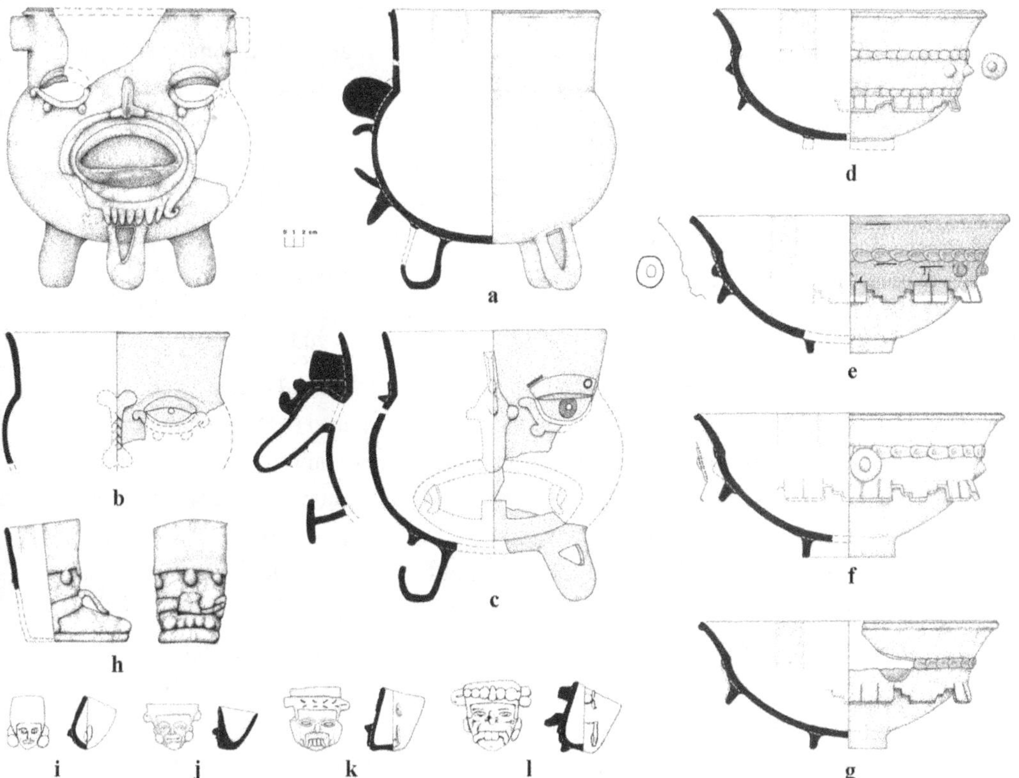

Figure 4.8. Pottery classified as "censer ware" from Santa Rita Corozal (see also figure 4.4aa and 4.4bb). Even though this is a single analytical category, the great variability of vessel forms is suggestive of specific multiple ritual functions. (Courtesy of D. Z. Chase and A. F. Chase, Corozal Postclassic Project.)

the archaeological record—most likely as part of calendric ritual (D. Chase 1985a, 1985b, 1986; D. Chase and A. Chase 1988, 2008). Traditional t-v-m analysis was not designed to draw these kinds of functional distinctions.

Conclusion

For better or worse, the current implementation of the type: variety-mode system of ceramic analysis in the Maya area is ready to be revamped. Rather than suggesting a completely new analytic framework, however, we would suggest the integration of t-v-m analysis with contextual analysis focused on reconstructable vessels, whenever possible. The process of ceramic analysis in the Maya area has become somewhat formulaic with many analysts assigning types and making counts with little attention paid to contextual and functional meaning. Without knowing exactly what vessel forms are present in a given context and what grouping of vessels constitute that context, analysts have difficulty placing the ceramics into a cultural milieu, which complicates the delineation of ceramic exchange and the interpretation of stylistic interaction. The focus on sherds, rather than on whole vessels or contexts, means that we have minimized the possibility of cultural interpretation, sometimes limiting expectations to the identification of types and varieties. Part of this focus is due to the need to process bulk ceramic material that has been excavated and is sometimes driven by permit requirements to analyze materials quickly and to develop type collections for viewing in national or regional collections (as in Mexico). But, as noted by Gifford (1976) in his influential conceptualization of t-v-m analysis, there is an abundance of sherd material in the archaeological record in comparison to whole vessels. And while detailing the multitude of sherd materials from an analytical standpoint was difficult enough, there also existed a not-always-correct assumption that a focus on reconstructable vessels encountered in specific subcomplexes would provide an incomplete ceramic picture or inhibit intersite comparisons. However, most collections of sherds, even those gathered by long-term large-scale projects and subjected to many years of analysis (such as those from Barton Ramie), represent only partial samples of the actual past. Thus, contextual analysis of recovered ceramics and a focus on recovering subcomplexes can substantially bolster traditional t-v-m analysis and potentially provide substantial alternative information relative to dating and cultural interpretations. Issues of mixed contexts, uneven breakage of sherds among forms and/or types, the probable existence of distinct and contemporaneous ceramic subcomplexes, and the functional analysis of ceramic materials are all easily masked when using t-v-m alone.

This chapter is not suggesting the abandonment of t-v-m analysis, which is still useful and necessary, especially in considerations of sherd-only collections and in comparisons among sites. Rather, we argue that Maya ceramic study can greatly benefit from additional modes of analysis that are specifically designed to develop and augment cultural interpretations. The examples selected here highlight the utility of combining contextual analyses and subcomplexes with more traditional t-v-m analysis as a means of making detailed functional and chronological interpretations that would not be possible through the use of t-v-m analysis alone.

Acknowledgments

The authors wish to acknowledge the long-term support of the Belizean Institute of Archaeology, specifically, Jaime Awe, John Morris, George Thompson,

Harriot Topsey, and Brian Woodye. We also wish to thank James Aimers for several detailed commentaries on earlier drafts of this chapter; he has helped us to better focus our arguments. The data reported in this chapter have been collected over 35 years of excavation in the country of Belize. A very early version of this chapter was presented at the 64th Annual Meeting of the Society for American Archaeology in 1999.

5

Ceramic Resemblances, Trade, and Emulation

Changing Utilitarian Pottery Traditions in the Maya Lowlands

ROBERT E. FRY

This chapter examines the role of exchange and emulation in assessing resemblances among regional ceramic assemblages. I review changing assumptions about the nature of ceramic production and distribution in light of recent research. Interest in exchange has tended to center on widely distributed polychrome serving vessels, while studies of utilitarian ceramics have tended to assume more localized production-consumption systems. In this chapter I concentrate on the information available from utilitarian ceramics, those used primarily in everyday household activities. I examine the evidence for specialized production and exchange in two regions—south-central Quintana Roo and northern Belize. In addition, I discuss the role of emulation in restructuring of both serving and utilitarian vessel production and distribution.

In this chapter I examine the similarities in assemblages among lowland Maya sites within a region. Most studies that try to establish affinities have concentrated either on shared presence of popular types and/or varieties, or on broad overall similarities without reference to the type-variety system. I show how patterns of resemblance of major shape categories of pottery that differ in demand structure and portability can give us useful insights into patterns of regional political and economic affiliation, as well as placement of sites in a regional site hierarchy.

Ceramic Production and Exchange Systems in the Maya Lowlands

There has been ongoing disagreement among lowland Maya ceramicists about the degree of specialization and scale of production of lowland Maya ceramics during the Classic period (Rice 1987a; Sharer 2005; Bill 1997; West 2002). Very few specialist workshops have been found (Becker 1973, 2003; Coggins 1975; Smyth et al. 1995). Instead, the presence of nonlocal materials in pastes, stylistic patterns, and unique configurations of lip and shape characteristics has been used to discriminate the products of localized workshops. It is now widely accepted that there was full occupational specialization for polychrome serving vessels, especially fine colloidal-slip polychrome vases and bowls (Ball 1993). Since Rands's pioneering work on Palenque-region ceramics (Rands 1967; Rands and Bishop 1980), we have known that there was some regional specialization in utilitarian ceramics, although the degree of specialization and scale of production have been controversial. Most utilitarian ceramics were consumed within regional systems (Hammond 1975; Hammond and Harbottle 1976; West 2002). However, even large coarse ware utilitarian jars, which might be expected to be very locally distributed through supply zone behavior (Renfrew 1975), can be shown to have been transported significant distances. Examples of the northern Belizean type Dumbcane Striated have been documented up to 100 kilometers from their production locations, possibly because water transport was available (Fry 1989).

Pottery production-distribution systems were on a large scale during the Classic period. Maya populations were consistently high (Culbert and Rice 1990), and there was heavy consumption of pottery in both elite and nonelite households in both the Late and Terminal Classic periods. In addition to regular household consumption and feasting events, it has become clear that major demand was also generated by massive pottery offerings in caves (Pendergast, 1969, 1971; Brady et al. 1997) and termination rituals and other renewal ceremonies at ritual structures and shrines (Fry 1969; Wille 2007). There is strong evidence from fall-off curves (Renfrew 1975) that locally produced wares were distributed through local and regional markets and major markets at central places (Fry and Cox 1974; Fry 1979, 1980; Bill 1997; Foias and Bishop 1997). Though some insist that redistributive systems are adequate to explain the patterning of the distribution of products of local workshops (for example, Rice 1987a, 1987c; Ball 1993), the scale of the system and the patterning of distribution (West 2002) argue against this position.

Nevertheless, clay and temper resources were so widely available throughout the Maya lowlands that industrial-scale production and specialization was probably unnecessary. The central Tikal market redistributed pottery from sources 8–12 kilometers from the market to places more than 20 kilometers distant. Though by Mesoamerican highland standards this does not seem a great distance, keep in mind that the population in the market area of Tikal in the Late Classic is estimated at slightly over 60,000 people (Culbert et al. 1990)—larger than estimated for the whole Valley of Oaxaca for much of its archaeological sequence until the Monte Alban III A phase (Blanton et al. 1982; Feinman et al. 1985; Kowaleski et al. 1989).

One of the major problems facing lowland Maya ceramicists is the inability to locate a significant number of pottery production locations. Here most of the evidence seems to be of fancier serving-form polychromes (Ball 1993), and even this has been questioned (West 2002). Becker (1973) and I have argued earlier that many production locations were dispersed in lower-density occupation areas at the edges of major sites (Fry and Cox 1974; Fry 1979). The pollution from firing and the location of good clay sources near *bajo* edges may have been major factors in such siting. At Tikal, fall-off curves of one major paste group indicated a zone of about four square kilometers as the likely location of a major production center in the northwest section of peripheral Tikal. The only possible firing area we found in peripheral Tikal was a deposit in the north Tikal earthworks adjacent to a causeway, which did have an unusual, thick, carbon-rich context. The pottery from this context was overwhelmingly of two shape classes (vases and pottery drums) with identical pastes. In some contemporary traditional societies in Mesoamerica, pottery was sometimes fired in open ditches, so as to better control the draft.

Some have proposed that much of the firing was done without enclosed kilns and thus would not leave much evidence except for ashy deposits, wasters, and props (Rice 1987c). Given preservation conditions in the Maya lowlands, it is likely that overfired and burnt sherds might have been susceptible to early deterioration. Such wasters were discovered in a context at Sayil, which is dominated by Puuc Slate Ware and identified as a possible workshop (Smyth and Dore 1992; Smyth et al. 1995).

There have been attempts to use standardization of attributes to assess the degree of specialization in Maya pottery production (Rice 1981, 1991; Beaudry 1984, 1987; Foias and Bishop 1997). Although logically this is a useful measure, I have reservations about using overly simple measures to assess standardization. For example, rim diameter, though showing a wide range of variation, should be studied to see if there are specific multiple modes. On one hand, plates and dishes of one paste class that have a wide range of variation in rim diameter could well be seen as reflecting a lower level of standardization and hence could erroneously be seen as products of a less specialized workshop or part-time producers. On the other hand, this may reflect the creation of easily stacked graded-diameter sets, common in very specialized workshops (figure 5.1). Sabloff and Rathje (1975) used the specific example of Muna Slate dishes to argue for a high degree of specialized production and commercialization for the Late to Terminal Classic Cozumel economy. Recently, Sarah Wille has discovered a stair-step distribution of rim diameters for large Terminal Classic bowls in a special deposit at the site of Chau Hiix, Belize (Wille 2007). This would indicate use of a graded series of bowls at the site.

Figure 5.1. Stacked set of contemporary Mexican bowls. (Photo by author.)

Another factor that should be kept in mind is the functional characteristics of differing shape classes. Not all attributes may be uniformly useful across shape classes in assessing standardization. For example, Foias and Bishop (1997: 280) note that narrow-mouth jars seem much more standardized than would be expected given the smaller demand for such vessels. Similarly, in my studies at Tikal, Uaymil, and Pulltrouser Swamp, I documented that the variation in rim diameter of such vessels is very limited. Such vessels constituted about 8 to 14 percent of the repertoire of shape classes. There are slight variations between regions, with Tikal specimens somewhat larger in diameter and the Uaymil examples smaller, but with a similar range and standard deviation within each region. It is likely that functional characteristics such as restricting spillage and ease of pouring seriously constrain orifice variability. Furthermore, most narrow-mouth jars presumably were water-carrying jars. Raymond Thompson's classic ethnoarchaeological studies of Yucatecan Maya pottery making (Thompson 1958) demonstrate that historically, water-carrying jars were very important as prestige goods, with several production centers dominating production, and under strong selective pressure. We do not need to abandon standardization tests, but we need to use common sense and functional studies to choose the appropriate variables to infer standardization.

Assessing Ceramic Similarities among Sites

Traditionally we have used the identification of specific types and varieties to place assemblages chronologically and show patterns of trade and influence. For smaller-scale regions, studies of paste variants and unique inclusions can identify local production-distribution systems (Rands 1967; Rands and Bishop 1980; Fry and Cox 1974; Fry 1979). There have been few attempts to try to assess measures of stylistic or technological resemblance among ceramic assemblages using variation *within* types and varieties or *within* broad shape classes. Traditionally, we infer resemblances because of the presence of similar types or even suites of types and varieties between or among sites. The concept of ceramic sphere is based on the shared presence of a suite of types and/or varieties among sites. But how do, say, Tinaja Red vessels from Tikal compare with Tinaja Red vessels from Uaxactún or more distant sites? Is there a pattern of similarity based on geographic distance? Or are the variations random in space? In many cases the lack of preservation of surfaces can make type-variety classification impossible for a sample of ceramics large enough to permit statistical studies. However, useful information may also be extracted by searching for patterning within major shape classes even in the absence of well-preserved surfaces. For example, in what specific ways do slipped large bowls from one site resemble those from another site or series of sites?

I experimented with such approaches while studying the ceramics recovered by the Uaymil Survey Project in southern Quintana Roo (figure 5.2) (Fry 1973b, 1974). In addition to traditional type-variety classification, I created a ceramic database using a codebook (Fry 1973a) in order to standardize formats for variables. This approach was pioneered in work in the Mexican Highlands and introduced into the Maya area by the Kaminaljuyu Project (Wetherington 1978a, 1978b). I developed a codebook for analyzing the ceramics from peripheral Tikal (Fry 1969) based in part on the Kaminaljuyu codebook. These programs were an attempt to go beyond what was by then traditional type-variety analysis to explore variability within types and varieties and to quantify this variability. We were also looking for new ways to measure degrees of standardization. Finally, there was a concern among some ceramic specialists that though type-variety was extremely useful for traditional cultural-historical reconstruction, many aspects of ceramic variability were not being effectively exploited by the system (Culbert and Rands 2007; Forsyth 1983). The addition of shape categories (Culbert 1993; Kosakowski 1987, 2003) and paste classes (Culbert and Rands 2007) was also initiated in the same period.

Information about 38 attributes was recorded for each vessel or each sherd or group of sherds representing a separate vessel (rim and diagnostic body

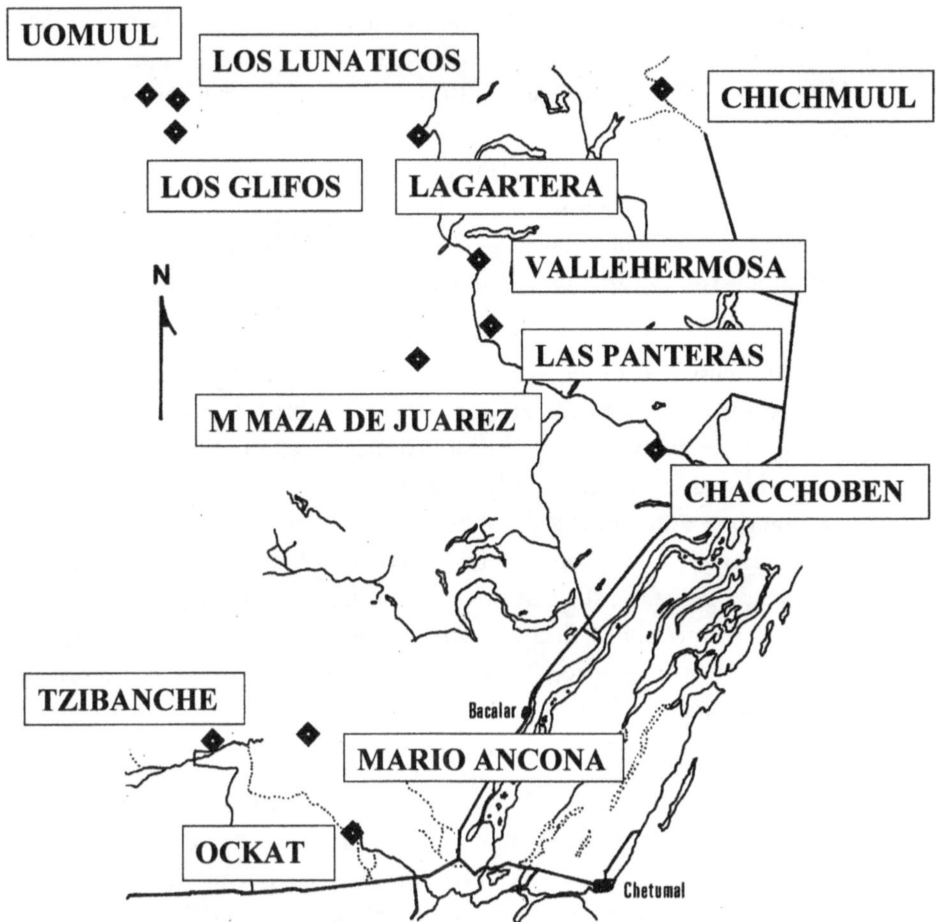

Figure 5.2. Map of sites in southern Quintana Roo studied by the Uaymil Survey Project. (After Fry 1987: fig. 1.)

sherds). These attributes reflected technology (for example, characteristics involved in production such as paste characteristics and firing characteristics), style (based on such characteristics as wall flare and curvature, decorative appendages, and so forth), and shape (based on a graded series of shape classes). A total of 4,437 rim or diagnostic body sherds representing separate vessels from 12 sites were analyzed.

In this study I discuss the results of only four of a series of studies on ceramic resemblances. Although it would be very informative to examine resemblances among types and varieties, in the case of the Uaymil Project, sample sizes were not large enough to provide statistically useful comparisons. In the current study I present results of the analysis of two major shape classes. Two of the most common shapes within the Uaymil zone (and also the rest of the Maya lowlands) are large slipped bowls and basins used for food preparation and storage, and unslipped wide-mouth jars used for storage of both solids and liquids.

The multidimensional scaling (MDS) approach I used in this analysis was one I used previously to assess patterns of production and consumption in the peripheries of Tikal, Guatemala (Fry and Cox 1974; Fry 1979, 1980), and to search for axes of variation reflecting social class in the same sample (Fry 2003a, 2003b):

> Multidimensional scaling is an analytic technique that places units or items compared by a measure of similarity or difference in a multidimensional space. Items that are very similar are placed in close proximity, while those that are significantly different are placed farther apart. One can interpret either the clusters or grouping of units or the axes on which they are arrayed. Solutions can be many dimensions down to a single dimension. Usually two- and three-dimensional solutions provide the optimal interpretability. Each solution can be seen as a model of the data in multidimensional space. The difference between the actual measures of distance and the models—that is, the goodness of fit—is indicated by a measure called stress. (Fry 2003b: 88)

Measures of technological and stylistic dissimilarity were created for all pairs of ceramic samples from sites in the study (see table 5.1). A profile of the characteristics of each shape class was created for each site. Coefficients of dissimilarity were created for each pair of sites based on deviations from the mean values for each attribute chosen. The formula for this measure is as follows:

$$IDt = \Sigma ni{=}1\ \Sigma mj{=}1\ (Xij - Yij)$$

where X_{ij} is the relative frequency at site X for the value *j* of variable 1, and Y_{ij} is the relative frequency at site Y for value *j* of the variable 1, *n* is the total number of variables, and *m* is the total number of values per variable.

These coefficients were then entered into a multidimensional scaling analysis program (KYST), which presents a graphic display of resemblances among sites in multiple dimensions (Kruskal et al. 1973).

In the cases presented, stress for the two-dimensional solutions was acceptably low and the additional information in the higher-level solutions showed no clear-cut patterns. In order to bring out further patterns in the ceramic resemblances, the final distances between sites in the multidimensional scaling solutions were used as inputs into a Johnson clustering program (Johnson 1967). This allowed us to cluster the sites, showing the degree of dissimilarity

Table 5.1. Attributes used in the analysis of pottery collected by the Uaymil Project from sites in east-central Quintana Roo

Stylistic attributes	Technological attributes
Wall or neck form	Paste color
Wall or neck curvature	Tempering material
Lip shape	Inclusions
Lip orientation	Temper to clay proportions
Wall-base form	Temper size
Interior surface treatment	Firing core
Exterior surface treatment	
Interior surface decoration	
Exterior surface decoration	
Location interior surface decoration	
Location exterior surface decoration	
Slip color	
Rim thickness	
Wall thickness	
Base thickness	

for each step of the clustering process. Of the alternative types of clustering available in the Johnson program, we chose the diameter method as the most useful. In this method, weighted centroids are calculated as each assemblage is added to the cluster.

The first analysis (figure 5.3) was of monochrome slipped bowls from the middle and later Late Classic from the 12 sites. This shows the resemblances of the bowls across a large region based on stylistic attributes. This gives a clearer-cut picture of regional stylistic resemblance than the solution for technological attributes, which is heavily influenced by types of clays available, tempering materials, and other variables less affected by stylistic choices. Not all 12 sites are included, since some had samples too small to be statistically significant.

The result of the multidimensional scaling of stylistic variables shows three broadly geographical clusters: an eastern grouping including the sites of Chacchoben and Chichmuul; a central-area cluster including Vallehermosa, Lagartera, Margarita Maza de Juarez, and a southern outlier of Ockat; and another major cluster that includes the western site of Uomuul and the centrally located site of Las Panteras. Though these are largely geographic groupings, the last cluster is of two fairly distant sites. Looking at the axes of variation, we can see

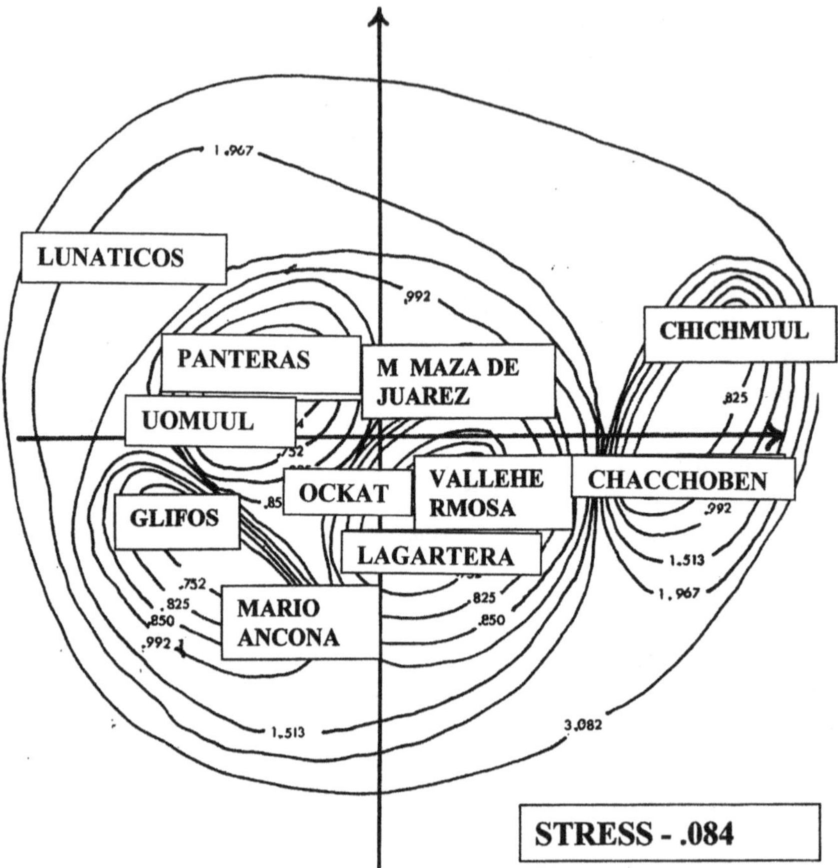

Figure 5.3. Two-dimensional MDS solution of stylistic resemblances of Late Classic slipped bowls from Quintana Roo.

that the horizontal axis tends to be an east–west geographical axis. The vertical axis, while less clear-cut, seems to reflect a north–south axis, with a few exceptions. Thus, geography does seem relevant to interpreting similarities among the collections of slipped bowls. The differences may reflect slightly differing periods of major occupation of the sites or at least of the ceramics we encountered in our small-scale excavations. Both Uomuul and Las Panteras had more Copo sphere ceramics and may date somewhat later than the other sites. Alternatively, they may have participated in a tighter economic and cultural relationship.

When considering similarities among collections based on technological attributes, we might expect that the resemblances among sites would be more clear-cut, hence there should be a lower level of stress. In addition, because fewer attributes were considered, we would expect to see a better fit and hence

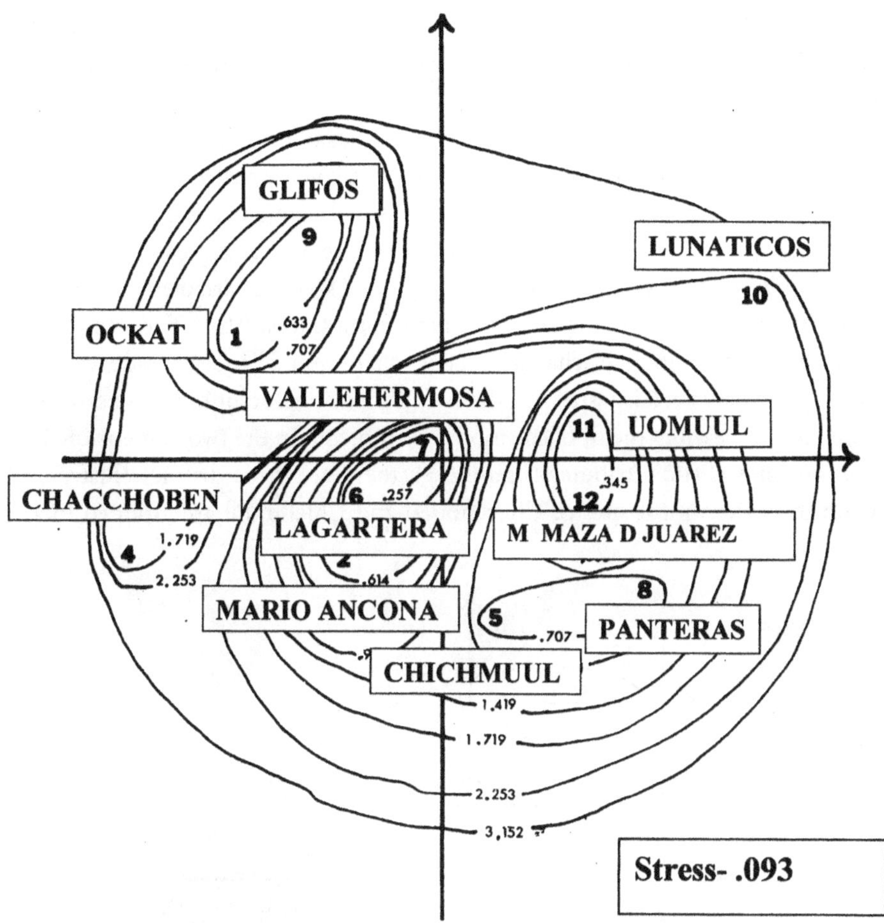

Figure 5.4. Two-dimensional MDS solution of technological resemblances of Late Classic slipped bowls from Quintana Roo.

lower stress. For technological attributes we should also expect that considerations of clay types and local geology would loom more importantly than geography. The MDS solution for technological attributes of slipped bowls (figure 5.4) is in many ways similar to that for stylistic attributes. Contrary to our expectations, stress, although similar, was actually higher for the technological attributes. Some of the clusters visible in the first solution have been rearranged. In part this may be because the solutions can be reversed and inverted while maintaining similar distances. In terms of axes of variation, there now is a different pattern. Though there is again an east–west axis on the horizontal axis, albeit a weaker one and reversed in orientation from the solution for stylistic attributes, there is a differing vertical axis. Those sites significantly above the horizontal axis are all smaller centers with smaller plazas and smaller public buildings. Thus, this axis reflects placement in the site hierarchy. Examination of the attributes used in the analysis indicates that this represents a quality factor. Collections for smaller sites have coarser pastes and more firing issues than those from more central places.

The third analysis was of stylistic characteristics of unslipped wide-mouth jars. These are often more massive vessels, usually considered less easily transportable and more likely to be circulated by supply-zone behavior (Renfrew 1975). Compared to the case with slipped bowls, there was a greater concordance between the solutions for technological and stylistic variables. This presumably reflects the more localized production traditions. The differences between collections should be sharper because there would be fewer trade wares blurring the pattern. Also, stress in the two-dimensional solutions was consistently lower, meaning the fit of the models was better. In the two-dimensional solution for stylistic attributes (figure 5.5), there are three distinct clusters. Again the easternmost sites of Chacchoben and Chichmuul are grouped to-

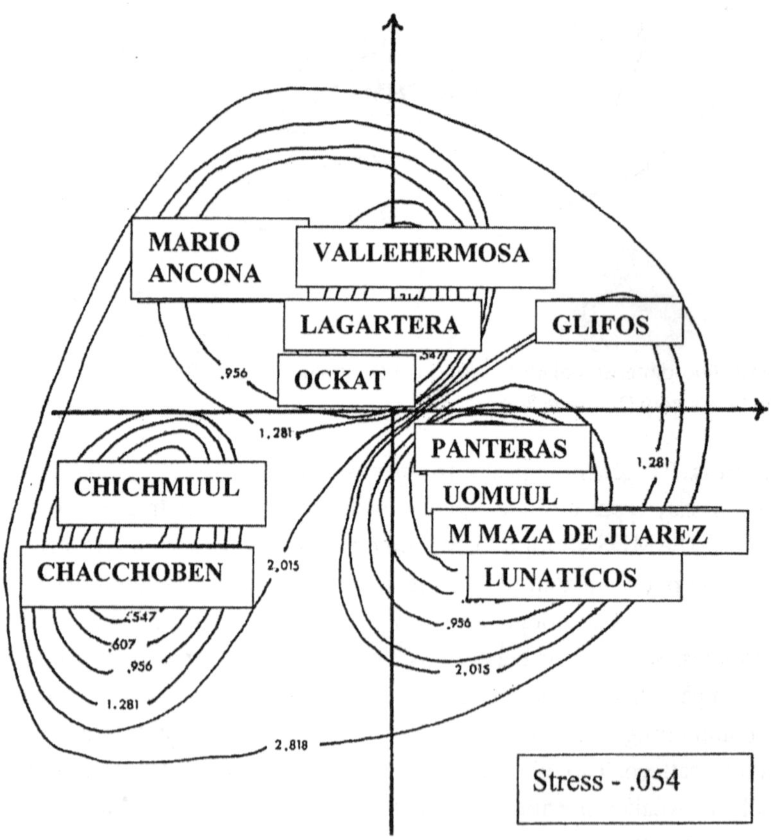

Figure 5.5. Two-dimensional MDS solution of stylistic resemblances of Late Classic unslipped jars from Quintana Roo.

gether. Nearby sites of Uomuul, Lunaticos, and Los Glifos are closely clustered in this MDS solution of stylistic resemblances. There is a broad division between northern and western versus southern and eastern sites. Overall, the pattern is remarkably similar to the solution for slipped bowls, showing that there is an overall structure to ceramic relationships involving quite discrete categories in terms of both function and portability. Studies of serving forms tend to replicate these patterns, as seen in shared types between sites.

The MDS solution for technological attributes of wide-mouth unslipped jars (figure 5.6) should represent supply-zone behavior most clearly, with more discrete clusters and spacing that more closely parallels the geographical distances between centers. Our expectations are confirmed. Closely spaced sites like Uomuul, Lunaticos, and Glifos are proximate in the solution. The same is true of Las Panteras and Margarita Maza de Juarez. Lagartera and Vallehermosa mark another closely spaced dyad. The clustering of Ockat with this group probably derives from the slightly earlier Late Classic samples at these

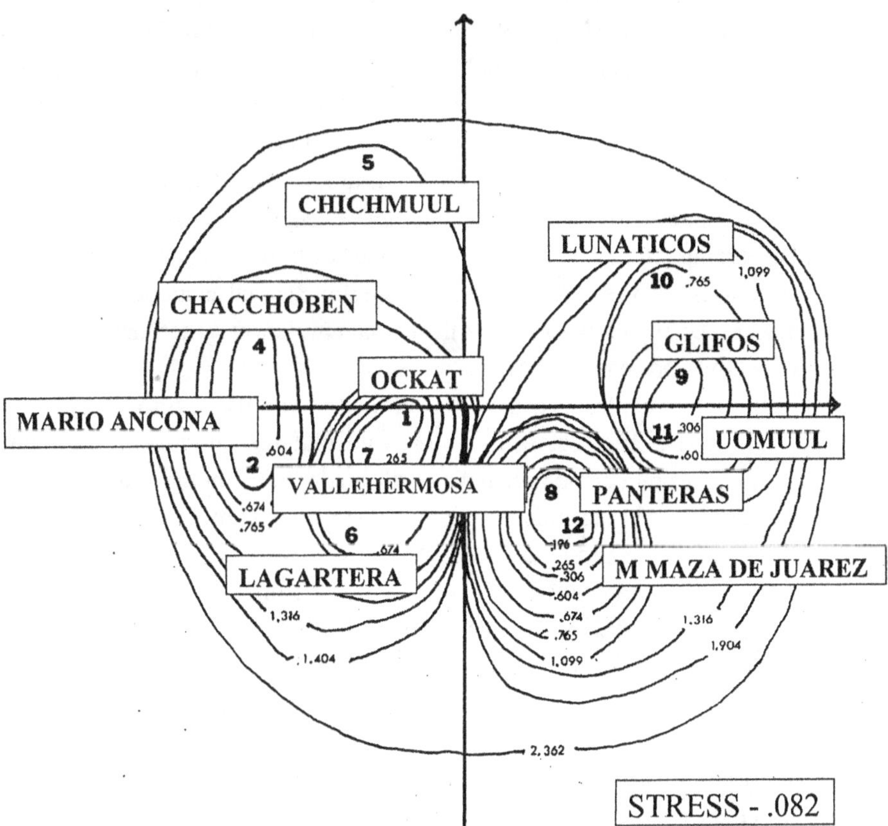

Figure 5.6. Two-dimensional MDS solution of technological resemblances of Late Classic unslipped jars from Quintana Roo.

three sites. Finally, there is a broader grouping of eastern sites. Unlike the situation with slipped bowls, there does not appear to be any differentiation in terms of higher- and lower-order sites in the settlement hierarchy.

One interesting feature of the above analysis is that it allows us to ask questions about relationships among sites that cannot be easily formulated using the traditional type-variety system of analysis. It also demonstrates how patterns of relationships among shape classes of pottery can differ significantly, and demonstrates a graphic means of displaying this patterning.

Trade and Emulation at the Panregional Level

In the previous section, I use multidimensional scaling to graphically represent patterns of similarity among assemblages. The results were inductively interpreted. The patterns revealed could have been a result of several factors. One obvious factor is temporal closeness, as indicated in the previous section. The close similarities of certain sites could have been due to a pattern of more intensive interaction either politically or commercially. Emulation of styles produced by this interaction would result in greater similarity. Alternatively, the exchange of pottery among interacting sites can also explain this pattern of resemblance. Imported pottery in volume would also result in a similar pattern. These alternatives, of course, are not mutually exclusive. Given the small sample sizes and scope of the Uaymil Survey Project program, we were not able to do sourcing studies of the relevant classes of pottery. However, given the differences among the paste classes from the sites, as well as subtle stylistic differences, especially in lip form, it is likely that emulation rather than extensive trade was the dominant pattern.

Ceramic similarities also have traditionally been used to show relationships among sites and regions in a more informal and nonquantitative manner. Similarities of assemblages have traditionally been thought to reflect not only chronological placement and cultural similarities but also political and economic influence and emulation. We know after decades of study that we can track political and cultural shifts in dominance through elite gift exchange and rituals (Adams 1968, 1971; Foias 2002; Sullivan 2002) and the popularity of trade wares and emulation of wares by local potters (Ball 1977a; Fry 1989). Most studies have concentrated on serving wares such as vases, plates, and bowls, often decorated with well-finished slips or polychrome decoration. However, in some cases this pattern of emulation can be seen in monochrome and unslipped coarse wares as well.

Widespread trade in a few well-made serving forms goes back to the Middle Preclassic, with small quantities of bowls of the fine-paste Savanna Orange

Ware widely traded in the southern lowlands. Such widespread trade seems actually to diminish in the Late Preclassic, with only a few imports such as Usulután wares and their local imitations from the highlands fairly widely circulated. The surprising uniformity of Late Preclassic ceramics, especially the Sierra Group red wares, throughout the lowlands is a remarkable development. The meaning of this uniformity has not been thoroughly explained. That this pattern extends into other regions such as the Grijalva Valley in Chiapas (Lowe and Agrinier 1960) may indicate that a growing cultural if not political dominance by thriving lowland Maya populations was a factor. This apparent uniformity may also mask more widespread regional and even inter-regional exchange. Reese-Taylor and Walker (2002) have noted the widespread distribution of a specific ceramic type (Zapatista Trickle-on-cream-brown) and shape class at sites as distant as El Mirador and Cerros. Several higher-quality varieties of ubiquitous types such as Sierra Red and Flor Cream may have been fairly widely exchanged.

During the Terminal Preclassic, the development of regional polychrome traditions heralds the changing to a pattern more common in the Classic period (Brady et al. 1998). Regionally circulated styles of polychromes tend to demarcate areas of political dominance and control.

This pattern continues in the Early Classic with the spread of polychrome serving forms with backgrounds of orange and cream, including basal flange bowls. In the Late Classic, we have the ubiquity in the central lowlands of Saxche and Palmar Orange polychromes, and finally the spread of slate wares from their center of origin in northern Yucatán. Some of the more elaborate items may well have circulated by gift exchanges or offerings during mortuary and other rituals, but simpler polychromes without functional glyphs, fine brushwork, or colloidal slips seem to have been circulated regionally among nonelite households and may well have circulated through market mechanisms sometimes with quite distinct boundaries. For example, Azcorra Buff-polychrome, a common Late Classic Belizean type produced in the New River drainage (sometimes called Pozito Polychrome), appears with some frequency in portions of the Pulltrouser Swamp settlement zone adjacent to the New River. However, the frequency drops sharply in the settlement zones closer to Nohmul, which is in the Rio Hondo drainage.

In most regions during the Classic period, utilitarian ceramics tend to show region-wide similarities. These do not necessarily correlate with boundaries of political control, though the latter probably shifted too rapidly to make much of an impact on slowly changing local traditions. Yet at certain critical times there are interregional patterns of emulation involving utilitarian ceramics. The previously mentioned period of great ceramic uniformity in the Late Preclassic is one such anomaly. I would predict that if someone did a multidimensional scaling analysis of Late Preclassic ceramics controlling for shape class for a broad geographic spread of sites, distances between sites would shrink compared to earlier and later periods. Ball (1977a) noted at Becán that there was a spread of Petén-like characteristics in the local tradition during the later Early Classic with the "Petenization" of utilitarian types to resemble Aguila Orange. Though with smaller samples, I noticed a similar shift in the same time frame from sites in the southern portion of the Uaymil survey zone. During the Late Classic we can see the spread of Copo sphere influence out of northern and north-central Yucatán into southern Quintana Roo and northern Belize, not only through trade wares such as members of the Thin Slate and Slate Muna groups and the adoption of such types as mainstays of the serving-class tradition, but also in the adoption of Copo sphere modes in utilitarian traditions. Northern Belize is interesting because in the Classic period, when the region becomes a more politically and cultural peripheral area, we see waves of imported wares and subsequent emulation first from the Petén region and then from northern Yucatán.

Figure 5.7. Local red slate ware annular-base basin from Chau Hiix, Belize. (Photo by author.)

I am especially interested in the adoption of local variants reflecting slate ware traditions. In northern Belize, as seen from the ceramics recovered from the Pulltrouser settlements, there was a somewhat unsuccessful attempt to emulate utilitarian slate ware ceramic modes. At Chau Hiix, farther south and farther from the source area, we have a few examples that successfully integrate local shape classes and modes with the pastes and slip characteristics on northern slate wares (figure 5.7). This may reflect interaction with the larger-scale polities in the New River lagoon area. Thus, local elites either had access to trade goods that local potters could copy, or may have even acquired privileged production secrets or recipes. Another possibility is that they actually imported craftsmen to shape local utilitarian traditions. Obviously, more detailed technical studies of these local slate wares may help resolve how this emulation came about.

Conclusions

I have examined the issue of ceramic similarities and differences at three differing levels: the local, regional, and interregional. At each level, differing attributes and combinations of attributes have differing information to provide about the functioning of systems of exchange, cultural influence, and emulation. The mechanisms for emulation of pottery styles need to be thought out more thoroughly, especially when it comes to utilitarian pottery. Were there technological factors that contributed to widespread adoption of certain modes, such as greater resistance to breakage, or cost-saving factors in pottery production? Or did changes in food preparation habits also contribute to such shifts? Emulation could thus have been in recipes and new food groups, requiring the necessary pottery technology in the wake of its adoption. Examples of this include the appearance of *comales* for preparing tortillas and chile grinders in the later Late Classic to Terminal Classic in the Maya lowlands. Another example of even greater interregional scope is the emulation of the chocolate pot form into the distinct southwestern U.S. ceramic traditions, accompanying the introduction of cacao consumption (Washburn et al. 2011; Malakoff 2011).

It should also be kept in mind that there might have been specific valued items contained in the pottery vessels that may have contributed to the wide distribution of certain types. Like the Classic Mediterranean amphorae that were used for wine, olive oil, and fish paste, there may well have been specialized jars and bowls for honey, spices, and other condiments. This may explain the findings of rare utilitarian types far from their production location.

There may have also been specific vessel functions that may not have been randomly distributed. For example, the unusual double-mouth jars of the type

Buyuk Striated (Chase and Chase 1987) are found in a seemingly random distribution in sites from northern Belize to central Quintana Roo but appear to be correlated with the presence of wells. It is possible that the double mouth functioned as a means of more rapidly filling the jars with less risk of breakage. The distribution of Buyuk Striated and related members of the shape class thus would correlate with the presence of wells.

The present study demonstrates some of the advantages of careful attribute studies of utilitarian ceramics. We can view patterns of relationships and also quantify those patterns in ways not feasible in traditional type-variety classification. Certainly we have just begun to tap the information available from more detailed stylistic, technological, and functional studies of the characteristics of utilitarian pottery.

Acknowledgments

The ceramics reported on in this paper include collections made by the Uaymil Survey Project, directed by Peter D. Harrison. Support for the project was provided by the Royal Ontario Museum. Ceramic analysis was also supported by grants from the Purdue Research Foundation, the American Philosophical Society, and the Ahau Foundation. Ceramics from Chau Hiix represent collection by the Chau Hiix Project, directed by K. Anne Pyburn. The Chau Hiix Project has been supported by Indiana University and also with NSF Grant SBR 9507. I am grateful for the assistance and insights provided by Scott Cox and Sarah Wille in formalizing these issues.

6

Type-Variety on Trial

Experiments in Classification and Meaning Using Ceramic Assemblages from Lamanai, Belize

JAMES JOHN AIMERS AND ELIZABETH GRAHAM

> I would hope that others working on Maya ceramics will address the issues I have raised here. The schemes we have now for dealing with the typology of the Southern Maya Lowlands clearly are not adequate. Perhaps Lowland ceramics are simply too diverse to be treated systematically by a single approach.
>
> Forsyth 1989: 10

Excavations at Lamanai since 1974 have produced an exceptional collection of pottery from the Terminal Classic and Postclassic periods (circa A.D. 960–1450), including several masterpieces of Maya art (Pendergast 1983/84). To date, however, published pottery (for example, Graham 1987; Pendergast 1982) has not been organized into types and varieties in accord with the type-variety system (Smith et al. 1960) but instead has been grouped and described as representative of successive phases based on stratigraphic contexts. A range of forms and colors has also been proposed as representative of these phases. Thus, the discussion of the Lamanai pottery has been primarily contextual, based on associations of objects from stratigraphic contexts.

With the stratigraphic framework established, at least in broad outline, three separate approaches to classification were implemented at Lamanai based on materials science (petrography, neutron activation analysis, and scanning electron microscopy) (Howie 2005), iconography (John 2008), and type: variety-mode (Aimers 2008, 2009).[1] Through the application of multiple approaches, we hope to reveal the strengths and weaknesses of the methods employed and thereby suggest ways in which these approaches contribute individually, and as a group, to our knowledge of pottery consumption and production at Lamanai. This chapter describes ongoing analyses and how we are proceeding, with emphasis on issues related to type-variety classification. This chapter is primarily a reflection on our use of multiple methods at Lamanai, with very brief indications of our findings. We are preparing an edited volume that will present the results in detail.

Contextual Analysis

Contextual analysis at Lamanai has meant that vessels from primary deposits have been considered together based on stratigraphic associations (for a discussion of the value of this approach, see Chase and Chase, this volume). The correlation of pottery forms and decorative styles on the basis of architectural and other stratigraphic contexts not only provides the basis for relative dating but also can be useful as a basis for hypotheses about the emic meaning of pottery within the Lamanai community. What do the elaborate, orange-red slipped and incised jars found smashed in Lamanai's Postclassic period burials suggest about burial ritual and concepts of the afterlife? Why were elements of more than 50 Chen Mul system (see Milbrath and Peraza, this volume; and Milbrath et al. 2008) anthropomorphic effigy censers smashed (or deposited after being smashed elsewhere) on top of Structure N9-56, "The Mask Temple," and what can this practice tell us about Lamanai's possible role in the Maya world as a pilgrimage destination (Howie et al. 2012)? What kinds of artifacts are associated with ceramics, and does this vary by context? Such questions have also been addressed by combining ethnohistorical information (for example, Roys 1962) with archaeological, art-historical, linguistic, bioanthropological, and ethnographic data (for example, Pendergast 1986).

What has been missing from the Lamanai studies is a way to compare pottery based on categories of form and surface treatment that are recognized and widely used by Maya ceramic analysts. Therefore, we have turned to the type-variety system of classification because comparability is one of its strengths. Type-variety has established a common language for the description of ancient pottery by organizing pottery hierarchically into wares, groups, types, and varieties based on stylistic similarity. These groupings have been the basis for both chronological and functional typologies. For example, in the Early Postclassic in the Belize Valley, the serving dishes that dominate the collection can be classified as the Augustine Red type (Aimers 2004a, 2004b). Perhaps of primary importance is the fact that types and varieties can be used as the basis for inferences about interaction among sites and regions. The extent and nature of interaction between Lamanai and other communities is a major impetus behind exploring the utility of type-variety classification at Lamanai.

Style and Interaction in the Maya Postclassic Period

The Postclassic period in Mesoamerica has been characterized as a time of "unprecedented population growth, a proliferation of small polities, an increased volume of long-distance exchange, an increase in the diversity of trade goods, commercialization of the economy, new forms of writing and iconography, and new patterns of stylistic interaction"(Smith and Berdan 2000: 286). Although all of these characteristics do not apply equally across Mesoamerica (for example, population growth), we do see ceramic evidence at Lamanai of increased trade and interaction and new "patterns of stylistic interaction." In order to understand this interaction, "a more comprehensive analysis of the distribution and significance of Postclassic styles and iconography" (Smith and Berdan 2000: 286) is needed, and our work is a response to that challenge in Belize: "Systematic site-by-site, subregion-by-subregion comparison and correlation of data must be undertaken for all of Belize. . . . Scholars working there need to increase communication between their many projects, including alignment of chronologies and typologies and collaborative construction of subregional culture-histories" (Demarest et al. 2004: 558–59).

We accept that style—in the sense of doing something in a particular way—can be defined as a form of nonverbal communication of information about identity (Wiessner 1990: 108). Both as individuals and as members of groups, people do things in ways (both consciously and unconsciously) that tell us something about them, or about how they want to be seen (that is, style can "lie"). Stylistic interaction is especially important if extant evidence that pottery rarely moved very far from its place of production is supported by future research. For the Late and Terminal Classic at Xunantunich (LeCount et al. 2002: 50) and in the Petexbatun region (Foias 2002: 233), exchange items made up only about 2 percent of the assemblages (for Tikal, see Fry 2003a, 2003b). Although trade increased throughout the Postclassic, most archaeologists report that the bulk of pottery remained locally made (for example, Arnold 1980; Drennan 1984; Hammond and Harbottle 1976; Rice 1980), and this is the case at Lamanai as well (Howie 2005).

Nevertheless, Early Classic data from sites along the coast of Belize and the Yucatán Peninsula, where there is no evidence of manufacture, show that pottery vessels, particularly polychromes, were being distributed inland via coastal networks (Graham 1994: 315–17, 330–31; Sierra Sosa 1999, 2001), and Fry (this volume and 1989) has noted that unslipped vessels sometimes also moved quite far. In terms of pottery production, Howie's materials science techniques have been instrumental in enabling the identification of local versus nonlocal vessels. They also reveal the extent of local knowledge of resources and production differences within sites and between sites and their peripheries. In terms of consumption, which is expressed through intra- and interregional relationships, our understanding of how the pottery from a given community reflects people's notions of what pottery should look like or what roles or demands the pottery should fulfill requires that we continue to refine our methods of stylistic analysis, including (but not limited to) type: variety-mode classification. The combined stylistic and technological diversity of the Terminal Classic and Postclassic period pottery at Lamanai indicates that trade was a crucial factor in its economy.

Type-Variety and Its Discontents

Type-variety classification has been postponed at Lamanai for several reasons. The first and perhaps foremost reason is the consideration that once vessels are classified according to types and varieties, the system becomes entrenched as reality, and thinking of ceramics outside of the structure of type-variety becomes difficult. Examples can be found in compositional studies that, outside of Lamanai, start with types as the basic framework rather than seek independently to develop an alternative classification system based on clay resources, where they originate, and how they were used. An important exception to the tendency to start with types is the Maya Polychrome Ceramics Project (see, for example, Reents-Budet et al. 1994), which combined instrumental neutron activation analysis (INAA) with studies of painting and design motifs to reveal particular artistic styles and even artistic schools and their possible points of origin. This work shows that the types created by the type-variety analyst may not always show a good fit with iconographic/epigraphic and/or materials science data, and there are, therefore, good reasons to develop complements to type-variety classification in the study of Maya pottery (see, for example, Culbert and Rands 2007).[2]

Another major problem in type-variety is the ware concept (the seminal discussion is Rice 1976). Wares have been defined either by surface treatment alone (for example, Usulutan Ware), or by a combination of paste and surface (for example, Fine Orange Ware), and therefore ceramic types with macroscopically different pastes have sometimes been classified as the same ware, sometimes not. Different approaches to ware can be linked to the different interests of researchers. Those interested in ceramic production or using poorly preserved samples have tended to privilege paste in their definition. These researchers have either used the traditional paste-plus-surface definition of ware or have adopted Rice's (1976) "paste ware" concept (although not always by that name), which classifies pastes at a hierarchical level above group. Because the hierarchical structure of type-variety requires that all varieties and types in a given group be of the same ware, this procedure tends to lead to a proliferation of type names if, for example, similar styles occur in different pastes (see chapters by Rice, by Cecil, and by Urban and colleagues, this volume). Researchers interested in stylistic comparison and consumer choice have tended to privilege surface characteristics, so paste variation has been treated as a modal quality of types (see, for example, Forsyth 1983) or has sometimes been used to define varieties (for example, Cayo Unslipped: Variety Unspecified [Buff]; Gifford 1976: 279), ultimately resulting in fewer type names. (For longer discussions that link these issues to Lamanai, see Aimers 2007a, 2009.)

At best, the ware category as traditionally defined (using paste and surface) is of "minimal analytical value" (Ball 1977a: 3), and a number of investigators have either abandoned it entirely (Willey et al. 1994), suggested that it be abandoned (Culbert and Rands 2007), or used some version of the paste ware concept. Howie's research at Lamanai has shown that vessels with different surface treatments (for example, slip colors or finishes) sometimes have the same paste recipes. Conversely, vessels that look identical were made using different paste recipes (Howie et al. 2003). The ware concept as traditionally used cannot represent this variation, because paste and surface are expected to covary and a given type cannot occur in more than one ware. These issues have been very important to us at Lamanai as we decide how to use type-variety most effectively.

Another challenge is a lack of consistency in naming types. Types that are stylistically similar from different places are often named separately, making comparison difficult. Reports sometimes include an intersite comparison section, but the proliferation of type names in the absence of integrative approaches means that archaeologists must be familiar with scores of ceramic types (often encompassing several varieties) in order to make inferences about interregional interaction. Conversely, when pottery objects from distant sites are given the same type names, this often masks significant variability in surface treatment and fabric, and this procedure often occurs without firsthand comparison of supposedly equivalent sherds or vessels (see Ball and Taschek, this volume). As Masson (2000: 70) noted, "the time is ripe for inter-site comparisons and collaborations to establish regional sequences," but this is challenging in light of varying definitions of ware, the differing ways that paste variation has been addressed, different approaches to naming, and the difficulty of examining disparate collections when deciding on type assignments (or a lack of effort to do so).

Inherent in some of the problems noted above is the fact that the methods used by different investigators to conduct a type-variety classification are influenced by at least two major considerations: (1) the nature of the sample; and (2) the research questions that are being addressed. At Lamanai, we have few of the sample-related issues that plague other projects. The sample is large, including hundreds of full or partial vessels and thousands of sherds. Also important is the fact that Postclassic pottery at Lamanai is usually well preserved, sometimes exceptionally so. Thus, the sample at Lamanai is large and well preserved enough to permit virtually any of the known variations of type-variety. Which, then, is the "correct" type-variety classification method to use at Lamanai? This can only be answered with reference to our particular research goals.

As Rice discusses in this volume and elsewhere (Rice 1987c: 284), type-variety classifications are not ends in themselves; they are taxonomic classifications created in order to address specific questions (see also Dunnell 1971a). Thus, although some archaeologists claim to use the "correct" type-variety method (in relation to the ware issue discussed above, or other issues) and therefore at least imply that the methods of others are inappropriate or simply wrong, the idea of a single, correct method of type-variety classification is probably not even an appropriate goal. The debate is similar to the old Ford-Spaulding debate about the reality of types, which is, as Rice (1987c: 284) has noted, "poorly phrased." Types are "real" because they "are non-random clusters of attributes that can be discovered and called types" (Hill and Evans 1972: 261). They are, however, "invented" in that the archaeologist must choose which attributes to observe in order to address particular questions. Similarly, lumping multiple pastes into types and describing them modally (or as varieties) and creating multiple paste wares at a hierarchical level above group are methods that can produce useful information, but only in relation to specific questions. At Lamanai, we recognize type-variety as a viable and potentially highly useful classification system because it is designed to represent stylistic choices; type-variety also facilitates consideration of the implications of these choices on a regional and interregional scale. Evidence of intersite and interregional interaction is essential in piecing together the political, economic, social, and religious aspects of the site's Postclassic period occupation, and our interest in type-variety classification at Lamanai flows from these interests.

Procedurally, the pottery is first sorted into types that share distinctive clusters of attributes in surface treatment and decoration but may include multiple forms (for example, jars and bowls). Groups comprise types that are similar in terms of color, surface finish, and forms. For this reason, groups have been compared to "super-types" (Smith and Gifford 1965: 501). Varieties, when established, are subdivisions of types dependent on minor but distinctive stylistic attributes (Gifford 1976: 9). As a result of Howie's (2005) research, we have decided that it is not useful to designate new varieties based on technology, a possibility raised in some discussions of type-variety (for example, Ball 1977a: 3) (see also comments on paste variation below). We recognize, however, that identification of types and varieties can in some circumstances entail a consideration of macroscopic technological qualities such as paste texture or inclusions, especially for unslippped ceramics (see below). Because decorative and iconographic attributes of ceramics from Terminal Classic to colonial times have undergone a separate analysis by John (2008), we are also in a good position to evaluate whether varieties based on incision, for example, are viable categories at all.

In our working analysis, groups will not be subsumed hierarchically under ware in the first instance because, as discussed above, the ware concept as traditionally incorporated into type-variety remains problematic. We hesitate to split stylistically identical vessels into different wares (and thus groups, types, and potentially varieties) based on paste alone, because our type-variety classification is directed, at least at this time, toward answering questions about consumer choice rather than production. The problem is complicated at Lamanai because paste does not vary macroscopically as clear-cut paste wares (in Rice's terms)—we see instead gradual variation. Materials analysis is being used to address these questions (see below), and until analyses are complete we will not make ware assignments of any kind.

Nevertheless, the potential strength of a category such as "ware" is that it can serve as a broad, integrative category above the level of the group. At this hierarchical level, pottery similarities should help us address questions of interaction at a very broad, perhaps interregional scale. These are exactly the reasons we are using type-variety at Lamanai, and it is therefore regrettable that the ware concept is so problematic.

Systems and Spheres in Type-Variety

Fortunately, type-variety as originally conceived includes two taxonomic levels designed for intersite and interregional comparison: ceramic system and ceramic sphere (Gifford 1960). Although type-variety was originally formulated to help address intersite ceramic similarities, these questions have been somewhat neglected as investigators have focused on developing specific site sequences (there are, of course, exceptions). (For spheres, see, for example, Ball 1976.)

Ceramic systems have rarely been used in type-variety reports (see Urban and Schortman 1987), yet they provide a way to group stylistically similar types from different sites: "[F]ocusing on surface treatment and decoration rather than technological and compositional features . . . they facilitate the recognition at the conceptual level" (Henderson and Agurcia 1987: 433). In an early article on systems, Wheat, Gifford, and Wasley (1958: 41) noted that "a ceramic system usually crosscuts wares." A useful quality of ceramic systems is that not only can they link local Lamanai pottery to known types elsewhere without ware designations, but group, type, and variety names are also not necessary. Thus, systems fulfill some of the roles of ware classifications but without the problems that have arisen in the use of ware, and we present two examples employing ceramic systems below.

At another level of analysis, pottery complexes can be assigned to spheres if they share "a majority of their most common types" (Willey et al. 1967: 306). Sphere membership (for example, definite and peripheral), based on the proportion of shared types (Ball 1976: 323) is thought to provide insights into "ceramic . . . trade networks, and regional economic integration" (Rice and Forsyth 2004: 52).[3] Michael Smith (2003: 35) concluded that "small polities characterized almost the entire area of Mesoamerica in Late Postclassic times," and Lamanai was almost certainly an important polity in the Late Postclassic. Grant Jones (1989) has suggested that it was part of the province of Dzuluinicob, unknown to Roys (Jones 1989: xx; Roys 1957), but even as part of the Chetumal province (Roys 1957) it was densely occupied and oriented toward trade and exchange (Graham 2004; Pendergast 1981, 1985a, 1985b). Trade goods from across Mesoamerica (Pendergast 1990: 173) suggest that the site may have acted as a "buffer" (Rathje 1972) or a gateway center (Hirth 1978) between the coast and the interior, including the Petén region, owing to its strategic location at the head of the New River, which leads to Chetumal Bay, and at the point where riverine and overland routes lead inland.

Both imported and stylistically similar ceramics can be used as a basis for inferences about alliance and economic networks (Brumfiel 1989; Schortman 1989; Stanton and Gallareta Negrón 2001; see also Bill, this volume). Along with the use of information from ethnohistorical sources, Postclassic pottery has great potential for contributing to the reconstruction of precontact political spheres (D. Chase 1982b; Rice and Rice 2004). We agree with Suhler and colleagues (1998: 168), who have noted that "using a variety of different kinds of ceramics was deliberate and meaningful to the Maya." They argue that the choices involved reflected cultural identity, which in turn was at least partially dependent upon political affiliation. Spheres as defined in the type-variety system can help us address these issues. Our focus in this chapter, however, is on systems, because a sphere-level designation is premature until the similarities between Lamanai types and types at other sites are better understood. We use several case studies in the next sections to highlight the role of systems in the type-variety classification process under way at Lamanai.

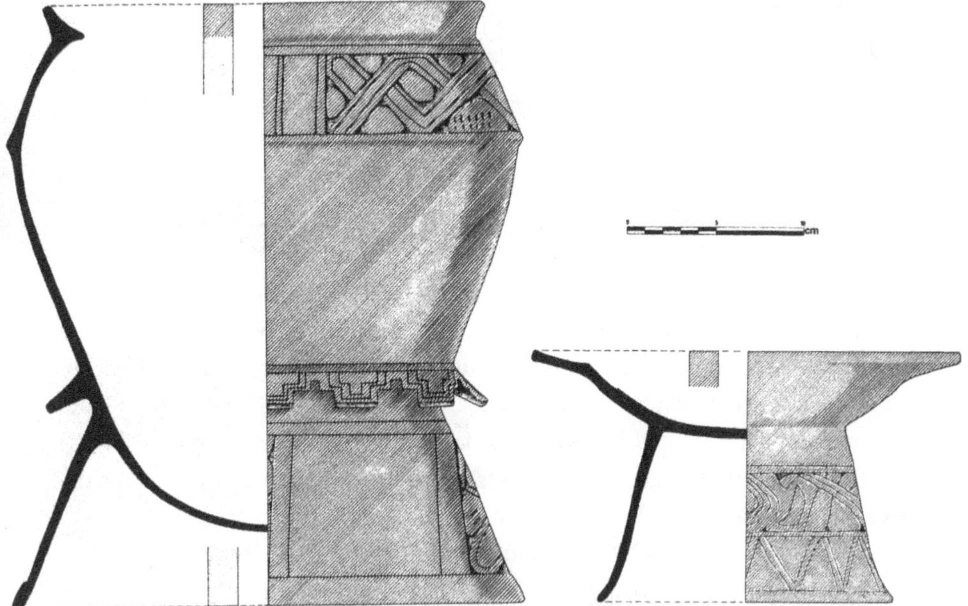

Figure 6.1. Pedestal-based jar and dish ("chalice") from Lamanai. (Drawings by Louise Belanger.)

Ceramic Systems at Lamanai: Buk Phase Orange-red Vessels

The vessels that have become emblematic of Lamanai are gouged-incised chalices and pedestal-based, flanged jars (figure 6.1) that at Cerros were named as members of the Zakpah Group (Ware Unspecified). They were divided into types based on surface treatment in the early facet of the Kanan ceramic complex (A.D. 1150–1300) by Walker (1990).

Established types of the Zakpah Group include Zakpah Orange-red: Variety Unspecified, Zakbeeb Incised: Variety Unspecified, and Zalal Gouged-incised: Variety Unspecified. Taken as a whole, ceramics of the Zakpah Group most closely resemble ceramics of Mayapan Red Ware (Smith 1971).

Thus, a preliminary designation for the Lamanai Buk phase orange-red vessels that are gouged-incised would be as follows:

System: Zalal Gouged-incised System

Systems are named after the type name of the first published type in the system (Wheat, Gifford, and Wasley 1958: 42). This does not imply that the type that gives the system its name was produced first.

Group: Zakpah Group

Type: Zalal Gouged-incised (Walker 1990)

Although there is a tradition of assigning types based on incision (or gouge-incision, and so forth), we suspect that such distinctions may be more appropriate at the varietal level when the form and finish of plain versus incised vessels are the same. Varieties are characterized by "lesser technological or aesthetic features as may indicate a minor regional or temporal departure from the standard" (Wheat et al. 1958: 36). Varieties are subdivisions of types generally based on "one or several minor attributes" (Gifford 1976: 9). "Attributes are the elements of construction, form, technique of decoration, or design that are combined in the formation of an artifact. . . . In pottery, such basic properties as temper, slip, form outline, kinds of paint, colors, and so on are attributes" (Gifford 1976: 9). (For useful comments on problems and contradictions in the designation of types and varieties, see Forsyth 1989.)

Alternatively, because incision and gouge-incision may have complex iconographic significance, an approach to classification in addition to type-variety might be more appropriate here as well, but when types have been established based on these attributes (as they have in this case) any attempt to revise the types down to varieties is bound to cause more confusion than benefits.

Variety: Varieties Unspecified

Aimers believes there are minor but covarying differences in form, finish, and incision style that may allow us to designate more than one variety at Lamanai, but this remains preliminary. Until we have examined a fuller range of Lamanai ceramics we follow Gifford (1976: 10) in using "Varieties Unspecified." Because Walker took a similar approach and did not designate varieties at Cerros (her sample consisted of three sherds), we may be able to link the Cerros sherds to varieties we designate at Lamanai.

Ceramic Systems at Lamanai: Buk Phase Unslipped Vessels

Systems are potentially even more useful for the preliminary classification of unslipped jars and bowls. Because unslipped utilitarian vessels are typically assumed to have been made locally, they are often given different names at different sites. The assumption that unslipped vessels were locally made is problematic, however, since as Fry (this volume and Fry 1989) notes, unslipped vessels were often moved far from their place of manufacture, and this would be expected at a site such as Lamanai if the vessels were exchanged for what they contained. An example of the problem of what to call unslipped vessels emerged at Lamanai because we have single sherds and whole vessels that resemble both Rio Juan Unslipped and Maskall Unslipped from the Belize Valley (Gifford 1976) as well as Pozo Unslipped from Macanché (Rice 1987b) (figure 6.2). Rice (1987b: 173) noted that Pozo Unslipped incorporates the range of variation in form and paste of Rio Juan and Maskall Unslipped. So, how should we name these at Lamanai? Options include using a familiar type name, a

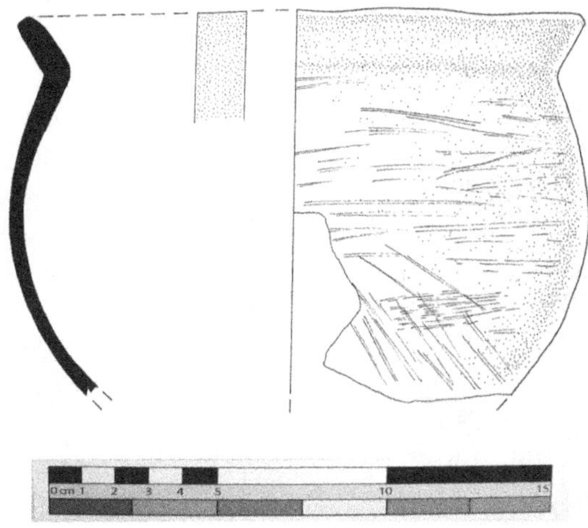

Figure 6.2. *a*, Pozo Unslipped system jar from Lamanai (drawing by Louise Belanger); *b*, photo of a Pozo Unslipped system jar rim from Tipu (photo by J. Aimers). Although these examples are from different sites, macroscopically they are indistinguishable.

name from a nearby site, or the creation of a new name if one assumes that unslipped ceramics were made locally. The problem lies in the fact that we do not yet know whether these ceramics were imported. Howie's petrographic analysis showed that many of the sherds in this style have paste compositions that may have been local or nonlocal (for example, her Calcite H and Quartz Sand classes; for descriptions, see Howie 2005: appendix X). Because we still do not have information that could link vessels in this style to any particular place (and they may indeed have been made in multiple places), we are placing these ceramics in the Pozo Unslipped system, which currently includes Maskall Unslipped, Rio Juan Unslipped, and Pozo Unslipped.

System: Pozo Unslipped System

Group

Sherds and vessels can sometimes (but not always) be sorted into the Pozo Group, the Maskall Group, or the Rio Juan Group (see explanation below).

Type

Over the years Aimers has examined and handled ceramics from the Pozo, Maskall, and Rio Juan groups in collections from Baking Pot, Tipu, the Petén Lakes, and the Mopán drainage, and in some cases specific types can be identified. For example, Maskall Unslipped is thin, hard, vesicular, and nearly black in color with angular calcite and some quartz temper and occasionally flecks of mica (Sharer and Chase 1976: 305). Maskall Unslipped typically includes a globular jar form with an outflaring (not outcurving) "collar."

Variety

In some cases, varieties of these known types are also recognizable. Rio Juan Unslipped: Variety Unspecified is tempered with quartz and calcite like Maskall Unslipped but is also characterized by lug and effigy handles on hemispherical bowls. Rio Juan Unslipped: Rio Juan Variety is similar but reddish in color without calcite; surfaces are rough and sandpapery because of the quartz temper.

But in cases where we cannot confidently assign original type and even variety names (for example, when classifying isolated rim sherds), we can simply assign the sherds to the Pozo Unslipped system. Members of this system (Pozo Unslipped, Maskall Unslipped, and Rio Juan Unslipped) are all common in the southern lowlands, so the system assignment alone enables us to quantify the fairly strong stylistic ties that Lamanai maintained with the southern lowlands in the Postclassic period, even as other unslipped types reminiscent of the northern lowlands became more common at the site (members of the

Navula Unslipped system; see Aimers 2008). Continuing connections to the southern lowlands are also indicated by John's iconographic analysis.

Consumer choices at Lamanai linked it to other communities in a web of stylistic emulation indicative of Lamanai's interregional affiliations and identity. As we further explore the various system relationships in our pottery sample, we will be able to say something about Lamanai's interaction with other sites. In the Postclassic period, Lamanai's strong stylistic ties to Mayapán and Tulum and to coastal centers including Marco Gonzalez (Graham and Pendergast 1989), Cozumel, Ichpaatun, and Santa Rita are clear but require further analysis and interpretation, as do rarer similarities between Cib phase ceramics at Lamanai and ceramics of the Rita Group at Santa Rita in the late facet of the Xabalxab ceramic complex (circa A.D. 1300–1532) (D. Chase 1984). Classifying on the basis of ceramic systems enables comparisons without requiring any of the other levels of type-variety designations (ware, group, type, or variety) until we are confident we better understand the production and consumption of these styles. Comparing ceramics at Lamanai with collections from other sites on the basis of ceramic systems can also help us to suggest a sphere designation for Lamanai.

Materials Science

Our work at Lamanai is testing some of type-variety's production-related assumptions, and Linda Howie has been assessing the range of variation in fabric and production technology of the pottery though thin-section petrography, neutron activation analysis and scanning electron microscopy (SEM). As noted above, type-variety is hierarchically structured so that a given type cannot occur in more than one ware (or paste ware), yet some pots that would be classified as the same type based on surface appearance have widely varying fabrics. Petrographic analysis allows us to recognize distinctive approaches to paste making and firing both across groups and within types, thus enabling us to test questions about ceramic production and consumption at Lamanai that type-variety cannot easily address. For example, Howie's work has demonstrated the complexity of pottery resource extraction and use and has shown substantial continuity through time in manufacturing technologies and production at Lamanai. Knowledge of where to get a variety of raw materials for pastes and tempers is not acquired quickly, so traditions persist even though formulae change, and there is a strong indication of continuity in the local knowledge base even though surface treatment and forms of vessels change.

We are working at Lamanai to see how best to articulate the materials science data with the stylistic analysis of type-variety (Rice 1976; see also Henderson and Beaudry-Corbett 1993). One option is that a fabric classification along the lines of paste modes be incorporated into the type-variety presentation of the Lamanai ceramics. In the case of unslipped pottery, there are some promising preliminary results of the combination of type-variety with materials science. For example, a large sample of coarse-tempered unslipped jar sherds was excavated as Lot 701 at Lamanai (a midden deposit along the edge of Structure N10-27). Formally, these look like a number of unslipped jar types from across the Maya lowlands throughout the Postclassic period. The most similar type Aimers has identified is Tsabak Unslipped from Cerros, which comprises three varieties (Tsabak Variety, Variety Unspecified, and Provisional Variety) (Walker 1990: 91–95). A large portion of the sample corresponds with the Provisional Variety, although the Tsabak Variety is also present. None of the Variety Unspecified, which Walker (1990: 94) suggested was imported to Cerros based on its distinctive micaceous paste, has been found at Lamanai. Given the close varietal-level similarities to Walker's descriptions, we are relatively confident in our designation of the varieties of Tsabak Unslipped, although in ambiguous cases we can also use the Tsabak Unslipped system assignment. Howie's (2005: appendix I) analysis of these sherds identified the consistent use of quartz sand temper (as at Cerros). Sources of the raw materials could be local or nonlocal, but Howie (2005: 639) notes that fabrics with high chert and chalcedony content may be from alluvial deposits "some distance to the east of Lamanai, between the coast and the Northern Lagoon drainage system."

Tsabak Unslipped is not known at Santa Rita (Walker 1990: 92), which suggests that Lamanai's ties, in this case signaled by the movement of vessels that may have contained some commodity, were closer to Cerros than to Santa Rita. Sherds and vessels at Lamanai that have been placed in the Navula Unslipped ceramic system (see Aimers 2009) also appear to have a different paste composition (Calcite H), suggesting that stylistic and petrographic data may, at times, covary.

Another productive combination of materials science techniques with contextual and stylistic analysis is presented in a study of a sample of the Chen Mul Modeled system anthropomorphic effigy censers from Lamanai. An examination of 50 feet from these censers showed that exceptional technological variability was in line with the high stylistic variability (Howie et al. 2012). Together, these findings suggest these censers were brought to Lamanai. Contextual information shows that these were deposited after structure abandonment and that the censers were probably broken elsewhere. Together, this information suggests Postclassic pilgrimage to an important religious structure after its abandonment but while Lamanai was still occupied.

Iconographic Analysis

The Late Postclassic ceramics of Lamanai are a local manifestation of a more general Postclassic International Style (Boone and Smith 2003) characterized by a widely shared symbol set (iconography). Both style and iconography appear to have been actively used to express social identity throughout Maya history (Ball 1993). Although part of the Postclassic International Style, the Late Postclassic pottery of Lamanai is a result of stylistic choices made by producers and consumers in a distinct community with specific interests and affiliations.

Like style, the iconography of Lamanai's elaborate Late Postclassic pottery provides clues to the site's external affiliations as well as the specific "figured world" of the Lamanai Maya (Brumfiel 2004; Holland et al. 1998; John 2008). What do these objects suggest about the cultural guidelines that structured life at Lamanai? How do Late Postclassic symbols at Lamanai differ from the Early Postclassic at the site, or from the Late Postclassic at other sites? Which animals and other beings are depicted on vessels (for example, through incised designs, tripod effigy feet, or appliqué), and what ideas might they represent? Jennifer John's research on the iconography of the Buk vessels suggests that incised motifs relate to the ritual use of the vessels, their contents, and the status of people with whom they were buried. Thus, it may be useful to consider some of the slipped Buk vessels as members of ritual subcomplexes, and the good contextual information from Lamanai should make the identification of pottery subcomplexes possible.

John's research shows that from the Terminal Classic through the Colonial period at Lamanai there are changes in iconography that may be the result of sociopolitical changes and increased contact with other regions, but these are incorporated into local traditions. For example, jaguar iconography and other symbols associated with dynastic rule in the Classic period seem to die out, but saurian imagery persists within recognizably local, Maya stylistic conventions.

Conclusions

Lamanai's exuberant Late Postclassic pottery includes many beautiful objects, but our work is also a fundamental step in an investigation of basic problems in type-variety method and theory that will continue at the site. Despite the often-noted problems, type-variety provides a standard language for site-to-site ceramic comparison, and that the ceramics from Lamanai be intelligible within the type-variety context is important. We believe that type: variety-mode classification is most productive when combined with other methods, as we have indicated with a few examples above.

Acknowledgments

We would like to thank the Institute of Archaeology, Belize for supporting this work. We would also like to acknowledge the people of Indian Church and the other members of the Lamanai Archaeological Project.

Notes

1. This chapter discusses the type-variety portion of what will eventually be a type: variety-mode classification.

2. We wrote the original version of this chapter for the 2005 SAA symposium from which most of the chapters in this volume are derived. We were thus pleased to see Culbert and Rands's 2007 article on alternative classifications and type-variety, which suggests we were not the only archaeologists thinking this way. Not everyone agrees wholeheartedly, however (see Adams 2008).

3. Rice and Forsyth (2004: 52) include "production organization" in their discussion of the uses of sphere designations, but Howie's research (particularly the great technological variation in Lamanai ceramic types) has made us somewhat wary of the value of spheres as indicators of production for ceramics found at the site.

7

Establishing the Cunil Ceramic Complex at Cahal Pech, Belize

LAUREN A. SULLIVAN AND JAIME J. AWE

When Awe (1992) first began intensive archaeological research at Cahal Pech in the 1980s, the primary goals of the project were to determine the nature of Preclassic Maya culture at the site and to more clearly define Formative period developments in the upper Belize River valley. At the time, the Formative period was still considered to be "one of the most enigmatic and often controversial eras in the study of Maya culture" (Awe 1992: 13), and data pertaining to this early phase of lowland Maya development were "quantitatively and geographically limited" (Awe 1992: 31). Excavations at sites such as Colha (Hester et al. 1982; Valdez 1987), Cerros (Freidel and Robertson 1986), and Cuello (Hammond et al. 1979) in Belize and Altar de Sacrificios (Adams 1971), Yaxhá-Sacnab (Rice 1979), Nakbe, and El Mirador (Forsyth 1989) in the Petén had just begun to identify and describe Formative occupation. However, there was still much controversy over the origins (Willey 1977), level of complexity (Ball 1977a), and material culture (Awe 1992) of these pioneering settlements. Problems with accurate dating and the original definition of the Swasey phase at Cuello (Andrews 1990; Kosakowsky and Pring 1998) also hindered accurate interpretation and evaluation. It was in the midst of these controversies that the distinct Cunil ceramic complex at Cahal Pech (figure 7.1) was originally identified and described as "typologically and stratigraphically a predecessor of the Jenney Creek Complex" in the Belize Valley (Awe 1992: 230). When Gifford (1976) first established the Jenney Creek complex at Barton Ramie, the early facet was "not documented stratigraphically" (Gifford 1976: 61), it was defined typologically. Furthermore, a start date for early facet Jenney Creek was never provided in Gifford's original analysis; however, late facet Jenney Creek was dated to 300–600 B.C. The new data presented here demonstrate that the Cunil

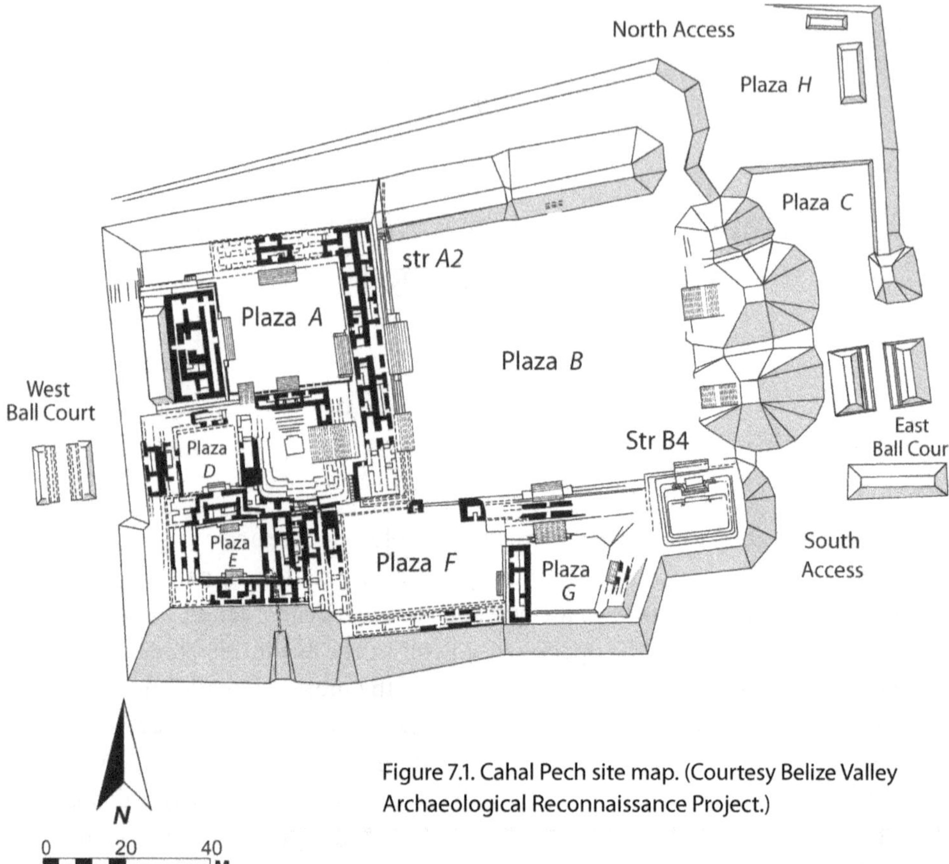

Figure 7.1. Cahal Pech site map. (Courtesy Belize Valley Archaeological Reconnaissance Project.)

complex is distinct from early facet Jenney Creek. Radiocarbon dates and stratigraphy support conservatively dating the Cunil complex to 1100–900 B.C., with early facet Jenney Creek beginning around 900 B.C.

The first Cunil pottery descriptions were based on approximately 250 ceramic sherds and two fragmented vessels that were stratigraphically isolated in the earliest construction levels of Structure B4, Plaza B, in the Cahal Pech site core (figure 7.2) and from mixed deposits at peripheral groups (Awe 1992). Subsequent excavations in 1994 and 1995 (Healy and Awe 1995, 1996) recovered additional ceramics from Structure B4, in a five-by-five-meter unit at the base of B4, and from a series of nine one-by-one-meter test excavations across Plaza B that were analyzed by David Cheetham (Cheetham and Awe 1996; Cheetham and Awe 2002; Clark and Cheetham 2002). These original excavations also provided a set of radiocarbon dates that placed the Cunil phase between circa 1100 and 900 B.C. (Awe 1992; Healy 2004 et al.).

In spite of these discoveries, there were some researchers who voiced con-

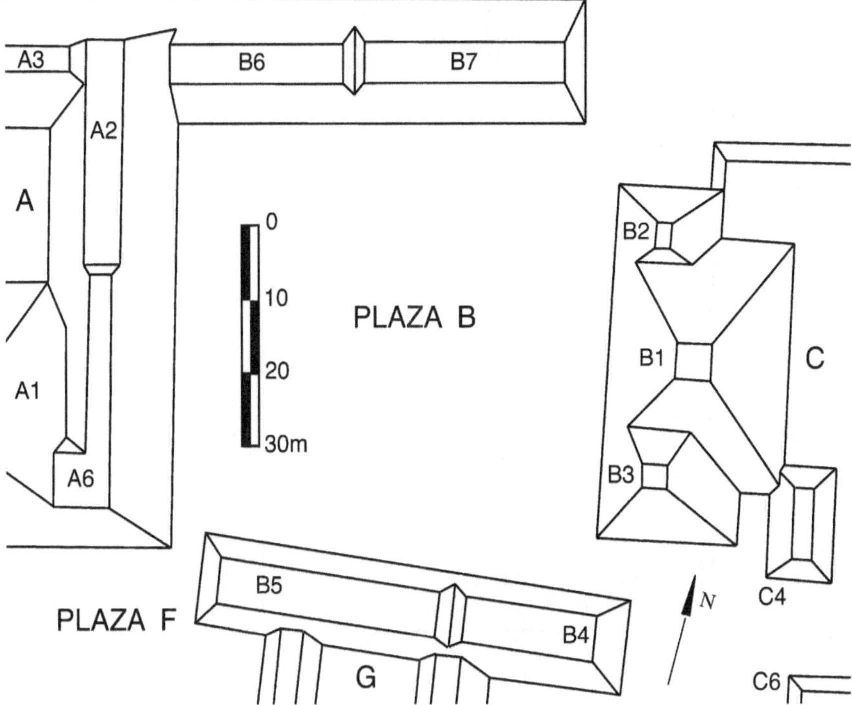

Figure 7.2. Cahal Pech Plaza B. (After Healey et al. 2004: 105.)

cerns with both the dating and the validity of the Cunil ceramic phase (Ball and Taschek 2004). In particular, Ball and Taschek (2004: 151) reported that they "found no traces whatsoever of the problematic 'Cunil' assemblage at Buena Vista." They also expressed concern over what they claimed were persistent and "continuing discrepancies, inconsistencies," and "contradictions" in the "descriptions of the 'Cunil' material" (Ball and Taschek 2004: 165). There is no question that the latter perspective was based on the fact that several of Cheetham's publications on Cunil (for example, Cheetham 1998; Clark and Cheetham 2002) did indeed present inconsistencies with the database and with the previous interpretation of the latter by Awe (1992). In view of these concerns, Awe purposely decided to delay further interpretations of the Cunil materials until such time as further investigations increased the sample size of Cunil phase cultural remains. Since then, new excavations into Structure B4 (Columns 7/2002, 8/2006, and 9/2007) have substantially increased the size of the ceramic assemblage and have confirmed the Cunil phase dating of the four lowermost levels (Levels 11–14) of Structure B4 (figure 7.3). Three radiocarbon dates from these new excavations support the original dating of the Cunil ceramic complex. The calibrated dates (two-sigma range) are 1120–910

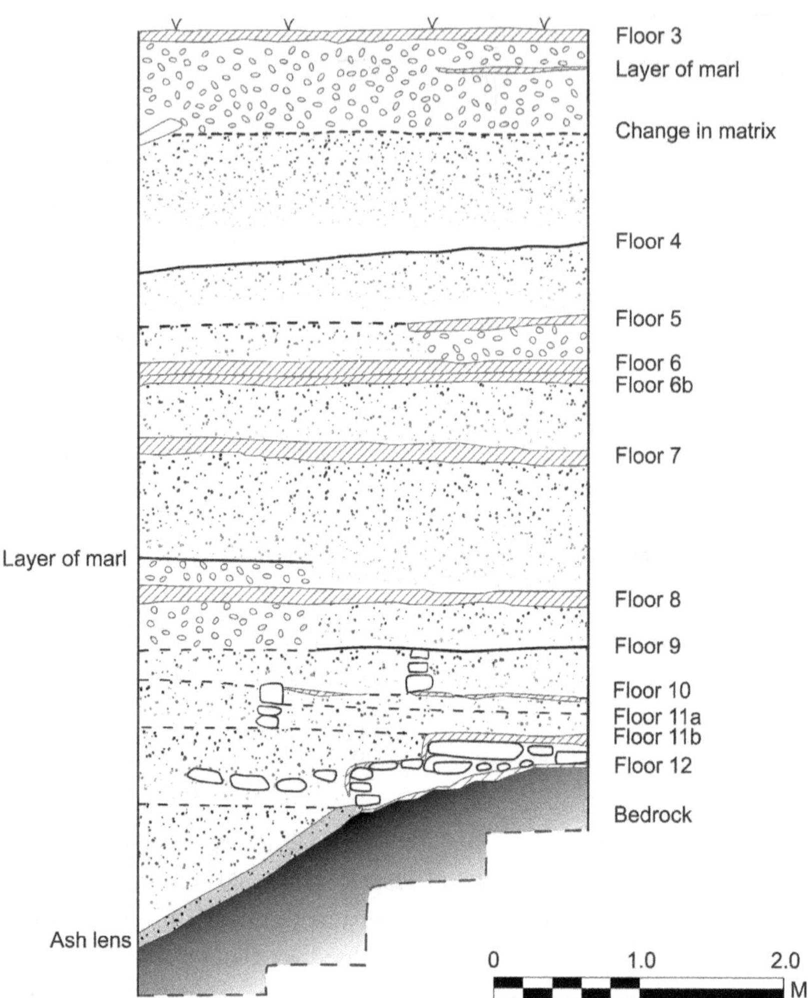

Figure 7.3. North Wall profile, Column 8/2006. Levels 11–14 are pre-Mamom. (Drawing by J. Awe.)

B.C. (Structure B4, Unit 8, Level 13), 1280–1010 B.C. (Plaza B, Operation 1v, Level 15), and 1360–1350 B.C. and 1310–1050 B.C. (Structure B4, Unit 9, Level 12) (Garber and Awe 2008b). These new data, in conjunction with a north–south trench across Plaza B (Garber 2005 et al.) plus excavations at Blackman Eddy (Garber et al. 2004) and Xunantunich (Strelow and LeCount 2001), have produced additional pre-Mamom remains and have provided considerable new information on the relationship between the Cunil and early facet Jenney Creek/Kanluk phases in the Belize Valley (Brown 2007; Sullivan et al. 2008).

One of the primary goals in our analysis of these new ceramic data (some 1,500 sherds) is to provide an accurate description of the Cunil ceramic complex at Cahal Pech and to present the Cunil ceramic assemblage in the standardized type-variety format (for example, Gifford 1976; Sabloff 1975) in order to facilitate future intersite comparisons (Sabloff and Smith 1969; Sullivan et al. 2008). While there is much debate about the usefulness of the type-variety system (Dunnell 1971a; Smith 1979; Lopez-Varela 1996; Culbert and Rands 2007), we found this traditional method extremely useful in our initial classification of this early ceramic collection. In fact, when the first Cunil deposits were uncovered in the 1980s, one of the first things many scholars asked for was traditional type-variety descriptions of the associated sherds.

Early ceramic analyses in the Maya area were focused on general regional descriptive classifications, as seen in Vaillant's work during the 1920s (Vaillant 1927) and later (by the 1930s) on more systematic stratigraphic sequences in order to develop better chronological control, as seen at Uaxactún (Thompson 1939; Smith 1955). These early studies used broad descriptive units of analysis; however, there were no standards in how to use and/or apply these units (that is, ware, type) (Smith et al. 1960). Underlying these early ceramic studies were a number of theoretical changes in Maya archaeology. These changes included a move away from a focus on ceremonial centers, mortuary practices, and associated pottery (that is, whole vessels) to the development of systematic settlement pattern studies concerned with problems of social structure, social and political organization, agricultural features, and the relationship of ceremonial to residential structures (Smith et al. 1960; Willey et al. 1965; Haviland 1966). R. E. Smith's 1955 volume on the pottery of Uaxactún was one of the first attempts to systematically analyze such a large body of ceramic data from the Maya area (Willey et al. 1967). Smith's (1955) book was groundbreaking in its comprehensive and meticulous ceramic descriptions as well as the fact that it provided some of the first evidence for Formative Maya occupation in the Petén region.

Concurrent with Smith's analysis of the Uaxactún data, archaeologists in the southwestern United States were in the process of developing the type-variety system with the intention of creating a more useful, flexible, and formalized nomenclature in ceramic analysis (Wheat et al. 1958; Willey et al. 1967). This system was applied to Maya pottery by Smith, Willey, and Gifford (1960) and refined at the "Conference on the Prehistoric Ceramics of the Maya Lowlands" in 1965 (Willey et al. 1967); it has since become the foundation and standard of many Maya ceramic studies. According to Smith and colleagues (1960: 333), types represent clusters of attributes and are considered to be unstable entities that can be "added [to] or subtracted from as ceramic knowledge increases." In other words, the definition of a type is never really completed but is continually refined (Smith et al. 1960; Adams 1971). One can see that this is a highly flexible system that can be and has been continually changed in order to reflect personal preferences and site-specific requirements (Gifford 1976; Valdez 1987; Adams 2008). The type: variety-mode system has been detailed and applied in a number of notable works, including the ceramics of Altar de Sacrificios (Adams 1971), Seibal (Sabloff 1975), Barton Ramie (Gifford 1976), Becán (Ball 1977a), Colha (Valdez 1987), Cuello (Kosakowsky 1987), El Mirador (Forsyth 1989), and Tikal (Culbert 1993).

One of the basic problems with any classification scheme developed for different types of material culture is the artificial nature of the categories constructed by the analyst. Once "idealized" types are created, there is often much debate over how to classify an artifact. In many cases, an artifact may not fit perfectly into a discrete type but is more realistically placed somewhere on a continuum between types. Nonetheless, these classification systems provide a useful way to organize data and provide an analytical framework for comparison of similarity and variability within and between assemblages and serve as a means to the end of inferring ancient cultural behavior (Dibble 2008). The authors believe that while the type: variety-mode method of classification may not answer every question about a ceramic assemblage, it is the best way to provide a common language for comparison of pottery between sites (see Rice, this volume).

One of the primary criticisms of the type: variety-mode system is the creation of too many type names when many "new" types can logically be placed into previously established categories (López Varela 1996). Ironically, in the first paragraph of the original type-variety article by Wheat and colleagues (1958: 34), they state "the proliferation of named types has alarmed many archaeologists" as one of the reasons for the creation of a recognized and agreed-upon classification scheme for prehistoric pottery. There is also the suggestion that one single typological system cannot account for all the potential variables in a collection (Culbert and Rands 2007). An example of this problem is seen in the identification and definition of wares. Rice (1976) notes that wares comprise both surface finish and paste composition, technologically independent variables that should be evaluated as such. She has used paste attributes to define paste wares (Rice 1976 and this volume). In reference to these problems with the traditional ware concept, Aimers (2007a) has called for the use of ceramic systems (part of the original type-variety model) as a way to classify pottery types that are related through style and surface treatment. Culbert and Rands (2007) suggest at least three different systems of classification using surface finish, forms, and paste. Ideally type-variety would be one of the various classificatory schemes integrated with others.

R.E.W. Adams (2008) proposes that the majority of problems associated with the type: variety-mode scheme are not with the method of classification but instead with its application. He highlights that this system has been highly successful in meeting its original intention to provide standardized comparative units of analysis. Problems in the application include a reliance on certain sources. For example, Gifford (1976) is relied on as "a sort of encyclopedia to be used uncritically" (Adams 2008: 223). Forsyth (1989: 7) also believes that the tendency to "fossilize" original classifications defeats the original intent for flexibility in the use of type-variety. As Smith and his colleagues stated, "The important point is, however, that the taxonomy must not preclude change, now or later. It must allow for reevaluation, revision, and subsequent shifting of units" (Smith et al. 1960: 337).

The authors believe that using the type: variety-mode system was the best way to begin a classification of the new Cunil assemblage in order to encourage, promote, and facilitate intersite comparisons. This method allowed us to organize sherds into different categories for initial assessment and evaluation (also see Brown 2007). We do agree that a detailed paste analysis is important to fully understanding this collection and have conducted preliminary petrographic analysis on some of the sherds. However, until further petrography and chemical analysis are conducted, the type: variety-mode system has successfully provided us with "analytical units that have comparative value" (Adams 2008: 222). Rice (this volume) echoes this belief in her statement "The type-variety approach works well at what it was intended to do—structure pottery descriptions for spatiotemporal comparison." As mentioned above, the analysis of Cunil material is centered on more than 1,500 pottery sherds recovered from three new excavation units into Structure B4 at Cahal Pech. The ceramic samples from each column were examined as individual units and grouped by level. Sherds were then sorted based on paste, surface treatment, and other readily visible attributes and roughly categorized into Cheetham and Awe's (2002) original ware and group designations. Rims and well-preserved body sherds were used to develop the type-variety descriptions. Diagnostic sherds used for type descriptions included those that showed some aspect of form (rim, handle, and so forth), sherds with decoration (incising, resist, and so forth), and well-preserved body sherds. Eroded body sherds were categorized by group and/or type-variety when possible. Separating unslipped Cunil sherds (Sikiya Group) from Jenney Creek/Kanluk (Jocote Group) sherds in the upper levels was difficult, and many of these sherds were simply categorized as "transitional" (Sullivan et al. 2008). In cases where the sample size was small, types were left unnamed and varieties listed as "unspecified." All of the new type names were registered for use with the Index of Mesoamerican Archaeological Nomenclature in *Ceramica de Cultura Maya* (Gifford and Kirkpatrick 1996). Vessel form and shape were described based on the definitions of primary classes and subdivisions provided by Sabloff (1975: 23–27). Vessel diameter from rim sherds was recorded when possible following Rice's approach (1987c: 222). Inclusion/particle size descriptions and shape are based on McCullough's method (1984). Sherds were examined macroscopically and with a 10X hand lens. Hydrochloric acid was used to detect the presence of carbonate inclusions per Pring (1977b), Kosakowsky (1987), and Ford and Spera (2007). In some cases, preliminary petrographic analysis was also used to identify inclusions (Sullivan 2006). A Munsell Soil Chart (2000) was used in a natural light setting to help standardize the color descriptions.

A critical part of this analysis included the hands-on examination and comparison of Cunil sherds with different ceramic collections at the Institute of Archaeology at Belmopan, the Peabody Museum at Harvard, and the University of Texas at Austin, as well as those from sites including Colha and Blackman Eddy (see also Ball and Taschek, this volume). Comparison with the Barton Ramie collection at the Peabody Museum has been particularly helpful in our ongoing analysis of levels containing both Cunil and Jenney Creek/Kanluk pottery. Another significant aspect of this study has been incorporating input from other ceramicists and scholars.

A ceramic workshop organized by Jaime Awe and James Aimers in July 2007 provided the opportunity for many scholars to examine collections from across Belize spanning the Formative to Postclassic time periods. This meeting was the first time that Cunil pottery was presented to a large group of ceramicists, allowing participants to compare and contrast the Cunil phase ceramics with those of the Swasey and Bolay complexes in northern Belize (Valdez et al. 2008) and with subsequent Jenney Creek phase materials from the Belize Valley. Many similarities have been noted with the contemporaneous Kanocha phase pottery at Blackman Eddy in terms of similar pastes, surface finish, forms, and decoration. In preliminary analyses, Garber and colleagues (2004) identified a utilitarian ware that is comparable to Belize Valley Coarse Ware and a dull-slipped ware much like Belize Valley Dull Ware. Decorative techniques such as postslip incising and differential firing are also noted in both the Cunil and Kanocha assemblages (Brown 2007) although the Cahal Pech material is much better preserved. Strelow and LeCount (2001) have also identified similar incised motifs on a collection of early sherds from Xunantunich. After much debate over the nature of these deposits, it was extremely gratifying for the authors to be a part of the discussion and debate that occurred at the conference. Subsequent discussions with Vilma Fialko, who is working on early deposits at Tikal, were also beneficial. She noted that there were modal, stylistic, and technological (especially paste) differences between the Cunil ceramics and the early pottery from Tikal. The early Eb phase at Tikal has been dated to "before 700 B.C.," with the late Eb phase dating to between 700 and 600 B.C. (Ponce de León 2003: 172). At best, Fialko noted just basic similarities and agreed with us that the early assemblages between the two sites clearly demonstrated greater regional differences than similarities during these early time frames. Comparisons with the Holmul assemblage (Neivens 2010) also suggest more or less independent ceramic traditions during this early time period, especially when compared to the Chicanel sphere of the Late Preclassic. It is our hope that a formal and accessible type collection of the Cunil pottery to be housed at the Institute of Archaeology will allow for continued dialogue with scholars working on similar deposits.

In sum, the type: variety-mode system helped us to successfully establish the Cunil ceramic complex at Cahal Pech. In this collection, two wares (Belize Valley Dull Ware and Belize Valley Coarse Wares), four ceramic groups (Uck, Cocoyol, Chi, and Sikiya), and 19 types have been successfully created (Sullivan et al. 2008) (table 7.1).

Table 7.1. Wares, groups, types, and varieties of the Cunil complex

Ware/Group	Type: Variety
Belize Valley Dull Ware	
Uck	Uck Red: Uck Variety
	Uck Red: Variety Unspecified (Orange)
	Uck Red: Variety Unspecified
	Baki Red-incised: Baki Variety
	Zotz Zoned Incised: Zotz Variety
	Mo Mottled: Mo Variety
	Mo Mottled: Variety Unspecified (Red)
	Kitam Incised: Kitam Variety
	Unnamed Brown Slipped: Variety Unspecified
Cocoyol	Cocoyol Cream: Cocoyol Variety
	Cocoyol Cream: Variety Unspecified (Resist)
	Cocoyol Cream: Variety Unspecified (Unslipped)
	Unnamed Ash: Variety Unspecified
	Unnamed Red-on-buff: Variety Unspecified (A)
	Unnamed Red-on-buff: Variety Unspecified (B)
Chi	Chi Black: Chi Variety
	Unnamed Black Punctated-incised: Variety Unspecified
Belize Valley Coarse Ware	
Sikiya	Sikiya Unslipped: Sikiya Variety
	Ardagh Orange-brown: Ardagh Variety

Belize Valley Dull Ware is characterized by a fine paste texture with volcanic ash, calcite, quartzite, and mica and/or hematite inclusions and dull slips associated with serving vessels. Belize Valley Coarse Ware is distinguished by a medium to coarse paste texture with calcite, quartz, quartzite, and small grains of mica and is associated with more utilitarian forms (Awe 1992; Sullivan et al. 2008). Some of the most distinctive pottery of the complex includes the grooved-incised types of the fine-paste Belize Valley Dull Ware. These sherds are characterized by a secondary decoration of grooved postslip incising placed on the interior of outflared plate rims with flat bottoms. One example from the Uck Group is Baki Red-incised: Baki Variety (figure 7.4), which has a dull red uniform slip that differs from the waxy red slips used during Kanluk times. Zotz Zoned-incised: Zotz Variety (figures 7.5–7.6) is similar to Baki Red-incised, with the addition of zones of brown and red, or brown and cream slip. The Uck Group also includes Kitam Incised: Kitam Variety (figure 7.7), which can be identified by thin postslip incised lines on incurving bowls with a multicolored slip. The motifs on these incised types have been discussed elsewhere and suggest that these early vessels may have been associated with ritual deposits and displays of wealth and prestige associated with the rise of social complexity (Awe 1992; Cheetham 1998; Brown 2007; Sullivan et al. 2008; Garber and Awe 2008a). The most distinctive Cocoyol Group sherds, also part of Belize Valley Dull Ware, are the creamy white sherds of Cocoyol Cream: Cocoyol Variety. These sherds have a smooth creamy paste with a dull "cream-coloured wash or thin slip" (Awe 1992). Unnamed Red-on-buff: Variety Unspecified (A) is one of the more interesting types in this group due to its similarities to Tower Hill Red-

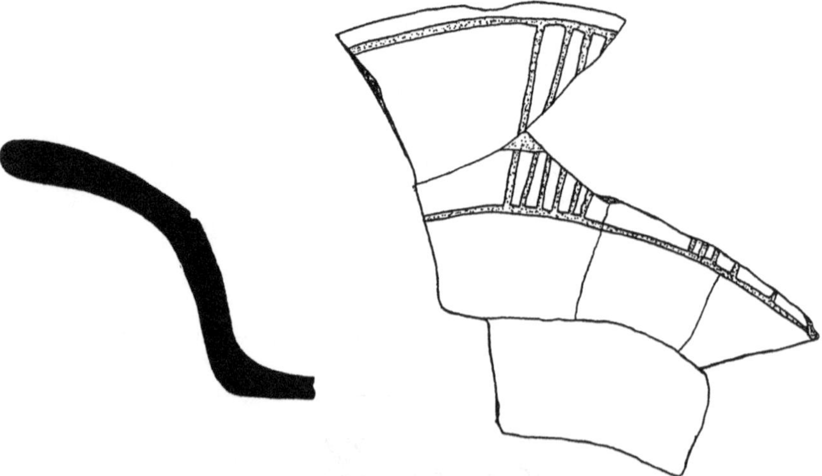

Figure 7.4. Baki Red-incised: Baki Variety. (After Awe 1992: 229, fig. 57b.)

Figure 7.5. Zotz Zoned-incised: Zotz Variety. (Photo by J. Awe.)

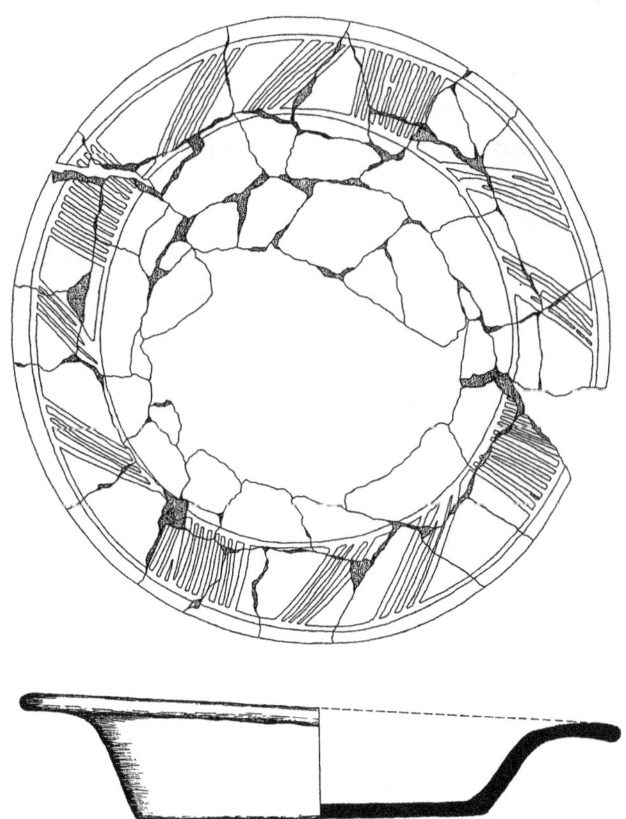

Figure 7.6. Zotz Zoned-incised: Zotz Variety. (After Awe 1992: 228.)

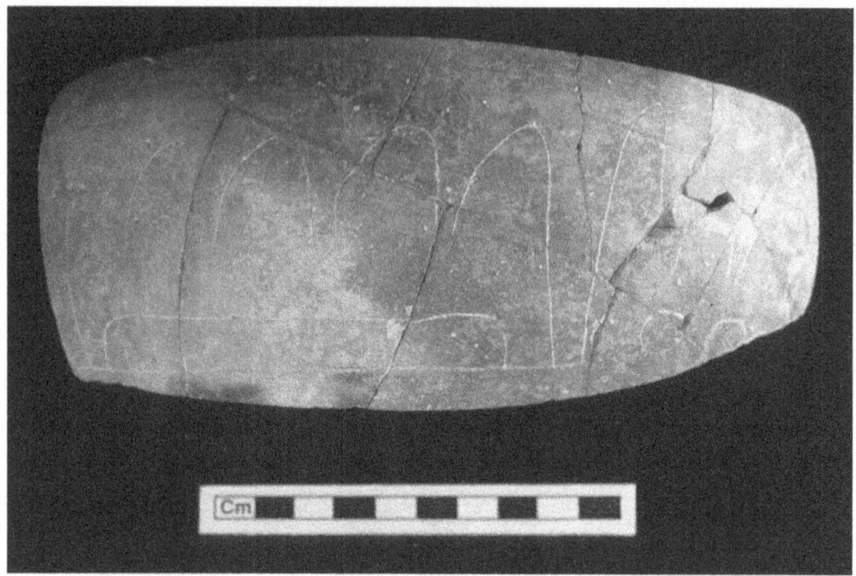

Figure 7.7. Kitam Incised: Kitam Variety. (Photo by J. Awe.)

on-cream found in early facet Kanluk deposits at Cahal Pech and in northern Belize. This type is represented by one rim sherd with a red slip on its interior, a buff slip on the exterior, and a red band that encircles the vessel exterior (Awe 1992; Sullivan et al. 2008).

Belize Valley Coarse Ware is dominated by the Sikiya Ceramic Group, specifically, Sikiya Unslipped: Sikiya Variety (figure 7.8). These unslipped sherds are characterized by extensive fire clouding and highly variable color that ranges from tan to brown to black, which is typically seen on jars (Sullivan et al. 2008). The Sikiya Unslipped body sherds from the upper levels are particularly difficult to distinguish from the later Jocote Group sherds. As noted in other collections (Smith 1955; Adams 1971; Forsyth 1989), ceramic styles may persist in time and precise classification may not always be possible. We believe this is especially true for these utilitarian types. Notwithstanding this observation, we should note that while filleting is very common on Jocote Orange-brown jars, it is atypical on Sikiya Unslipped vessels. As our analysis continues on the transition from Cunil to early facet Kanluk we hope to better identify and describe these types of sherd groups, thus keeping with our goal to revise and restructure our type-variety classification as needed.

The type-variety analysis of the Cunil pottery successfully revealed that it is quite different from what follows in the Jenney Creek/Kanluk complex, allowing for a clear distinction between these two ceramic complexes. Overall characteristics of the Cunil ceramic complex include a prevalence of dull slips

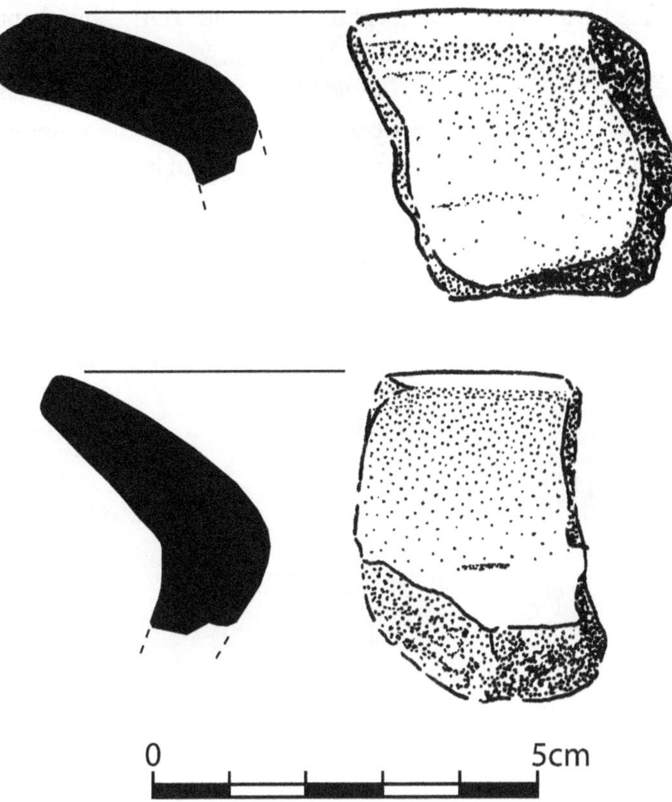

Figure 7.8. Sikiya Unslipped: Sikiya Variety. (Drawing by J. Awe.)

that are not waxy, the absence of Mars Orange types, an absence of spouted jar forms, few examples of filleting, the presence of preslipped incised types and decoration that are not seen in Jenney Creek or in Swasey/Bladen and Bolay assemblages, local varieties that do show ties to Swasey/Bladen and Bolay assemblages from northern Belize (Valdez et al. 2008), and less standardization in ceramic types between the Belize Valley, northern Belize, and the Petén region than during subsequent times (Sullivan et al. 2008). Our hope is that the initial type descriptions of the Cunil material represent a "work in progress" that will continually be refined with future ceramic analyses at Cahal Pech and other sites.

Acknowledgments

The authors would like to thank the following individuals: M. Kathryn Brown, James F. Garber, Paul Healy, Jim Puc, Myka Schwanke, the Institute of Archaeology, and the hardworking members of BVAR and BVAP. This chapter has also benefited from conversations with Richard E. W. Adams, E. Wyllys Andrews, George Bey, Laura J. Kosakowsky, Lisa LeCount, Nina Neivens, and Fred Valdez Jr. Last but not least we would like to thank the volume editor, Jim Aimers, and the reviewers for their constructive and insightful comments.

8

Technological Style and Terminal Preclassic Orange Ceramics in the Holmul Region, Guatemala

MICHAEL G. CALLAGHAN, FRANCISCO ESTRADA-BELLI, AND NINA NEIVENS DE ESTRADA

One of the purposes of this volume is to address ancient Maya ceramic exchange and interaction using concepts of style and the application of multiple analytical methods to ceramic data sets. Style in archaeology is a thorny issue, and many scholars have had great difficulties setting forth a working definition of this term (Conkey and Hastorf 1990; Hegmon 1998; Sackett 1990; Wobst 1977). Where style resides in an archaeological object, what it comprises, and what functions it performs in society can vary greatly within and between artifact classes and prehistoric cultures. In the present chapter, we apply the concept of technological style in combination with multiple ceramic analytical techniques to the study of red versus orange serving vessels in the Holmul region of Guatemala during the close of the Late Preclassic period (A.D. 150–250).

Ceramic artifacts used in this study come from seven years of excavation directed by Estrada Belli in the Holmul region. The Holmul region is located in the northeastern department of Petén near the present-day Belizean border. The site of Holmul was initially investigated in 1911 by Raymond Merwin of Harvard University (Merwin and Vaillant 1932). Holmul garnered attention early in the archaeology of the Maya lowlands for its Building B in Group II, a masonry structure with ten burial chambers containing pottery and remains dating sequentially from the Late Preclassic (350 B.C.–A.D. 350) through Early Classic periods (A.D. 350–550). More recent mapping and excavations have revealed approximately seven major archaeological sites within a seven kilometer radius of Holmul: two large ceremonial and administrative centers (Holmul and Cival), separated by approximately seven kilometers and six minor centers (T'ot, K'o, Hahakab, Hamontun, La Sufricaya, and La Riverona) varying in area and in number of monumental pyramidal structures and plaza groups.

While changes in slip color (from red to orange) and surface finish (from "waxy" to "glossy") of serving vessels dating to the close of the Late Preclassic and beginning of the Early Classic period have been well documented by previous scholars (see Pring 2000 for an excellent synthesis), only recently have researchers begun to study other technologies associated with these surface changes (Brady et al. 1998). One of the goals of the present study was to determine whether orange-slipped serving vessels produced during this time displayed other changes in technology aside from surface characteristics.

The study of ceramics from the Holmul region revealed a change in technological style (specifically, aspects of paste recipe) from Late Preclassic red serving vessels to Early Classic orange serving vessels that coincided with the change in surface technologies. The primary importance of this research is that the results show that changes in technological style were not merely "skin deep" but included changes in paste recipes and perhaps even firing processes. These changes in technologies represent different patterns of production and could be representative of larger changes in the ceramic economy of the Holmul region taking place during the close of the Late Preclassic period. While it is difficult to know for certain why these changes occurred, we believe they were inextricably tied to larger changes taking place in the political, economic, and social realms of ancient Maya society during this time, and we offer a brief explanation at the close of this chapter.

Technological Style

Heather Lechtman (1977, 1993; Lechtman and Steinberg 1979:154–57) was influential in forwarding the concept of technological style in the study of archaeological artifacts with her work on ancient Andean craft production systems. As the term implies, seemingly mundane aspects of production technologies can be considered stylistic themselves. Furthermore, this style is not "passive" in the sense of Sackett's (1990) isochrestic variation—that is, resulting from heavily ingrained motor habits or arbitrary, yet consistent, technological choices on the part of craftspeople. Lechtman argues that the technologies employed in the production of any artifact do not exist in isolation from social, political, and religious concerns. Production technologies can be informed by worldview, group-specific ideologies, and even social networks.

In her work, Lechtman supports this argument with a study of ancient Andean metallurgy. Through experimental archaeology and archaeometry she demonstrates that the time-consuming and complicated technologies that ancient Mochica metallurgists used to create the color of gold or silver on the surface of a metal object reflected a worldview in which "the essence of the object, that which appears superficially to be true of it, must also be inside it. In fact, the object is not that object unless it contains within it the essential quality" (Lechtman 1984:30). More recently, Gosselain (1992:82) has suggested that technological style can be used as a means to identify and understand social identity. He explains that technological style "is founded upon the ethnographically verified assumption that similar aims can always be reached in different ways, but that the choices artisans make essentially proceed from the social contexts in which they learn and practice their craft. . . . [S]tudying technical style offers an opportunity to explore the deepest and more enduring facets of social identity." Because we view the social relationships and ideological value systems within which these vessels were made as being inextricably linked or embedded in their physical creation, we refer to any aspect of this process as "production" rather than "manufacture" throughout this chapter.

It was our intention to extend the framework of technological style back in time to the end of the Preclassic and beginning of the Classic period with the study of a long-debated set of archaeological artifacts, "Protoclassic" orange serving vessels. Similar studies of technological paste style have been performed on Middle Preclassic ceramics from the site of K'axob, Belize (Bartlett 2004) and Postclassic ceramic types in the Petén Lakes region (Cecil 2001b). The orange serving vessels we discuss here, especially the first polychrome pottery, appears in the archaeological record of the lowlands during what has previously been referred to as the Protoclassic period—a loosely defined time frame beginning at approximately 75 B.C. and ending at approximately A.D. 400 in the Maya lowlands (Brady et al. 1998).

The "Protoclassic" Period in the Maya Lowlands

The chronological placement, culture-material correlates, and economic and sociopolitical changes that took place during the Protoclassic period have long been the subject of intense debate in Maya archaeology (Adams 1971; Brady et. al. 1998; Hammond 1974, 1977, 1984; Pring 1977a, 1977b, 2000; Sharer and Gifford 1970; Sharer and Traxler 2006; Sheets 1979a, 1979b; Willey, Culbert, and Adams 1967; Willey and Gifford 1961). Recently scholars have proposed a number of chronological and culture-historical correlates to isolate this period in time; we draw upon those syntheses here.

Brady and colleagues (1998) address the chronological placement of the Protoclassic period in terms of ceramic evidence. They divide the Protoclassic in the Maya lowlands into two facets—an early (75 B.C.–A.D. 150) and a late (A.D. 150–400)—both based upon significant changes in ceramic modes. In brief, the first facet witnessed the introduction of matte- or waxy-finish orange-brown ceramic types (for example, Iberia Orange and Ixobel Orange), as well as the production and exchange of pottery displaying the Usulután mode of drip-like decoration (through application of true-resist technology or positive painting). The second facet saw the introduction of glossy-finished orange types (for example, ceramics of the Aguila Orange Group), including those with polychrome painted decoration (for example, Ixcanrio Orange-polychrome), as well as continued production and exchange of matte-finished types (for example, ceramics of the Aguacate Orange Group).

Brady and colleagues (1998) also address the confusing use of the term *Protoclassic* by previous researchers. Building on Willey's (1977) observations, they note that the term has become increasingly complex because of (1) its association with a phase of Maya cultural evolution, (2) its use in referring to specific traits of certain ceramic assemblages, and (3) its use as a chronological time period in Maya prehistory. They urge future researchers to use the term only in reference to ceramics displaying specific modes that appear during the two facets of time 75 B.C.–A.D. 150 and A.D. 150 to as late as 400. Furthermore, they urge researchers to spell the term with a lowercase *p* (that is, "protoclassic") and never hyphenated, in order to avoid confusion with previous use.

We agree with Brady and colleagues' (1998) arguments about the confusing nature of the term *Protoclassic*. However, we believe that this time period bore witness to more than changes in ceramic modes. Previous research cited in a recent synthesis by Reese-Taylor and Walker (2002) focuses on a number of significant culture-historical changes that occurred during the close of the Late Preclassic period. These changes included (1) increased signs of warfare and site abandonment along preexisting trade routes; (2) a massive reorganization of trade patterns after the collapse of El Mirador; (3) signs of the first royal burials in tombs and plazas of major centers such as Tikal, Caracol, and Holmul; 4) usurpation of the supernatural realm by elites through the construction of ceremonial architecture in the form of mythical places at major site centers and the possibility that elite shamans began taking on roles of deities and sacred ancestors at important ceremonial events; and most important as concerns this research, (5) the introduction of a subcomplex of orange-slipped polychrome pottery displaying "tags" of ideology representing rebirth (such as mammiform supports, which Reese-Taylor and Walker relate to representations of breasts from the goddess Ix'chel) and symbols that eventually become associated with Classic period elites (such as the weave, mat, or "pop" pattern as well as early representations of the *ahau* glyph).

In summary, the close of the Late Preclassic period at some sites is marked by dramatic political, economic, and social changes. Based on Brady and colleagues' (1998) ceramic markers and Reese-Taylor and Walker's (2002) culture-historical correlates, we believe this period warrants the use of a distinct term of reference. Like Brady and colleagues (1998), we prefer to discontinue use of the now confusing term *Protoclassic* and will therefore refer to this period as the Terminal Preclassic period. We defer to Brady and colleagues' dating based on ceramic markers that are, not surprisingly, coeval with Reese-Taylor and Walker's (2002) culture-historical changes. Of course, adoption of the early and late facet ceramic modes as well as the appearance of the culture-historical changes mentioned above did not occur simultaneously at every site across the lowlands. Therefore, the dating of the Terminal Preclassic period within any site is subject to the appearance of local data. In the following section we address the chronological placement and culture-historical correlates of the Terminal Preclassic period within the Holmul region.

The Terminal Preclassic Period from the Perspective of Holmul

To date, no site in the Holmul region has shown ceramic evidence for participation in Brady and colleagues' (1998) Terminal Preclassic period early facet (75 B.C.–A.D. 150). Based on the appearance of Ixcanrio Orange-polychrome material and radiocarbon dates (discussed below), the late facet begins at approximately A.D. 150 in the Holmul region and ends with the introduction of Tzakol I ceramics (namely, Actuncan Orange-polychrome and Boleto Black-on-orange types) at approximately A.D. 250.

New excavation campaigns by the Holmul Archaeological Project between 2003 and 2007 in Building B of Group II at Holmul expanded the sample and chronological control of Terminal Preclassic ceramics in the Holmul region (Callaghan 2006; Estrada-Belli 2003, 2004, 2006, 2010). A new tomb was located below the two tombs encountered by the 1911 expedition, Rooms 8 and 9, which contained most of the Terminal Preclassic complete vessel sample from Holmul. This interment contained the remains of a single male individual in extended position. An Ixcanrio Orange-polychrome tetrapod rested on his pelvis. Below it were the decayed remains of painted stucco, which may have been pages of a stucco-coated codex or other stucco-coated perishable object. A small tubular jade bead necklace pendant was the only item of personal adornment. The vessel, among the many recovered in the region, was of the finest quality. The possible painted book and the jade necklace, while certainly denoting a high-ranking status for the interred, would not qualify this as a richly furnished tomb, especially when compared to later tombs in the same edifice. In contrast to the relatively simple funerary furnishing was the tomb's architecture, featuring upright stone slabs as walls and four large lid stones as roof.

While relatively unimpressive compared to other elite interments of the period, the significance of this tomb lies in the fact that it is cut into the floor of a Late Preclassic temple platform, that it is the first of a long sequence of elite interments in the Building B structure, and that it provides a secure date, by AMS assays on bone collagen from the interred skeleton, to A.D. 150. This tomb's date and its stratigraphic position at the beginning of the sequence of tombs containing orange polychrome vessels in Building B reaffirm Brady and colleagues' (1998) placement of the beginning of the second facet of Terminal Preclassic ceramic development, heralding the introduction of polychrome painting on orange-slipped vessels at A.D. 150.

The superstructure built above this tomb may thus represent one of the earliest documented examples of funerary temples. The iconography associated with the frieze of the Early Classic period version of this building (phase five) is further evidence of this (Taube 1998). Funerary temples are an architectural type yet to be documented in the Preclassic period but fairly common in the Classic period and are directly related to Maya secular authority (Houston 1998; McAnany 1998; Taube 1998). Finally, this Terminal Preclassic elite tomb and others found looted at nearby Cival and Hamontun represent additional tangible signals of the changes occurring in Maya society at about A.D. 150. During this period, elite interments were for the first time placed within public buildings, appropriating spaces that were typically reserved to the conjuring of supernatural forces. Another tangible signal of changing social realities in the Holmul region stems from the appearance of elite interments not only at the major ritual center of the region, Cival, but also at those sites that undoubtedly must have housed elites of secondary political status within the Holmul region throughout the Late Preclassic period, such as those of Holmul and Hamontun.

Terminal Preclassic Orange Gloss Ceramics and Maya Cultural Process

Terminal Preclassic orange gloss pottery exhibits a combination of Preclassic and Classic period ceramic traits along with its own unique characteristics (Smith 1955: 22). Classic period characteristics include glossy surface finish, red-and-black-on-orange polychrome painting, and some aspects of vessel form including composite bowl shapes. Preclassic characteristics include thick vessel walls and the presence of four supports, or "tetrapods." Traits unique to orange gloss ceramics include fashioning the tetrapod supports into "mammiform" shapes, as well as vessel forms such as the tetrapod cylinder vase and the plate with swollen cylindrical supports. Orange gloss pottery of the Termi-

Figure 8.1. Location of the Holmul region and other Terminal Preclassic sites. (Map by Michael G. Callaghan.)

nal Preclassic period was first discovered in 1911 among funerary offerings of tombs within Late Preclassic Building B at the site of Holmul, Guatemala, by Raymond Merwin (Merwin and Vaillant 1932) (figure 8.1).

Maya archaeologists have tested many models aimed at understanding the function and meaning of Terminal Preclassic orange gloss ceramics. Because these vessels appeared to be evolutionary links between Preclassic and Classic period ceramic styles, archaeologists first believed they represented a transitional cultural phase between the Preclassic and Classic periods (Willey, Culbert, and Adams 1967). However, after years of excavations at other Maya sites yielded relatively few examples of Terminal Preclassic orange gloss ceramics (see discussion in Brady et al. 1998; Callaghan 2008a; Pring 2000), it became clear that the vessels could not be indicative of a pan-lowland phase of cultural evolution.

Because the majority of Terminal Preclassic orange gloss and orange matte pottery (similar in form but lacking glossy surface finish) was found in the eastern portion of the Maya lowlands, and because of their similarity to vessels found at sites in El Salvador dating to the same time period (Sharer 1978), scholars next hypothesized that this type of pottery was brought to the Maya lowlands by invaders or refugees from the southeastern periphery (Sharer and Gifford 1970). Volcanism and climatic activity were thought to be the cause for migration of southeastern populations into the lowlands (Sheets 1979a, 1979b). However, further comparison between the ceramic material found at sites in El Salvador and the eastern lowlands area revealed that similar Terminal Preclassic pottery in the eastern lowlands was made locally and only certain style modes traveled from El Salvador into the Maya heartland (Hammond 1974a, 1984; 1977; Pring 1977a). Further excavation and tighter ceramic and radiocarbon chronologies at sites in El Salvador also revealed that the potential cause of population movements out of El Salvador, the eruption of the volcano Ilopango, occurred much later than the introduction of orange gloss ceramics to the Maya lowlands (Dull et al. 2001).

Scholars are currently applying models derivative of more traditional political economy approaches to understand the introduction of orange gloss ceramics during the Terminal Preclassic period. In these models, orange gloss pottery constituted part of a new political economy and served as a form of social currency that materialized political or trade relations (Brady et al. 1998: 33; Fields and Reents-Budet 2005: 214–17; Pring 2000: 42; Reese-Taylor and Walker 2002: 104–5; Walker et al. 2006: 665). In this type of model, orange-slipped pottery would have been considered a type of prestige good with its production and/or distribution controlled by groups of elites seeking to gain or maintain social status and political authority.

However, a simple study of the distribution of Terminal Preclassic and early facet Early Classic orange-slipped material reveals that this type of material is not restricted to elite contexts at sites in the lowlands. This pottery is most often found in ritual contexts such as *chultuns* (Forsyth 1989: 10; Pring 2000: 117; Thompson 1931: 284–88), caves (Brady 1989; Ichon and Arnauld 1985), burials (Anderson and Cook 1944: 84; Gann et al. 1939; Merwin and Vaillant 1932; Pring 2000: 106; Willey and Gifford 1961), and caches (Culbert 1993) but also in construction fill of seemingly nonelite architecture or features (Dillon 1977; Pring and Hammond 1985). Furthermore, as the primary author's (Callaghan 2008a) recent study and this chapter show, production patterns are far too complicated to support a traditional prestige goods model. As we detail below, the results of the study suggest that changes in technological style between red and orange serving vessels of the Late Preclassic, Terminal Preclassic, and early facet Early Classic periods may have been more informed by pan-lowland changes in worldview and perhaps even reorganization of regional social structures.

Method, Sample, and Design

The primary purpose of this study was not merely to identify technological changes in orange-gloss serving vessels of the Terminal Preclassic period but to study those potential changes within the framework of the political economy model outlined above. It was the first author's original intention to test the hypothesis that orange-slipped pottery was a type of prestige good and functioned as a kind of social currency. Taking into account the limitations of the current sample from the Holmul region, correlates for prestige good production and exchange would have been (1) the identification of restricted technologies used in the production of orange-slipped pottery, (2) a restricted number of producers manufacturing orange-slipped pottery, (3) restricted distribution of orange-slipped pottery to elite contexts both within the Holmul region and elsewhere in the Maya lowlands, and (4) evidence of production and exchange reaching outside the Holmul region.

Because ancient Maya ceramic production areas are notoriously difficult to identify in the archaeological record (Fry 2003 and this volume; Masson 2002; Nichols et al. 2001; Stark 1992), the units of study for this investigation were whole vessels and diagnostic rim sherds from Late Preclassic monochrome red material (Sierra Red: Sierra Variety) (figure 8.2), Terminal Preclassic orange polychrome material (Ixcanrio Orange-polychrome: Ixcanrio Variety) (figure 8.3), early facet Early Classic monochrome orange material (Aguila Orange: Variety Unspecified) (figure 8.4), early facet Early Classic black-on-orange material (Boleto Black-on-orange: Boleto Variety) (figure 8.5), and early facet Early Classic orange polychrome material (Actuncan Orange-polychrome) (figure 8.6). From this point forward, we refer to these specific type-varieties by only their full type names. The sample consisted of rim sherds and whole vessels from the medium-sized (25–30-centimeter rim diameter) composite bowl shape-class. We refer to these units of study as "type-forms" (see Foias 1996). A type-form is a subset of a type that includes vessels of only a given shape and size. For example, Actuncan Orange-polychrome composite bowls with diameters measuring between 20 centimeters and 25 centimeters are considered medium-sized bowl type-forms of Actuncan Orange-polychrome types in this study.

Rim sherds of Sierra Red, Aguila Orange, Ixcanrio Orange-polychrome, Boleto Black-on-orange, and Actuncan Orange-polychrome ceramics were selected from four types of contexts at the sites of Holmul, Cival, La Sufricaya, K'o, and Hamontun in the Holmul region dating to the Late Preclassic through early facet Early Classic periods. The four types of contexts included (1) burials, (2) caches, (3) primary deposition middens, and (4) redeposited middens in construction fill.

In accordance with the hypothesis stated above, if glossy orange-slipped pottery was produced and circulated within a prestige goods system, we expect it to have been produced by a small group of artisans who possessed knowledge of restricted ceramic technologies (for example, paste recipes, firing technology, and surface finish), with production possibly controlled by elites. In contrast, preexisting, contemporaneous, and seemingly unlimited in distribution, red ceramics of the Sierra Red Group would have been produced by a potentially larger group of production units using unrestricted technologies. Beginning with aspects of type-variety classification and continuing with modal analysis, diversity studies, petrography, and instrumental neutron activation analysis (INAA), Callaghan examined the difference between paste, firing, forming, and surface finish between the red- and orange-slipped ceramics.

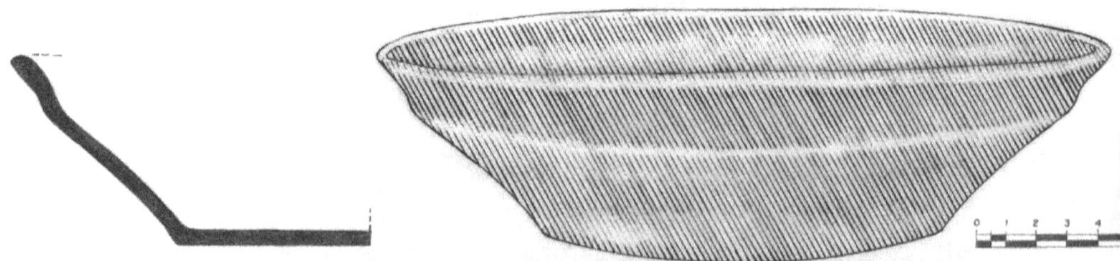

Figure 8.2. Sierra Red composite bowl form. (Drawing by Fernando Alvarez.)

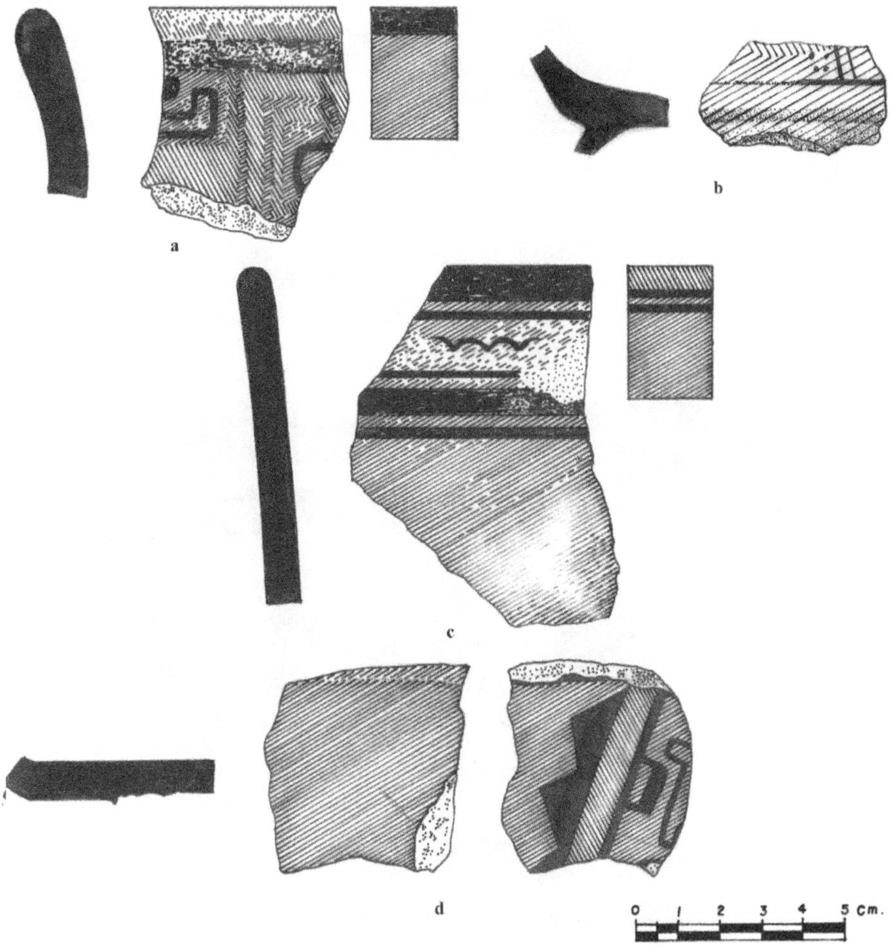

Figure 8.3. Sherds of Ixcanrio Orange-polychrome composite bowl forms. (Drawing by Fernando Alvarez.)

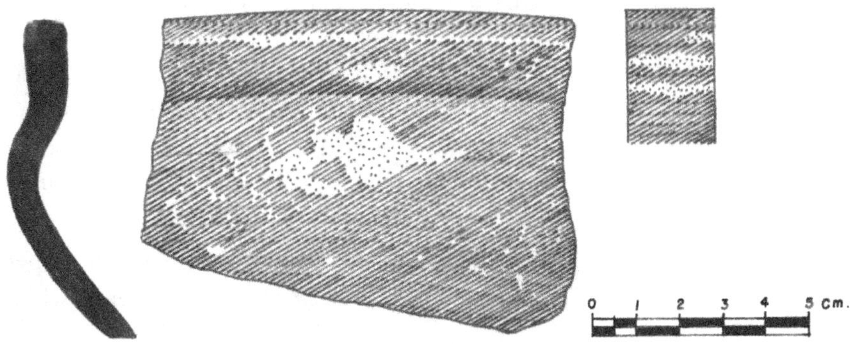

Figure 8.4. Aguila Orange composite bowl form. (Drawing by Fernando Alvarez.)

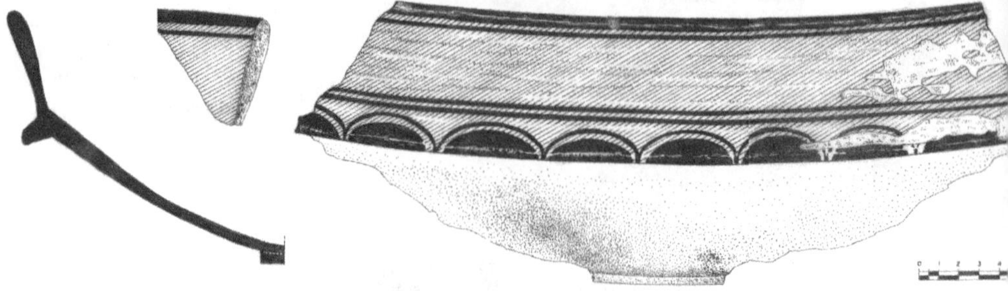

Figure 8.5. Boleto Black-on-orange composite bowl form. (Drawing by Fernando Alvarez.)

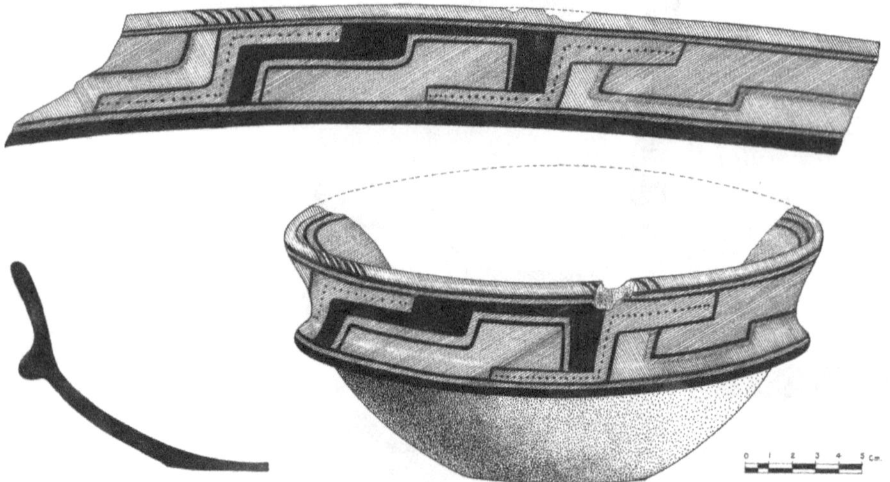

Figure 8.6. Actuncan Orange-polychrome composite bowl form. (Drawing by Fernando Alvarez.)

Here, we report only on the paste data from the ceramic analysis (results of other analyses can be found in Callaghan 2008a). The paste study comprised a three-tiered method of compositional analysis. The purpose of this type of analysis was to (1) characterize the mineralogical and chemical composition of pastes within the five type-forms, (2) seek to identify any restricted technologies in the form of paste recipes by unique mineral and chemical combinations associated with specific ceramic type-forms, (3) characterize the potential geologic origin of paste recipes used within each tradition, and (4) test a complementary methodology for paste composition analysis in which paste fabric and inclusions were classified according to microscopic visual properties, petrographic mineralogical properties, and chemical properties all within the same analysis.

Analysis began by using a simple stereomicroscope. Paste variants within each tradition were identified based upon the first major inclusions within a degree of texture (for example, fine, medium, coarse) for each sherd. Analysis revealed three major medium-textured paste groups based upon three major inclusion types: (1) crystalline calcite, (2) gray calcite, and (3) ash. Callaghan was able to further subdivide these three major groups based upon major secondary inclusions. In the second tier of analysis, thin sections of one sherd from each of these seven subgroups from each site in the region were created and used in the petrographic analysis. These same samples were then subject to third-tier-analysis INAA by researchers at the Missouri University Research Reactor (MURR). Results from all three analyses were then compared to one another in an effort to see whether the methods yielded similar, albeit complementary, results.

Results

A list of all paste variants and their distribution within type-forms of the red- and orange-slipped traditions is presented in table 8.1. A number of patterns are immediately recognizable in the data. The first is that the composite-bowl type with the most variation in paste recipes is Actuncan Orange-polychrome, followed by Ixcanrio Orange-polychrome and Boleto Black-on-orange. The

Table 8.1. All paste variants of composite bowls

	Sierra (n=22)		Aguila (n=29)		Boleto (n=15)		Actuncan (n=18)		Ixcanrio (n=7)	
Inclusion type	#	%	#	%	#	%	#	%	#	%
Crystalline calcite	4	18	1	3	3	20	3	17	1	14
Crystalline calcite and white calcite	1	5			2	13	1	6	1	14
Crystalline calcite and gray calcite	8	36					1	6		
Crystalline calcite	9	41							2	29
Crystalline calcite and orange sherd							1	6	2	29
Gray calcite			26	90	7	47	3	17		
Gray calcite and white calcite			2	7	2	13	1	6		
White calcite									1	14
Ash							2	11		
Ash and crystalline calcite							6	33		

great variation in paste of all three painted type-forms potentially suggests that each of these was produced by a number of different production units using their own specific paste recipes. Both traditions of monochrome ceramics show the least variation. Interestingly, it appears that the lateral-angle bowl form of Sierra Red contains fewer paste variants than any other type-form in the study. It also appears that some paste recipes (specifically, the crystalline calcite variants) crosscut type-forms, while others (namely, gray calcite and ash recipes) are found only in the orange type-forms. This supports evidence for continuity in paste recipes between all the type-forms. Furthermore, in Callaghan's (2008a) extended analysis, flaring bowl forms of Sierra Red vessels were also seen to exhibit gray-calcite-and-ash-based paste recipes, further suggesting continuity in production and a lack of complete restriction in the paste preparation process.

To further quantify the patterns above, Callaghan performed separate studies of richness and evenness on the stereomicroscope paste variant data. The results are presented in table 8.2. A simple category count reveals that more paste variants make up the Actuncan Orange-polychrome type-form. However, this could be due to a difference in the sample sizes between the five type-forms. Therefore, Margalef's Index was calculated for each of the five type-forms. Margalef's Index calculates species richness while controlling for unequal sample sizes (see Magurran 2003). The results confirm data from the simple category count and show that paste variants are richer (there are more variants) in Actuncan Orange-polychrome, Ixcanrio Orange-polychrome, and Boleto Black-on-orange material than in Aguila Orange and Sierra Red. Finally, through calculating the standard deviation of paste variants within each type-form, Callaghan quantified evenness. The data show that paste variants are more evenly distributed within the painted type-forms as opposed to the monochrome red and orange material. In sum, richness and evenness measures reveal that paste variants are more diverse within type-forms of the Terminal Preclassic and early facet Early Classic orange ceramic industries as opposed to the Preclassic red industry. This could indicate that more producers were involved in the production of the later orange material in comparison to the earlier red monochrome material.

Petrographic analysis of thin sections from eight subgroups of the major paste groups identified in the stereomicroscope analysis revealed specific mineralogical characteristics of the inclusions that defined each group. Petrographic mineralogical characteristics correlate directly to the stereomicroscopically observed major inclusions in each group. These mineralogical groups, based first upon analysis with the stereomicroscope and second on petrographic analysis of thin sections, are correlated in table 8.3. These groups

Table 8.2. Diversity data for all paste variants of composite bowls

	Sierra (n=22)	Aguila (n=29)	Boleto (n=15)	Actuncan (n=18)	Ixcanrio (n=7)
Category count	4	3	5	8	5
Richness (Margalef's Index)	0.97	0.59	1.48	2.42	2.06
Evenness (Standard Deviation)	3.7	14.15	2.35	1.75	0.55

Table 8.3. Major stereomicroscopic and corresponding petrographic paste variants

Stereomicroscopic variant	Petrographic variant (PV)
Crystalline calcite	Sparitic calcite (PV1)
Crystalline calcite and white calcite	Sparitic calcite (PV1)
Crystalline calcite and gray sherd	Sparitic calcite and sherd (PV2)
Crystalline calcite and orange sherd	Sparitic calcite and sherd(PV2)
Gray calcite	Peloid calcite (PV3); peloid calcite and bioclasts (PV4)
White calcite	Crypto-crystalline calcite (PV5)
Ash	Ash (PV6)
Ash and crystalline calcite	Ash and sparitic calcite (PV7)

comprise (1) a crystalline calcite or sparitic calcite variant, (2) a gray calcite or peloid calcite variant, and (3) an ash or volcanic glass variant. Petrographic analysis further refined the eight subgroups of paste variants, allowing Callaghan to recognize inclusions present in paste fabrics but not visible with a simple stereomicroscope (such as calcite bioclasts within the pastes of gray calcite/peloid material) and to correct any misclassifications of the stereomicroscopic analysis that occurred because of similarities in surface characteristics between mineral inclusions (namely, the potential similarity between gray calcite/peloid grains and crystalline calcite/sparite grains at the microscopic level). As the reader may note, calcite and ash were the only major inclusion groups identified in the sample. However, through both stereomicroscopic and petrographic analysis, Callaghan was able to further subdivide the calcite group into two major groups consisting of two specific types of calcite: sparitic calcite and peloid calcite.

Along with characterizing inclusions on the mineralogical level, petrographic analysis also allowed for the creation of five unique groundmass or paste fabric groups. Groundmass consists of individual clay particles that are not visible even at the greatest magnifications of the petrographic microscope, as well as any other inclusions smaller than the size of silt (0.0625 millimeters) visible with the petrographic microscope at a magnification of 150X. The compositional characteristics of the groundmass may best represent the compositional characteristics of the source from which the ceramic paste was fashioned.

The five types of groundmass correlate directly to the three major paste variants and eight subvariants (table 8.4) with the crystalline calcite/sparitic calcite variant comprising groundmasses 2–4, the gray calcite/peloid calcite comprising groundmass 5, and the ash variant comprising groundmass 1. If we extend the idea that paste groundmass may characterize geologic sources, it is possible that crystalline calcite/sparite ceramics were fashioned from clays either heavily mixed with or containing naturally occurring sparite limestone. Gray calcite/peloid ceramics may have been made from a clay source heavily mixed with or containing naturally occurring grains of peloid limestone. Finally, ash-tempered ceramics may have come from a relatively pure clay or a clay devoid of many naturally occurring inclusions and later heavily processed to sift out any form of inclusion.

The third tier of the paste analysis, INAA, was performed by Michael D. Glascock and Jeffery Ferguson as part of a National Science Foundation subsidy program of the Archaeometry Laboratory at the University of Missouri, Columbus. INAA further supplemented the results of the petrographic analysis by confirming that the three main paste groups were, in fact, chemically distinct, based upon concentrations of strontium, calcium, and chromium. While INAA did not distinguish chemical differences between clay types within the three major inclusion classes based on secondary inclusions, it did distinguish chemical differences between the three major inclusion classes. (This is the reason for the presence of only three INAA groups in table 8.5 in contrast

Table 8.4. Petrographic paste variant and groundmass type

Groundmass type	PV1	PV2	PV3	PV4	PV5	PV6	PV7
Pure clay				2	4		
Spherical sparite	11	10					1
Subspherical sparite	11	13					1
Streams of sparite	1	5					
Clay and peloids			20	12			

with the seven petrographic groups in table 8.3.) The gray calcite/peloid group constituted a chemical group with high strontium levels designated Group 1 by Glascock and Ferguson. The ash group contained relatively low levels of both strontium and calcium and constituted Group 2 of the chemical analysis. Finally, the crystalline calcite/sparitic calcite group was characterized by high levels of calcium but lower levels of strontium in comparison to Group 1 and therefore made up the third group, Group 3 of the chemical analysis (figures 8.7 and 8.8). Type-forms fall out according to their major inclusions within the three chemical paste composition groups (table 8.5). Because the INAA data mirror the stereomicroscopic and petrographic data, the same measures of diversity in paste composition for orange-slipped ceramics as well as continuity in the crystalline calcite variants between the orange and red ceramics are mirrored as well. The INAA data reported on here are admittedly brief. The relationship between mineral inclusions and chemical characteristics forms the basis of a forthcoming article by Ferguson, Glascock, and Callaghan. The authors use the data here only to show the complementary pattern of stereomicroscopic, petrographic, and INAA data.

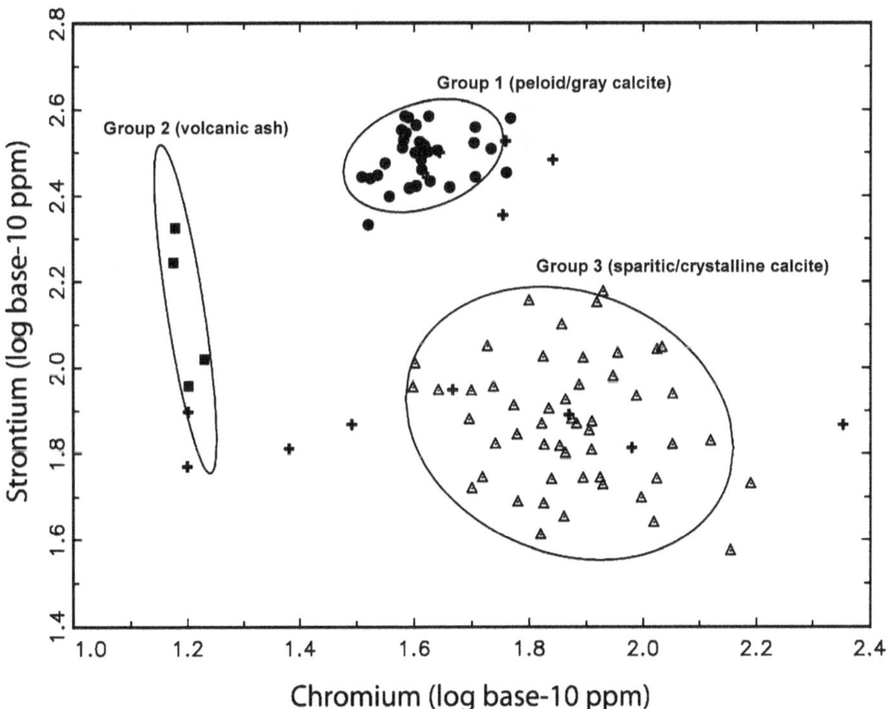

Figure 8.7. Bivariate plot of strontium and calcium-corrected chromium base-10 logged concentrations showing the three compositional groups and the unassigned samples (plotted with a "+" symbol). Ellipses represent a 90 percent confidence level for membership in a group.

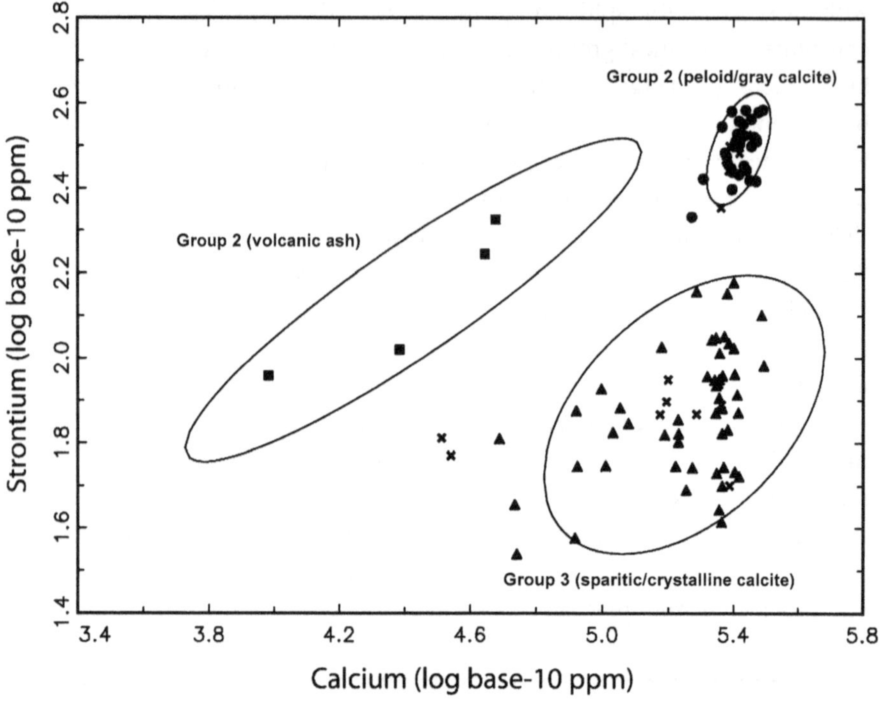

Figure 8.8. Bivariate plot of uncorrected calcium and strontium base-10 logged concentrations showing all three compositional groups. Unassigned samples are plotted with an "x" symbol. Ellipses represent a 90 percent confidence level for membership in a group.

Table 8.5. INAA groups and type-forms

Type-form	Group 1	Group 2	Group 3	Unassigned
Sierra			8	
Aguila	10		1	1
Boleto	9		3	
Actuncan	2	3	4	
Ixcanrio	2		3	1

After performing a Mahalanobis distance analysis with other samples already in the MURR database, Glascock and Ferguson found relatively few signs of direct matches. The most similar sherds to the Holmul material in the database come from sites recently excavated in the Petén Lakes region. The lack of matches in the database could support the idea that the sherds in this sample were produced relatively locally in the Holmul region and not traded at a distance. However, the lack of matches could also be a product of a small sample of sherds from the Petén area in the present MURR database.

Discussion

The goal of this research was to identify any changes other than surface characteristics in the technology of orange gloss ceramics and to understand the degree of restriction of these technologies in order to test the model of prestige goods production. Separate richness and evenness analyses of paste variants within the composite bowl type-form of red and orange traditions suggest that orange polychrome ceramics were produced using more recipes than ceramics of the monochrome red and monochrome orange traditions. This may reflect the number of production units involved in these two traditions of ceramics and correlate to orange polychrome ceramics being made by more production units than the two other traditions. The results reported here, along with previously reported results (Callaghan 2008a), also suggest that paste recipes used to fashion monochrome orange and polychrome orange composite bowls arose out of preexisting recipes in the Holmul region—in the case of the analysis reported on here, specifically, the crystalline calcite/sparitic calcite/Group 3 paste variant.

In summary, the data suggest that orange-slipped pottery of the Terminal Preclassic and early facet Early Classic periods may have been produced using quantifiably different paste recipes from monochrome red pottery of the Late Preclassic period, but (1) these recipes did not show strong signs of restriction or exclusivity, and (2) these recipes were not "invasive" to the Holmul region but arose out of existing local recipes. Because of these results, we can rule out a purely external origin for the introduction and production of orange-slipped ceramics in the Holmul region during the Terminal Preclassic period, as well as the notion that all aspects of production were controlled by elite groups and these ceramics functioned strictly as a type of ceramic prestige good in a new form of political economy.

When we return to the concept of technological style, we can see that the shift in paste preparation techniques may have reflected changes in the Terminal Preclassic period social structure or worldview. As discussed previously by Callaghan (2008a, 2008b), orange-slipped ceramics represented a dramatic change in every aspect of the ceramic production process, encompassing not only surface finish and decoration but also paste, form, and firing techniques. However, and as scholars have noted previously (Brady et al. 1998; Pring 2000), aside from the type and style of Terminal Preclassic period polychrome painting, none of these techniques was completely new to the Maya lowlands prior to the introduction of Terminal Preclassic period orange-slipped ceramics. What was new during the Terminal Preclassic was this specific combination of paste, form, firing, surface finish, and decoration modes and a clear shift away from previous production techniques. The data suggest to us that this shift was not the result of passive choices within the realm of isochrestic variation, the introduction of foreign pottery or technologies into the Maya lowlands, or even a change in political economy due to the control of craft production by a new group of political elites (or old groups practicing new strategies of social control). Rather, the shift in technologies *may* have been due to the conscious choices of pottery producers during the Terminal Preclassic period to break from traditions of the past and reflect a reorganized social structure that emerged in unison with reorganized political, economic, and religious systems that more closely resembled Classic period systems.

Drawing a close parallel between Lechtman's (1977) original study of ancient Andean metallurgy and the production of Terminal Preclassic orange-slipped pottery may be somewhat simplistic, but we cannot help but call attention to the similarities. The change in paste recipes during the Terminal Preclassic and early facet Early Classic periods—specifically, the steady abandonment of the use of the crystalline calcite and sherd temper variants—in the production of orange serving vessels may have represented a change in worldview reflected in the production process. Scholars in the Maya lowlands (Bartlett 2004) and other world regions (Smith 1989: 61; Sterner 1989) have noted the social implications of including crushed sherd from older pots in the paste fabrics of new ceramic material. These scholars call attention to the social link created between the present producers and the pots they are making with past producers, the pots they have made, and even the owners of those pots, when old crushed sherd is added to the paste of a new vessel. The new vessel essentially takes on certain inalienable qualities of the old vessel's social history, its owners, and producers along with the present producers and owners (see also Milbrath and Peraza, this volume).

Perhaps ceramic production technologies during the Terminal Preclassic reflected a shift in worldview away from the importance of including past histories in the creation of new vessels and represented a move toward more neutral or perhaps even more individualized or regional ideologies. This would correlate well to the lengthy process of increasing regionalization of lowland Maya political organization taking shape during the Early and Late Classic periods (Matthews 1991). While this particular theory is purely conjectural at this time, it nonetheless shows us that archaeologists can gain another entry point into the study of changes in worldview and social structure through the application of the concept of technological style.

Conclusion

Despite the small sample size, this research and other related analyses (Callaghan 2008a, 2008b) cause us to rethink models concerning the significance of the introduction of glossy orange serving vessels in the Holmul region during the Terminal Preclassic period. Production and distribution data show that this type of ceramic material was not exclusively produced and exchanged outside of the Holmul region, nor can it be considered part of a traditionally defined ceramic prestige goods system. Through the application of the concept of technological style, we have shown that the production and exchange of this kind of orange-slipped pottery may have represented a shift in worldview and reorganization of social structure that took place in tandem with the now well-known reorganization of contemporary political, economic, and religious systems at many lowland sites during the Terminal Preclassic period. Furthermore, with the application of the framework of technological style, production and exchange studies of orange- and red-slipped serving vessels move beyond the realm of craft production studies and into the realm of the study of ancient social practice. Finally, methodologically, this study has shown how different forms of compositional paste analysis need not contradict one another but instead, when taken together, can create a holistic complementary study of the paste preparation process. The results of this analysis suggest to us that we can gain a better understanding of prehistoric cultural processes, not to mention the relationship between ceramic style and social interaction, through this combination of practice-based theoretical frameworks and the application of multiple analytical methods.

9

Acanmul, Becán, and the Xcocom Phenomenon through a Type-Variety Looking Glass

Resolving Historical Enigmas through Hands-On Typological Assessments

JOSEPH BALL AND JENNIFER TASCHEK

> The type-variety method is not analysis, and you are not "analyzing" ceramics when you use it. Type-variety is classification—a method for classifying pottery and potsherds into comparable units and categories and then using these to intercompare sites and the degrees of equivalence, similarity, and distance between them.
>
> Robert Sonin to Joe Ball, 1970

The ruins of Acanmul lie approximately 25 kilometers northeast of Ciudad Campeche and 15 kilometers inland from the present Campeche coast (figure 9.1). It is a medium-size regional center of the type and magnitude classified as a "Rank 2" site by Nicholas Dunning (1992: 88–91, table 5.3), including among its known remains at least four pyramidal structures exceeding ten meters in height; a ballcourt; four large, functionally distinct architectural complexes incorporating multiple vaulted buildings and acropolis platforms; and numerous sculpted columns and architectural wall panels (figure 9.2).[1]

The center core occupies a low limestone knoll, Isla Acanmul, that rises an irregular 10 to 16 meters above the surrounding sea-level bottomland at the northern end of the Río Verde valley. Actually the floodplain of the ancient river—today renamed Río Hontún—this channelway consistently floods to canoe-navigable depths during the annual early summer through winter rainy season and so provides direct protected egress to the gulf, some 15 kilometers downstream. There is a well-preserved riverine "*embarcadero* group," or port facility, complete with a descending stone stair and wharf on the south bank of the ancient channel about 1 kilometer south of Isla Acanmul.[2]

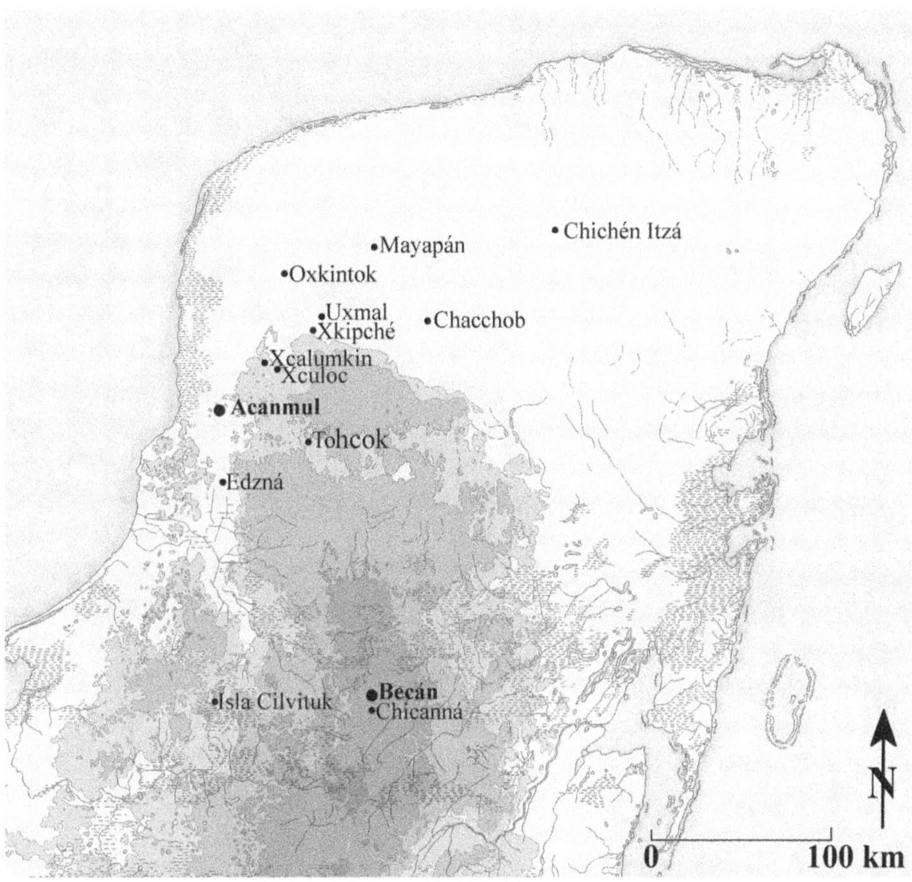

Figure 9.1. Areal map showing sites mentioned in text and other key centers. (Map by Jennifer Taschek.)

Isla Acanmul was occupied at least as early as the Middle Preclassic and has yielded evidence of plastered courtyard floorings and platforms dating to this time (Ball and Taschek 2007a). Continuous settlement and growth over the Preclassic led to the emergence of a good-sized architectural center complete with its own ballcourt by the third to fourth century A.D. (Tankab phase), and by the early seventh century (Chel phase), Acanmul had attained the magnitude and complexity of a significant regional center, or *batabil,* with a pyramid-defined central plaza and two functionally distinct, restricted-access architectural complexes. Architecturally and ceramically, the center was a participant in the Early Oxkintok–Western Puuc cultural tradition well known from Oxkintok, Xculoc, Xcalumkin, and other sites in the Yucatán-Campeche border zone. This remained so well into the ninth century (Pa'xil phase), the focus of this chapter.

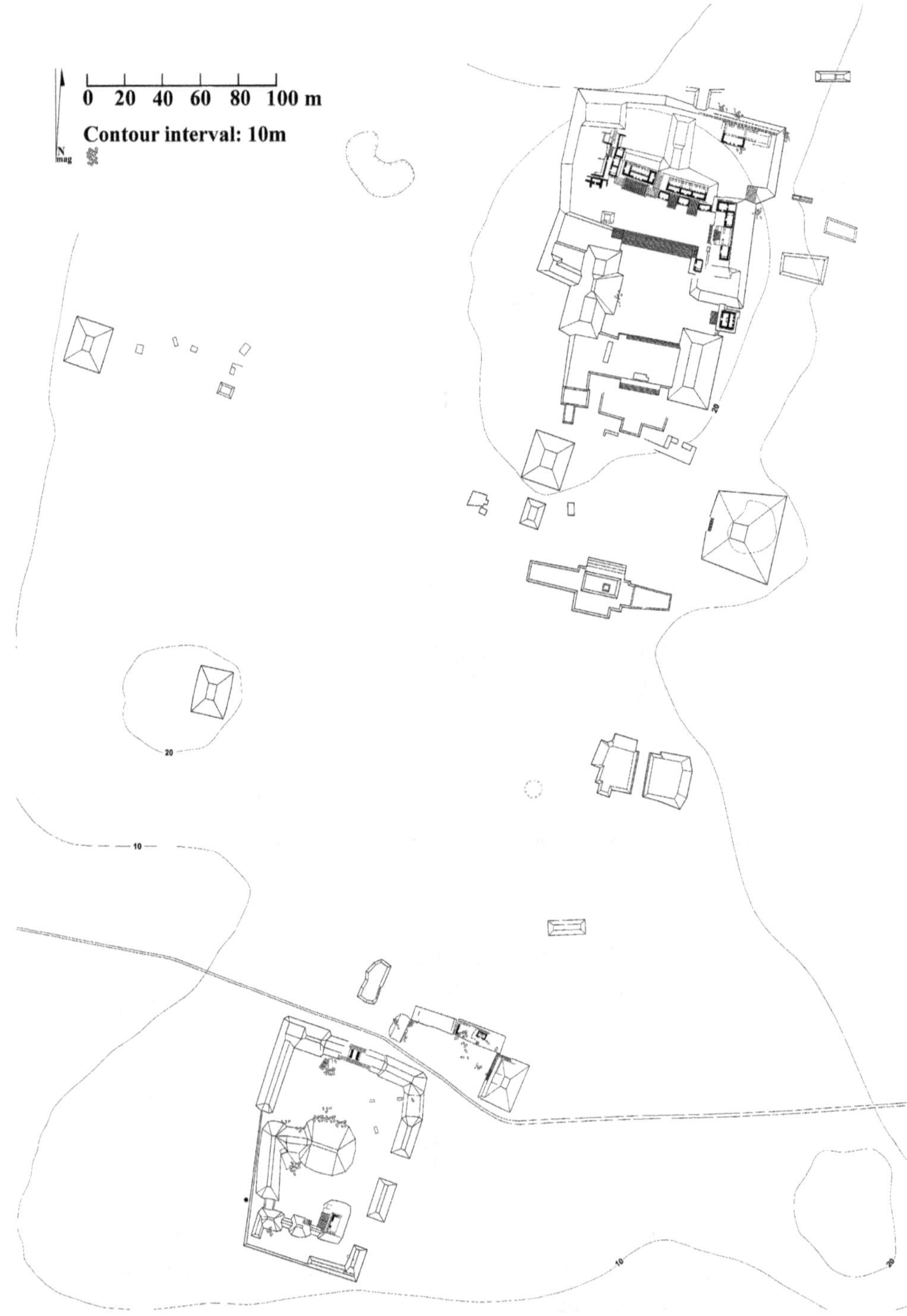

Figure 9.2. Plan view of Acanmul site core. (Map by Jennifer Taschek.)

Overall, Acanmul is typical of medium-size centers of the Classic era throughout the Maya lowlands and presents few attributes special to itself. That said, the site's brief systematic study has produced data leading to a number of provocative lines of inquiry and future investigation. One involves the fate of the center's elite population and its attendants following what appears to have been the seizure of Acanmul by interior northwestern peninsula or northern coastal plain (perhaps Itza) forces sometime in the mid-ninth to mid-tenth century A.D.[3] and the associated demolition of much of the center's regal-residential and public ceremonial architecture. Complexes and buildings razed included portions of the main palace compound and its north-side *audiencia*;[4] the central ballcourt; and several columned range buildings and associated pyramidal platforms from which sculpted columns were pulled down and rolled into heaps in adjacent courtyards. Several multistory residential apartment buildings—similar to Structure IV at Becán—were deliberately imploded and then filled with rubble to provide irregular open cores for overbuilding. A number of structures and groups were preserved and utilized, some being refurbished and enlarged. Among these were the main administrative acropolis (Group A) and—more significantly—at least one of a series of embarcadero plaza groups or riverine port facilities located about a kilometer south of the center's core on the south bank of the Río Hontún (see note 1). On the basis of ceramic and other artifactual evidence, we believe an occupying force remained at Acanmul for an undetermined period, and we suspect that final abandonment of the site was linked directly to the failure of the Chichén Itzá center, polity, and economic system of which they were a component part. One way or another, the intrusive Machil occupation coincided broadly with the occupational florescence and failure of Chichén Itzá.

All this is well documented in the on-site archaeological record and is far from extraordinary. More intriguing is what happened to the resident Late-Terminal Classic elite occupants of Acanmul at the time of the documented incursion. We believe that we have determined at least some part of the answer as to their fate and that it is documented in the occupational histories, depositional contexts, and varietal-level ceramic and lithic identities tightly linking Pa'xil phase Acanmul and early Xcocom phase Becán via the peripheral Chenes zone Puuc-style center of Tohcok in east-central Campeche or the regal-ritual city of Edzná (see figure 9.1). These identities include traditional type-variety attributes of surface finish, form, and decoration but importantly extend to paste variants as well.[5] Involved in all cases are limited quantities of what are conventionally recognized as "elite" or limited-availability wares that are moderately well to well represented at Acanmul but appear only in limited numbers and contexts at Becán. We believe the latter to be actual vessels from central Campeche that reflect only a relatively brief period of availability and circulation by northern immigrants (see Rovner 1975; Rovner and Lewenstein 1997). The data underpinning our hypothesis follow.

We should note that it is imperative to keep in mind that what matters was the sudden and unheralded appearance of the entire, conjoined constellation of wares concerned, not the occurrence of any one of the specific individual types or modes. Any of those alone or even all as isolates could easily have owed their presence to any number of possible mechanisms such as gifting, exchange, or local mimicry among others. What matters and is crucial to our argument was the intrusive appearance of the full assemblage as an integrated assemblage, and this is what is documented by Becán's archaeological record.

The Pa'xil Complex, Cehpech Ceramic Sphere

The late Late Classic Pa'xil Cehpech ceramic assemblage at Acanmul developed directly out of the local full Late Classic Chel complex and is marked by both developmental continua in several wares and the appearance of some new exotics and disappearance of others. Among the local ware traditions, narrow-mouthed/strap-handled jars, basins, bowls, and tripod dishes in plain and trickle-decorated (oxidized, reduced, and mixed variants) Puuc Slate Ware qualitatively and quantitatively interfingering from deposit to deposit with flaky, low-luster Campeche gloss ware developmental ancestors and contemporaries continued as the predominant constituent. Following closely in abundance are unslipped plain/striated jars, bowls, and "buckets," many with asphaltum-black trickle. Larger jars and food-service forms—tripod dishes and plates—are abundant in a range of decorative variants of Celestun Red Ware and its Pa'xil derivatives, Nimun Brown and Fine-paste Celestun Red. Rounding out the majority local wares were large, T-rim basins of Holactun Black-on-cream (Cahuich Coarse-cream Ware/Holactun Slate Ware), another Chel continuance.

Excepting some smaller, lighter vessels, all of the foregoing are seen as "local"—perhaps *regional* would be a better term here—products for general, quotidian domestic use circulating via the general economy (Ball 1993; Ball and Taschek 1992). Most of these local production traditions continued in some form in the subsequent Machil phase.

Minority or specialty wares present in Pa'xil that we assign to a "luxury" or "elite" status include Ticul Thin-slate vases, bowls, and tripod dishes and plates in both clear and purplish dendritic-marked pearly gray slips. Incised, gouged-incised, impressed, and molded-carved decorative variants are represented. Acanmul examples are decidedly distinct from the brownish to olive Chenes thin slates (see Williams-Beck 1994, 1999) and noticeably more soapy in luster than more northern Puuc zone examples. They are literally identical to early Xcocom Becán pieces, however.

Also present is a previously undesignated "thick thin-slate" (first recognized and discussed but not defined by Michael P. Simmons [1981])—Muncul Thick Thin-slate—that we believe to be transitional between the Late Classic "medium" slate wares and true thin slate. Other tight Xcocom identities include Sayan Red-on-cream hemispherical bowls and Zanahoria Incised polychrome tripod grater-dishes. The correspondences between the Acanmul Pa'xil and Becán early Xcocom materials are the closest the authors ever have seen between two geographically distant assemblages and do represent true identities in all observed attributes. What is critical to stress, therefore, is that we see these not as interacting contemporaries but as sequential, with Pa'xil dating to approximately A.D. 790~800 to 840/860~880 and being continuous with and out of its local predecessor assemblage, Chel, and followed by early Xcocom ("*a*") at Becán, dating from roughly 830/860 to 890~910/930~950 (see note 3) and representing a discontinuous intrusive entity (see Ball 1977a; Rovner 1975; Rovner and Lewenstein 1997).

Pa'xil ended abruptly, an event we associate with the successful ninth-century attack on, large-scale symbolic demolition of, and subsequent revitalization of Acanmul and its port facilities and the establishment of the associated Machil ceramic complex. As already noted, this involved a continuance of many quotidian domestic wares together with the appearance of a battery of replacement fine wares. We will not consider Machil further here, as our focus is on Pa'xil and what happened to it, in addition to the (possible) fate of its associated user-population.

Becán: Reassessing the Chintok and Xcocom Ceramic Assemblages

During and following visits to Becán and the collections stored at the Centro Regional de Campeche, Instituto Nacional de Antropología e Historia (INAH) in 2001 and 2003, the authors began to seriously reconsider Ball's (1973, 1977a) early 1970s formulations, datings, and interpretations of the late ceramic assemblages from that site. We have since come to a number of conclusions that differ radically from those of 35 years ago (figure 9.3). Serendipitously, these reassessments of Becán's ceramic and cultural histories coincided with tantalizing new findings at Acanmul and other northern sites. What emerged were a number of provocative new avenues for research involving Becán, Acanmul, Edzná, and Tohcok, among other sites. We explore some of those possibilities here.

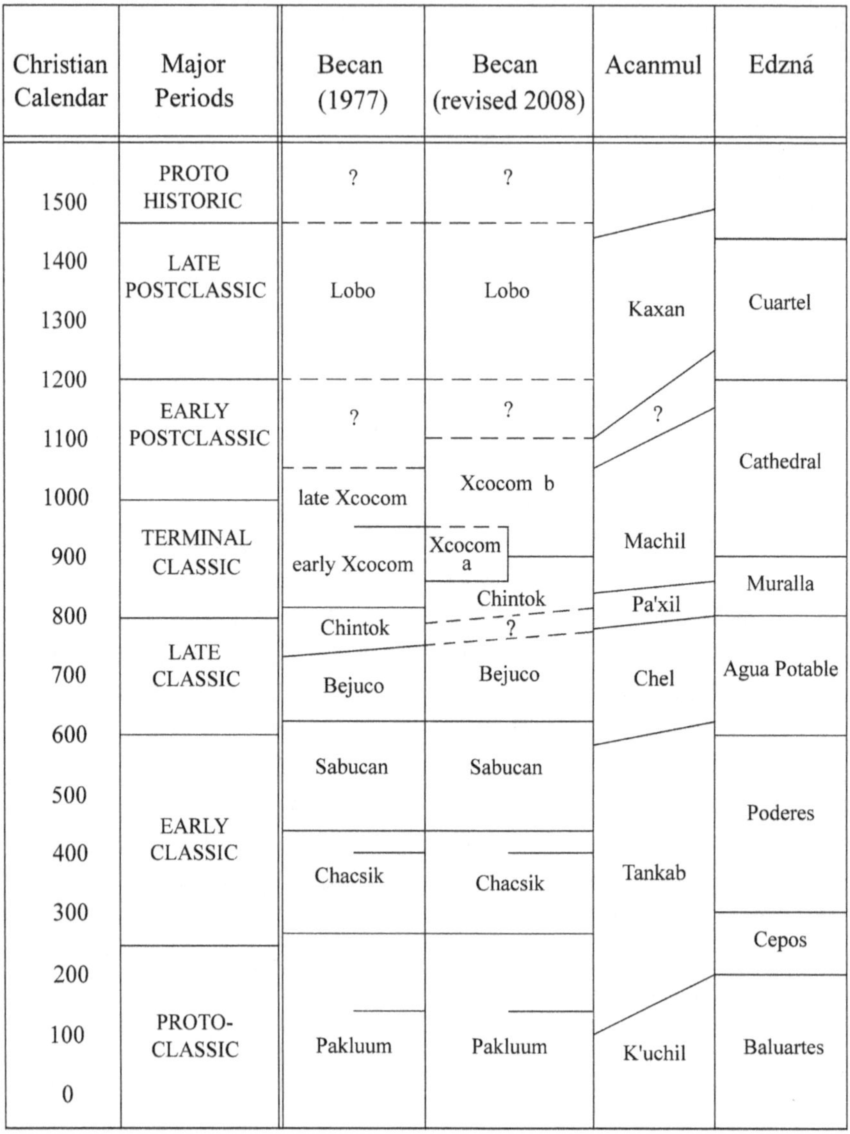

Christian Calendar	Major Periods	Becan (1977)	Becan (revised 2008)	Acanmul	Edzná
1500	PROTO HISTORIC	?	?		
1400	LATE POSTCLASSIC	Lobo	Lobo	Kaxan	Cuartel
1300					
1200					
1100	EARLY POSTCLASSIC	?	?	?	Cathedral
1000		late Xcocom	Xcocom b		
900	TERMINAL CLASSIC	early Xcocom	Xcocom a Chintok	Machil	Muralla
800		Chintok	?	Pa'xil	
700	LATE CLASSIC	Bejuco	Bejuco	Chel	Agua Potable
600					
500		Sabucan	Sabucan		Poderes
400	EARLY CLASSIC	Chacsik	Chacsik	Tankab	
300					Cepos
200					
100	PROTO-CLASSIC	Pakluum	Pakluum	K'uchil	Baluartes
0					

Figure 9.3. Chronological chart comparing original (1973, 1977) and revised (2008) Becán, Acanmul, and Edzná Classic-Postclassic ceramic phase sequences. (Chart by Jennifer Taschek.)

Chintok

The "Chintok complex" was and remains the most poorly documented ceramic assemblage at Becán (Ball 1977a: 133–34). Its original definition and dating were based weakly on factoring in mixed-core deposits in constructions overlying and underlying pure depositional contexts dating to the very well defined and heavily represented Bejuco Tepeu and Xcocom assemblages, accompanied by an analysis of which types and modes were not present rather than which were. This was a process considerably facilitated by the near total typological and modal discontinuities between Chintok and Bejuco on the one hand and, on the other, the fact that Xcocom and its facets were defined by the simple, coeval additions of several specific types and modes to a Chintok "base." In truth, the senior author is now convinced that its definition and existence owed as much to early 1970s conventional dogma regarding the "expected" existence at Petén-linked sites of a traditional Tepeu 1, 2, 3 sequence as to actual archaeological realities. Project research directors E. Wyllys Andrews IV and Richard E. W. Adams also strongly encouraged the definition of a Chintok complex.

The authors have carefully reexamined Chintok and Bejuco, with special attention to the securely dateable exotic pottery, polychromes, and decorative modes definitely associated with each as well as those not represented—such as Fine Gray Ware—and also have reviewed the distributions and depositional circumstances of the two as represented in the 1969–73 National Geographic Society–Middle American Research Institute Program and the more recent (1999–2002) INAH project directed by Luiz Evelia Campaña. Our conclusions, presented here, are at considerable variance with those reached in the early 1970s.

First, while Bejuco remains essentially as defined with some additions, its contextual distributions, depositional stratigraphy, and imported exotics (for example, Ball 1977a: figs. 28b, c, d; INAH collections, personal observations, 2001, 2003) clearly point to a small but significant original shortening of its true duration, and we now would date the Becán Bejuco phase as circa A.D. 620/630 to at least circa 760~770. This accords far better with the overall archaeological picture from both the site and the surrounding hinterland.

Conversely, review of all data pertaining to Chintok, both typological and distributional, supports a temporally shallower span than originally proposed. We would draw its inception forward in time from around A.D. 730/750 to about 790~800 or even later. How late Chintok might have lasted is complicated by its now-perceived likely overlap or even identity with Xcocom, as discussed below.

For all practical purposes, Chintok *is* Xcocom sans the exotics and homologies that define the "early" and "late" facets of the latter complex. In fact, while there is a complete and total disjunction between Bejuco ceramics and the diagnostic groups and types that characterize the Chintok core (Traino Brown; Pixtun Trickle-on-gray; mottled Achote Black), all of the former continue into and through both aspects of Xcocom (see Ball 1977a: 133–40). This extends even to the quintessentially local unslipped-striated (Encanto Group) pottery that spans Chintok and Xcocom but differs markedly from its Bejuco predecessors (Ball 1977a: 134–35). All this was noted 40 years ago, but its significance was not recognized. In concert, these data very much suggest a real occupational discontinuity or break. It now appears highly possible—in fact probable—that the Becán Late Classic collapse actually corresponded with the end of Bejuco and that the center sat abandoned for at least some length of time (indicated by the question mark on figure 9.3) before the reoccupation and refurbishment by regional hinterland and more exotic populations, reflected in the appearance of Chintok/Xcocom ceramics.[6]

Judicious review of the hinterland settlement data also indicates only a scattered and light Chintok or Xcocom presence outside the Becán ditch-and-parapet system, in contrast to heavy, dense Bejuco and earlier population (Thomas 1981). There is a decided concentration of Xcocom occupation in standing vaulted structures on platforms, both in close proximity to the center and elsewhere, but only a sparse and ephemeral Xcocom or Chintok presence farther afield (Thomas 1981). All this suggests a very different scenario from that of decline but continuity and subsequent invasion put forward 40 years ago, and it indicates a far more complex local cultural history than the one then proposed.

The duration of non-Xcocom Chintok is extremely difficult to determine on the available data; however, severely compressing the "phase" much better fits the known depositional and distributional data for the assemblage and far better accords with the overall archaeological record than do the formulations of 40 years ago (Ball 1973, 1977a). In the end, "Chintok" may in fact be nothing other than Xcocom sans the exotics and fine wares used to define the "early" and "late" facets or "a" and "b" subcomplexes (see below) of that complex's urban (site core) aspect (see Ball 1986: 400–402). In that case, hinterland occurrences of Chintok and Xcocom potentially are partly to largely or even entirely contemporary both with each other and with "urban" Xcocom and actually reflect not temporal variation but differing ceramic consumption and circulation spheres and differential access to exotics. Systematically, what actually are present are not two separate ceramic complexes but three subcomplexes defined by exotics and fine wares. All that is needed to test this is some limited but thoughtful and strategically focused fieldwork at Becán and in its hinterland.

Xcocom

Since its original definition in the early 1970s and recognition as an intrusive, possibly "elite" complex defined by a suite of "Northern" or "Puuc" ceramic and lithic indicators (Ball 1973, 1977a; Rovner 1974, 1975), Xcocom has undergone two important modifications and refinements. The first of these, suggested independently by Irv Rovner (1975) and Charles Lincoln (1986), involved redefining the sequential "early" and "late" facets of Xcocom as synchronous "Xcocom *a* (Gulf-oriented)" and "Xcocom *b* (Caribbean-oriented)" subcomplexes (Ball 1986: 400–402). The second refinement, suggested by Ramón Carrasco (1989), proposes extending the full duration of Xcocom well into the eleventh century or even later (Ball and Taschek 1989: 193n15). This is certainly a possibility based on the radiocarbon determinations and architectural associations that Carrasco reports, but further support for such late dating would be welcome.

From the start, the generic "Northern" or "Puuc" derivation of the intrusive elements defining Xcocom was evident both from the independently formulated type-variety classification of the ceramics and their observational comparison to existing ceramic collections from throughout the lowlands, and from Rovner's pathbreaking lithic analysis and comparative typology (Rovner 1974, 1975; Rovner and Lewenstein 1997). Both analyses identified a generic "northwestern" or "Puuc" origin area for the new elements defining "early" Xcocom or Xcocom "*a*," but neither could then be more specific, and both identified the intrusion as an aggressive invasion (Ball 1973, 1977a; Rovner 1975; Rovner and Lewenstein 1997). Thirty-five years of additional investigations and data have significantly altered the latter situation. In the intended methodological and theoretical spirit of this volume, we wish to stress that the conclusions reached and resulting interpretations presented rely not on "match my sherds to the published illustration/description" comparisons or literature reviews but on personal, hands-on examinations of pertinent collections and *muestras* at multiple facilities in Campeche, Yucatán, Tabasco, Chiapas, Guatemala, and Belize over the past thirty and more years. Such experiential familiarities are sine qua nons for such syntheses as the present one, an argument that the authors have made repeatedly since the 1970s (Ball 1980: 121; Ball and Taschek 2007a: 175).

Briefly stated, we now believe Rovner's (1975: 219) early assessment to be correct: "the limited distribution of early facet material suggests it is not a true chronological facet but an intrusive group occupying specific structures during the course of the Xcocom phase. Late facet Xcocom material in many respects is derived from Chintok material and at Chicanná is intermingled with Chintok indicating a direct Chintok to late facet Xcocom sequence. In this sense, late facet Xcocom probably wholly overlaps early facet Xcocom in time."

Accompanying the "early facet" assemblage was a bifacial chert point with a distinctive narrow, elongate shouldered body and a relatively short, rounded stem (figure 9.4). Within the Río Bec collections, this point type had a limited distribution appearing almost exclusively at Becán Structure IV in both use-related refuse deposits and mortuary contexts of "early" Xcocom constitution.

The point type is also known from Uxmal, Xkipché, Santa Cruz, and Chacchob in the Puuc zone proper (Rovner and Lewenstein 1997: 132; Braswell, personal communication 2008) and was present in our late Chel/Pa'xil collections from Isla Acanmul. Both Ball (1973, 1977a) and Rovner (1974, 1975; Rovner and Lewenstein 1997) describe considerable other data linking the overall content of "early" Xcocom with the Campeche-Tabasco Gulf Coast and the generic "Puuc" culture area or wider northwestern lowlands. Here we elaborate further, adding a number of what we believe to be significant details.

First, Chintok as here redefined either *is* incipient Xcocom sans any exotica or foreign elements, or so rapidly evolved into Xcocom as to make their complex-level distinction essentially pointless. Its later, evolved state is represented not only by "late" facet Xcocom *b* deposits (per Rovner 1975: 219) but also by "early" Xcocom *a* ones. The differences are in the exotics and influences represented, which, as Charles Lincoln (1986: 170–71) has pointed out, reflect

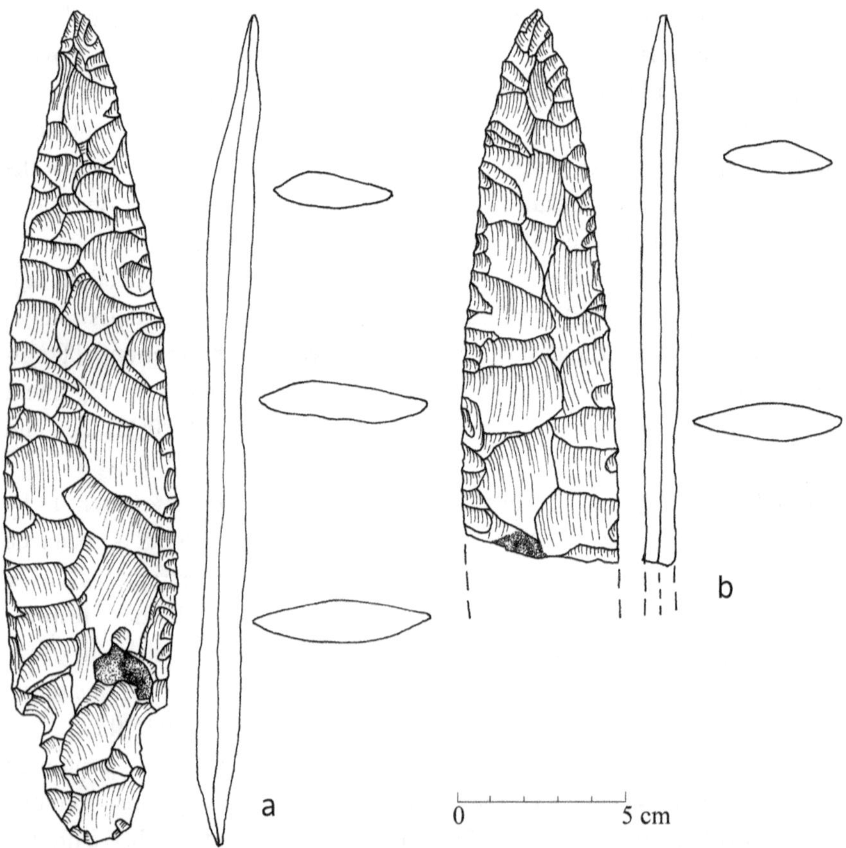

Figure 9.4. Diagnostic "early Xcocom" or "Puuc" lance points: *a*, from Becán, Structure IV chamber burial; *b*, from Acanmul palace refuse. (Drawings by Jennifer Taschek.)

differential access situations rather than chronological separation, although we would maintain that the latter could have been a contributing factor as well. A partially synchronous, partially sequential, but temporally overlapping alignment probably describes the actual relationship of the Xcocom subassemblages better than any other (see figure 9.3).

Second, the early Xcocom (*a*) intruders arrived not as invaders but as refugees. Their accompaniments included both favored personal effects and the means for continued access to at least some of these, as well as at least some craftspeople or artisans able to introduce into the local industries a small number of manufacturing traditions of surface finish and decoration (Pixtun and Dolorido groups [see below]).

Finally, ultimately, the Xcocom *a* refugees originated from Acanmul and represented the southward flight of that fallen center's surviving inhabitants. Natural topography suggests an easy retreat southward to Edzná; Xcocom *a* ceramic indicators also point to that center (see below). These could, however, also reflect continuing commonalities between the larger Becán and Edzná potting communities that first become evident in the short-lived Chintok assemblage. A natural corridor links the Edzná Valley southward to Laguna Cilvituk and its settlements, and we have previously discussed the overland connection from these eastward to Becán (Ball and Taschek 1989). An alternative route of flight directly eastward from Acanmul would have taken the hypothetical refugees out of and away from the canoe-accessible bottomlands of the Río Hontún drainage and into the rolling hill country of the southeastern Puuc-Chenes zone. Just over 50 kilometers east of Acanmul, the medium-size center of Tohcok experienced violent demolition and haulage displacement of at least several of its standing Late/Terminal Classic buildings and its ballcourt, similar to what occurred at the former center (personal observations, 2004). Stored ceramic collections at the site indicate a largely Chenes-like tradition, but sufficient late western Puuc materials are present to suggest either a connection to that zone or the transient presence of the displaced Acanmul population. We lack adequate data to resolve this issue: Ball favors the Edzná route while Taschek believes a Tohcok-Chenes retreat more plausible. In either case, what the data do support is identification of the intrusive Xcocom *a* population with the survivors of Isla Acanmul's capture and occupation (see note 2).

Comparative Type-Variety Data

We have wrestled with how best to present the ceramic evidence supporting our contentions given the severe space limitations applying to this presentation, and we have concluded that what we can best do here is delineate the ceramic units defining "early" Xcocom (*a*)—and "late" Xcocom (*b*) when applicable—and indicate their putative relationships to Pa'xil and, if appropriate, to the Terminal Classic Muralla complex at Edzná. Full and convincing data-based documentation will have to await more extended treatment via a lengthier venue. Not wishing to impose our own peculiar "outsider's view" on the work of others (Forsyth 1983; Benavides 1997), we do not here offer any comments regarding possible Edzná (Muralla)–Becán (Xcocom) relationships but simply note identities, similarities, and parallels. We reiterate the critical importance of the conjoined appearance of the full assemblage as an assemblage rather than the simple occurrence of any one or more of these otherwise not unusual Terminal Classic fine wares.

Identities (Figure 9.5)

Thin-slate Ware Ticul Group (Figure 9.5a–e)—Ticul Thin-slate: Ticul Variety; Muncul Thick Thin-slate: Muncul Variety; Chencoyi Black-on-thin-slate: Chencoyi Variety; Xul Incised: Xul Variety; Tabi Gouged-incised: Tabi Variety

All occur in Xcocom *a* (early) use-related and mortuary contexts. Ticul Thin-slate and Xul Incised are also present in Xcocom *b* deposits. Variety-level identities in macroscopically comparable paste variants (see note 4) are abundant in Pa'xil (Acanmul) and also characterize Muralla (Edzná).

Puuc Red Ware Teabo Group (Figure 9.5f)—Teabo Red: Teabo Variety; Tekax Black-on-red: Tekax Variety

These types are present in Xcocom *a* use-related contexts. The Acanmul and Edzná distributions are the same as for the Ticul Group.

Cream-polychrome Dolorido Group (Figure 9.5k–l)—Dolorido Cream-polychrome: Dolorido Variety; Zanahoria Scored: Zanahoria Variety

Both occur in Xcocom *a* and Xcocom *b* use-related contexts, and the Dolorido type is also present in a rich, Xcocom *a* chamber burial. Both types occur as rare, introduced exotics in Pa'xil, and Dolorido Cream-polychrome is similarly so represented in the Edzná Muralla complex.

Fine Orange Paste Ware Altar Group (Figure 9.5g)—Altar Orange: Altar Variety; Tumba Black-on-orange: Tumba Variety; Trapiche Incised: Trapiche Variety; Pabellon Molded-carved: Pabellon Variety

All occur in Xcocom *a* use-related and mortuary contexts. Simple hemispherical dishes of Altar Orange or Silho Orange also are present in Xcocom *b* deposits and are present in high frequencies in Pa'xil as introduced exotics. Altar Orange is reported only as a rarity at Edzná.

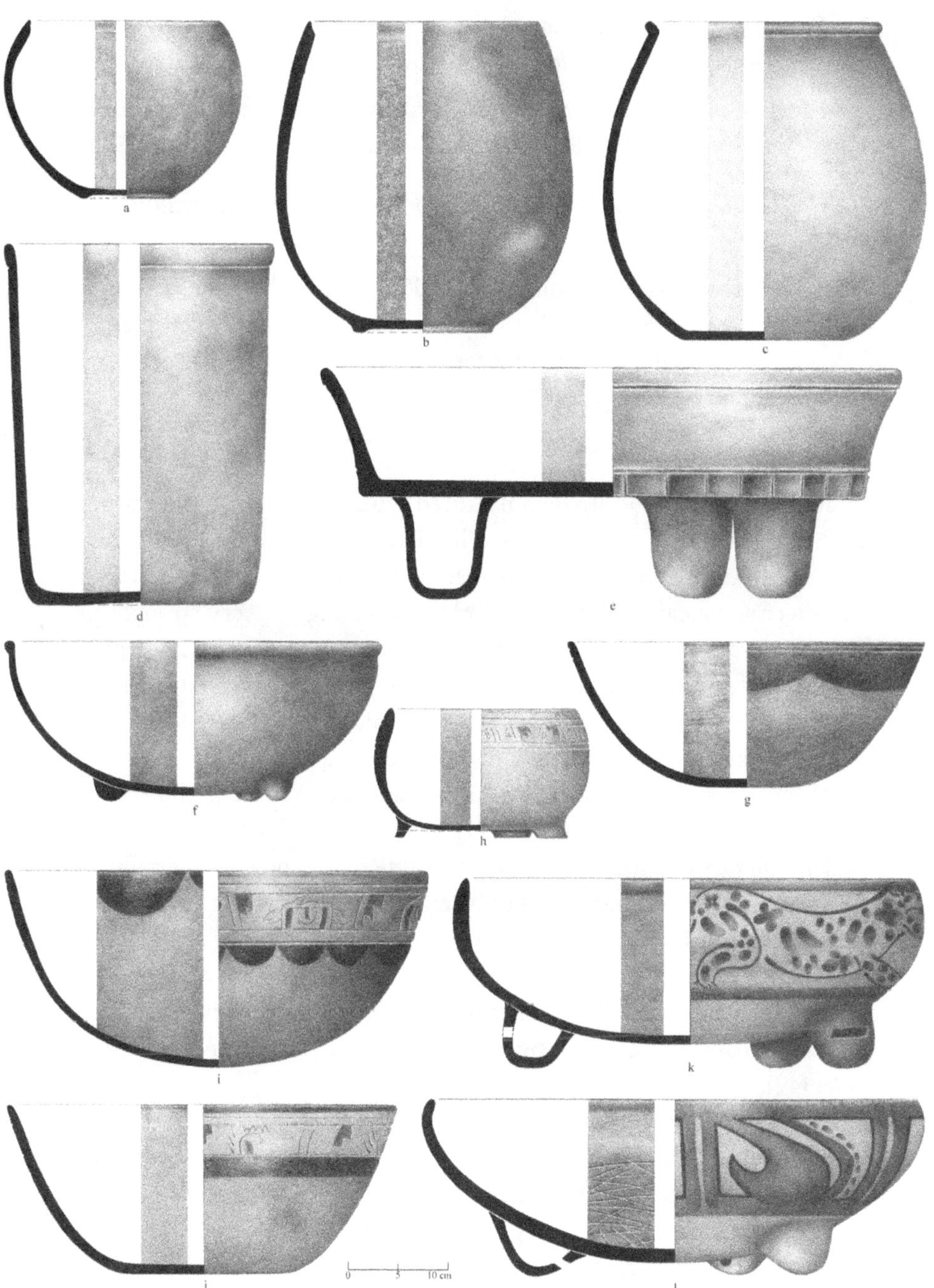

Figure 9.5. Select Acanmul (Pa'xil)–Becán (Xcocom *a*) ceramic identities: *a–b*, Muncul Thick Thin-slate; *c–d*, Ticul Thin-slate; *e*, Xul Incised; *f*, Teabo Red; *g*, Tumba Black-on-orange; *h–j*, Provincia Plano-relief; *k*, Dolorido Cream-polychrome; *l*, Zanahoria Scored. (Drawings by Jennifer Taschek.)

Fine Orange Paste Ware Balancan Group (Figure 9.5h–j)—Balancan Orange: Balancan Variety; Provincia Plano-relief: Provincia Variety

These are present in Xcocom *a* use-related contexts and in high frequencies in Pa'xil as introduced exotics. Provincia Plano-relief occurs as a rarity at Edzná.

Fine Gray Paste Ware Chablekal Group—Chicxulub Incised: Chicxulub Variety

This is an extremely rare Xcocom *a* exotic although it is abundant at Acanmul and reasonably well represented at Edzná. Its absence from the Becán assemblage likely reflects the lateness of Xcocom and consequent unavailability of the ware (Foias and Bishop 2005).

Homologies (Figure 9.6)

A number of clearly locally manufactured types occurring in both aspects of Xcocom so closely resemble late Chel-Pa'xil Muna Group slate wares in surface appearance, coloration, form attributes, and decoration—although not in technological or slip/paste fabrics—as to suggest very strongly that they were efforts to reproduce the latter by Xcocom potters utilizing physically disparate materials and firing techniques. These include Pixtun Trickle-on-gray (figure 9.6a; Ball 1977a: 63), Torote Pale Brown (figure 9.6b–c; Ball 1977a: 30), and an undesignated light brown basin and jar group (Ball 1977a: 29). These and a small number of others—Tancachacal Slate (Ball 1977a: 37) and Chumayel Red-on-slate (Ball 1977a: 62)—*may* first appear late in Chintok, lending further credence to the possibility that Xcocom essentially represents the melding of intrusive Pa'xil ceramics and ideas and existing local industries at Becán.

It should also be noted that of three formal adult Xcocom burials recovered at Becán and Chicanná, two were accompanied by what can only be described as rich Pa'xil assemblages, one by a solitary Pixtun Trickle-on-gray jar (Ball 1977a: 149).

While the case presented is hardly conclusive, taken in concert the combined evidence is undeniably suggestive of the identification of the Xcocom *a* assemblage and its population with displaced refugee elites from the overrun Acanmul center. In addition to typological identities and homologies linking the Terminal Classic ceramics of the two sites, we recall attention to (1) the sudden, effectively unprecedented appearance of Xcocom wares at Becán, especially with respect to "elite" fine wares and associated exotics; (2) the effectively concurrent termination and disappearance of the content-comparable Pa'xil complex at Acanmul in conjunction with the violent seizure, selective

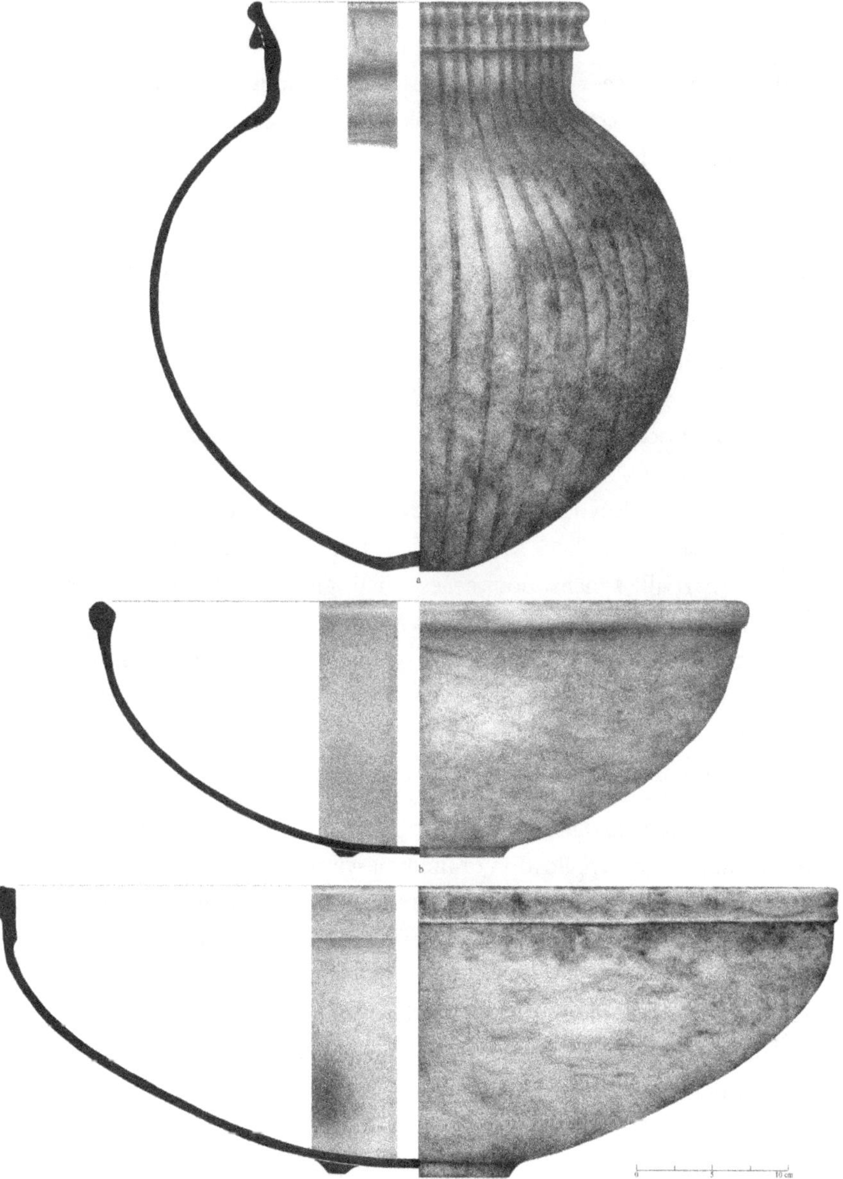

Figure 9.6. Select Acanmul (Pa'xil)–Becán (Xcocom *a*) ceramic homologies: *a*, Pixtun Trickle-on-gray; *b*–*c*, Torote Pale Brown. (Drawings by Jennifer Taschek.)

destruction, and occupation of that center by northern plains Maya (Itza?); and (3) the stratigraphically documented developmental roots of Pa'xil in its local, Late Classic predecessor, the Chel complex. Taken together, we find the evidence compelling even if not conclusive.

Conclusion

In this chapter, we reexamine the nature, chronology, and cultural historical significance of the Xcocom and Chintok ceramic assemblages at Becán in light of new data and findings from Acanmul, central-west Campeche. We do so using the comparative powers of hands-on, physical examination-based type-variety assessments of the Late and Terminal Classic ceramics and their sequences at the two sites against the larger pan-lowland ceramic landscape. The results of this exercise include

- redating the appearance of the Chintok assemblage from circa A.D. 730~750 to circa 790~800+ and identifying a likely ceramic disjunction and occupational hiatus between the Bejuco and Chintok/Xcocom phases;
- support for the Rovner-Lincoln hypothesis that the chronologically defined "early" and "late" Xcocom *facets* might better be understood as at least partially synchronous access-distinguished *subcomplexes*;
- circumstantial identification of the Xcocom intrusion as the arrival of displaced refugee-elites from the overrun Acanmul center; and
- arguable resolution of the likely fate of the Acanmul Pa'xil population following the seizure of that center and its riverine port facilities by northern invaders (Itza).

Grounded in archaeological data, these inferences ultimately are products of a careful and rigorous application of the type-variety method and the comparative chronological alignments and intersite relationships that such application can enable. We emphasize again that effective use of the method in this way must be based on direct, hands-on examinations and comparisons of collections rather than literature-based "match the illustration" exercises. The former work and can be powerfully effective; the latter do not.

No faunal analyst, no human osteologist, no biological taxonomist would ever even seriously consider let alone actually make specific, positive identifications based solely on line drawings and truncated verbal descriptions, but many Maya ceramic typologists have come to do so routinely. They do so despite the fact that while every rabbit femur, every spondylus valve, every human phalange is fundamentally the same, pottery vessels and sherds vary enormously in surface coloration, luster, tactile qualities, formal modes, paste and tempering attributes, and more. Just how reliably and validly can someone who has never physically handled and examined ceramic samples from Mayapán, Chichén Itzá, Barton Ramie, Altar de Sacrificios, or Becán evaluate the true comparability of their own sherds to those of any of the latter based on

Smith 1971, Gifford 1976, Adams 1971, or Ball 1977a? Not very well, we would argue—not very well at all.

There is another aspect to this issue. All too commonly, "identification" itself has become a process of "matching" collected sherds or vessels to previously published illustrations and descriptions—or at least to those most closely resembling the in-hand materials. This is simply not acceptable and has been an important factor in engendering the justifiable skepticism regarding the value and reliability of type-variety studies now too often encountered among other Maya scholars. The remedy is simple. All that is needed is a return to the basic, routine practice of approaching a collection by sorting it; describing it; provisionally establishing tentative types and groups—and only then bringing in the literature to verify these. This was the approach expected of and underpinning type-variety systematics as originally defined (Gifford 1960, 1976; Smith, Willey, and Gifford 1960), and this is the only means by which it can be and still is operationalized validly (for example, Ball 1977a, 1980; Forsyth 1983; LeCount 1996; López Varela 1989; Matheny 1970; Robles Castellanos 1990). The all-important comparative step and comparisons discussed above should follow next, and only next.

This is work, and harder and slower work than matching sherds to pictures, but 50 years after its inception, this potentially powerful approach is in need of some serious review and overhaul. Today some use it well; some abuse it awfully. Let's look to these failings now and restore type-variety to its onetime effectiveness and credibility.

The ever more frequent doubts and criticisms regarding the utility and reliability of the type-variety approach really result more from the increasing slipshoddiness and looseness with which the system has come to be applied than from any inherent failings of the method itself. Some regional theaters are worse than others, but the general fault is widespread and endemic in Maya ceramic studies. The past 15 years have seen other domains of Maya archaeology grow significantly in rigor and sophistication, but in many respects ceramic studies have backslid. Perhaps it is time for those engaged in the nonphysicochemical typological and modal study of Maya ceramics to become a little bit less "postprocessual" and a little bit more "processual" in their practice. As a self-disciplinary start, we suggest that future type-variety/mode descriptions and comparisons include as a formal, regular feature an explicit statement as to what specific collections were personally physically examined by the analyst in determining the types, varieties, and groups of their samples and the bases of any comparative/contrastive arguments. A return to such rigor and conscientiousness in analysis and reporting would constitute a significant positive step toward restoring the onetime repute and reliability of the type-variety approach. At a minimum, it would provide other researchers with some sound basis on which to evaluate the potential reliability of reported identifications and comparisons, as well as the potential validity of derivative interpretations. This would go far toward restoring the utility and value of the system as originally envisioned.

In the end, type-variety is neither an analytical method nor a panacea for classifying and comparing ancient pottery assemblages—although it can be a powerful tool for accomplishing the latter and establishing chronologies and intersite alignments and relationships. To do so validly and effectively, however, it needs to be used thoughtfully, carefully, rigorously, and responsibly, and that is the real message of this chapter.

Type-variety is about imposing order on chaos.

Richard E.W. Adams to Joe Ball, 1970

Acknowledgments

We thank Jim Aimers for the invitation to contribute to this volume. This paper reflects the efforts of multiple separate research programs and their participants, and all who contributed to the extensive ceramic and larger archaeological databases involved. We especially thank Lorraine Williams Beck for inviting us to participate in the 2003–5 Proyecto Acanmul phase of her larger Proyecto Historía Regional Diacrónica: El Cuyo, Acanmul y San Francisco de Campeche. The Acanmul research was supported financially and logistically by the Consejo Nacional de Ciencia y Tecnología de México (CONACyT); the Universidad Autónoma de Campeche; the San Diego State University Campanile Foundation; San Diego State University; and several private donors from the greater southern California San Diego region.

Importantly complementing the rich "historical" databases available to us, INAH Becán Project Director Luiz Evelia Campaña generously accorded us access to the newer ceramic collections from her recent investigations at the site. We also acknowledge Tohcok site guardian Hector Montejo for providing access to the onsite ceramic bodega. Our examinations of collections from other sites—from Edzná and Calakmul to Oxkintok, Chichén Itzá, and so many more—have spanned some four decades and owed their facilitation to so many individuals and agencies that we can reasonably only make note of the generosity and hospitality of all and offer our most sincere gratitude to them. We hope that this chapter and its message will serve as a rewarding professional acknowledgment of the fruits of their courtesy, a blanket statement of deep appreciation to all.

All illustrations were produced by Jennifer Taschek, and the vessels depicted in figures 9.5–9.6 all are based on actual sherds and vessels. The authors assume full and sole responsibility for any and all errors of fact, presentation, or interpretation, or any other shortcomings from which the final product may suffer.

Notes

1. First reported in 1927 (Quintana 1927) and surveyed by H.E.D. Pollock (1980) in 1940, Acanmul was "rediscovered" in 1994 by Lorraine Williams-Beck and Edmundo López de la Rosa (1999) in the course of an extensive survey of the central western Campeche inland coastal plain. Complementary programs of mapping, excavation, and architectural restoration were initiated at the site in 1999 by the Universidad Autónoma de Campeche (UAC) and the Centro de Campeche of the Instituto Nacional de Antropología e Historia (Ojeda Mas 2007; Williams-Beck 2001). The ceramic data presented in this chapter derive from the authors' participation in the UAC project during the summers of 2003–5.

2. Williams-Beck (personal communication, 2004) has remarked on the possible existence of at least two additional such groups elsewhere along this relict bank; however, the authors were not personally able to visit the reported locales, nor have they seen any recorded or tangible evidence supporting their existence.

3. More precise datings of these events, including the termination of Pa'xil and the appearance of Xcocom *a* remain to be established. We are awaiting the processing of two suites of radiocarbon determinations for the fiery destruction of Groups A and B at Acanmul, which should contribute significantly to accomplishing this. In the meantime, it should be understood that the events involved might have taken place anytime from as early as A.D. 820/840 to as late as 860/880, with the Xcocom *a*/*b* interface occurring anywhere from about A.D. 890/910 to 930/950. The specific assignments employed in this chapter and table 9.1 represent informed selections based on a host of pertinent data synthesized in Ball 1986, Ball and Taschek 1989, and Lincoln 1986.

4. We use *audiencia* to describe a building type consisting of two back-to-back ranges of individually accessed rooms flanking a central portal connecting one seemingly more "public" plaza or courtyard with a more "private" or restricted-access counterpart, which is typically associated physically with high-status occupancy and other activities. Functionally, the audiencia was both a screen and a controlled-access passageway between more public and more private zones of high-status social activity (Ball and Taschek 2001: 200).

5. Paste variants were defined and compared macroscopically rather than petrographically or instrumentally, although this is a field expediency for which it obviously would be preferable to substitute high-resolution petrographic or physicochemical lab analyses. While such are ever more frequently being used effectively for focused, limited-sample special studies (e.g., Clayton 2005; Foias and Bishop 2005, 2007; Rands 1967; Reents-Budet et al. 2000; Smyth 1995), the practicalities of multicollection physical examinations continue to require a more seat-of-the-pants approach to paste variant identification and

comparison. The senior author still travels with a small kit containing a Munsell Soil Book, a 10X geologist's comparator with grain size and sorting reticules, and a simple soil grain size and angularity matchbook chart. These are fully adequate for basic recording of descriptive comparative data on paste color and texture and temper type, size, and distribution. These tools are not perfect but far better than "eyeballing" or nothing at all.

6. Similar scenarios also would apply at Chicanná and several other local monumental sites. The revisionist chronology proposed plainly holds serious ramifications for the dating and cultural histories of the areal architectural traditions, but these are far beyond the scope of this chapter to explore.

10

Looking for Times

How Type-Variety Analysis Helps Us "See" the Early Postclassic in Northwestern Honduras

PATRICIA A. URBAN, EDWARD M. SCHORTMAN, AND MARNE T. AUSEC

Let us begin by making clear what we intend to accomplish in this chapter: we will not discuss the theory or practice of typology in general or of type-variety analysis in particular.[1] In short, this is not a meditation on classification. Instead, it is an account of how the type-variety approach was used to examine a specific problem: ascertaining the presence of Early Postclassic (hereafter abbreviated as EPC) occupation in three areas of northwestern Honduras: the middle Ulua drainage, also known as central Santa Barbara (hereafter, MUSB); the Naco Valley (NV), approximately 40 kilometers to the west and north of the middle Ulua; and the Middle Chamelecon-Cacaulapa zone (MC-C), immediately south and west of Naco and north and west of the middle Ulua (figure 10.1).

Although Urban was introduced to ceramic analysis as an undergraduate, she first deeply engaged with type-variety analysis during her graduate apprenticeship on the Quirigua project (1977–79), under Robert Sharer's instruction. In subsequent work pursued by her, Schortman, and Ausec, the system has been adapted in several ways. First, following Sharer, a greater emphasis has been placed on modes, which we define in the following way: a mode is a variable that exists as a possible variation within a specific attribute class. For example, "neck form" is an attribute class, and within that, we recognize these (a noninclusive list): neckless; outflared; convex (opposite of outflared); straight vertical; and straight at an angle. Then, to categorize the neck fully, we combine one of these modes with a mode for the attribute "junction of neck and body." These can be, again not inclusively as follows: no break to body interior or exterior; break to body on both interior and exterior; rounded exterior, break on interior; rounded interior, break on exterior; and rounded exterior,

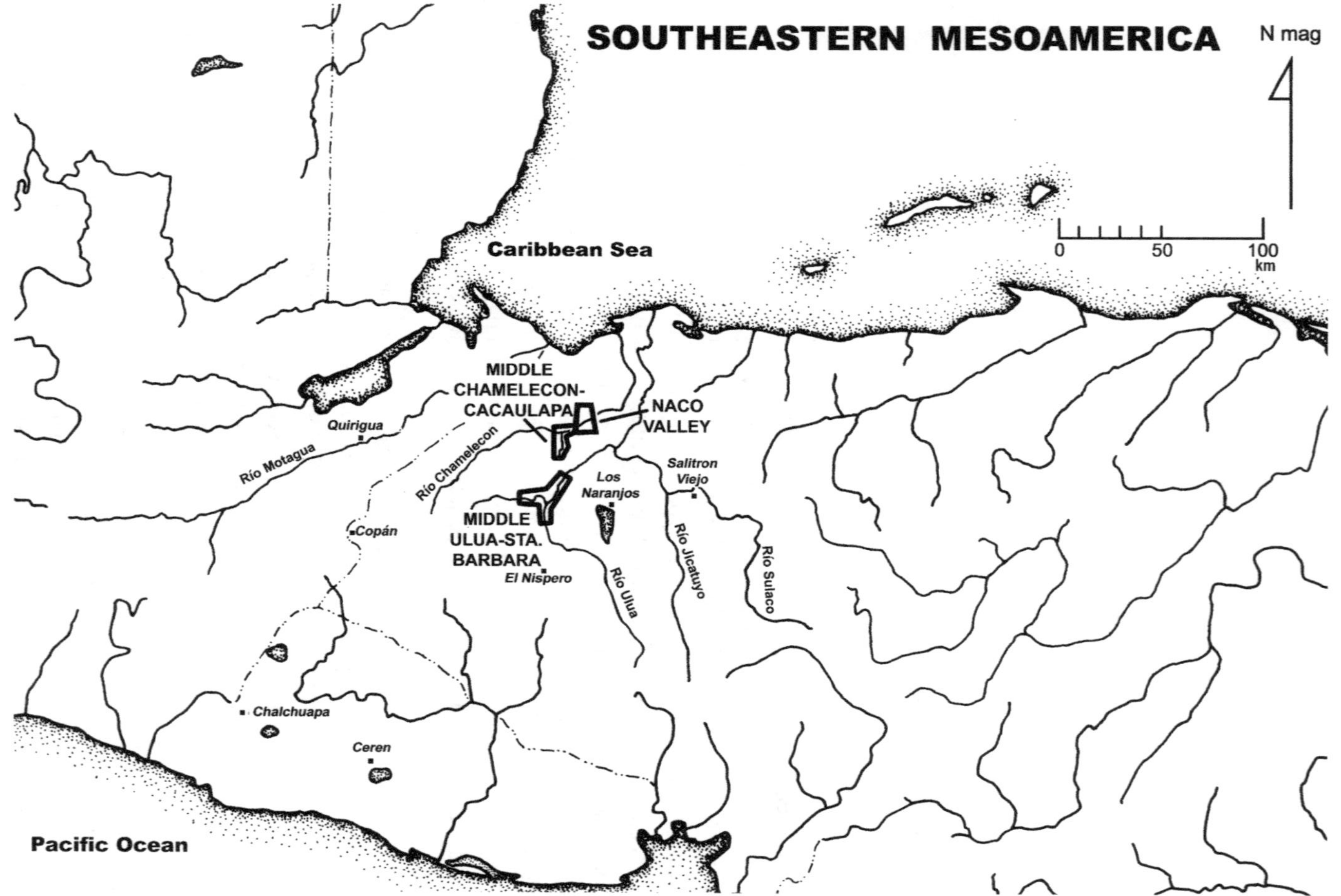

Figure 10.1. Map of Northwestern Honduras showing areas and sites mentioned in the text. (Map by Patricia Urban.)

beveled or double-break on interior. The resulting combination has a specific designation in an extensive coding system that includes lip shaping, the forms of and connects between rims, necks, walls, bases, handles, flanges, as well as other attributes.

Examples of coding sheets can be seen in figures 10.2 and 10.3: figure 10.2 illustrates the first half of the range of variation we record in lip shaping, while figure 10.3 shows the first half of the variations we recognize in a jar category we call "flaring-necked." We also include an example of an actual readout (a term with an unknown origin, but the word we have always used) to show

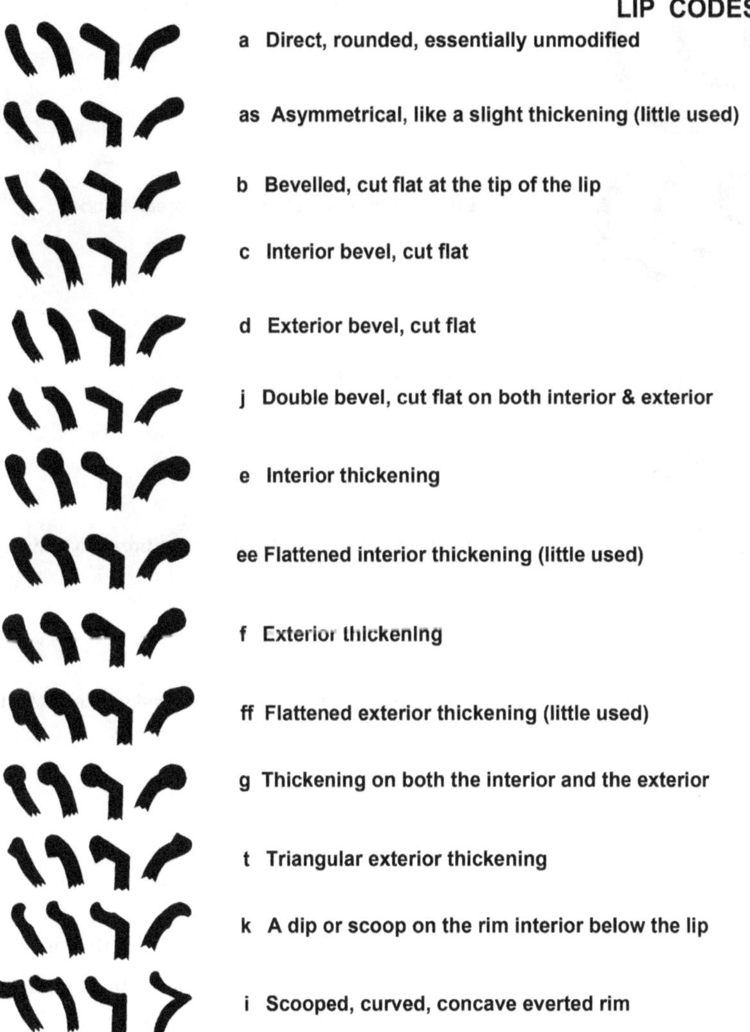

Figure 10.2. Sample of lip form coding sheet.

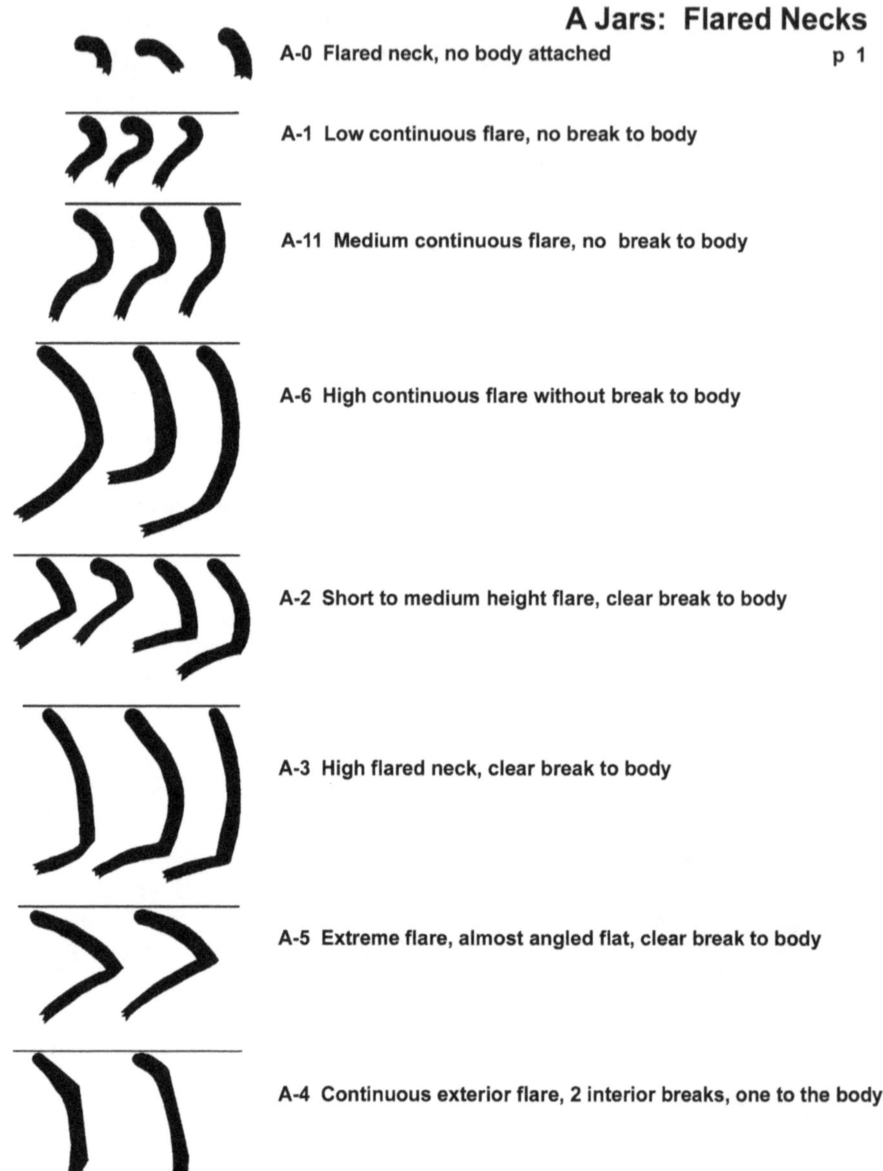

Figure 10.3. Sample of jar neck form coding sheet.

how coding is done in the field (figure 10.4). "Doing a readout" is the process of sorting and recording ceramics from an individual lot ("lot" is an excavator-defined spatial unit, generally 1 meter on a side and 10 or 20 centimeters deep if arbitrary levels are employed, of variable thickness if cultural and/or natural strata are being followed). The result is a "readout sheet," and that is what is

PVC READOUT | Date 21 Jul 02 | S 1 of 2 | Bag 1 of 2 | Readout by | Excavator 44 | Str. # | LOT 16AB/021

Type-Variety	Form (b,j,s)	Rim Code	Lip Code	R.A. Quantity	Base Code	Base Quantity	Handle Code	Handle Quantity	Body Quantity	Other Code	Other Quantity	T-V Total ENTER ONCE
JIC	j-	IND		3				-	83 2			88
MAG 9	j	H-φ	a	3					9			12
CHAMP	b	X-φ	o	1								1
CHAMP 9	b								3			3
PN 9	j b	IND		3			+b	1	174 4			182
MAP 9	j j	IND H-φ	 a	1 2					12			15
PIT	j	A-φ	l-f	1								12
	j	H-φ	a	1								
	b b	Z-φ Z-φ	o a	1 1								
	b	Z-φ	l	3								
	b	Z-φ	u	1								
	b	X-φ	o	1								
	b	X-5	o	1								
	b	X-6	l-f	1								
	b	X-7	a	1								
PIT	j b	IND		5					340 29			374
MAN 9	j						stp bf	1	14	nkb	1	16
ARA	b				rng	1			6			7
MPO 9	b b				fb-sb fb	1 1			3			5
SJ	b b	Z-φ X-7	a a	1 1								2
SJ 9	j b	IND IND		4 1			stp bf	1	182 11			199
MARL 9	j								5			5
CAC	j	A-φ	a	3								20
	j	A-11	a	1								
	j	G-1	l-i	1								
	j	A-1	a	1								
	c c	X-φ	a	1			sb comal	1 1				

Artifacts 1= ocarina 2= worked sherds 2= ladle stems 2= fig frags 1= sherd disk | Non-Pottery Discards | Sherd Discards 0

Specials (describe; cont. on reverse) C | Lot Total ENTER ONCE 941

Comments Heavily eroded, med to very small sherds; most in small-very small range. Hard to tell bowls from jars. PIT is extremely eroded. CAC: the 2 items coded as plates are comals—recorded on sherd table

Temporal Info: 1. LCl 2. 3. Probable TCl Possible Evidence 1 Evidence 2 Evidence 3

LOT NUMBER 016AB/021 P 1 of 2

Figure 10.4. Completed readout sheet.

shown in figure 10.4. Additions to all parts of the system are made yearly as new items are found.

Second, because of the nature of the assemblages in our areas (described below), attention to paste composition is crucial; this introduces complexity with respect to numbers of taxa, but splitting decorative categories on the basis of paste ware (Rice 1976) allows close attention to shifting frequencies of types and varieties, which we believe reflect change through time in workshop locations, as well as new decisions about materials that were made by artisans within a single, long-inhabited locale.

Third, because of the use of the same formal, finishing, and decorative modes on a variety of paste wares, the "system" concept is important to our analysis. Henderson and Agurcia (1987: 432) define a ceramic system as sets of "homologous types that are related in terms of aspects of decoration: design elements, element execution, design field layout, and the like." Above the level of the system is the "supersystem," designed to call attention to how systems are related. Beaudry-Corbett and Henderson say that "Groupings with considerable variability in decorative techniques are designated as supersystems and then partitioned into systems. The types assigned to a single system represent a continuous temporal span and, typically, reflect a continuous spatial distribution as well" (1993: 1–2). The ceramic system and supersystem were emphasized by the Instituto Hondureño de Antropología e Historia during its memorable "Rolling Sherd Shows," initiated by Ricardo Agurcia in 1988 when he was its *gerente*. In these, archaeologists working in Honduras came together in an attempt to standardize, if not operating procedures and fundamental classification theory, at least nomenclature. Given the prevalence of decorative modes across space in the Honduras portion of Southeast Mesoamerica, the system proved, and proves, a good way to clarify stylistic relationships over the entire zone. We also use it within our specific area for the same reason: to make clear stylistic relationships among types allocated to different groups, with groups nesting within paste ware categories.

An example of supersystem-system-type-variety classification is the Jicatuyo Supersystem (Henderson and Beaudry-Corbett 1993: 294–95), which includes red-on-natural painted items. Within the Jicatuyo Supersystem, there are five systems. One of these—the Magdalena System—is named after Magdalena Red-on-natural from the Naco Valley. The Magdalena System encompasses five types; most have only one variety, but the types Magdalena and Marimba (from the Sula Valley) have three and five varieties, respectively. Thus, 11 taxa at the varietal level are combined within one system and are further related to 37 other type-variety units within the Jicatuyo Supersystem. In practice, use of the supersystem appears to have died out, but the system is employed from time to time for comparative purposes.

Fourth, we use the group classification often, because of our hierarchical view of attributes. Let us take the example of orange slip. This decorative and functional attribute is seen, most often, on bowls. Orange-slipped vessels can then serve as the basis of both bichromes and polychrome decorated items. A typical polychrome bowl has a black lip or sublabial interior band, below which is a red band and a second black band. The remainder of the decorative field is divided by angled lines in black, red, or a combination of both, and the subfields thus produced contain figures such as birds, dancing monkeys, or crabs done in red and/or black. The interior base is generally not painted. So, if we have a bowl wall piece that has no paint, does it come from a plain orange-slipped bowl or from an unpainted portion of a bi- or polychrome? Since we do not know, we put that piece in a "group only" category, that is, a residual class composed of what remains after the clearly identifiable pieces are classified. The "group only" category is also used for items for which we can see the orange slip but that may not show paint, because the sherd has been damaged in some way, generally by erosion. The result is large numbers of body sherds, as well as some rims, in the "group only" categories, and some bodies, but all rims with identifiable decoration, in the type and variety classes.

Fifth, we have developed ways of recording information that traditional type-variety analysis does not address. For example, because we have encountered ceramic workshops, we came up with ways to preserve information about firing errors; to understand function, we record use wear, sooting, and other meaningful bits of data. Overall, type: variety-mode analysis (TVM for short) remains the bedrock of our ceramic studies, but we continue refining the system to expand the range of information it can capture.

In sum, over the 77 or so combined years of experience we have with ceramic analysis, we have looked at other ways of classifying ceramics and, as some would express it, have intensively "interrogated" our own TVM approach, modifying the system each year. The system does *not* get simpler with time, and indeed the amount of data leading to useful knowledge increases as the system gets more complex. The complexity slows analysis, but TVM remains an efficient way to record large quantities of information in a relatively short time. For us, the balance remains satisfactory, and we will continue to tinker with TVM whenever and wherever we work: we are sure that it beats the alternatives even though it does not, on its own, answer all questions concerning the use and manufacture of ceramics.

A Note on Terminology and Temporality

In this chapter, we must attend to a vexing question: the temporal placement of Tohil Plumbate pottery. The senior author first became acquainted with Plumbate through her undergraduate course on ceramic analysis; Shepard's classic (1956) volume was a central text, and her 1948 work was also used. Then and during all the authors' subsequent graduate work, Plumbate was considered to be a marker of the Early Postclassic, and this is how we have traditionally viewed it. Recently, the temporal position of Plumbate has been reviewed by many writers. Some accept Tohil Plumbate in particular as diagnostic of the early Postclassic (Fash 2004; Manahan 2000, 2004; Smith and Berdan 2003). Others view it as a hallmark of the Terminal Classic (A. Chase and D. Chase 2004; Chinchilla et al. 1997; Demarest 2004; Ringle et al. 2004; Suhler et al. 2004). Elsewhere, Tohil Plumbate is seen as extending from the late Terminal Classic into the initial phase of the Early Postclassic (Carmean et al. 2004; Rice and Forsyth 2004; Taube et al. 2005). Cobos (2004) places it in the Late Chichen Itza phase, which spans the Terminal Classic and Early Postclassic. Hector Neff, a notable expert on Plumbate, also straddles the temporal divide, sometimes referring to Plumbate as Early Postclassic and at other times placing it at the end of the Terminal Classic (for example, 2001, 2003).

During our work in the Middle Ulua/Santa Barbara area, we perceived Tohil Plumbate as an Early Postclassic marker that appeared as a package with Las Vegas Polychrome and Pachuca obsidian. Based on four C assays, ceramics, and stratigraphy, we defined the Late Classic in the MUSB as A.D. 600–850. Because no clear Terminal Classic occupation was indicated by any of these three lines of evidence, we extended the Late Classic to A.D. 950, with the Early Postclassic following immediately after. For Naco Valley research, where we found neither green obsidian nor more than one sherd of Plumbate, we still believed Plumbate to be an Early Postclassic manifestation. We continue such usage here and define the Late Classic as A.D. 600–850, the Terminal Classic as A.D. 850–950, and the Early Postclassic as A.D. 950–1250. Finally, for the Middle Chamelecon-Cacaulapa zone, we began with the assumption that Plumbate dated to the Early Postclassic.

As discussed below, this simple equivalency can no longer be fully sustained. Rather, Plumbate and its fellow travelers—Pachuca and Ucareo obsidian and Las Vegas Polychrome—are found with materials (for example, "fine paste ceramics") that are characteristic of the Terminal Classic in neighboring regions; the temporal placement is supported by radiocarbon assays and stratigraphy. Thus, for the MCC, there appears to be a bridging period, neither purely Terminal Classic nor quite Early Postclassic. For this segment of our chapter, however, we continue to speak of Plumbate as an Early Postclassic marker in order to maintain consistency with the other areas we discuss. The MCC temporal periods, then, follow the dates given above for the Naco Valley.

The Middle Ulua–Central Santa Barbara Area

At the core of the MUSB is the site of Gualjoquito, which lies on the east bank of the Río Ulua just north of where it is joined by the Río Jicatuyo. The zone encompasses 135 square kilometers, of which 28 were surveyed. Our project here was chronically underfunded, and thus less clearing excavation was done in this zone than in the other two regions; artifact samples were concomitantly reduced. Overall, we recovered 400,000 sherds, about 97,000 of which were analyzed (the TVM analysis is discussed in Urban 1993a). The collection derives from excavations at 62 sites out of the 261 settlements recorded during survey. Most sites in this area had multiple construction and occupation components. Postclassic occupations, both Early and Late, tended to be the last parts of long sequences, and only a few single-component EPC sites were located. These rare sites and sealed deposits at the main site of Gualjoquito were welcome discoveries indeed. On the whole, the persistence of decorative modes such as wavy line, multiple point incision combined with red paint, as well as formal modes such as the pyriform jar shape, rendered ceramic studies here difficult—or so we thought at the time.

In reality, this zone is the easiest of the three discussed here, in terms of distinguishing EPC remains, for several reasons. First, there are new TVM taxa that appear in the EPC complex: one of these emerges within a previously existing ceramic group, while two are new ceramic groups in two new paste ware categories. (Table 10.1 shows the actual numbers of types and varieties for the Classic, Terminal Classic, and Early Postclassic in all regions.) Second, six taxa disappear entirely. Almost all of these are polychromes, and their absence is striking. Third, there is a reduction of varieties in another distinctive decorative group: red-on-natural vessels that sometimes have incised designs in addition to the painted motifs. Fourth, two categories with white slips—a mode that stands out in the MUSB—seem to die out completely in the EPC.

The fifth and final reason that the EPC is readily visible is based on two factors. Ceramics are evenly distributed across the zone; the most marked difference is that taxa with coarser pastes are more common in the north of the research area than in the south. Thus, the analytical units that exist are found everywhere. The other aspect of importance is that there are clear nonlocal markers, that is, imported items: Plumbate and Las Vegas Polychrome; and green (Pachuca) obsidian. Las Vegas Polychrome most likely comes from within Honduras but southeast of the MUSB zone. These three categories are found at sites of any size and complexity in the MUSB, although in extremely small quantities. Nonetheless, finding these materials in clear contexts allowed us to characterize the EPC complex in ways that enable its recognition whether or not the markers are present.

For the above reasons, then, "seeing" the EPC in the MUSB area is relatively easy. Even if the imported markers are not present (because of small samples), shifts in local taxa are obvious enough that the period is clear. There is a lesson

Table 10.1. Numbers of paste wares, groups, types, and varieties in the Middle Ulua–Santa Barbara area, Naco Valley, and Middle Chamelecon–Caculapa zone

Middle Ulua–Santa Barbara Area	Late Classic			Terminal Classic			Early Postclassic		
Paste ware	Group	# of types	# of varieties	Group	# of types	# of varieties	Group	# of types	# of varieties
Aguacatales	Aguacatales	2	4						
Chorrera	Chorrera	5	8				Chorrera	3	3
Picicho	Picicho	1	1				Picicho	2	2
Santa Rosita	Santa Rosita	6	6				Santa Rosita	3	4
Quecoa							Quecoa	3	3
Uncana							Uncana	2	2
Totals	**4**	**14**	**19**	**n/a**	**n/a**	**n/a**	**5**	**13**	**14**

Naco Valley	Late Classic			Terminal Classic			Early Postclassic		
Paste ware	Group	# of types	# of varieties	Group	# of types	# of varieties	Group	# of types	# of varieties
Jicaro	Jicaro	4	5	Jicaro	4	4	Jicaro	1	1
	Magdalena	2	5	Magdalena	4	7	Magdalena	1	1
				Higueral	1	1			
La Champa	La Champa	4	8	La Champa	4	7	La Champa	3	3
Monte Grande	Monte Grande	3	5	Monte Grande	5	8	Monte Grande	1	1
Manacal				Manacal	1	4			
				Agua Sucia	1	3			
El Brazo				El Brazo	2	5			
El Chaparral				El Chaparral	1	2			

Calpules				Calpules	1	2			
Cacaulapa				Cacaulapa	1	3	Cacaulapa	1	1
Los Culucos				Loc Culucos	5	5			
Junquillo				Junquillo	1	2	Junquillo	1	2
Fulano				Fulano	1	1	Fulano	2	2
El Exito				El Exito	1	1	El Exito	2	2
Totals	4	13	23	15	33	55	8	12	**13**

Middle Chamelecon-Cacaulapa	Late Classic			Terminal Classic			E arly Postclassic		
Paste ware	Group	# of types	# of varieties	Group	# of types	# of varieties	Group	# of types	# of varieties
Pueblo Nuevo	Pueblo Nuevo	2	2	Pueblo Nuevo	3	3			
	Mapache	4	4	Mapache	4	4			
				Tascalapa	2	2			
	Chululo	3	5	Chululo	3	3			
Pitones	Pitones	2	3	Pitones	2	3			
	Manuel	3	3	Manuel	3	3			
				Campo Deportivo	1	1			
	Mal Paso	3	3	Mal Paso	3	4			
Canoas	Canoas	2	4	Canoas	2	4			
	Santa Clara	2	3	Santa Clara	3	3			
	Coroza	3	3	Coroza	3	3			
Canoas Crude				Canoas Crude	1	1			
				La Pita	2	2			

(continued)

Table 10.1. (*continued*)

Middle Chamelecon-Cacaulapa	Late Classic			Terminal Classic			E arly Postclassic		
Paste ware	Group	# of types	# of varieties	Group	# of types	# of varieties	Group	# of types	# of varieties
San Joaquin	San Joaquin	3	5	San Joaquin	3	5	San Joaquin	1	1
	Marcelina	4	5	Marcelina	5	6	Marcelina	1	1
	Tumbo	3	3	Tumbo	3	3	Tumbo	3	3
	Amapa	4	5	Amapa	4	6	Amapa	1	1
Cacaulapa	Cacaulapa	3	3	Cacaulapa	4	5	Cacaulapa	1	1
	Jocomico	1	5	Jocomico	1	7	Jocomico	1	1
				Temblor	1	4	Temblor	1	1
	Olola	1	4	Olola	1	6			
Monte Redondo	Monte Redondo	2	4	Monte Redondo	4	5	Monte Redondo	2	3
	Lumbana	1	3	Lumbana	1	3	Lumbana	1	3
				Don Anselmo	1	1			
	Cavas	1	2	Cavas	1	2	Cavas	1	1
				Terrero	2	3	Terrero	2	3
	La Laja	3	3	La Laja	3	3	La Laja	1	1
Tanque							Tanque	2	3
							Carbonera	1	1
Rabona							Rabona	1	5
Cerro de la Cruz							Cerro de la Cruz	1	4
Sarnoso							Sarnoso	4	4
Totals	20	50	72	27	66	95	17	25	37

to be learned from this zone, however: reliance on markers can be misleading if those markers are present in small frequencies.

The Naco Valley

The Naco Valley comprises an area of 96 square kilometers in the Sierra de Omoa of northwestern Honduras. The valley is cut by the Río Chamelecon and prior to the past 15 years of development held 467 Precolumbian sites. In excavations at 69 rural sites and in the large site, La Sierra (468 surface-visible structures), over 3,000,000 pieces of pottery were recovered. Of these, just over 850,000 have been analyzed, and these constitute the data used herein. The typology as it existed by 1992 is discussed in Urban 1993b; since the publication of that chapter, further analysis has made revisions in the system, and these are reflected in the current work.

Naco is an example of an area in which Early Postclassic deposits are not immediately recognizable. The peak of ceramic diversity in Naco is the Terminal Classic, for which we have 12 macroscopically identified paste wares (see table 10.1 for the numbers of types and varieties), while the Late Classic has only three. For the Early Postclassic, there are seven paste wares, and none are new. The Fulano paste (a name chosen by A. Wonderley and published in his dissertation [1981]; it is not related to Fulano from the Yucatán) is present in the Terminal Classic in minute quantities, as is the El Exito paste ware. The two have a much larger representation in EPC materials and continue to grow in frequency into the Late Postclassic. The Fulano and El Exito paste wares, taken together, then, are the only clear signs that an EPC component exists. All other evidence from local ceramics is negative, that is, the period is notable for the *absence* of earlier types, not the presence of specific categories.

Definition on negative evidence is not comfortable, but we believe it is accurate, due to the presence in the valley of a few single-component EPC sites where the assemblage could be clearly defined. Because of these analyses, it has been possible in mixed deposits or areas with complex occupation patterns to tease out those taxa directly relevant to the EPC from confounding ones, enabling temporal placement.

Why is there no other, clearly *positive* evidence for the EPC? In a phrase, because there are no imports: in the 850,000+ sherds analyzed, a single piece of Plumbate was found, and less than a handful of Las Vegas Polychrome sherds. In the field, Las Vegas was noted in a few more lots, but the taxon rarely turned up in the sample chosen for analysis. Thus, if one relied on clear markers, either local or imported, the EPC would be "invisible." Instead, we look here to the absence of categories and to concomitant shifts in relative frequencies of surviving categories.

The Middle Chamelecon-Cacaulapa Zone

The Middle Chamelecon-Cacaulapa area (MCC) presents challenges both different from and similar to those seen in the Naco and middle Ulua valleys. If one looks only at the major site of El Coyote, the Early Postclassic appears to be obvious; if one looks at the rest of the territory, the EPC does not exist. This paradox is even more mystifying because the MCC is quite small by comparison with the other two regions: only 24 square kilometers, with 127 sites. For this chapter, we use a sample from 10 of the 20 excavated rural sites, with a total of 29,895 sherds. El Coyote materials are a sample of 38,150 sherds from 10 of the site's 55 distinct settlement zones, not all of which have been tested by excavation. Overall, in the MCC we have recovered at least 1.8 million sherds and have analyzed about 250,000, just over 13 percent. This chapter excludes ceramic materials from the site of Las Canoas, the locale with the most ceramic debris. Las Canoas is a ceramic production site largely dedicated to the manufacture of vessels with their natural orange-brown surfaces decorated in red paint. Using Canoas' frequencies would only muddy an already confusing situation. That said, let us begin with the clear case, El Coyote.

The site's 312 structures are divided into several clear groupings. On the northeast is an open area with long, low structures, including the platform with the largest basal area of any at the site and a small ballcourt. The planning of the Northeastern Cluster is distinct from areas to the west and east where the bulk of the site lies: the space is open, with no clear plaza arrangements. In contrast, the northern section of the rest of the site is dominated by a large plaza (101 meters north–south by 51 meters east–west) surrounded by temples and elite residences. South of this is an area of large residential platforms around small plazas, flanked on its west by a ballcourt. The remainder of the site, which contains the majority of the platforms, has small structures loosely arranged around irregular plazas. This zone, roughly 150 × 135 meters, resembles the crowded portions of La Sierra in the Naco Valley, as well as rural sites in all three regions.

Ceramics from the Northeastern Cluster have clear EPC markers: Tohil Plumbate, occurring at a frequency of 1.3–1.9 percent per lot, and Las Vegas Polychrome, which runs at about 0.5 percent. The remainder of the Northeastern Cluster subassemblage has new types and varieties using paste wares different from those of the Classic period. The trend in pastes is to greater coarseness, both in the matrix and in the aplastic inclusions. The latter are angular, poorly sorted, and as large as 0.5 centimeters. Decorations on the new taxa continue some Classic period modes, such as red wash/slip, but for the most part the vessels are less well finished and sport reduced decoration: for example, there are no polychromes or bichromes, and surfaces are so poorly smoothed that the large temper is at least visible on, and often protrudes from, surfaces. The corpus of forms is augmented by a new bowl shape seen in no other period, but otherwise the shapes are those familiar from the Classic but with a revival of the *tecomate* form previously seen in Preclassic materials. There are also holdover types from the Classic, in greatly diminished quantities. In addition, there is a small quantity of Terminal Classic fine-paste markers (0.15 percent, as compared to 0.78 percent fine-paste items in the Terminal Classic materials). These Early Postclassic lots have no Terminal Classic markers save the fine pastes, while Terminal Classic lots, in addition to the fine-paste items, have 0.9 percent of other diagnostics characteristic of Terminal Classic.

The Northeastern Cluster yielded fewer sherds compared to the rest of the site; due to their paucity, we examined 60–70 percent of the total number and thus feel confident in our characterization of the subassemblage. Despite the small quantities of EPC sherds, they and materials from earlier MCC periods fall into more taxa than do the assemblages from our other regions; the information on MCC types and varieties by temporal period is summarized in table 10.1. Clearly, an abundance of categories is one of the difficult aspects of this area's assemblage.

Other lines of evidence that support the EPC temporal placement of the Northeastern Cluster materials are the large quantities of Pachuca (green) obsidian (amounting typically to 25 percent of the blades in any lot), Ucareo obsidian in small quantities, Las Vegas Polychrome, and C determinations (a burnt beam likely representing the end of major activities in the Northeastern Cluster falls out at A.D. 960–1040, two-sigma calibrated maximum; McFarlane 2005).

Green obsidian, Plumbate, and Las Vegas Polychrome are found in other areas of the site, as are the new types and varieties. The quantities of new local taxa as well as the imported items are much lower outside of the Northeastern Cluster than within it. Whether this reflects variations in EPC population densities or in access to imports is not clear. It may be that those residing in the newly built northeastern complex enjoyed heightened access to the foreign ceramics and obsidian that define EPC occupation vis-à-vis their contemporaries who continued to reside in other portions of the center. We agree with McFarlane (2005) that the Northeastern Cluster residential and architectural distinctions mark a change in leadership.

Outside of El Coyote, the EPC does not exist, if one relies on the package of imported ceramics and obsidian as the phase's determining characteristics: no Plumbate is recorded in analyzed lots; a few sherds of Las Vegas have been seen in the field but were not recorded in analyzed lots; and the number of Pachuca obsidian blades is fewer than the fingers of one hand. In contrast, the carbon assays indicate that final-phase rural (and Las Canoas) occupation coincides with that at El Coyote. Thus, if there is EPC at El Coyote, it must exist in the rural sites as well. How, then, can we "see" this elusive period?

Taxa indicative of the Terminal Classic are not common in the rural zones: only 0.7 percent of the subassemblage is constituted by clear markers such as local and imported fine-paste, modeled-carved, molded, and incised items, with an emphasis on fine pastes imported from the nearby Naco Valley. Nevertheless, there are clear temporal trends in decorative modes and the pastes on which they appear. First, orange-slipped vessels, painted or not, decline in the Terminal Classic from Late Classic levels and are nonexistent in the few lots that we believe (on a variety of grounds) to be either EPC or transitional Terminal Classic–EPC. Second, red-on-natural decoration declines in frequency. Third, red washes and slips increase. Fourth, whether items are decorated or not, tan pastes decline and orange-browns increase in frequency, while within each broad color grouping, pastes become coarser, following the pattern discussed above for El Coyote. This trend is summarized in figure 10.5 with respect to undecorated materials. All four of these trends appear at El Coyote in the Terminal Classic and continue in the EPC.

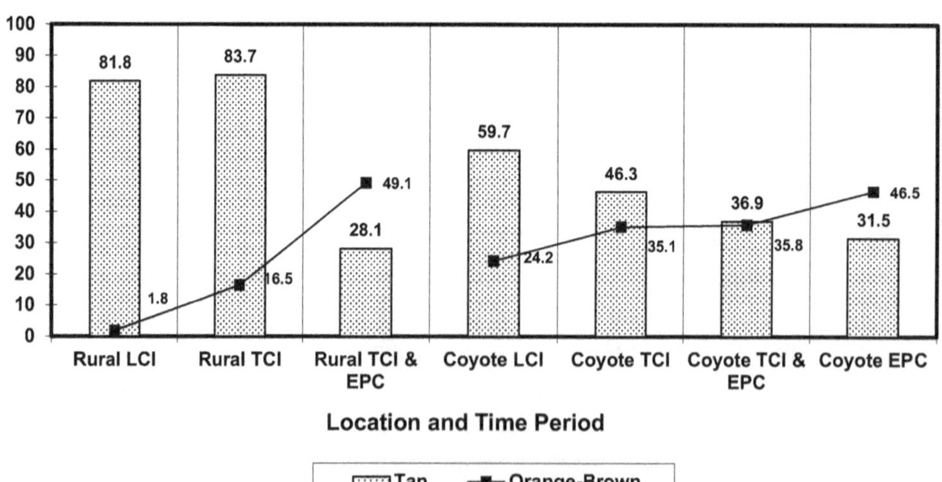

Figure 10.5. Graph comparing trends in paste composition, Middle Chamelecon–Cacaulapa rural area and El Coyote.

In rural areas, then, the EPC can be detected in ceramics only by paying close attention to shifting frequencies of local and imported Terminal Classic "markers," decoration on local types, and paste composition. In short, as in the Naco Valley, the MCC rural Early Postclassic is characterized by the *absence* rather than the presence of types, varieties, decorative modes, paste wares, and imports. The period exists but is hard to see without attending to ceramic details and finding other lines of supporting evidence.

The El Coyote situation, in contrast, resembles that of the Middle Ulua/ Santa Barbara area: in both areas, striking imported ceramic and lithic items indicate the EPC. Even in their absence, however, the EPC could be detected at El Coyote using the same criteria operative for rural subassemblages.

In sum, in the MCC there is a clear Terminal Classic complex, as well as an EPC complex that is variably represented across the area. In addition, we suggest that there may be a subcomplex that bridges the temporal gap, characterized by imported Plumbate and Las Vegas pottery, Pachuca and Ucareo obsidian, and a few fine-paste ceramics. This complex is differentially present in the area, to date seemingly restricted to the major site of El Coyote, and within that site, most obviously seen in the Northeast Complex.

Discussion

The three areas under consideration partake of a common set of trends, yet within these, show individual variation. Here we look briefly at each set of trends, highlighting similarities and differences.

Paste Wares

In all areas, the most common pastes used in the Postclassic are among the coarsest in each sequence. The impression of crudeness stems from the large quantities of inclusions, the sizes of the aplastics, and, usually, their angularity. The most notable example of heavy aplastics comes from the Cacaulapa area: Cerro de la Cruz, which looks more like sand and chunks of limestone lightly held together by clay than it does a useful clay recipe. In the Naco Valley, the alterations in pastes occur gradually, with Postclassic formulas the end points of long-term change. The same is true of the MUSB area, although here the changes are not as extreme.

The Postclassic recipes in all areas resemble those from the Preclassic, which leads to problems of identification. TVM analysis comes into its own when dealing with this problem in several ways. The system's ease in tracking finishing modes, along with decorative, stylistic, and formal mode changes, helps the analyst identify the often-subtle differences that help to distinguish the eras under study. Some of these are highlighted below. Type: variety-mode analysis also allows rapid study of large quantities of materials in the field. This also helps tease out temporal differences at a point in one's studies when sampling strategies can be altered to help clarify problematic deposits.

At the same time, the Terminal Classic assemblages also have distinctive "fine paste" ceramics that continue into the Early Postclassic, or, as in the case of the middle Ulua region, new ceramics with finer pastes come into use in the Postclassic itself.

Surface Finish and Decoration

In all three areas, Postclassic utilitarian wares are less well finished than in all earlier periods. Exterior surfaces are more irregular, often undulating or with wide depressions. Temper is not pushed down into the clay, contributing to surface irregularity through bumps and pits, and burnishing is rarely used. Orange slips decline in frequency and are partially replaced by red washes and slips.

Some complexly decorated types continue from the Classic, and in these instances the same motifs and techniques appear but are more poorly executed. This is most notable in the continuations of red-on-natural decoration, with and without incision, in the MUSB, where changes were obvious enough that we assigned varietal names to the later red-on-natural materials. In our other two areas, we continued the preexisting Classic designations. White slips are more prominent in the Postclassic than previously, in all three zones, with little change from earlier times in their quality. In the MUSB, the white slips disappear by the Late Postclassic. Simple plastic decoration remains the same through time in all zones: wavy fillets are applied; faces (anthropomorphic and zoomorphic) are made with appliqué, incision, punctation, and modeling; and simple incised designs still decorate handles. No form of plastic decoration is common, however, save for the crude cross-hatching on jar handles.

New decorative modes are rare in the Postclassic, with the exception of the Naco region's bichromes, Nolasco and Victoria, which come into prominence only in the Late Postclassic.

Forms

In all areas there is continuity in forms from period to period. At the same time, there are some shifts in frequencies: for example, in all three zones, tecomates, common during the Preclassic, come back into use in the EPC after falling into desuetude during the Classic. Modal preferences in bowl and jar forms are retained as well, as are regional distinctions: an example is the pyriform jar, which dominates MUSB assemblages but is rare in the other two regions. In the Naco and Cacaulapa areas, however, there are new forms in the Postclassic. Naco's Postclassic residents produced open bowls with outflared walls, elevated on tripod supports—often bird effigies—a combination not attested to previously. In the Cacaulapa area, a new form of restricted-orifice bowl with a very small everted rim appears in the EPC.

Finally, all three zones have two other changes in common. First, all show increases in *comales* in the Postclassic. This shift begins at the end of the Classic in the Cacaulapa area, where the variation in comal wall profiles is greater than in the neighboring territories. Second, *molcajete* (grater) bowls appear for the first time in all three zones, beginning at the end of the Classic. These are recognized not by their wall profiles but by the treatment of the basal interior surface. Turning a basic bowl into a molcajete requires having relief on the bowl interior. At the simplest this is accomplished by incised cross-hatching, an approach found in all the zones. In the Naco area, some of the interior incised designs are curvilinear, and in addition, there are molded curvilinear molcajete bases. The molding is not seen in the MUSB, but a few examples have been encountered in the MCC. The variation in molcajete bases can also be considered decorative: as long as there are high and low surfaces to hold the materials being ground, the nature of the designs seems to be irrelevant. Unfortunately, in no area are there enough molcajete bases to determine a design grammar.

Simplification of the Assemblages

In all of the areas presented, Postclassic assemblages are less complex than those of earlier time periods: the number of paste wares decreases; there are fewer ceramic groups; and within groups, there are fewer types and varieties. The range of variation in forms is reduced through time as well: the most popular shapes from the Classic continue on, but minor forms disappear. Finally, many decorative modes end with the Classic, and there is little or no innovation in decoration in the EPC.

Summary

All three of the regions considered here follow similar general shifts in ceramics from the Classic through the Postclassic. Yet within these broad similarities lie a host of local differences, discussed above.

In all three areas, the authors and those who assisted them in the field have found that type: variety-mode analysis is not merely a sufficient tool for most aspects of ceramic analysis but is positively beneficial in several regards: handling large volumes of finds; pinpointing important trends while in the field;

and differentiating among similar items through attention to, primarily, decorative and surface finish modes. Type: variety-mode analysis is not suited to the study of function, but data addressing questions of function can be collected in parallel with the sorting and recording needed for the TVM classifications. The criticism that TVM analysis does not take into account technological variables, particularly paste, is also not borne out in our investigations. Because of the areas in which we have worked, we have been forced to acknowledge the importance of macroscopic paste differences and have included these variables within the TVM taxa at the topmost level of the paste ware. Although technical studies are not yet completed, we are pleased to say that to date, our TVM categories have been largely supported by petrographic and neutron activation characterizations.

Conclusions

Consideration of the three zones discussed above gives rise to several conclusions with potential significance outside of northwestern Honduras. The dominant theme is generalization. To begin, the available data indicate that a researcher cannot project interpretations derived from one area onto another. The MUSB zone is a day's walk from El Coyote, which is situated near the southern edge of the defined MCC area, and the Naco and MCC zones are contiguous. The conventional wisdom we had learned in graduate school, to whit, Las Vegas Polychrome and Plumbate were the markers of the Early Postclassic, held true in MUSB but not in Naco or the rural MCC. Therefore, looking for these markers, and not finding them, would erase the presence of Early Postclassic occupation.

Nor can we generalize within regions unless we are willing to accept the possibility of major errors. The stark contrasts between the MCC's El Coyote and rural sites, as well as the confounding nature of Las Canoas, mean that any typology based on the one large site would not work well in rural areas; nor would a typology for rural areas be applicable without alteration at, say, El Coyote; and finally, a system based on Las Canoas would be useful only there. It is necessary to examine subassemblages derived from the entire range of site sizes, complexities, and locales in order to understand fully the nature of Precolumbian life.

The third conclusion is that large samples are necessary to get a full (or at least fuller) grasp of the ceramics, their temporal shifts, and thus the larger picture of life and times. Some of the markers discussed above would have been invisible in smaller samples. In addition, small samples would not provide data for assessing subtle frequency shifts within local taxa. What is "big enough"?

We hesitate to say, because we realize that our wide purview is unusual. Ceramics were scarce enough in the middle Ulua area that we were able to look at roughly 30 percent of the entire regional assemblage. In Naco, we aimed for 20 percent overall, but not all sites were examined with the same intensity. In the MCC, the studied percentage of the take varied greatly: at Las Canoas, which has produced hundreds of thousands of sherds each season, 7–10 percent is enough (or all we can manage), whereas in the parts of El Coyote that were constructed and used in the Early Postclassic, the scarcity of material dictated that we look at 60–70 percent. Other parts of El Coyote were studied less intensively; overall, we have examined on average 13 percent of the MCC materials. Large samples in rural areas did not include many markers, while even small samples from Coyote could contain—but not necessarily did contain—ample signposts for temporal periods.

Fourth, it is very important to consider site functions. We could not use Las Canoas for any calculations in this paper because the quantities of particular paste categories are highly unusual: the orange-brown wares are apparently made there, and thus the percentages of materials based on these pastes, instead of being in the 2–24 percent range, depending on site and paste formula, are in the 30–60 percent range. This leads, however, to a question that we cannot adequately address here: how does one know if relative frequencies are unusual, and thus likely indicative of manufacturing? Again, a partial answer is testing at a range of sites and obtaining good-sized samples, whatever that means in a given area.

Finally, one needs to be flexible and to impart that flexibility to anyone engaged in ceramic analysis. For example, one cannot assume that a particular form is always wedded to a particular type or variety; rather, one should be ready to add forms, adjust TVM descriptions, and be in every way prepared to change perceptions and the system. Part of the flexibility is being willing to add different recording methods—even new, crosscutting typologies—to capture a variety of data classes. As J. O. Brew once wrote, "We must classify our material in all ways that will produce for us useful information. . . . We need more rather than fewer classifications, different, classifications, always new classifications, to meet new needs" (Brew 1946: 65). A proliferation of typologies might make us cringe and even feel dismay, but the return is worth the effort.

Acknowledgments

Each area was examined under the codirectorship of the two senior authors. Naco was the site of Urban's dissertation research from 1975 to 1979, and she returned to the valley between 1988 and 1996, with E. M. Schortman as codirector and the junior author as, first, a student (1988), then laboratory director (1990, 1995–96; during the latter time, she also pursued doctoral work). Central Santa Barbara (MUSB) was investigated from 1983 to 1986, under the codirection of Urban, Schortman, and W. Ashmore; S. Smith Duggan was laboratory director. Finally, the ongoing Middle Chamelecon-Cacaulapa (MCC) project began in 1999, with Urban, Schortman, and Ausec as codirectors in 1999–2000, and was subsequently pursued by Urban and Schortman (with M. Stockett and W. McFarlane as assistant directors in 2002; E. Bell in that capacity in 2004; and L. Schwartz and M. Esqueda in that position in 2008).

Our work in Honduras is done under the auspices of the Instituto Hondureño de Antropología e Historia. We are grateful to all *gerentes* who headed IHAH during our 34 years of work, as well as heads of the Region Norte, under which Naco and the MCC fall. Over the years many individuals have done basic laboratory work—washing, numbering, counting, and recording of artifacts—and we are highly appreciative of their efforts. For the past several years, much of the logistical and laboratory work has been overseen by Jorge Bueso Cruz, intrepid right-hand man and good friend. We also thank the by now almost 200 students and staff members who have joined us over the years: without them, our database would be much, much smaller than it is—but maybe that would be a good thing? Funds for our projects have come from a variety of sources: Kenyon College, the National Science Foundation, the National Geographic Society, the National Endowment for the Humanities, the Fulbright Foundation, and Wenner-Gren have provided most of these greatly appreciated assets. Kenyon has also allowed us generous amounts of time for, and the directorship of, the Kenyon-Honduras Project, in which undergraduate students have been enrolled since the summer of 1983. Kenyon has provided us with a niche; we hope our exploitation of it has been beneficial to all concerned.

Note

1. In addition to "classic" works such as Ford 1954; Shepard 1956; Wheat, Gifford, and Wasley 1958; Gifford 1960; Rouse 1960; Smith, Willey, and Gifford 1960; and Rice 1987c, we have found Adams and Adams 1991 to be inspirational.

11

Slips, Styles, and Trading Patterns

A Postclassic Perspective from Central Petén, Guatemala

LESLIE G. CECIL

The techniques that various sociopolitical groups of Postclassic Maya in central Petén used to slip their vessels reflect differences in resources, manufacturing recipes, and decorative programs. Through visual and chemical analyses of the slips and paints used by these groups (primarily the Itza and the Kowoj), I am able to detect changes in slipping technology through time and across the Petén Lakes region, to demonstrate that the Early Postclassic Snail-Inclusion Paste Ware slipping technology is similar to the Late Classic polychrome slipping technology and to show that by conjoining slip and paint chemical data (technology) with decorative program data (styles) of central Petén Postclassic pottery, Early Postclassic Petén trade patterns can be inferred.

When comparing Late Classic polychrome pottery to Early and Late Postclassic polychrome pottery in the central Petén Lakes region, one is immediately aware of the differences in quality of technological and decorative execution such as complexity of designs (motifs and number of colors), fire clouding, and vessel forms. These changes correspond to changes in central Petén environmental conditions and sociopolitical reorganization that resulted from a change in Maya society after the Late Classic period. However closer mineralogical and chemical analysis of Snail-Inclusion Paste Ware pottery from Nixtun Ch'ich', Ixlú, Zacpetén, and Tipu indicates that Petén Postclassic potters to some extent attempted to continue Late Classic polychrome pottery technology.

In addition to increasing our understanding of general slipping technology, chemical characterization of the Snail-Inclusion Paste Ware Postclassic slips and paints also contributes to our knowledge of manufacturing technology and trade. This information was obtained with the use of laser ablation inductively coupled mass spectroscopy (LA-ICP-MS) analysis. When this information is combined with instrumental neutron activation analysis (INAA) of the same ceramic pastes, our understanding of trade patterns during the Early Postclassic and the Late Postclassic periods also improves.

Sociopolitical Geography of the Central Petén Lakes Region during the Postclassic Period

In central Petén, ethnohistorical research has indicated that the Itza and Kowoj (as well as other sociopolitical groups) occupied territory in the region in the sixteenth and seventeenth centuries (Jones 1998: 18). Spanish documents and Postclassic to Colonial period (thirteenth through eighteenth centuries) native histories of these groups (especially the Itza) record their presence, their various alliances in Petén, and their repeated movements to and from northern Yucatán. The documents suggest that Petén was divided into administrative provinces headed by and named after a dominant lineage, each controlling several subprovinces throughout the area (figure 11.1).

The Itza controlled the southern and western basin of Lake Petén Itzá, an area stretching from Lake Quexil west to Lake Sacpuy, with their capital, Nojpetén (or Taiza), on modern Flores Island (Boot 2005; Jones 1998; Jones et al. 1981). The Itza may have been an alliance of multiple sociopolitical groups (Jones 1998). Their Late Postclassic ruler, Kan Ek', claimed ancestry from Chichén Itzá in the northern Yucatán Peninsula, and he stated that the Itza mi-

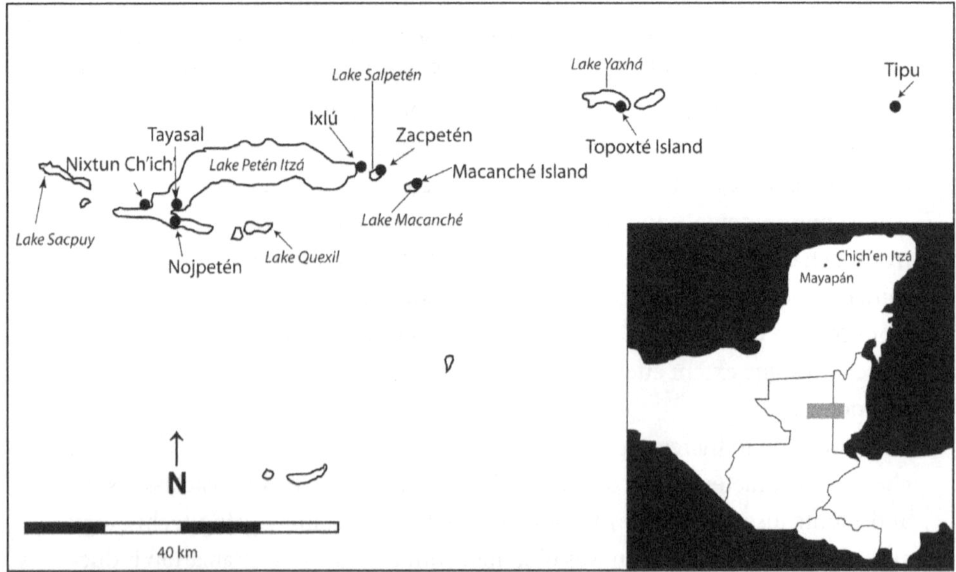

Figure 11.1. Central Petén archaeological sites. (Modified from Cecil 2001: fig. 1.)

grated from Chichén Itzá when it fell at approximately A.D. 1200 (Edmonson 1986; Jones 1998; Roys 1933).[1] In A.D. 1695, AjChan, Kan Ek's nephew, also claimed that his deceased mother was from Chichén Itzá, and "members of the Itza nobility were still living there in the seventeenth century and successfully avoiding Spanish recognition" (Jones 1998: 11). Additionally, lists of married residents in A.D. 1584 and A.D. 1688 record Can (Kan) as the most prominent name in Hocaba and Sotuta, and Ek' commonly occurs in the Cehpech and Cochuah provinces (Roys 1957: table 1). Although this indicates a later migration of Itza to central Petén, many scholars (Boot 1997, 2005; Rice et al. 1996; Schele and Grube 1995; Schele et al. 1995; Schele and Mathews 1998) state that epigraphic and archaeological materials suggest that Itza origins might have been in central Petén in the Classic period, and portions of the Itza may have begun migrations to and from the northern Yucatán as early as A.D. 900. Regardless of their migration history, the Itza were present at Lake Petén Itzá when Cortés traveled through Petén on his way to Honduras in A.D. 1525 (Cortés 1976: 219–85).

Itza architecture is characterized by formal open halls, raised shrines, and architectural sculptures that include raptorial birds, coyotes, serpents, and small phalli and turtles (Pugh 1996: 206–11; D. Rice 1986; Rice et al. 1996). Associated with the temple structures on an east–west axis are caches of east-facing human skulls placed in rows or caches of two human crania (Duncan 2005). Similar associations of architecture and crania are found at Chichén Itzá (Duncan 2005; D. Rice 1986; Rice et al. 1996).

The Kowoj controlled the northeastern area of Lake Petén Itzá and the east-central Petén Lakes (Lake Salpetén and possibly Lake Yaxhá and Lake Macanché) (Jones 1998). They claimed to have migrated from Mayapán around A.D. 1530; however, they too may have had a series of earlier migrations to and from Mayapán, of which one occurred after the fall of that site (circa A.D. 1450) and the last may have been circa A.D. 1530 (Cecil 2001b, 2004; Rice et al. 1996). Petén Kowoj kinship patronyms were linked to those of prestigious individuals at Mayapán (Jones 1998: table 1.1; Roys 1957: table 1), and the *Chilam Balam of Chumayel* stated that the guardian of the east gate of Mayapán was a Kowoj (Roys 1933: 79).

The main architectural pattern shared by the Petén and Yucatecan Kowoj is the temple assemblage (Pugh 2001a). First defined by Proskouriakoff (1962) at Mayapán, this complex is present at Topoxté Island and Zacpetén; variants also occur at Ixlú and Muralla de León in central Petén (Pugh 2001b: 253), Tipu in western Belize (Cecil and Pugh 2004), and Isla Cilvituk in Campeche, Mexico (Alexander 1998). In addition to temple assemblages, ossuaries and individual skull deposits are common among the Kowoj (Duncan 2005).

Snail-Inclusion Paste Ware Pottery

The Itza and the Kowoj manufactured pottery made from lacustrine gray carbonate clays, as is evident from the plethora of this pottery at all of the Postclassic archaeological sites in central Petén and western Belize. Snail-Inclusion Paste Ware (see also Adams and Trik 1961; A. Chase 1983; Cowgill 1963; and Rice 1987b) pottery is characterized by a variable gray-colored clay with red, pink, or black slips. In central Petén, the ceramic pastes vary from dark gray (10YR 5/2, GLEY1 4/N) to gray (5YR 6/1) to light gray (2.5YR 6/1) to tan (10YR 6/3) and to reddish brown (5YR 5/6). Snail-Inclusion Paste Ware pottery is easily identified by its inclusion of lacustrine shells (some whole and obviously living in the clays and others crushed and most likely culturally added). In addition to snails, the sherd pastes also contain calcite (euhedral, polycrystalline, and cryptocrystalline), quartz, hematite, biotite, and chert.

Bullard (1973), Chase (1979), and Rice (1987) have noted that the Trapeche ceramic group represents Early Postclassic manufacture, and Chase (1979), Rice (1987b), and I (Cecil 2001) have noted that Early Postclassic Paxcamán ceramic group sherds tend to exhibit variable-colored pastes (often without an abundance of shell inclusions) that range from tan to light gray and tend to be more sandy in texture (or are tempered with volcanic ash) than the Late Postclassic Paxcamán ceramic sherds, which are light to dark gray throughout with the distinctive shell inclusions.

Within the ware category there are three different slip colors: red (Paxcamán ceramic group), pink (Trapeche ceramic group), and black (Fulano ceramic group). In general, Paxcamán ceramic group red (10R 4/6 to 2.5YR 4/8) and black (7.5YR 3/1 to 2.5Y 2.5/1) slips have a low luster, and the majority have a matte finish. Pink (2.5YR 5/6 to 5YR 5/6) slips result from double slipping: the primary slip near the sherd surface is red or brown, and it is covered by a thin, translucent tan to creamy secondary slip with a waxy feel (Cecil 2001b, 2004). Decoration on Snail-Inclusion Paste Ware sherds includes black (Ixpop Polychrome, Yamero Polychrome, and Mul Polychrome types), red-on-paste (Macanché Red-on-paste, Sotano Red-on-paste, and Picté Red-on-paste types), and red-and-black (Sacá Polychrome type) painted decorations, incising (Picú Incised, Mengano Incised, and Xuluc Incised types), and, on some sherds, both painting and incising (Doña Esperanza type).

Analyzing Snail-Inclusion Paste Ware Slips

Visual Examination of Slips

The first method of analysis was a visual examination of the slips and paints used on Snail-Inclusion Paste Ware pottery. Feel of the slips is an important criterion when attempting to separate slips that may have an unusual texture (in this case double slipping) (see also Rice, this volume). Using feel of the slips as a distinguishing characteristic, I separated those sherds with a waxy, smooth slip from those with a matte finish. With a 10X hand lens, I was able to determine which slips were the result of double slipping. From there I selected the best candidates (thick, noneroded slips) for petrographic analysis. When examined using a polarizing light microscope, double slips were apparent. I also selected three Trapeche ceramic group sherds with visually obvious double slips to examine with a scanning electron microscope. Under high magnification, the double slips were also apparent.

In addition to slipping technology that could be determined through a visual examination, I also noted decorative motifs (when possible), decorative programs, blackened rims, and overall quality of sherd decoration (how well the design was executed, how much erosion had taken place, and whether or not an underslip in the design panel existed).

LA-ICP-MS and Chemical Group Recognition

LA-ICP-MS was chosen because of its success with analyzing slips and paints in situ. Because separating the Postclassic slip and paint pigments from the sherd paste without also including part of the sherd paste in the analysis is very difficult, LA-ICP-MS is the ideal technique: it is unlikely to penetrate beyond the level of the slip and/or painted decoration, as the laser ablates only the first five microns (Cogswell et al. 2005; Neff 2003; Speakman 2005). Thus, the resulting chemical compositions do not include chemical analysis of the underlying pottery sherd paste composition, and one can interpret information about the slips and paints.

Fifty Snail-Inclusion Paste Ware exterior slips (31 Paxcamán Red, 15 Trapeche Pink, and 4 Fulano Black) were selected for analysis via LA-ICP-MS at California State University–Long Beach. In addition to the exterior slips, 15 decorative paint samples from the sherds themselves (8 black and 7 red) were analyzed.[2] Forty-six elements were analyzed (detailed specifications of this methodology are available in Cecil and Neff 2006: 1485–86).

Upon completion of the LA-ICP-MS data collection, compositional groups were determined (for more details, see Glascock 1992). Compositional groups can be viewed as "centers of mass" in the compositional space described by the measured elemental data. Groups are characterized by the locations of their centroids and the unique relationships (for example, correlations) between the elements. Decisions about whether to assign a specimen to a particular compositional group are based on the overall probability that the measured concentrations for the specimen could have been obtained from that group.

Initial hypotheses about source-related subgroups in the compositional data can be derived from noncompositional information (for example, archaeological context, decorative attributes, and so forth) or from application of various pattern-recognition techniques to the multivariate chemical data. In this case, I used principal components analysis (PCA) as a pattern-recognition technique to search for subgroups in the yet-unexplored data set. Principal components analysis creates a new set of reference axes arranged in decreasing order of variance in the data set. Data can be displayed on combinations of the new axes, just as they can be displayed on the original elemental concentration axes (for example, bivariate plots). Generally, compositional differences between specimens can be expected to be larger for specimens in different groups than for specimens in the same group, and this implies that groups should be detectable as distinct areas of high point density on plots of the first few components.

It is well known that PCA of chemical data is scale dependent (Mardia et al. 1979), and analyses tend to be dominated by those elements or isotopes for which the concentrations are relatively large. As a result, these data were transformed into log concentrations to equalize the differences in variance between the major elements such as aluminum (Al), calcium (Ca), and iron (Fe), on one hand and trace elements, such as the rare-earth elements (REEs), on the other hand. In the end, plots of the first two or three principal components as axes display group separation and the relationships of the various elements responsible for the compositional groups.

Results

Visual Examination

While the majority of the Postclassic slipped pottery is characterized by a low luster or matte finish, much of the Early Postclassic pottery represented by the Trapeche and Paxcamán ceramic groups from Zacpetén and Tipu have waxy or glossy slipped surfaces. The waxy slipped surfaces are most likely due to a translucent (or light cream-colored) overslip or resin and burnishing or are a result of the application of two different colored slips (double slipping). The waxy Paxcamán and Fulano ceramic group slips seem to have been produced by the application of a translucent overslip (or resin), whereas the Trapeche ceramic group slips appear to have been produced by a double-slipping technique. The characteristic double slipping is the result of the potter first applying a darker red or reddish-brown slip color and then applying a cream-colored slip over the darker color. In places where the slip has begun to erode, one can see the two slips. This is also confirmed through petrographic thin section and SEM images (figure 11.2). At this time there is no way to determine whether the double-slipped pottery was fired after each slip was applied, but Rice (1987b) has hypothesized that this may be the case.

a)

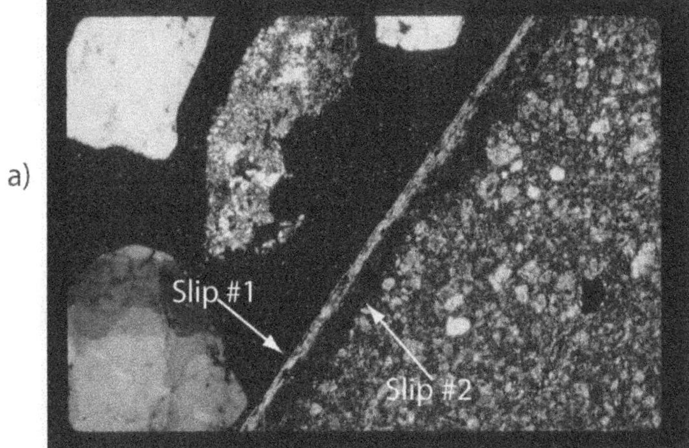

b)

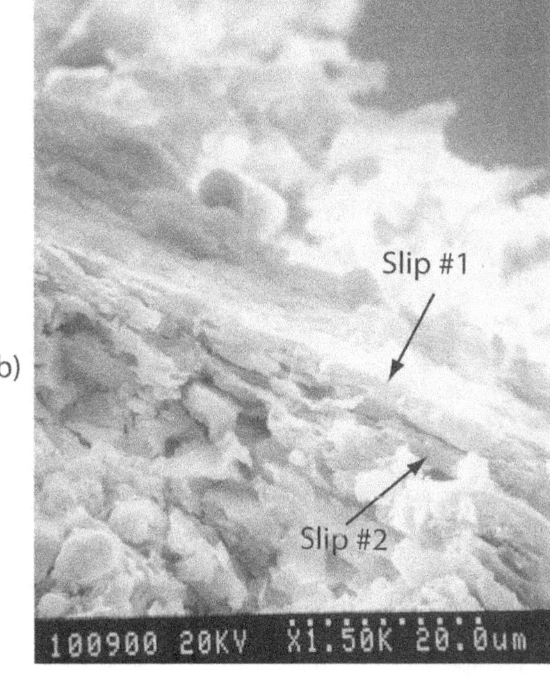

Figure 11.2. *a*, Thin section of Trapeche ceramic group sherd (ZTr 8112) demonstrating two slips (XPL); *b*, SEM image of a double slip of Trapeche ceramic group sherd (ZTr 30310) under X1.50K magnification.

In addition to the slipping technique, some Early Postclassic pottery (monochrome and polychrome) has an intentionally darkened rim (figure 11.3d). In rare instances, the band appears to have been painted; however, more often than not the black rim band is a result of firing technology—a very intentional firecloud.

Below the rim (blackened or not), decorated pottery typically has a series of circumferential bands that serve as boundaries for the area to be decorated.

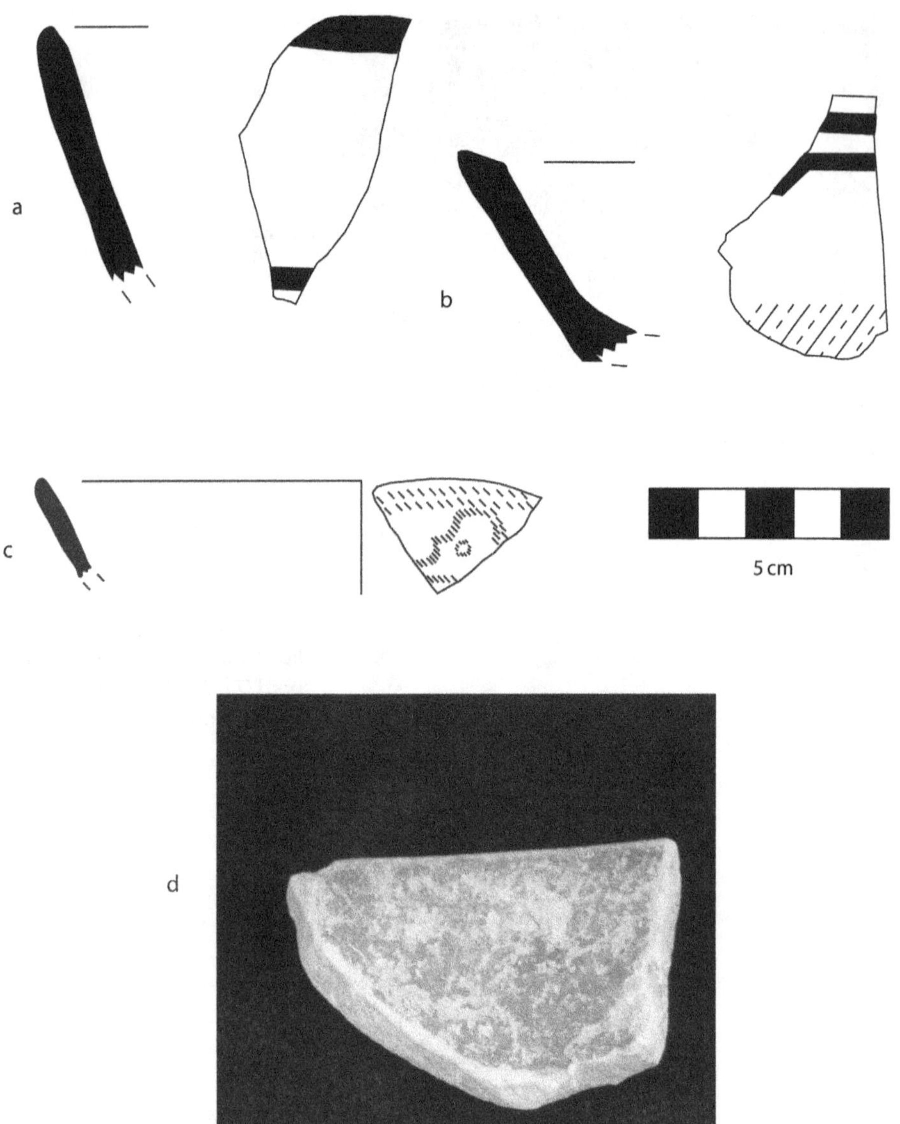

Figure 11.3. Early Postclassic period pottery: *a–b*, Mul Polychrome from Zacpetén; *c*, Picté Red-on-paste from Zacpetén; *d*, photograph of Paxcamán Red: Escalinata Variety sherd from Nixtun Ch'ich' showing black rim. (Images and drawing by Leslie Cecil.)

Between the circumferential bands are various motifs. Postclassic designs typically consist of a repeated motif that is repeated three or four times in the banded area. The repeated motifs are separated by a series of vertical bands. Many Postclassic motifs within the designated decoration area of a vessel resemble Late Classic hieroglyphs (see also Rice and Cecil 2009). Some of the decorative motifs include glyphic elements occurring in isolation, or the same motif is repeated three or four times in the paneled areas. Some of these motifs include the hook or curl, *pop*, *ajaw*, and various sky-band elements, which include *ak'b'al*, *lamat*, and the beard and scroll or *ilhuitl* motif (for a discussion of the meaning of the different Postclassic elements, see Rice and Cecil 2009). Unfortunately, very few Early Postclassic Trapeche Pink sherds have noneroded motifs. Where decoration does occur, the remnants of the motifs appear to be curvilinear motifs or some variant of a hook or curl (figure 11.3a, b, c). The exception to this general trend is seen in the Machanché Island Trapeche collared bowls with intricately carved reptilian and mat motifs (Rice 1987b: figs. 51 and 52).

Chemical Analysis

When the slips of the 50 Snail-Inclusion Paste Ware pottery are plotted based on these chemical compositions, statistically significant compositional groups exist. The Trapeche ceramic group pink slips separate into two distinct compositional groups (figure 11.4a). Group 1 represents all but one Trapeche slip excavated from Zacpetén, one sherd from Ixlú, and three of the four Fulano black slips. Group 2 contains all of the Trapeche slips from Nixtun Ch'ich', all but one slip from Ixlú, and one Trapeche slip from Zacpetén.

Unlike the Trapeche and Fulano slips, the Paxcamán ceramic group slips do not form statistically significant compositional groups (figure 11.4b). However, there are three clusters that may have cultural significance (and may be statistically significant with a larger sample size). Each cluster has samples from the four archaeological sites, and there are no patterns as to decoration type and exterior slip. Therefore, there may have been three different zones or raw materials used for the exterior slips of the Paxcamán ceramic group exterior slips.

Because of the small number of Snail-Inclusion Paste Ware red and black paints analyzed, they had to be combined with other Postclassic ceramic groups (Clemencia Cream Paste and Vitzil Orange-red wares) to make any significant statements about the differences in composition. The Snail-Inclusion Paste Ware red paints separate into two compositional groups that show similarities with red paints used on Clemencia Cream Paste Ware pottery (Cecil and Neff 2006: 1488–89). The black paints separate into three compositional groups (Cecil and Neff 2006: 1489). One group represents black painted hook motifs (Ixpop Polychrome) from all of the archaeological sites. The second group represents red-and-black painted motifs (Sacá Polychrome) on pottery excavated from Zacpetén. The final group represents three black paints on pottery from three different sites (Nixtun Ch'ich', Ixlú, and Tipu).

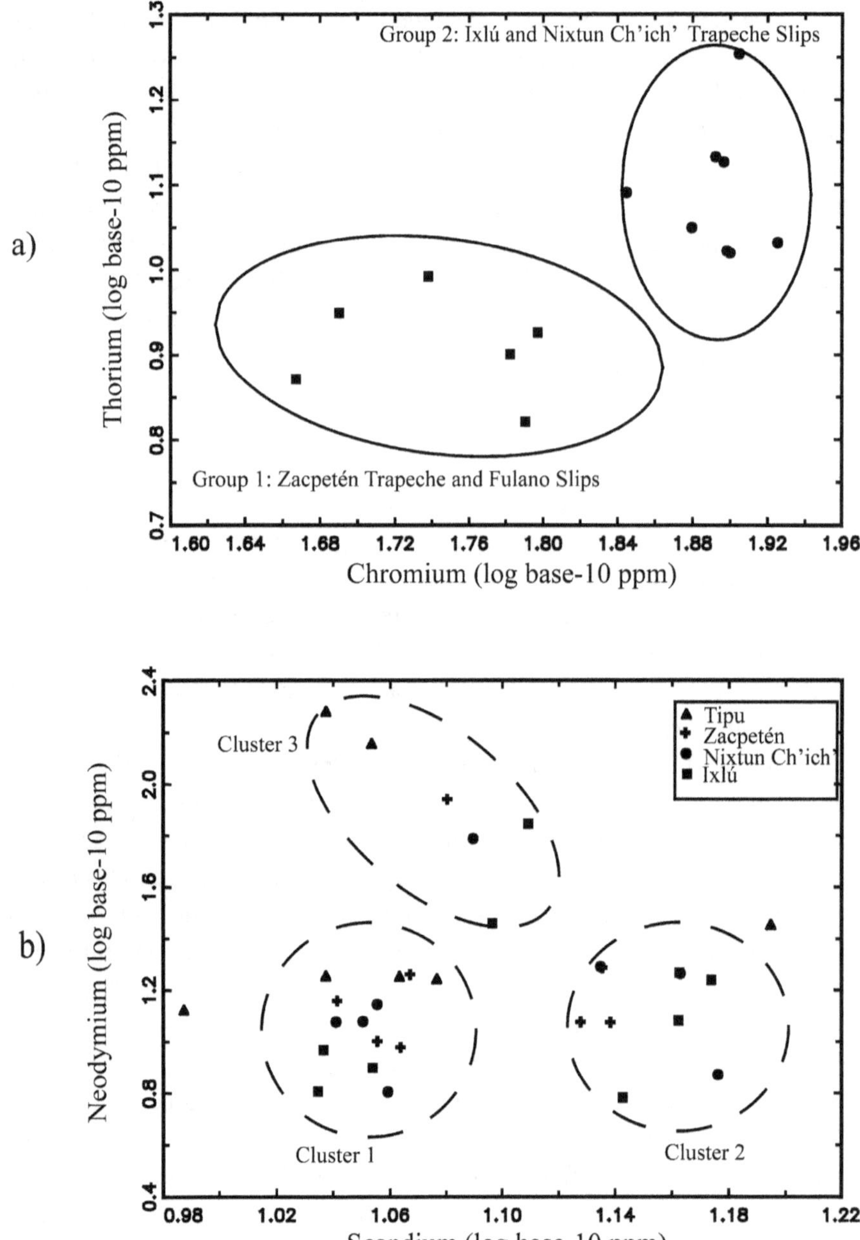

Figure 11.4. *a*, Bivariate plot of chromium and thorium base-10 logged concentrations showing the separation of Trapeche and Fulano ceramic group slips. Ellipses represent 90 percent confidence level for membership; *b*, Bivariate plot of scandium and neodymium base-10 logged concentrations showing separation of Paxcamán ceramic group slips. Dashed ellipses do not indicate confidence intervals.

Discussion

Connections to Late Classic Manufacture

Decorated Postclassic pottery produced by social groups in the Petén Lakes area may be an attempt to re-create Late Classic polychrome pottery and themes such as ritual ceremonies. This can be seen through four characteristics of Postclassic decorated pottery: double slipping; black rims; decoration panels; and decorative motifs.[3] If these types of surface finishes and decorations are indicative of Early Postclassic Maya potters attempting to re-create Late Classic polychrome surfaces, it may also suggest that people at these archaeological sites may have lived in the Petén Lakes region early in the Postclassic period.

Earlier Petén Postclassic potters tried to copy Late Classic polychrome waxy/glossy slipped surfaces. Coe and Kerr (1998: 141) state that the Codex Style pottery surfaces were the result of a manipulation of two slips or colorants and that the Petén Gloss Ware surfaces may have been a result of a clear coat of an organic material or a lacquer-like substance or resin applied after firing. Double slipping of Late Classic pottery also has been discussed by Reents-Budet and colleagues (1994: 211–16), who suggest that first a base slip (usually white) was applied, then a painted decoration was added, and then a second slip may have been added. "More gloss may be obtained by applying thin layers of terra sigillata to a pre-fired (bisque) and possibly pre-slipped vessel and lightly polishing the slip in either a semidry or [a] dry stage" (Reents-Budet et al. 1994: 211). This would produce a high-gloss vessel, or what may be also categorized as a waxy slip.

Waxy/high-gloss slips are not unique to Late Classic Maya pottery. This same quality of slip is also characteristic of northern Yucatán slate wares of the Early Postclassic period. Brainerd (1958: 27, 52–54, 68, 70), Smith (1971: 148–55, 174–77), and Smyth and colleagues (1995: 121–22) describe Puuc Slate, Thin Slate, and Chichen Slate wares as having a polished slip that varies in soapiness and translucence and in color from brown to gray to pinkish with variable cream, brown, or gray streaks and rootlet markings. All of these slip descriptions also include the term *waxy*, with Thin Slate Ware pottery having a less pronounced waxiness (Brainerd 1958: 53; Smith 1971: 154–55). There is no mention as to how many times the slate wares were fired.

Obviously, the Petén Early Postclassic surfaces are not identical to those of the Late Classic period or the northern Yucatán slate wares, but they are the result of double slipping. While the idea is the same, Postclassic differences seen in Petén pottery may be due to the difference in available resources and the lack of knowledge of the new resources on the part of Postclassic potters. However, the double slipping of the Trapeche ceramic group and the waxy nature of some of the slips of the Trapeche, Fulano, and Paxcamán ceramic groups at Ixlú, Zacpetén, and Tipu are intentional.

In addition to slipped surfaces, some sherds (Paxcamán Red: Escalinata Variety) have black painted and/or fire-clouded rims and a red- to red-orange-slipped body (Cecil 2001: 131–34). Although Postclassic black rims are not common, the rim color does not appear to be accidental. In some cases, it may have been painted; however, most blackened rims appear to be the result of differential access to oxygen during firing. Because no other portion of the vessel is fireclouded, the blackening of the rim is likely to be not the result of fire clouding but the result of intentional placement in a firing situation where the rim area would lack oxygen during firing.

These black rims resemble some Late Classic polychrome pottery (Reents-Budet 1994). The majority of the Late Classic polychrome pottery with black rims have been classified as Ik'-style polychromes (for example, K533, K680, K1439, K1452, K1463) that were manufactured at Motul de San José (immediately northeast of Nixtun Ch'ich') (Halperin and Foias 2010; Reents-Budet et al. 2007). The tradition of black rims is not unique to the Late Classic or Postclassic periods, as they also occur on pottery that dates to the Mamon or Chicanel period.

Postclassic decorative panels also resemble those of Late Classic polychrome vessels but are less elaborate (Kerr 1989, 1990, 1992, 1994, 1997, 2000). Typical Postclassic decorative panels are marked by a double circumferential band toward the rim and a single circumferential band along the bottom of the panel. Double banding on the bottom of the decorative panel also appears; however, it is rare. On occasion, jars have triple banding to mark the top of the design panel. The black or red panel bands are painted over a light tan to light orange undercoat. This undercoat is analogous to Late Classic polychrome decorated areas. Panel dividers (a single vertical line) typically divide the decorative panel into two or four parts. Many Late Classic polychrome plates have similar decorative panels and divisions.

Possible Manufacturing Locations for Postclassic Slipped Pottery

The Trapeche and Fulano Black ceramic groups have two chemically distinct paste compositional groups: (1) sherds from Nixtun Ch'ich' and Zacpetén; and (2) sherds from Zacpetén and Ixlú (figure 11.5, upper image). There are also two chemically distinct slip compositional groups: (1) Trapeche pink slips on pottery excavated from Ixlú and Nixtun Ch'ich'; and (2) Trapeche pink and Fulano black slips on pottery excavated from Zacpetén (figure 11.5, lower image). While there is no clear correlation between slips and pastes from Zacpetén, samples from Nixtun Ch'ich' and Ixlú are chemically distinct (figure 11.5).

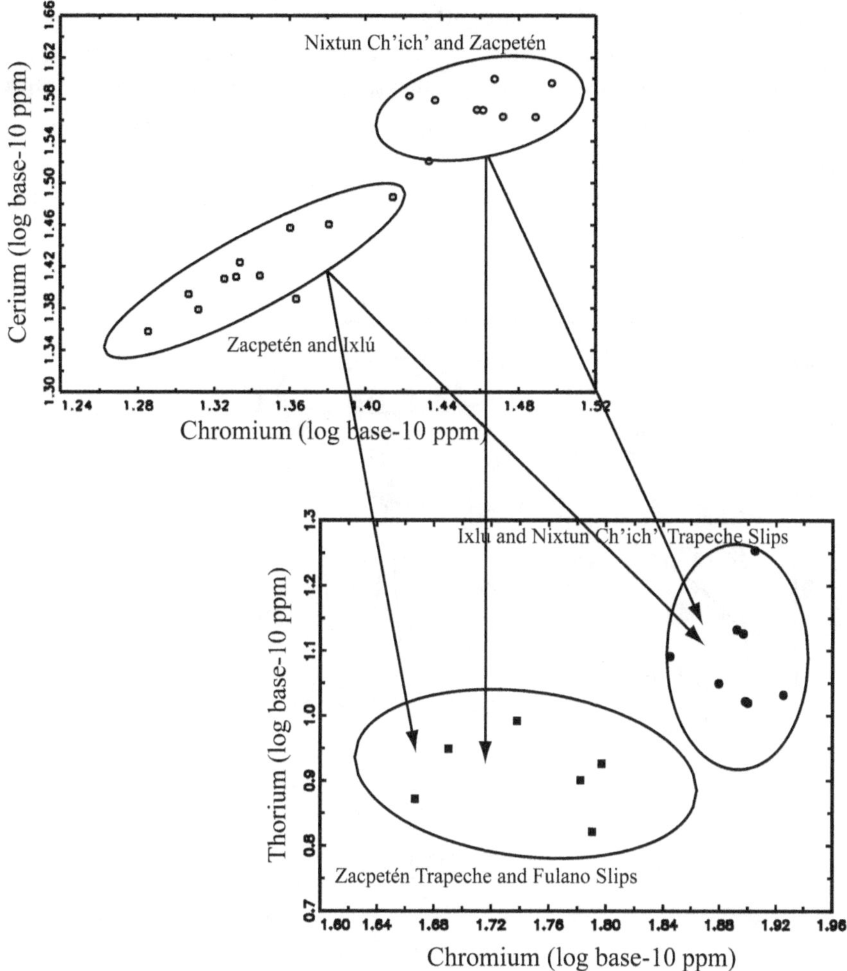

Figure 11.5. Bivariate plots of Early Postclassic period Trapeche and Fulano ceramic group pastes (*upper*) and slips (*lower*). Arrows between the plots indicate sherd associations between paste and slip confidence interval groups. Ellipses represent 90 percent confidence level for membership.

There appear to be two recipes for the pink slips—one representing manufacture of pottery excavated at or near Zacpetén and one representing manufacture of pottery excavated from Nixtun Ch'ich' and Ixlú.[4] Interestingly, none of the pink-slipped pottery has been excavated from Tipu.

Even though Snail-Inclusion Paste Ware pottery has the potential to be manufactured from any number of lake clays in the region and the Paxcamán ceramic group slips did not form statistically significant compositional groups, combining the paste compositional data (Cecil 2009) with the slip data discussed above enables the inferring of zones of manufacture. Late Postclassic Snail-Inclusion Paste Ware pottery (Paxcamán ceramic group) has three chemically distinct paste compositional groups (figure 11.6, upper image). Group 1 presents pottery high in cryptocrystalline calcite and quartz from Zacpetén and is decorated with red-and-black decoration; the group also presents black-decorated pottery from Ixlú and Tipu. These slips are all in a single cluster (the clusters reflect chemical composition groups of slips), suggesting one place of

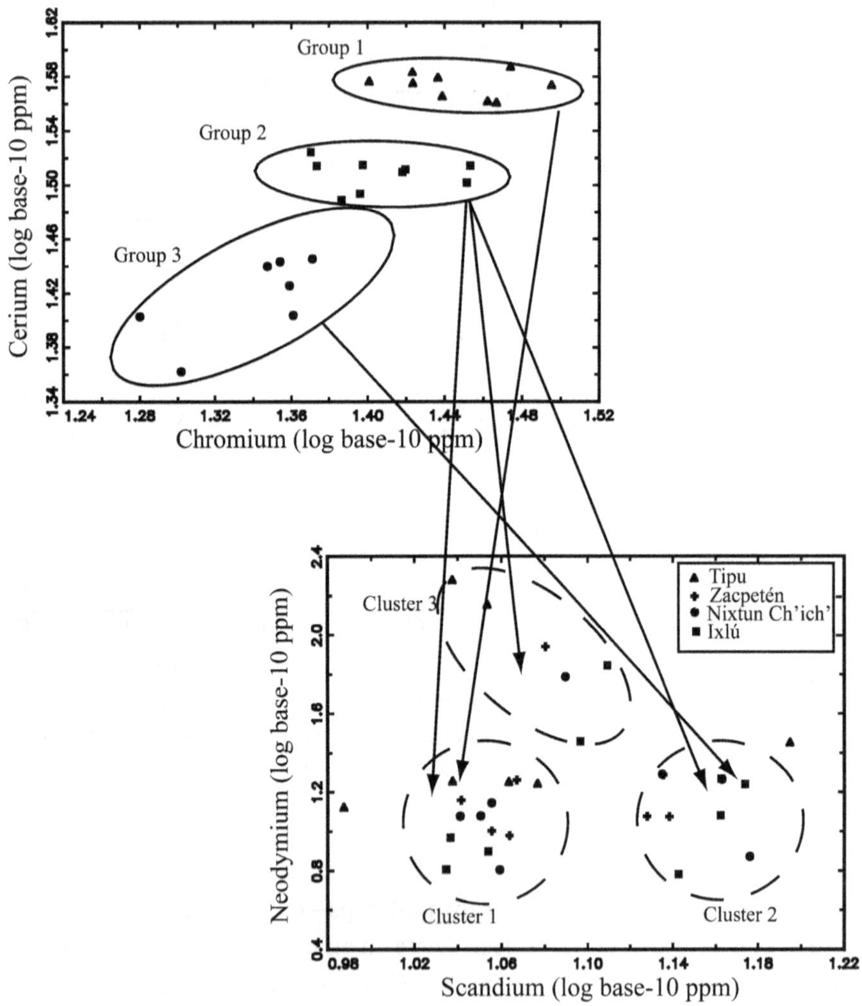

Figure 11.6. Bivariate plots of Late Postclassic period Paxcamán ceramic group pastes (*upper*) and slips (*lower*). Arrows between the plots indicate sherd associations between paste and slip confidence interval groups. Solid ellipses represent 90 percent confidence level for membership in the Paxcamán ceramic groups; dashed ellipses do not indicate confidence intervals.

manufacture (figure 11.6, lower image). Pastes of Group 2 have lower frequencies of cryptocrystalline calcite and higher amounts of iron and primarily consist of undecorated sherds from Nixtun Ch'ich' and incised sherds from Ixlú, Tipu, and Nixtun Ch'ich.' This chemical composition group demonstrates the largest variability in slips, suggesting a variety of slip recipes (all three clusters) and possible locations of production. Finally, Group 3 (pastes, upper image) lacks cryptocrystalline calcite, quartz, and iron and contains pottery from Zacpetén that is decorated with red-and-black or red-only motifs, as well as minor amounts of undecorated pottery from Ixlú and Nixtun Ch'ich.' These red and black paints are chemically distinct from those that are members of Group 1. All of the slips for Group 3 fall into Cluster 2. Therefore, potters at Zacpetén may have produced two different clay recipes used for the different decorative programs. People at Tipu may have manufactured the incised pottery (all with the *ilhuitl* motif) and traded it to Ixlú, as is suggested by the differences in pastes and slips. Additionally, two paste and slip recipes also exist that correspond to the association of the communities of Nixtun Ch'ich' and Ixlú.

Bringing It All Together

During the late Terminal Classic to Early Postclassic periods, new types of architecture and pottery indicate that new sociopolitical groups may have entered into the area (Cowgill 1963; D. Rice 1986, P. Rice 1987b, among others). Several archaeologists have stated that the Itza may have migrated to the Petén Lakes region from northern Yucatán before or during this time period. In addition to the Itza presence, the Yalain and Mopan sociopolitical groups may also have been present in the area, perhaps as remnant populations of the Late Classic inhabitants after the collapse (Boot 1997; Jones 1998). The pottery with the thick, waxy double slips and those with compact ash pastes suggest that social groups, and potters, remained in the area and continued traits of Late Classic period polychrome manufacture. While there are similarities in Early Postclassic slipping technologies to those of slate wares in northern Yucatán and the Early Postclassic potters of central Petén may have imitated northern Yucatán slipping technologies, I suggest that the stronger association is with pottery and the traditions of central Petén because the similarities go beyond slipping technology alone, to include blackened rims and decorative modes that resemble those of the Ik' polychrome pottery manufacture of Motul de San José.

There appear to have been two general manufacturing zones for the Early Postclassic period Trapeche and Fulano ceramic groups: the eastern lakes (perhaps around Zacpetén) and the western lakes (centered at Ixlú or Nixtun Ch'ich'). In addition to the Snail-Inclusion Paste Ware pottery, it is likely that the Itza, the Yalain, and/or the Mopan manufactured and traded the "new" Early Postclassic period orange-paste pottery (Vitzil Orange-red Ware) throughout the central Petén Lakes region. The distribution pattern of these wares suggests that boundaries may not have been established or enforced, and the corridor from the Petén Lakes to Tipu may not have been under any one sociopolitical group's control.

At approximately A.D. 1250, sociopolitical groups from northern Yucatán migrated to central Petén. At this same time, double slips and blackened rims drop out of the Petén Postclassic design repertoire. In general, the Kowoj arrived and occupied territory in the east and the Itza controlled territory in the west (Jones 1998).[5] The Kowoj occupied Topoxté Island and most likely Zacpetén (Pugh 2001b) at that time and produced white-paste pottery (for an extensive discussion, see Cecil 2009) with at least four different paste recipes (pastes with volcanic ash; pastes with cryptocrystalline calcite dominant; pastes with quartz, chert, chalcedony, hematite, and calcite inclusions; and pastes with quartz, chert, chalcedony, hematite, calcite, and biotite inclusions) and two decorative modes (red and red-and-black painted decoration) (Cecil 2001b, 2009).[6] In general, pottery decorated in red and red-and-black painted motifs (regardless of paste color—orange-red, gray, or white) are associated with the Kowoj and occur predominantly at Zacpetén, with lesser amounts at Tipu (Cecil 2001b). During the Late Postclassic period, Kowoj at Zacpetén were re-creating the Kowoj-specific decorative modes on gray-paste pottery (Snail-Inclusion Paste Ware, Macanche Red-on-paste, and Sacá Polychrome types). Postclassic potters also appear to have been using different slips for different decorative programs (Cecil and Neff 2006). Examination of the paste and slip clusters may permit the suggestion that a manufacturing zone existed at or around Zacpetén and that trade occurred between Zacpetén and sites to the east. In contrast, incised pottery with the *ilhuitl* glyph and thick glossy slips characteristic of Tipu manufacture appears to have been produced at Tipu and traded to the west (only as far as Ixlú). This may reflect the ethnohistorical account of the Itza temporarily losing control of Tipu and then regaining it after A.D. 1618 (Jones 1998). To the west, paste Group 2 represents pottery excavated from the archaeological sites of Nixtun Ch'ich' and Ixlú. This pottery is undecorated and represents the largest diversity in slips. Thus, the Itza appear to have utilized a larger resource base when manufacturing their pottery; alternatively, a more extensive trade may have occurred that we have not yet been able to detect.

Nevertheless, these data demonstrate that various chemical composition groups were established that reflect the differences in paste, slip, manufacturing, and trade characteristics that are associated with pottery from the archaeological sites of Nixtun Ch'ich', Ixlú, Zacpetén, and Tipu in the central Petén Lakes region. When these data are examined in light of the ethnohistorical and archaeological record, changes in manufacturing characteristics and trading patterns throughout the Postclassic period can be recognized. During the Early Postclassic period, pottery from all of the sites seems to suggest that potters in the central Petén Lakes region were making similar pottery or that trade was not restricted. In addition to similar manufacturing traditions and unrestricted trade, some potters were attempting to continue the Late Classic pottery technique of creating hard, compact pastes that were then painted with polychrome decoration and waxy slips. The Late Postclassic period is characterized by migrations of sociopolitical groups from the north as well as the manufacture of sociopolitical-group-specific decorative programs and paste groups.

While these data advance our understanding of the pottery manufacture and trade practices of the Itza and Kowoj, more research needs to be conducted to obtain a clearer view of Maya life at the time of Spanish contact. More extensive excavations at archaeological sites in Itza territory as well as analyzing possible clay and pigment raw material sources will undoubtedly better define Itza technological styles as well as further defining local trade that involved Nixtun Ch'ich', Ixlú, Zacpetén, and Tipu.

Acknowledgments

This research was funded by the National Science Foundation (Grants BCS-0228187 and SBR-9816325 [Dissertation Improvement Grant]), in part by a grant from the U.S. Department of Energy Office of Nuclear Energy, Science and Technology (Award no. DE-FG07-03ID14531) to the Midwest Nuclear Science and Engineering Consortium under the Innovations in Nuclear Infrastructure and Education program, and Proyecto Maya Colonial of Southern Illinois University–Carbondale. I would like to thank Michael D. Glascock, Hector Neff, and Prudence M. Rice for their assistance in this research project, as well as Jim Aimers for inviting me to write a chapter for this volume. I would also like to thank IDAEH for the necessary export permit. All errors and omissions are my own.

Notes

1. The fall of Chichén Itzá at approximately A.D. 1200 is currently debated given the reworking of the ceramic record. The A.D. 1200 date comes from the *Chilam Balam of Chumayel* (Edmonson 1986; Roys 1933) as well as Jones's (1998) interpretation of the eth-

nohistoric record. Until the ceramic record debates in north-central Yucatán have been resolved, I am using this date.

2. The original data set included Snail-Inclusion Paste Ware pottery as well as Vitzil Orange-red and Clemencia Cream Paste wares. One hundred exterior slips and 41 paints were analyzed. Principal components analysis was done with the total data set to allow for testing of Mahalanobis distances and chemical group memberships.

3. Many of these double-slipped sherds also have volcanic ash inclusions in the ceramic pastes.

4. In the absence of analyzing raw clay sources or minerals used in slips, the analyst can suggest possible manufacturing zones based on the provenience postulate and the criterion of relative abundance. The provenience postulate (Weigand et al. 1977: 24) can be applied to chemical compositional groups by demonstrating that there is "greater variation in chemical composition between sources than with them." The criterion of relative abundance (Bishop et al. 1982) suggests that the archaeological sites with the highest quantity of an artifact, in this case pottery, may represent the place/zone of manufacture (or stated another way, the place where a type of pottery is made most likely has the most of that pottery type in the excavations). Therefore, if one slip chemical composition group represents pottery from Ixlú and Nixtun Ch'ich' and another represents pottery from Zacpetén, it can be suggested that there are two different places of manufacture.

5. Kowoj-specific architecture at Topoxté Island dates to before A.D. 1250 (Hermes and Noriega 1997). Therefore, it is not beyond the realm of possibility that the Kowoj were established in central Petén by A.D. 1250.

6. For more information about Kowoj-specific pottery characteristics, see Cecil 2009 and Rice and Cecil 2009.

12

Mayapán's Chen Mul Modeled Effigy Censers

Iconography and Archaeological Context

SUSAN MILBRATH AND CARLOS PERAZA LOPE

Full-figure effigy censers are best known from Mayapán, a major regional capital in the lowland Maya area during the Late Postclassic period. The southern boundaries of this polity are not certain but may well have included Petén, where ceramics and architecture show some specific overlaps with Mayapán (Andrews 1984; Milbrath and Peraza 2003b: 24, fig. 1; Pugh 2003). Effigy censers found at abandoned or partially abandoned Classic and Terminal Classic period sites in the Yucatán Peninsula, such as Champotón, Cobá, Kulubá, and Edzná, are thought to indicate veneration of ancestors and ancestral Maya sites in the Late Postclassic period (Barrera et al. 2003; Benavides 1981: 98; Miller 1982: fig. 101; Millet 1992).

This article is an overview of the effigy censer type known as Chen Mul Modeled, first identified at Mayapán, the most important Maya city in the northern Maya lowlands between A.D. 1150 and 1450. As will be seen, examination of the origin and chronology of these effigy censers indicates a local origin, even though there are possible precursors at Epiclassic sites. We also discuss the archaeological context of the effigy censers in burials, ritual caches, and both ceremonial and residential structures at Mayapán, in contrast to the more limited contexts at other sites. Few imports of effigy censers from Mayapán appear at these sites, suggesting that production of effigy censers was localized. Also, Mayapán has a much larger repertoire of deities represented in effigy censers, and a number of gods from the Maya codices can be recognized. As will be seen, central Mexican deities are also depicted in the corpus, but they are much more limited in number.

Effigy censers are the most important type of ceramics found at Mayapán (figure 12.1). The Chen Mul Modeled type, originally defined by Robert Smith (1971: 206–212), is part of the Unslipped Panaba Group of Mayapan Unslipped

Figure 12.1. Mayapán Chen Mul Modeled censer representing God N. (Photo by Susan Milbrath, courtesy of INAH.)

Ware of the Tases ceramic complex (A.D. 1250/1300–1450). Smith reports that Chen Mul Modeled effigy censers constituted 45.9 percent of all the sherds in the Tases phase, indicating the dominance of effigy censers in the material excavated by the Carnegie archaeologists during the 1950s. Ceramic frequencies for more than ten seasons (1996–present) of Instituto Nacional de Antropología e Historia (INAH) excavations at Mayapán have not yet been tabulated, but we estimate that fragments of Chen Mul Modeled effigy censers represent at least 25 percent of the total ceramic deposits. Thus, even though we focus here on only one type of ceramics (Chen Mul Modeled type, Chen Mul Modeled variety), it represents the single most important type at the site. As we will see, local copies of this type were made at numerous sites throughout the Maya area. The distribution of these censers seems to overlap with regions where the Yucatecan languages (Yucatec, Lacandón, Itzaj, and Mopán) were spoken at the time of the conquest in the Yucatán Peninsula, the Guatemalan Petén, and Belize. Although linking ethnic groups with ceramic types is certainly fraught with problems, the broader censer complex we refer to elsewhere as the Chen Mul Modeled *system* (Milbrath et al. 2008) does seem to overlap with the distribution of the Yucatecan languages.

The Chen Mul Modeled type is characterized by medium- and large-sized effigy censers with figures that are attached in an upright position to a cylindrical vase with a flaring pedestal base and rim. A concave floor with openings (also found in the pedestal sides) provided a draft for burning copal, fragments of which are sometimes found on the floor along with fire-blackening marks. The figures themselves are hollow and attached at the head and buttocks to the vase. The elbows are bent, most often with hands raised and holding some form of offering. The figures are painted in multiple colors that include black, white, red, orange, yellow, blue, green, and turquoise. They have well-shaped hands with tapering fingers, usually showing fingernails. Toenails are also shown on feet with modeled toes, although occasionally the toes are merely incised. Molds were used for four basic face types to produce a variety of deity images. For example, a straight-nosed youthful face could be embellished to form the Maize God or Quetzalcoatl. Eyes usually have painted pupils, in contrast to the perforated pupils found on effigy censers from Belize, the Petén, and the coastal areas of Yucatán (Smith 1971: 212, fig. 67).

Origins and Chronology of Chen Mul Modeled

Numerous scenarios have been proposed for the origin of Chen Mul Modeled effigy censers, which first appeared in the transition between Mayapán's Hocaba and Tases phases, around A.D. 1250–1300 (Milbrath and Peraza 2003b: 7, table 1). Recent analysis of radiocarbon dates discussed below indicate that the Chen Mul Modeled type is as early as A.D. 1220–1310 (sample 32, Peraza et al. 2006: tables 1, 2). This places the development midway through the Postclassic period. Earlier precursors of the Chen Mul Modeled type have been proposed by a number of researchers.

Lamanai in Belize, a large site that had a continuous occupation from the Late Classic through the Postclassic, has early examples of effigy censers.[1] Elizabeth Graham (1987: 81–82, 85, fig. 5.b; 2004: 235, fig. 4.b) suggests that at Lamanai large standing figures attached to censers, found perhaps as early as the Buk phase (currently dated to approximately A.D. 960–A.D. 1200/1250) (Graham 2008), seem to anticipate later censers more closely resembling those of Mayapán. This is an intriguing thought, but with so few known examples from these early contexts at Lamanai, it seems premature to suggest they are predecessors of the Mayapán effigy censers. Also, there are other possible precursors to the Mayapán-style effigy censers.

Smith (1971: 205, 256) suggests that the Chen Mul Modeled censer type was introduced to Mayapán from the east coast of Yucatan, even though he notes that the entire complex of Mayapán's Tases ceramics is more closely connected to ceramics of the west coast. Full-figure effigy censers can be traced back at least to Cehpech times on the east coast, where they occur with Puuc Slate Ware at Xcaret (circa A.D. 800–1000; Smith 1971: 255). Effigy censers at other east coast sites, such as El Meco and Tulum, are dated contemporary with Chen Mul Modeled at Mayapán (Robles 1986; Sabloff et al. 1974: 412).[2]

Another possible origin point for the effigy censer form proposed by Smith (1971: 205) is in Petén. Subsequent research indicates that the effigy censer form in Petén probably does not predate the apogee of the effigy censers in the Tases phase at Mayapán (A.D. 1250/1300–1450). At Macanché, the sample of Patojo Modeled effigy censers seems to be confined to the Late Postclassic and Protohistoric (Rice 1987b: 184–87, tables 4, 6, figs. 61–64, plates XIII, XIV). Associated radiocarbon dates at Zacpetén suggest that the censers date circa A.D. 1300–1500, with the earliest sample (A.D. 1290–1430) marking the collapse of Structure 764, so the censers themselves are earlier (Pugh 2003: 420–21, figs. 8, 9, table 1). But with such a long time span for the sample, it cannot be used to demonstrate an early appearance of censers at the site.

Another source of inspiration is proposed by Raymond Sidrys (1983: 139), who notes that an interchange between the Zapotecs and Mixtecs overlaps with the appearance of effigy censers in Yucatan, and he says, "Terminal Classic Zapotec/Mixtec ritual effigy urns may have served as evolutionary prototypes for Mayapan style effigy censers." The Zapotec urn tradition of the Terminal Classic period as an inspiration for the Mayapán censers is also mentioned by Smith (1971: 255) and Marilyn Masson (2003: 197). Nonetheless, the function of Zapotec urns as funerary vessels seems entirely different from the role of effigy censers used for ritual offerings of incense.

Effigy incense burners (*xantiles*) are found as early as the Epiclassic period at Cacaxtla and Cholula (McCafferty 2007: 222, fig. 8.3). They represent a possible precursor to Mayapán effigy censers because they performed the same function and are similarly associated with altars. Xantiles belong to the Mixteca-Puebla tradition of the eastern Nahua confederacy, which linked Cholula with the Mixtecs and Zapotecs (Pohl 2007). One possible point of contact for the eastern Nahua and Yucatec Maya was in trading centers such as Xicalango in Campeche, near the border of Tabasco. Ultimately, the Epiclassic censers at sites such as Cacaxtla in Tlaxcala may be linked with Classic Maya censers from Chiapas and Tabasco that have complex figures attached to the front of the censer body (Pérez Suaréz and Zabé 1999: 66).

Masson (2003: 197) proposes an alternative source of an inspiration from the Gulf Coast. Effigy censers from Veracruz, dated on stylistic ground between A.D. 1000 and 1500, have standing figures and vessel flanges like the Mayapán censers, but the stylistic details of the figures differ and they seem more closely related to seated xantile figures from the same area, like those illustrated in the Los Angeles County Museum of Natural History's exhibition catalogue (Hammer 1971: 86–87). The development of effigy censers on the Gulf Coast may have been mediated through Tabasco and Chiapas, where we see the greatest elaboration of Late Classic effigy censers.[3] Some of the Late Classic censers have attached figures, either seated or standing, as at Palenque and Comitán in Chiapas and at Teapa and Tapijulapa in Tabasco (Pérez Suaréz and Zabé 1999: 66). And in neighboring Campeche, closer to the site of Mayapán, Late Classic effigy censers with standing figures have been found at Calakmul (Boucher and Palomo 2000: fig. 8).

In any scenario of origins, it is most important to pinpoint the earliest forms at Mayapán itself. Full-figure effigy censers may date back to the Cehpech phase at Mayapán, dated A.D. 800–1000 by Smith (1971: 255). Unfortunately, he provides no illustrations or discussion of the archaeological context of these pieces. Furthermore, Cehpech material is now dated to a longer time span, extending into the Postclassic, perhaps as late as 1250/1300 (Milbrath and Peraza 2003b: 5). Another prototype for Chen Mul Modeled effigy censers mentioned by Smith (1971: 135–36, 255) is the Hoal Modeled type characteristic of the Hocaba phase (A.D. 1100–1250/1300). They apparently predate the development of Chen Mul Modeled censers in the Hocaba-Tases transition around A.D. 1250 (Smith 1971: 135–36, 255; Milbrath and Peraza 2003b: table 1).[4]

Like Chen Mul Modeled, Hoal Modeled type effigy censers are made of Mayapan Unslipped Ware (figure 12.2; Smith 1971: 135–36, 195–96, figs. 68a2, 3).[5] The surface is embellished with low-relief modeling and some appliqué ornamentation, and a white coat of paint on the figure served as a background for painted decoration.[6] Because the Hoal Modeled effigy censers largely predate Chen Mul Modeled, the type could be a precursor of the more refined forms developed in the Tases phase.

Even though the Carnegie project linked the introduction of Chen Mul censers to changes in religious practices associated with the Cocom faction

Figure 12.2. Mayapán Hoal Modeled effigy censer. (Photo by Susan Milbrath, courtesy of Regional Museum of Anthropology, Palacio Cantón.)

and the Canul mercenaries they brought from Tabasco in Katun 1 Ahau (A.D. 1382–1401; Pollock et al. 1962: 8; Smith 1971: 256), Smith (1971: 136) proposed a date of A.D. 1300 for the introduction of Chen Mul Modeled effigy censers based on analysis of ceramic lots. Masson (2000: 258, table 6.8) originally proposed a later date for the introduction of effigy censers, coinciding with Katun 1 Ahau (1382–1401). Analysis of radiocarbon dates for Mayapán has pushed back the earliest architectural construction to the eleventh or twelfth century (just prior to Structure Q162a; Peraza et al. 2006: 158). New evidence from excavations indicates a violent event in the fourteenth century at Mayapán, and Marilyn Masson (personal communication, 2006) suggests that the introduction of Chen Mul Modeled censers is associated with this disjunction, an event dating around A.D. 1382. Nonetheless, Chen Mul Modeled effigy censers, seen as a marker for the later Tases deposits, are linked to dates as early as A.D. 1220–1310 (Sample 32) with a two-sigma range (95.4 percent probability). This date and others suggest that the earliest possible introduction of Chen Mul Modeled at the site would be around A.D. 1250, and the weight of evidence suggests an association with new Cocom-Itza religious practices (Milbrath and Peraza 2009: 190).[7]

Archaeological Context and Use of Chen Mul Modeled Censers

Censers are found associated with a wide variety of contexts at Mayapán, including burial cists, ceremonial middens, and caches found in ceremonial structures and a few residential constructions (Smith 1971: 106–9, 112). Censers were rare in residential contexts, and when found they invariably were in burials. Censer caches are associated with altars in colonnaded halls, shrines, round structures, and pyramid temples (Adams 1953: 149; Peraza et al. 2006: table 2). Censers in pyramid temples were renewed over time, such that fragments of multiple figures have been found. The archaeological contexts for Chen Mul Modeled effigy censers at Mayapán are quite varied, but censer use was not practiced uniformly across Mayapán (Peraza and Masson 2005; Masson and Peraza 2012). Generally more than one censer was found in ceremonial structures, except for Structure Q89, a skull platform (or *tzompantli*) that had a single censer representing an aged god that may be Itzamna (Masson and Peraza 2006, 2012).

The Monkey Scribe censer found behind the temple of Structure Q58 may have been the focus of worship in this temple around the time of a revolt that ended Mayapán's tenure as a political capital around A.D. 1450 (Milbrath and Peraza 2003a, 2003b). Other effigy censers are known from this structure, but the Monkey Scribe was the only one found nearly intact. It probably was displayed in this temple before it was removed from the altar and thrown down during the revolt.

Individual burials and mass burials (ossuaries) contain fragmentary effigy censers that may have served some funerary function, as at Santa Rita (D. Chase and A. Chase 1988: 51, fig. 26). In contrast to the burial practices at Santa Rita, many effigy censers at Mayapán were not complete when placed in the graves (Masson 2000: 239; Thompson 1957: 602).[8] In one rapidly abandoned residential structure (R86), however, a burial cist was reopened and complete censers were deposited along with other ritual paraphernalia (Masson and Peraza 2006). Burial Cist 2 in Structure R86 included censers representing Xipe, Tlazolteotl, and the Diving God, suggesting foreign contact through east coast trade routes, but there were also more conservative Maya deities represented, such as Chac and Itzamna (Peraza and Masson 2005; Masson and Peraza 2012). The burial of so many censers is unlike the situation in the central area of the site, where censers were displayed in groupings in structures around the Central Plaza.

Some colonnades have groups of censers arranged in front of the altar. Seven censers were found in situ grouped around an altar in Structure Q81; although broken, most could be completely reconstructed (Smith 1971: fig. 67). In contrast, the altar of another colonnade (Structure Q54) excavated by the INAH project in the 2003 season had a group of four censer figures in front of the altar, but there were a large number of missing pieces. The censers were probably broken elsewhere and set up in a fragmentary condition in front of the Q54 altar. Among this group (Lot MY-03-2190) there was a skeletal god and a deity standing on a turtle, as well as a "step-eyed" god (figures 12.3, 12.4). Originally, investigators believed that only four censers were in the group (Lot MY-03-2190; Milbrath 2007a; Peraza et al. 2004: 19, foto 14). It now appears that there were at least seven, with three more censers found near the altar: a censer representing Quetzalcoatl-Kukulcan (Lot MY-03-2035) and two other fragmentary censers with this same lot number.[9]

In Structure Q64 (Sala de los Incensarios), excavated in the 1999–2000 field season, the lower portion of four figures and their pedestal bases were found in front of the altar, along with fragments that indicate they had been broken intentionally (Peraza et al. 2003a: 18, foto 39). Another fragmentary censer found nearby represents an old god broken in situ (Lot MY-99-0268, quadrant 8-N [Peraza et al. 2003a: foto 41]). There are at least ten censer bases linked with Structure Q64, but many were so fragmentary that the associated figures could not be reconstructed (quadrants 8-O, 9-O, 10-O [Peraza et al. 2003a: fotos 42–44]). It is possible that they were broken elsewhere and only some fragments were deposited in Structure Q64.

Censers found in midden deposits are so fragmentary that they probably were smashed in one location and the sherds were dumped in another place (Adams 1953: 146; Masson and Peraza 2012; Smith 1971: 111–12, table 22). Smashing censers might be related to fabrication of new censers. One colonial period source recounts that new clay "idols" were made using ground-up fragments from older ones, thereby transferring the power of the deity image (Chuchiak 2009: 146).

Effigy censers found broken in situ on the top of structures or widely dis-

Figure 12.3. Step-eyed Maize God from Structure Q54, Mayapán (Lot MY-03-2109). (Photo by Susan Milbrath, courtesy of INAH.)

tributed in ceremonial middens seem to provide evidence of cyclical renewal ceremonies. Censers were not only containers for burned offerings of copal to communicate with the gods but also apparently played a role as idols in calendric ceremonies (Thompson 1957: 601; Tozzer 1941: 161, note 827). Their link with calendar rituals can be deduced from study of ethnohistorical evidence

Figure 12.4. Skeletal deity from Structure Q54, Mayapán (Lot MY-03-2109). (Photo by Susan Milbrath, courtesy of INAH.)

and the context of the censers. Broken censers found sealed in the different renovations of the Serpent Temple on top of the Castillo (Q162) provide evidence for renewal ceremonies or other forms of calendric rituals described by Friar Diego de Landa. Landa says that it was the custom that each idol should have its own brazier, and he notes that they performed a ceremony to renovate the clay braziers during the festival of Yax, when Chac was honored and the priests consulted the prognostications of the Bacabs (Tozzer 1941: 161). During another renewal ceremony in the festival of Pop, the first "month" (*veintena*) of the year, the priests of Chac lit a new fire to burn incense in braziers (Tozzer 1941: 151–52). Effigy censers may also have been used in the ceremonies marking the year end (Uayeb) that were integrated with the New Year ceremonies (Masson 2000: 241; Tozzer 1941: 136–49).

Chen Mul Modeled effigy vessels that are not incense burners may have been used in year-end rituals. A number of well-preserved effigy vessels have been found in caches (Smith 1971: fig. 64a–d, i–o; Peraza et al. 2003a: 136). At Santa Rita, Diane and Arlen Chase (1988: 72) interpret cache deposits of modeled figures (Kol Modeled) as offerings made during the Uayeb rites that were cached because they could not be reused once the offering was made, in accord with Landa's account of Uayeb rites (Tozzer 1941: 166).

Based on Landa's description of *katun* idols, some of the effigy censers may have served as markers for longer periods of time (D. Chase and A. Chase 1988: 72; Tozzer 1941: 166–69). Landa notes that there were actually two katun idols, and the older idol eventually fell into disuse and was taken away. Apparently after the censers were replaced by new effigies, the old ones were reverently disposed of once they had completed their ritual cycle, much as is seen in the case of contemporary Lacandón practice (McGee 1998: 42–45). Identical paired effigy censers have been found in the recent excavations of Mayapán in two adjacent contexts, with an almost complete example found in Q152a and a virtual duplicate found in a more fragmentary state buried nearby between Q151 and Q152a. Similarly, at Santa Rita, pairs of effigy censers included one almost complete example and another more fragmentary effigy, suggestive of the paired katun idols described by Landa (D. Chase and A. Chase 1988: 85). This is further supported by the fact that one pair was associated with an altar where katun ceremonies may have been performed.

External Contacts Evident in the Distribution of Effigy Censers

Comparing the censers from the center with those from the periphery yields information about the nature of the censer cult as it spread throughout the lowland Maya area in the Postclassic period.[10] Censers at other sites are most often associated with pyramid temples or shrines, in contrast to those of Mayapán, which are more widely distributed.

Censers appear at a number of sites that had their apogee in an earlier period, representing offerings made at time when only a small population resided at or near the site. Censers were found associated with a Postclassic shrine constructed on top of earlier structures at both Champotón and Cobá (Folan et al. 2003; Navarrete et al. 1979:78). Effigy censers at Chichén Itzá are found as late offerings in Terminal Classic and Early Postclassic pyramid temples, principally in the Osario and the Templo de las Mesas, located alongside the Temple of the Warriors (Schmidt 1994, 2006). At Chichén Itzá, there is evidence of a small Late Postclassic population associated with pilgrimage routes to the site. Chichén was never totally abandoned, and the censers were surely locally produced, because they have a distinctive style and iconography.

One Classic period site thought to have been abandoned proved to have Postclassic residential structures and censer workshops. At Dzibanché in Quintana Roo, censers found largely intact in collapsed buildings were originally thought to be offerings brought by pilgrims, but recently Postclassic houses and a significant occupation have been found (Nalda and López Camacho 1995; Nalda 2005: 246n7). Large deposits of smashed censers indicate use in rituals elsewhere at the site, and some of the censers seem to have been buried after being broken (Nalda, personal communication 2005). This may be the case at Lamanai as well (Aimers, personal communication 2009). These ceremonial deposits, like those at Mayapán, may be compared with ritual dumps of censer fragments that are apparently related to calendric rituals in Belize (D. Chase and A. Chase 1988; Russell 2000).

Trade and pilgrimage routes linked Mayapán to the coastal regions of Yucatán and Belize and to the inland Maya area of the Petén Lakes region, where Postclassic effigy censers are relatively abundant (Bullard 1970; Milbrath et al. 2008; Pugh 2002; Rice 1987b).[11] Zacpetén and Topoxté both show specific overlaps with Mayapán in terms of architecture and effigy censers (Pugh 2003; see also Cecil, this volume). Molds for making censers have been recovered from Macanché Island and also from sites on Lake Quexil and Lake Salpetén (Rice 1987b: 203, fig. 68), indicating local manufacture. At Topoxté, the censers were found in a terraced temple known as Structure C (Bullard 1970: 278, figs. 4, 18), and a similar context is evident at Zacpetén, where they were also found associated with temples (Structures 605 and 764; Pugh 2003: 420–22, figs. 9, 11).

Formal and stylistic differences are notable when comparing effigy censers from other sites with those of Mayapán. The censers of Mayapán are generally larger (averaging 50 centimeters high) than those from other sites, with the possible exception of Champotón. At Mayapán, censers representing the eyes with painted pupils are more common, whereas censers depicting pupils with punched holes are characteristic of sites in Belize, the Petén, and also Champotón (Sidrys 1983; Milbrath et al. 2008). Even though William Bullard (1970: 304, figs. 18–22) noted only minor differences between the effigy censers of Mayapán, Quintana Roo, and Topoxté, the examples he illustrates from Topoxté on Lake Yaxhá and those from the Petén Lakes region (Mancanché on Lake Macanché and Punta Nimá on Lake Petén-Itza, and Zacpetén on Lake Salpetén) are sufficiently different that they are now identified as a distinct ceramic type (Patojo Modeled; Pugh 2003: fig. 8; Rice 1987b: 184–92, fig. 61).

Generally, the Petén effigy censers that are more complete have the arms held out at chest height, with relatively crude, clawlike hands, whereas the Mayapán figures are most often posed with the upper arms by the figure's side and the elbows bent and lower arms extended with finely modeled hands. Petén examples show the eyes rimmed all the way around, most often without apparent eyelids, and they tend to be oval in shape with deep punctures for the pupils, unlike the more naturalistic eye forms of Mayapán. The costuming is repetitive, most often featuring a mat pectoral, an element known from the Mayapán repertoire but certainly not the dominant costume feature at the site.[12]

Effigy censers from Tulum have been described as almost identical to Chen Mul Modeled examples (Sabloff et al. 1974: 412), but they are generally smaller and more crude than those from Mayapán, and they have a distinctive paste (Tulum Buff Paste). The east coast examples also lack the calcareous coat that serves as a ground for multiple colors seen among the few known examples of small effigy censers at Mayapán (Smith 1971: 208).

Although the type designation of Chen Mul Modeled has been applied to ceramics from Champotón and El Meco (Forsyth 2004: 33; Robles 1986: fotos 42–44), these effigy censers seem to be a local expression of a broader style that we identify as the Chen Mul Modeled system (Milbrath et al. 2008; for more on systems, see Aimers and Graham, this volume; Bill, this volume; and Rice, this volume). Champotón has a local effigy censer tradition that evokes Mayapán, even though trace element analysis indicates that the censers were locally made (Forsyth 2004; Bishop et al. 2006). The quality of the Champotón effigies is somewhat inferior to those at Mayapán. There are specific stylistic differences, especially in the rudimentary treatment of hands and feet; nonetheless, Champotón censers are closely related to those of both Mayapán and Lamanai (Milbrath et al. 2008: figs. 6–9).[13]

Censers from Mayapán represent a wider range of deities than are found at other lowland Maya sites. Analysis of the distribution of different deities at outlying sites is preliminary, but some patterning is clearly evident. The Maize

God is relatively common at Mayapán and Chichén Itzá, but the Merchant God and associated depictions of cacao so plentiful at Mayapán are not evident at Chichén Itzá (Milbrath et al. 2008). The Diving God, appearing at various sites in Quintana Roo (Martos 2002: 33; Nalda and López Camacho 1995), is rare at Mayapán, with only four examples known to date (Masson and Peraza 2012). At Zacpetén, the predominant deity seems to be Chac, whereas at Mayapán this god is relatively scarce and the deity most commonly represented is Itzamna (Pugh 2004; Thompson 1957: 622). Itzamna is also the predominant figure in the effigy censers of Santa Rita, although figures of Chac, God K, Xipe, and Quetzalcoatl have also been identified in collections from the site (Nielsen and Anderson 2004: 84). At Champotón, there are some overlaps with Mayapán, such as the Death God, the Merchant God, and a warrior god with a shield, but the range of figures that can be identified as specific deities seems more restricted. This site also includes a number of representations of Tlaloc, a deity not known among the censers of Mayapán, even though Tlaloc-Chac combinations are known from smaller effigy cups (Milbrath et al. 2008; Taube 1992: fig. 73b, c). Despite the absence of Tlaloc in the effigy censers of Mayapán, there are a number of effigy censers representing other deities prominent in central Mexico (Taube 1992: figs. 63a, 64a, 65a, 66a, 68c; Thompson 1957).

One feature that seems to be shared broadly among the effigy censers in the lowland area is the braided breastplate, seen on a number of examples from Petén, Belize, and Mayapán. Merideth Paxton (2004: 107) compares this "necklace" to an image on Madrid Codex 21c and to a painted image on Structure 16 at Tulum. This breastplate sometimes appears combined with an oval pectoral, as in an example from Dzibanché identified as Itzamna (Nalda and López Camacho 1995: 23), but at Mayapán this feature is apparently associated with imagery of God N (figure 12.1), as discussed in the next section, which focuses on the deities represented at Mayapán, where the closest counterparts to the gods of the codices are to be found.

Iconography of Mayapán's Effigy Censers

Chen Mul Modeled effigy censers were clearly idols at Mayapán, representing a new form of worship because earlier censers largely lacked representations of deities (Smith 1971: 255). They reflect both a religious change and expanding trade contacts beginning around A.D. 1250. The effigy censer cult apparently spread in association with the Cocoms, a faction of the Itzas at Mayapán who claimed descent from Kukulkan and built temples modeled on those of Chichén Itzá (Masson 2000; Milbrath and Peraza 2003b, 2009).

Some of Mayapán's Chen Mul Modeled censers are linked with Postclassic deities represented in codices from central Mexico, while others relate to Postclassic Maya codices and murals from Maya sites such as Tulum and Santa Rita (figures 12.1, 12.3, 12.4; Boucher and Palomo 2005; Milbrath and Peraza 2003a, 2003b; Taube 1992; Thompson 1957: 608–12). And at least nine Mayapán censers represent Xipe, a central Mexican god who is distinguished by closed eyes shaped like crescents and by flayed skin, which is most easily seen on the arms (Peraza and Masson 2005; Masson and Peraza 2012). Even though Karl Taube (1992: 105–12, 121–22, figs. 56, 64) suggests that Xipe may be linked with the Maya God Q, he makes it clear that the closest central Mexican counterpart for God Q is seen in a complex of blindfolded gods who are quite separate from the Xipe complex.

The roster of Maya deities represented by censer figures includes at least ten different gods known from the Maya codices, with the most common being representations of Chac (God B), Itzamna (God D), the Death God (God A), the Maize God (God E), and the Merchant God (God M). Some of the aged deities may actually be God N, who has a quadripartite aspect as a Pauahtun. The Pauahtun in Landa's account of Uayeb ceremonies is a counterpart for the opossum in the Dresden Codex (pages 25–28 [Thompson 1972]). The four opossum Mams in the Dresden Codex Uayeb pages are closely related to God N, a quadripartite god associated with the yearbearers (Taube 1989). God N is also among the katun images represented on page 6 of the Paris Codex.

Images of God N may not be common among the censers of Mayapán, but there are at least two examples that possibly formed a set of katun idols, as noted previously. One old god effigy vessel apparently representing a Pauahtun was found in Structure Q152a, and a duplicate figure was found nearby (figure 12.1). The aged god wears a mat pectoral with an oval shell at the center representing the Mexican *oyohualli*, a rattling pendant made of mussel shell (figure 12.1).[14] The clawed toes of the Mayapán effigy figure resemble an opossum, the animal alter ego of God N (Taube 1989, 1992: 92–99). The Uayeb pages of the Dresden Codex depict an opossum on page 26 wearing a braided breastplate with an oyohualli pectoral that is virtually identical to that of the censer figure (figures 12.1 and 12.5). This is the only representation of the oyohualli pectoral with a braided breastplate in the surviving Maya codices.[15] Other examples of the oyohualli on the interlaced breastplate are known from fragments of censers at Mayapán (Smith 1971: figs. 73c1, c2) and the representations of aged deities from sites such as Santa Rita (D. Chase and A. Chase 1988: fig. 26a). The interlaced breastplate on effigy censer figures has been interpreted as cotton armor worn by warriors, but its appearance on elderly gods and on the opossum Pauahtun of the Dresden Codex would seem to invalidate this interpreta-

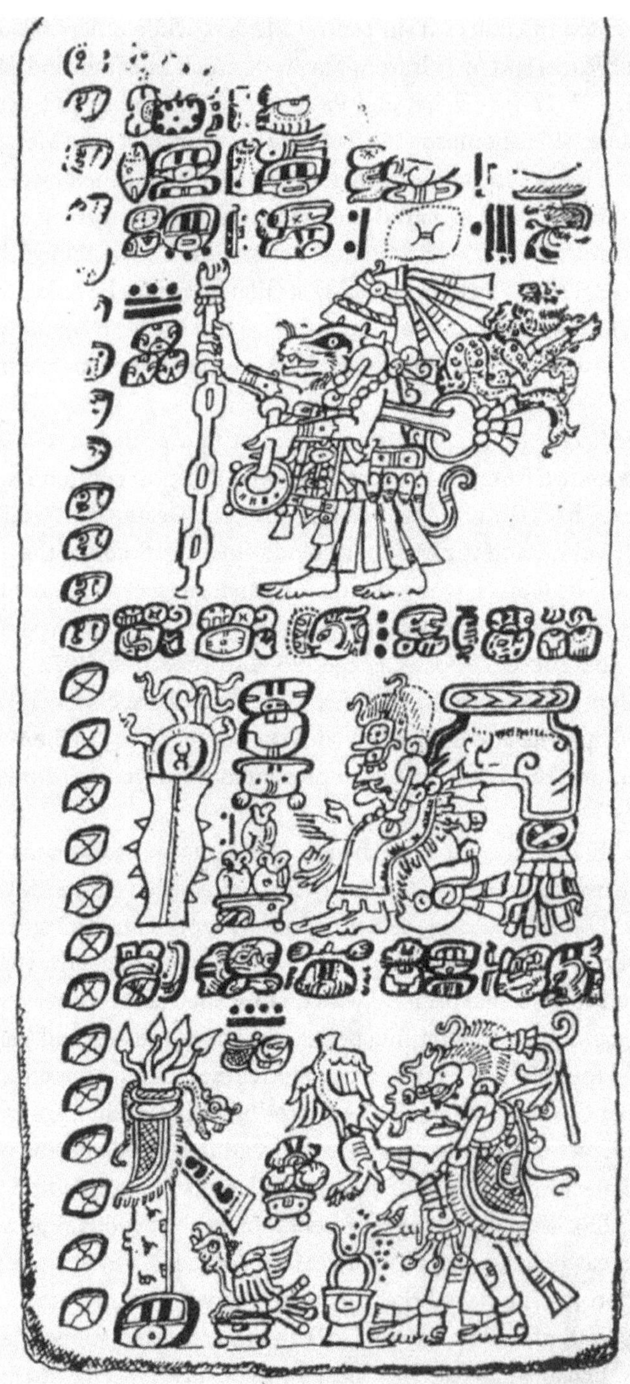

Figure 12.5. Dresden Codex 26 [56], Opossum or Mam wearing an oyohualli on a braided breastplate in the Uayeb ceremonies preceding the New Year. (After Villacorta and Villacorta 1976.)

tion, especially because it is never seen on armed figures in the codices. The toothless (aged) God N never appears to be armed in the codices. None of the armed figures, be they warriors or hunters, wear the braided cotton pectoral, and the lack of an association with warrior imagery argues against identifying this form as cotton armor.[16]

The aged Itzamna is represented frequently in the censers of Mayapán (Thompson 1957: 622). He may be linked with the central direction in the Madrid Codex cosmogram (75–76), where the creator couple is seated beneath a stylized world tree symbolizing the ceiba. A connection with incense burners and the symbolism of ceibas is made more explicit in a colonial period source that says incense was burned beneath the ceiba in the center of village plazas in Yucatán (Vásquez 1941: 84–88). In the codices, Itzamna is the counterpart of God D, who is sometimes shown in the katun ceremonies, as on Paris Codex 11. God B and God N represented among Mayapán's effigy censers also find parallels in the Paris Codex katun pages.[17] There are, however, many Mayapán censers representing enigmatic gods, a situation parallel to that in the Madrid Codex Uayeb pages, where a number of deities are not easily identified.

Among the gods of the year-end ceremonies (the Uayeb) in the codices, a number are related to figures represented in censers. These include a black god (God M?), God A, and God E (all associated with the Cauac Yearbearer dates on Codex Madrid page 34); God E is also associated with the Kan Yearbearers on page 35. God A, God E, and God D in the Uayeb pages of the Dresden Codex (25–28) all relate to censer deities identified at Mayapán. Arranged vertically from top to bottom in the sequence proposed by the Brickers (Bricker and Bricker 2011: table 6.1), Dresden Codex page 25 represents God K (or God B?), God K, and God G (or God D?) associated with the Ben Yearbearers; page 26 depicts Chac Bolay (a jaguar), God G, and God K associated with Etznab Yearbearers (figure 12.5); page 27 shows God E, God D, and God A with the Akbal Yearbearers; and page 28 has God A, God A', and God D with the Lamat Yearbearers). In the Dresden Codex, the first of each set (on top of the page) are "burdens" carried by opossums (counterparts for God N?) in the Uayeb year-end ceremonies.

The Madrid Codex (63c–64c) shows a series of six gods attached to vessels that look very much like effigy censers (Graff 1997). They represent gods known from the repertoire of Mayapán censers (Peraza and Masson 2005). Based on their glyphic names and traits, Donald Graff (1997: 162, fig. 5-17) identifies the Madrid Codex deities as Itzamna (God D), the Death God (Ah Cimil or God A), possibly God N, an Akbal variant of God A (probably God A'), God R wearing God N's headdress, and another representation of Itzamna, although the name glyph does not confirm this identification and the beard suggests instead a link with the aged Sun God (God G) represented on Codex Madrid 108b (Taube 1992: fig. 22b). God A and God D are well represented among Mayapán's effigy censers, and God N is also found among the corpus.

Position and Relationships between Different Chen Mul Gods

Groups of censer figures are known from several colonnades, providing evidence of positioning of different deities in relation to one another. Structure Q54, a colonnade on the west side of the Central Plaza (quadrant 10-J) excavated in the 2003 season, has a group of at least seven censers with four positioned in front of the altar (Peraza et al. 2004: 19, foto 15). The censer on the north side of this group represents a fragmentary figure standing on a turtle. Positioned directly to the south is the Death God (God A), with skeletal ribs (figure 12.4). The adjacent censer (to the south) is too fragmentary to be identified. The censer farthest to the south in the group of four depicts a god with a stepped cutout that replaces his eyes and cheeks, and face paint that is blue with darker blue dots that may be numbers (figure 12.3). Nearby, the excavators found a headless effigy censer with a spiral wind shell diagnostic of central Mexican images of Quetzalcoatl, very much like the more complete example found in Structure Q81 (Smith 1971: fig. 67a). Two other censers found in quadrant 10-J include a bearded figure with hollow eye sockets and fangs, perhaps representing the Sun God (God G), and a god whose fragmentary face has twined cord earrings. Similar earrings appear on images of Chac represented on a lidded effigy vessel found in a cache in Mayapán Structure Q164 (Shook and Irving 1955: fig. 7m; Smith 1971: fig. 63a) and on an effigy censer depicting Chac found at El Meco (Martos 2002: 32). The twined cord earrings might be a diagnostic trait of Chac (God B).

Perhaps the most interesting in the altar group is the figure with a stepped facial cutout and maize foliation on the headdress (figure 12.3). The youthful features and maize foliation suggest that the censer figure represents the Maize God (God E). This figure has a counterpart in the Madrid Codex (27a–28a) where five gods with stepped designs on their cheeks have maize foliation in their headdresses. The five gods all have a vertical column of numbers on their bodies, with black numbers representing intervals read bottom to top (9, 4, 8, 5, in solid black) and red numbers the *tzolkin* coefficients (9, 13, 8, 13, outlined in black to represent red). The black numbers represent intervals that total 26 days, the appropriate intervals for the red tzolkin coefficients found interspersed between the black numbers (compare figure 12.6). Reading from bottom to top, the numbers are the same on all the figures. Adding the interval 9 to any date bearing the coefficient 13 will yield a date with the coefficient 9,

Figure 12.6. Madrid Codex 74, Step-eyed Maize Gods. (After Villacorta and Villacorta 1976.)

the first of the red coefficients on the bottom of the column on the Madrid Codex figures. Adding the next interval in black, 4, brings the count to the red coefficient of 13, which is the next number in the red tzolkin sequence. The following interval in black, 8, results in a day with the red coefficient 8; adding the last interval in black, 5, brings the coefficient back to 13. At this point, the count cycles on to the adjacent figures, each associated with a 26-day period, for a total of 5 × 26 days in the Madrid sequence (130 days total). A similar set of five gods appears on Codex Madrid 73–74a with well-preserved numbers and glyphic names (figure 12.6). The numbers are also to be read from bottom to top, with black numbers marking the same intervals of 9, 4, 8, and 5, which alternate with red numbers that record the appropriate tzolkin coefficients of 9, 13, 8, and 13. The text on Madrid 74a contains five pairs of glyphic collocations that identify each of the associated figures as the Maize God, with the first pair of collocations read as *nal u kuh*, meaning "God E is the deity" (Victoria Bricker, personal communication 2010).

On the step-eyed maize god censer, traces of paint on the cheeks may be effaced numbers, suggesting another link with the Madrid Codex deities. An intriguing detail on the step-faced censer figure is an earring depicted in the form of a luminous ray, a costume element worn by lunar goddesses associated with maize in the Tulum murals (Milbrath 1999: 148; Miller 1982: plate 28).

In Structure Q81, a colonnaded hall on the north side of the main plaza, a well-preserved effigy censer representing Quetzalcoatl-Kukulcan was found among a group of seven effigy censers (Cache 33, Late Lot C72). The censers in Cache 33 are the most complete grouping known to date (Smith 1971: fig. 67). They were arranged in a pattern around the altar with three cached objects aligned north–south (figure 12.7).[18] The large effigy censer (68 centimeters high) depicting Quetzalcoatl-Kukulcan was on the east side of the entry, and a smaller figure (40.5 centimeters high) of a warrior with a shield was on the west side (figure 12.7, #3, #4; Smith 1971: figs. 67a, e).[19] This warrior may be another form of Venus god, in which case two different Venus gods guarded the entry to the altar shrine in Q81.

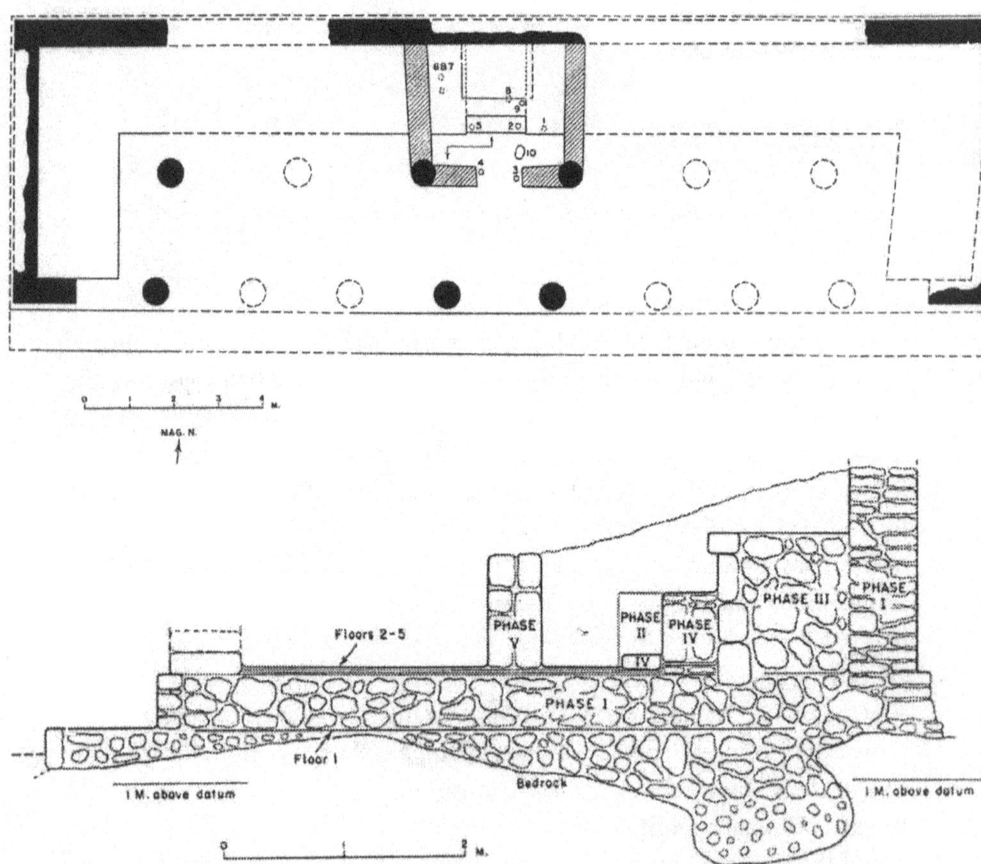

Figure 12.7. Location of effigy censers and other figures in Cache 33, Lot C72 in Structure Q81. (After Winters 1955: fig. 1.)

The pair of gods located at the center of the altar are identified by Eric Thompson (1957: 606–8, 615–16) as the Maize God and Chac (figure 12.7, #2, #5; Smith 1971: figs. 67b, d; Winters 1955: fig. 3c, d, h, i). The pair on the northwest side of the Q81 shrine represents Itzamna, an old god with a flowered headband, paired with the whiskered Merchant God (Figure 12.7, #6, #7; Smith 1971: fig. 67c, f; Thompson 1957: 604–10).[20] This figure closely resembles another whiskered god from the east side of the shrine that probably represents a second image of the Merchant God (Figure 12.7, #1; Smith 1971: fig. 68b6).

Both whiskered deities wear a bird headdress and headband with two rows of beads and a third row of oval shapes that could represent shells or cacao (a beaded headband is also found on God N; see figure 12.1). A bird headdress, whiskers, and a beard appear on another censer depicting the Merchant God, which is more easily identified as the Merchant God by his prominent Pinocchio nose (Smith 1971: fig. 68b9; Thompson 1957: fig. 1e). Structure Q54 also had a whiskered god with a beard, possibly another representation of the Merchant God, although the bird headdress is lacking.

An effigy censer representing a Monkey Scribe excavated at the base of Structure Q58 clearly blends traits of Maya and central Mexican deities (Milbrath and Peraza 2003a: figs. 1–2). The Monkey Scribe is well known in Maya art (Coe 1978); however, traits such as the flowered headband suggest links with the central Mexican monkey god associated with artisans, an animal alter ego of Xochipilli, the "prince of flowers" (Milbrath and Peraza 2003a: 122). This censer figure has numbers on his tongue and on the vegetal scrolls that flank the figure. The numbers represent 20-day intervals appropriate to a Uinal count, and they are clearly related to gods shown with "number trees" in the codices (Milbrath and Peraza 2003a).

A sample of 265 censers was plotted in the context of different architectural complexes to determine differing frequencies, and some clear patterns emerged (Peraza and Masson 2005; Masson and Peraza 2010). In this sample, the most common gods represented are the Maize God, Chac (God B), the Merchant God (God M), Itzamna (God D), and an old god of uncertain identity. There was a concentration of Venus gods in a group on the Central Plaza comprising Structures Q79, 79a, Q80, and Q81 (Peraza and Masson 2005). The Venus gods can be linked to Tlahuizcalpantecuhtli, a deity known from central Mexican codices. Xipe is also fairly common, as are female effigies (some identified only by hair parted in the center).

Carnegie excavations recovered only two effigy censers portraying Tlazolteotl and nine of Xipe, and recent excavations have found no more examples of Mexican deities, so foreign deities remain about 3.8 percent of the total sample of censers (Masson and Peraza 2010: 6, fig. 11, table 2). Thompson (1957: 621) noted that two elite residences (Q208 and R86) had a concentration of central Mexican deities. Two figures of Xipe and one of Tlazolteotl were found in Lot A110 in Structure R-86, an elite residence that also had Mexican artifacts (Thompson 1957: figs. 2a, 2b, 4g; Smith 1971: fig. 68b10).[21] Tlazolteotl and Xipe, often represented in the central Mexican codices, are also seen in Mayapán's stucco sculptures on Structure Q163, which is a late addition to the Castillo (Milbrath and Peraza 2003b: figs. 19, 21a, table 1). The period of contact with central Mexico probably began in the Tases phase (Milbrath and Peraza 2003b: 30; Milbrath 2005).[22] Study of the central Mexican deities suggests that foreign influences in the censer cult came as a result of trade contact with the central highlands that apparently peaked around Phase II of the Aztec Templo Mayor (A.D. 1375–1420). This interchange involved trade in Maya blue to central Mexico (Milbrath and Peraza 2003b: 30).[23]

Final Remarks

Sites actively occupied in the Late Postclassic period have large deposits of smashed censers and groups of effigy censers associated with altars and burials. Clearly, effigy censers were used in many forms of ceremonies, including funerary rites and calendric rituals. The effigy censer form is most highly developed at Mayapán, where these censers are most numerous and varied. There is also some evidence of chronological changes in the effigy forms at Mayapán. The origins of the effigy censer cult remain uncertain, but possible prototypes appear at Mayapán in the Early Postclassic and the precursors may be found in the eastern Nahua zone of Puebla and Tlaxcala during the Epiclassic. This area may have been in close contact with Tabasco through trade, which served as a repository for Maya traditions that cycled through the eastern Nahua area and back to the Maya area in the Postclassic, perhaps via Veracruz.

Mayapán effigy censers predominantly represent Maya deities, but many are not easily linked with gods in the Maya codices. Nonetheless, because numerous deities in the codices have not been identified under the standard system developed by Paul Schellhas and expanded by Taube (1992), it may be that further study of the more obscure deities in the codices will result in more overlaps with the censer figures of Mayapán, such as the Maize God represented with a stepped face that has been identified here for the first time. With the exception of Tlaloc-Chac combinations, central Mexican deities represented in effigy censers are confined to Mayapán, indicating that this site served as the primary point of exchange with the greater central Mexican area.

Regional thematic traits or iconographic clusters also seem to be evident, such as the prevalence of the Diving God on the east coast and the Tlaloc images at Champotón. Many Late Postclassic sites seem to have a recognizable local or regional style of effigy censers, as in the case of the Late Postclassic Petén and Champotón. The Chen Mul Modeled system effigy censers reflect an integration of the Postclassic world through ideology and trade. Rituals incorporating effigy censers linked distant sites, and these objects of reverence may have occasionally been physically moved among sites. The intriguing evidence of intersite contact seen in the censer complex is rich territory for further study. Indeed, someday it may be possible to test Marilyn Masson's (2000: 262) hypothesis that local leaders controlled the development of the censer cult because the effigies seem to be increasingly generic farther away from Mayapán.

Acknowledgments

Our thanks to the Foundation for the Advancement of Mesoamerican Studies, Inc., for funding the study of the Mayapán censers (Grant no. 05025, 2005–6). We also thank the Mexican National Institute of Anthropology and History (INAH) for permission to photograph pieces from Mayapán, Champotón and other sites with effigy censers. Sylviane Boucher and Yoly Palomo of the Ceramoteca, Centro INAH, Yucatán, and Blanca Gonzaléz, director of the Regional Museum of Anthropology, Palacio Cantón, were very helpful during the process of photography. We also acknowledge the contributions of the team of archaeologists working at Mayapán, especially Wilberth Cruz Alvarado, whose help was invaluable. Our thanks go also to Victoria Bricker for commenting on discussions related to the codices.

Notes

1. In comparison with those of Belize, the Mayapán examples are larger, more colorful, and more impressive (Sidrys 1983: 262–65). Although most Belizean examples seem to lack a calcareous coat with surface painting, remnants of this coating appear on the Lamanai examples, suggesting that the coating may not be preserved in the more humid southern areas (Aimers, personal communication 2009).

2. Effigy censer sherds at the east coast site of El Meco, generally confined to the upper two levels at the site, are linked to the Tases complex, contemporary with the Tases phase at Mayapán (Robles 1986: tables 1–6, fotos 42–44). They are quite similar to those from Mayapán, although the figures are generally smaller. The paste seems to be different and the proportions make the figures seem squat in the few published examples of whole censer figures from El Meco (Martos 2002: 32).

3. Late Classic effigy censers in Chiapas have wide flanges and complex decoration with a maximum of seven tiered figures, but by the Postclassic wide flanges atrophied and the tiered deities telescoped into a single image (Goldstine 1977: 409). Tiered censers from

Palenque were actually censer stands for deep conical containers used for burning incense to communicate with the gods and ancestors, and the figures symbolize the cosmic tree forming an *axis mundi* (Cuevas and Bernal 2002; Rice 1999; Rands et al. 1979: 21). Study of censers from the Palenque region indicate that censers with standing figures are generally later and may be related to stone censers from Balankanche, near Chichén Itzá, some of which represent figures with attributes of Xipe Totec (Rands et al. 1979: 23).

4. Smith's (1971) analysis suggests that Hoal Modeled was found in middle lots (transitional Hocaba between and Tases) and was later replaced by Chen Mul Modeled effigy censer forms in the Tases phase (Lots C88–C93; Shook and Irving 1955; Smith 1971: fig. 68a). There are, however, very few examples of the type illustrated, two from the Middle Lot C90, and at least one is said to be from a Late Lot (C94; Smith 1971: fig. 68a).

5. The censer in figure 12.2 was found in Lot C90 with a Cehac-Hunacti composite-type pedestal censer with appliqué spikes, a type most typical of the Hocaba phase at Mayapán (Milbrath and Peraza 2003:7, fig. 2; Smith 1971: fig. 31b), resembling the ones depicted in the Madrid Codex (36b and 60a) and Dresden Codex 26b [56b] in the Uayeb pages.

6. Based on photo captions in Smith's volume and an example examined in the Palacio Cantón collection, the size up to the vase rim seems to range from 24 to 32 centimeters. The heads and headdresses are missing in the examples illustrated by Smith, but most likely the head forms would not prove to be useful, because of the small sample. The heads may have been mold made like the corpus of Chen Mul Modeled effigy censers of the Tases phase (Smith 1971: fig. 66a).

7. Other samples linked with this ceramic type show a two-sigma range that spans from A.D. 1240 to 1470 (Samples 9, 13, 15, 16, 19, 22, 25, 30; Peraza et al. 2006: 168, 170–72, tables 1, 2).

8. Smith (1971: 114–18) suggests that ossuaries are repositories for sacrificial victims and the associated ceramics were swept-in debris, with the exception of Ossuary 4, which had grave furniture, including a Navula Tripod and a Chen Mul Modeled effigy cup (Smith 1971: fig. 31q, 63j). Only a few of the 13 individual burials profiled by Smith had Chen Mul Modeled effigies, and at least one of these is actually in a postconstruction midden associated with Q214 (i.e., Late Lot C-74, Burial 51 [Smith 1971: 115–117, table 24]). Although Burial Cist 2 in R86 had abundant effigy censers, it seems to be a deposit made in haste after the tomb was looted, according to Proskouriakoff and Temple (1955: 357). The high concentration of effigy censers in this residential structure could be misleading. For example, Chuchiak (2009: 142) concludes that the distribution of effigy censers at Mayapán was concentrated in house and palace mounds with few effigy censers found in temple complexes, leading him to suggest the censers were used in private worship, rather than as public cult idols. Nonetheless, Masson and Peraza (2006) conclude that censers were not that common in residential contexts, and when they are found they are in burials. Also, it is clear that effigy censers were an important component in serpent temples at Mayapán, especially Q58 and Q162 (Milbrath and Peraza 2003a: 16, 2003b).

9. One censer in quadrant 10-0 was found in the same lot as three pieces of jade (MY-99-0290; Peraza et al. 2003a: 170, table 136).

10. Bradley Russell (2007) proposes that Mayapán's censer cult spread throughout most of the Maya lowlands in the period following Katun 1 Ahau (1382–1401).

11. Some intersite connections involving censers followed a route from south to north, as in the case of a censer from Calakmul (Dominguez 1994: foto 17) that is very similar to fragmentary examples from sites occupied in the Late Postclassic in the Petén.

12. Examples from Topoxté incorporate a censer form with a pedestal base and a smoothly rounded body, not unlike those of Mayapán, but the Zacpetén examples use a different censer vessel form. A reconstructed censer from that site shows a large figure (38 centimeters high) with the censer vessel itself only about a third of that size, and the figure's body has exceptionally large arms and hands, unlike the well-proportioned figures at Mayapán (Pugh 2003: fig. 8). Nonetheless, one unpublished censer fragment from Timothy Pugh's excavations at Zacpetén more closely resembles Chen Mul Modeled figures of Chac (Smith 1971: fig. 67d).

13. James Aimers (personal communication 2007) notes that links between Lamanai red wares and those of Mayapán, as well as the similarity of the Chen Mul–style censers, suggest that Mayapán and Lamanai were in close contact. Despite the comparisons with Mayapán effigy censers, Champotón lacks the red wares that link Mayapán and Lamanai.

14. The effigy censer has the oyohualli and mat combination associated with aged God D (Itzamna) in the Late Postclassic murals of Santa Rita (Taube 1992: fig. 14d). The censer figure, however, lacks the flowered headband characteristic of definitive examples of Itzamna in the corpus of censers at Mayapán (Smith 1971: fig. 32k, 67c; Thompson 1957).

15. The oyohualli itself is more commonly found in central Mexican art and seems to have been introduced in the Maya area in Terminal Classic Maya relief sculptures representing the aged God N at Chichén Itzá (Taube 1992: figs. 46f, g).

16. The clearest representation of Postclassic warriors is seen in the Venus pages of the Dresden Codex (46–50). One of the Venus warriors on page 46 may be an elderly aspect of God L with only a few teeth. And on Dresden 14c, God L is clearly aged (toothless) and does not appear in a warlike context. In contrast, on Dresden 60 he is a youthful warrior with a Muan bird headdress, holding a shield, an atlatl, and a dart or spear with a captive figure at his feet. In the scene above, the aged God N stands unarmed facing an attack by two youthful warrior gods. In the Madrid Codex, the situation is more complex because so many deities seem to be toothless. Among the armed deities is the aged Sun God, God G (Madrid 90d). Some armed gods are toothless but appear to be hunting gods (Madrid 50b, 51c). The Merchant God is also armed and apparently toothless (Madrid 52–55). Youthful hunting gods are also represented with arms (Madrid 40b).

17. Among the deities represented in the katun pages of the Paris Codex pages, we see an enthroned deity receiving offerings from a sequence of gods. Bruce Love (1994: fig. 3.6) described most of these as "unidentified deities," but we believe it is possible to identify God E (Paris 3); possibly God C, with a Tun headdress (Paris 4); possibly God B (Paris 5—compare Dresden [62]); God N, with a spiral shell (Paris 6); God K (Paris 7); a turkey god (Paris 8); Lord 6-Sky, possibly a variant of God G (Paris 9); God CH (Paris 10—Taube 1992: fig. 28h); and God D (Paris 11).

18. A Mayapán Red Ware cache vessel was in the center (Middle Lot C71a), and to the south a limestone turtle (Lot C72) was located near the entry to the shrine (figure 12.7, #9–10; Winters 1955: fig. 2i–k). To the north there was a turtle effigy vessel, the turtle

surmounted by a fanged male holding an interlaced band decorated with maize foliation (figure 12.7, #8 [Cache 32, Lot C71]; Smith 1971: fig. 64d; Winters 1955: 383–84, fig. 3q, r). Lot C71a (a Middle Lot) was deposited before the group of seven effigy censers in Lot C72, which is defined as a Late Lot by Smith (1971: appendix B).

19. Discussing the warrior figure, Howard Winters (1955: fig. 3f, g) suggested that the missing face was that of an old god and the missing arm was represented by a hand holding maize, both fragments found in the same cache. This seems improbable because maize iconography is not generally seen with warriors and youthful features are the norm among warrior figures. We identified the missing head as a youthful face (13 centimeters high) in the same Cache 33 and the missing arm as one with a hand holding an atlatl in the same deposit (Milbrath and Peraza 2007; Smith 1971: 69g, 70a24). This arm (17 centimeters long) might seem too large for a figure measuring 40.5 centimeters high, but effigy censers have arms that are generally large in proportion to the body. Unfortunately, we were not able to see whether there is a possible match, because the body of the warrior is in the Palacio Cantón bodega while the youthful face and the arm with the atlatl are in a separate collection (the INAH *ceramoteca*).

20. Another pair of censer figures was located in front of the altar and on the northwest side of the altar, but no pair was found on the northeast side, resulting in an asymmetrical array of gods around the shrine (figure 12.7).

21. Smith (1971: appendix B) classified Lot A110 as a Middle Lot, suggesting these central Mexican deities appeared as early as A.D. 1250–1300. Nonetheless, there is considerable mixing in the Middle Lots, and whether the Middle Lots represent a valid chronological subdivision is not clear.

22. To help determine whether there were changes in iconography over time, a study should be undertaken of censer fragments associated with buildings that are clearly late, such as the two colonnades (Q161, Q163) that are the final additions to the Castillo (Q162). The Carnegie report on the excavations of Q163 is brief but does position the colonnade as later than the west stairway of the Castillo, a structure that overlies an earlier pyramid (Q162a); however, ceramic lot numbers are not specified in this description or in the brief mention of Q161 in the Carnegie yearbook (Pollock 1954:277–78). Further excavations by INAH archaeologists in Q161 revealed a bench substructure (Q161-sub) in Stratigraphic Trench 8 (Lots 0307 to 0307-5), but the effigy censer fragments have not been studied to date (Peraza et al. 1997: 93, 133–34). A Chen Mul Modeled lidded effigy vessel representing Chac (Lot 0307-2) was found in this trench in the second level (the third layer beneath the surface), well above the early bench found in the fourth level. Excavations conducted in Q163 and Q163a involved two stratigraphic trenches (Peraza et al. 1999: 96–97, 103, 117), but these have not yet been studied in terms of the iconography of censer fragments.

23. Possibly effigy incense burners that appear in Templo Mayor offerings reflect a borrowing from the Maya area, since effigy censers are not typical of Aztec art. These Aztec forms, however, are more probably inspired by effigy censers from Veracruz and the xantiles from that area and from Puebla and Oaxaca.

13

Problems and Prospects in Maya Ceramic Classification, Analysis, and Interpretation

JAMES JOHN AIMERS

In various ways, the chapters in this book examine the use of pottery in interpretations of the lives of ancient Maya people. In the spirit of the symposia from which most of them are derived, each chapter addresses issues of general method and theory related to type-variety and modal classification with specific examples derived from fieldwork. In this conclusion, I reflect upon some of the concerns that have been raised about type: variety-mode classification in this volume and elsewhere, and I consider some of the ways these may be addressed.

Criticisms of type: variety-mode are described below:

- The hierarchical structure of type-variety downplays variability in both the appearance of artifacts and the rate of change (see Hammond 1972). This is an old criticism levelled at all typological approaches, but it misses the point of classification, which is to "organize chaos" in relation to a particular problem (see the final quotation from Richard Adams in Ball and Taschek's chapter). Inevitably, some variability is lost in any classification (see also Rice, this volume).
- A similar complaint is that type-variety data cannot be reused for new analyses (Smith 1979). Again, this old notion relies on the mistaken idea that a single classification can be good for all purposes (see discussions in Brew 1946; Dunnell 1971a, 1971b). For a concise response to this idea, see Ball (1979b).
- The question of whether type-variety classification deals with culturally meaningful units has been raised by Pendergast (1979) and many others (for example, Chase and Chase, this volume). The historical context of this issue is discussed by Rice in this volume and I return to it below. Regardless of one's position on the emic reality of type-variety *units*, the

chapters herein show that the type: variety-mode *approach* can provide a productive starting point for the construction and investigation of questions about ancient Maya culture that run the gamut from ideology to economics.

- Foias (2004: 144) notes that type: variety-mode classification privileges surface treatment and decoration, whereas "morphological and paste characteristics have been devalued" (Foias 2004). This is true for many studies (which is one reason why many reports include what are most accurately called type-variety rather than type: variety-mode classifications). A neglect of shape data has been noted frequently and is relatively easy to address either within type-variety descriptions or separately (for example, Sabloff 1975; Smith 1955). More problematic has been a lack of consistency in dealing with paste variation and a lack of clarity about reasons for highlighting it or downplaying it, another issue I return to below. The neglect of morphological and paste characteristics is not an inherent limitation of the type-variety system (as the contribution here by Urban and colleagues shows) but is an aspect of how the system has been used by some analysts.
- Lincoln (1985) and others have noted that some pottery styles continue from one period to another but some analysts give identical pottery in consecutive phases new names (see comments in Forsyth 1983: 5; Adams 1971: 30). This is one of the issues that seems to depend on the predispositions of the analyst, just as lumping and splitting do, and clearer methodological statements may help (see comments below). Bill's chapter makes suggestions about these sorts of issues (for example, her "macro-traditions").
- In the first part of the twentieth century, there was an implicit (Kidder 1915, 1917) or explicit use of concepts derived from evolutionary biology in pottery classification. For example, Colton suggested that pottery types in a ware had "a genetic relation to each other" (Colton and Hargrave 1937: 11). Brew's (1946: 53) response to this was dismissive: "Phylogenetic relationships (i.e., relationships of descent) do not exist between inanimate objects." Nevertheless, the evolutionary analogy has continued to be important (for example, in the work of Neff and Shennan and in Ball's use of ceramic "homologies" and "analogies") and to some degree controversial. Concerns about the use of evolutionary analogies are reminiscent of recent debates about approaches to objects that suggest that they have life histories and forms of agency (see, for example, Aimers 2010, 2012; Arnold 2007: 110; Gell 1998; Kopytoff 1988). This issue is beyond the scope of this volume (but for a useful discussion see O'Brien and Lyman 2003).

What can we take from these criticisms? Most of them have been around for decades, and none of them negate the fact that if the system did not have more benefits than liabilities it would have been abandoned years ago. We do not use type-variety out of blind faith in tradition, even if classification sometimes seems to be perfunctory and unrelated to broader research goals. Type-variety is an efficient way to describe and summarize the range of variation in a ceramic collection, and it can be done rapidly with large samples at a low cost.

As Rice notes near the end of her contribution, type-variety fosters communication. This has become especially clear to me since joining the Lamanai project in 2002. Pendergast resisted the use of type-variety nomenclature there because of his conviction that it helped him little in understanding the Maya. Nevertheless, in the first years of my work there, people would ask me, "What is the Postclassic pottery of Lamanai like?" Until I became familiar with similar types in the area and farther to the north, I would launch into lengthy physical descriptions: "There are orange/red-slipped chalices and jars with elaborate curvilinear incising . . ." and so forth. The descriptions of the forms that followed would also be lengthy. When it became apparent to me that the vessels I was describing were stylistically analogous to Zalal Gouged-incised pottery at Cerros, Belize, my descriptions of the vessels became much shorter and my discussions of their significance much longer: How far is this type (or members of its ceramic system) distributed? How does its chronological position at Lamanai compare to other sites? In what contexts is it found? Type-variety terminology provides a very useful and efficient common language. So while it is true that the designations themselves may *inherently* tell us virtually nothing about Maya life, type-variety terminology does makes it easier for us to focus on cultural issues instead of description.

Thus, I believe that type: variety-mode classification facilitates insights about the Maya although it cannot (and clearly was never meant to) tell us everything we want to know about the Maya. I agree with Pendergast and the Chases that contextual associations (which can be used, for example, to establish subcomplexes) tell us much more about the Maya than do sherds from fill. Furthermore, although one can sometimes identify a well-known type without reference to context, the creation and validation of taxa must be the result of some sort of investigation of context, and that context can be expanded from an individual excavation unit to virtually the entire Maya lowlands (and, as Milbrath and Peraza show in chapter 12, potentially beyond). Criticisms of the use of type-variety without reference to context are more appropriately directed at studies that use type-variety without regard to context than at the system itself. Type-variety nomenclature provides a starting point for efficient systematic comparison of pottery, something that contextual descriptions can do only inefficiently and less reliably. If only for the reason that it is so widespread, all Mayanists should have some familiarity with it.

The important issue of context in type-variety came up in relation to the legacy of James C. Gifford in correspondence among myself, the Chases, Joseph Ball, and Carol Gifford as I prepared this volume, and it is worth highlighting because Gifford (1976) is so influential. As both Joseph Ball and Carol Gifford pointed out in their correspondence with me, Gifford's 1963 dissertation was written in the late 1950s and early 1960s as type-variety was still being formulated. James Gifford (1963) argued that types were emically real and thus had a phenomenological reality beyond their context (see also Rice's comments in this volume), and this earlier discussion was included virtually unchanged in the 1976 volume published after his death. Nevertheless, Gifford's ideas—and certainly those of others—had continued to evolve since his dissertation. Willey (in Gifford 1976: viii) says as much in the foreword to the volume, noting that ceramic research had "flowed along swiftly" between 1963 and the publication of the 1976 volume, and although Gifford's introduction "may seem dated" it was included for its historical value and as an unusually detailed procedural statement.

Even so, as Ball pointed out, a close reading of Gifford's work (1976: 10) shows that he did recognize the importance of context in defining varieties, at least, and there are comments peppered throughout the 1976 volume that suggest as much (see especially various references to context in Gifford 1976: 21–24). It is also clear that Gifford considered the situation at Barton Ramie far from ideal, especially for dating (see Gifford 1976: 37). Gifford (1976: fig. 213) also shows contextual associations of vessels that are referenced in the type descriptions.

Few people now agree with Gifford's suggestion that types are simultaneously analytical constructs and emically real, and even by 1976 these ideas had largely fallen out of favor. In his review of the Barton Ramie volume, Adams (1977: 970) noted that Gifford's view that type-variety analysis would in itself identify emically real ceramic units "has been rejected by most of his colleagues," but this did not negate that Gifford's type-variety units are "logically rigorous and tightly observed. . . . As such, they are excellent 'etic' units with which to attempt to establish ancient cultural categories or 'emic' units." A great irony of all of this, as Ball (personal communication, 2011) pointed out, is that those who today consider matching excavated sherds to published illustrations as a form of "analysis" are in practice denying the need for contextual validation and in some sense supporting Gifford's ideas of the phenomenological reality of types while simultaneously following a method that could not be further from Gifford's. According to Ball, this version of (so-called) "analysis" would have "appalled" James Gifford.

The "realness" or "arbitrariness" of type-variety taxa and what are relevant attributes (to us, or to the Maya) are issues that ultimately underlie not only many criticisms of type-variety but also many of the inconsistencies in its use. Perhaps the question should be phrased as "emically real to *whom*?" Consumers may have cared little, if at all, whether their large black-slipped incurving bowls (for example, those we would designate as Mount Maloney Black) were produced by one workshop or fifty, using one paste recipe or one thousand. Ethnography suggests that what mattered was their appearance, form, and function as large bowls suitable for certain tasks; production locus and paste recipe may have had virtually no emic significance for ancient consumers. To potters making decisions during production, however, characteristics of manufacture *must* have mattered, and it seems unlikely that their own products versus those of others could have been anything other than an emic reality to them. Questions of manufacture and production are also central to those of us interested in trade and exchange. As I discuss further below, basic preconceptions about what was culturally important to the ancient Maya (particularly questions about production versus consumption) structure most type-variety studies, but they are not always made explicit.

Multiple Classifications: Challenges and Prospects

For decades, it has been noted that one solution to many of the problems described above lies in multiple classifications. Examples range from the now-famous statement by Brew (1946: 65) about the need for "more rather than fewer classifications" through Ball's (1979b) "Reply to Smith" to Culbert and Rands (2007) to many of the chapters in this book in which various approaches are combined. Cecil, Callaghan and colleagues, Rice, Aimers and Graham, and to some extent Urban and colleagues use materials science techniques with type-variety; Chase and Chase argue persuasively for the centrality of contextual information; and Milbrath and Peraza augment their study of a single pottery type with ethnographic and ethnohistoric research and analogy, including iconography. As in the study of pottery economics (see Pool and Bey 2007: 28), this volume shows that "multidisciplinary" or "integrated" approaches have become ever more popular.

From early on, the importance of the incorporation of modal analysis with typology has been recognized in Maya pottery studies (for example, Sabloff and Smith 1969; Smith et al. 1960: 331), particularly because modes of all sorts (for example, decorative or paste modes) are often temporally sensitive. The various attributes of a type, like the various components of a phase, usually do not "change simultaneously, like the change of a billing for a vaudeville show" (Brew 1946: 73; see also Rouse 1939). For example, the piecrust rims on Terminal Classic Cayo Unslipped jars in the Belize Valley constitute one of the few reliably observable changes from the earlier Late Classic, and notched flanges on Belize Group dishes are a useful way to distinguish Terminal Classic examples from similar but earlier Late Classic ones (LeCount 1996: 145; Aimers 2004a: 79). Because modes should be based on a single attribute or small cluster of attributes, they are inherently more specific than any larger package of modal qualities that may be associated with a single type. So when type-variety is used primarily for chronological assessment, a careful modal analysis is likely to be more reliable than a typological assignment alone.

Especially since the seminal work of Shepard (1956), materials science techniques (for example, thin section petrography) have been increasingly important in Maya pottery studies, and they have been particularly powerful when incorporated with various forms of stylistic analysis (for example, in the study of Petén polychromes). In my discussions of ceramic classification and analysis over the years, however, I have found that some archaeologists appear to assume that *all* of our questions about Maya pottery production and exchange can be solved with petrography and other materials science techniques. I am not so optimistic. For example, Plog and Upham (1989: 214) offer cautionary comments from a five-year study in north-central Arizona where petrographic research has been extensive:

> We are not sure even now, after a substantial investment of time and research dollars, that petrographic analysis is the appropriate technique to resolve problems of identifying manufacturing localities and patterns of local and regional exchange. We are sure, however, that after analyzing hundreds of sherds that our sample is simply too small. We believe that to resolve the questions we have raised we will require data from thousands of sherds from a number of different localities. It is important to emphasize that virtually all petrographic studies of ceramics, including our own, have relied on far too small a sample to be able to draw firm conclusions about the nature of constituent variability in pottery made at a particular locality, let alone across regions.

The issue becomes even more marked in the Maya area when we take into consideration that the "vast majority of pottery was made and consumed locally" (Pool and Bey 2007: 36; see also Arnold et al. 1991). Furthermore, many materials science–based studies still use type-variety to organize comparison, which only reinforces the need for rigorous attention to type-variety methods. For example, petrographic data on types from different sites cannot be very useful if types are confused or misidentified, and I believe this is a common occurrence.

The fact that modal classification and materials science can be done separately from type-variety or along with it reminds us of the flexibility of the system and the value of multiple classifications. The idea that there could ever be one all-purpose form of classification reminds me of the modernist approach to the world as one that can be known objectively. The alternative, which acknowledges multiple forms of rightness in classification, is appealing to the postmodern mind but is difficult and messy. One of the main issues this question raises is the comparability of types and typologies.

Consistency and Comparability

Whittaker and colleagues (1998: 131) note that "consistency in classification is one of the most studiously ignored problems in discussions of archaeological typology." This is partly a result of the fact that different people see different things in any given sample. Even with Munsell soil color charts, my 2.5 YR 6/8 might be someone else's 2.5 YR 5/8. Consistency in classification is also complicated by "disagreement in the choice of attributes that are considered important in defining types" (Whittaker et al. 1998: 158). It is understandable that someone with experience in petrography, for example, might notice and make finer distinctions based on temper than do others, who may privilege surface or shape. Finally, some sherds or vessels never seem to fit into a given type, or they have the characteristics of multiple types (see comments by Sullivan and Awe in this volume). Detailed definitions of classes and setting explicit criteria for inclusion can help (Beck and Jones 1989; Daniels 1972), but as Adams and Adams (1991) discuss, there are limits to this. The various Late Classic red types described in Gifford 1976 come to mind here—I have read Gifford's detailed descriptions hundreds of times, but identification of red dishes still seems at times "something of a mystical art" (Dunnell 1971b: 116), and multiple archaeologists will frequently disagree on type assignments.

Whittaker and colleagues (1998) argue that the best typology is not simply the one that works best for any particular data set or research question(s) but one that facilitates interobserver consistency (see Hill and Evans 1972 for more on the issue of "best" typologies). This is an important point because multiple classifications in Maya pottery studies tend to use type-variety as a central language and different typological assignments can lead to different interpretations. Chronological assessments are an obvious issue, but broader culture-historical interpretations are also implicated. I have seen sherds identified as Augustine Red and Paxcamán Red that are quite unlike the Paxcamán and Augustine Group materials I have seen in the Belize Valley and the Petén Lakes region and are much more similar to pottery in the Zakpah Group at Cerros and Lamanai. These differences are not trivial: the Augustine and Paxcamán Groups are most abundant in western Belize and especially Petén, and thus reasonably can be taken to represent interaction with these areas, whereas the Zakpah Group is known mostly from northern Belize. Some people may view type-variety primarily as a language, but it is never far removed from its use in interpretations of ancient Maya beliefs and behavior.

An important way to address interobserver variability is to make collections more easily available. The *ceramoteca* at INAH Mérida is an excellent example, and individual archaeologists are usually generous about allowing others access to their collections. In 2006, I visited collections from Isla Cerritos (Rafael Cobos), Champotón (William Folan and Linda Florey Folan), Caye Coco (Marilyn Masson), the Petén Lakes region (Prudence Rice and Leslie Cecil), the Mopan drainage (Juan Pedro Laporte), INAH Mérida and Chetumal, and several small museums. Planning for this took almost a year, however, and although it was one of the most productive seasons of my career, acquiring funding for it was very difficult (several applications in the United States through the years failed, but the British Academy saw the value of it). I find it frustrating that so much funding continues to emphasize pulling yet more material from the ground, while finding money for basic comparative studies is very difficult. Ironically, the least expensive of techniques—stylistic and formal analysis—is one of the hardest to fund. Lab work continues to be, it seems, the domestic labor of the archaeologist and undervalued in relation to excavation, and high-tech methods seem to have more cachet than even the most rigorous and productive low-tech methods. Similarly, it is very difficult to find funding for storage, an issue we are familiar with at Lamanai and one with which the nation of Belize continues to struggle. Most funding agencies do not find collections research or comparative collections appealing, despite their central importance to making sense of what we dig up.

Reflexivity

Many of the problems raised above can be ameliorated by clearer methodological statements. As early as 1946, Brew (1946: 45) noted that archaeologists have a "professional obligation" to state the assumptions that underlie their conclusions—in other words, to be reflexive. Reflexivity has been most evident in archaeology in considerations of the biases one might hold about, for example, gender roles or social structure in the past, but it is often absent methodologically (although most of the work of Michael Schiffer on formation processes seems to fit the bill). How do my preconceptions and goals lead me to approach pottery in certain ways? What biases do I bring to the (sorting) table? How can I make these predispositions clear? The answer, as cultural anthropologists and others have shown, is to talk and write about them. Full-scale monographs about pottery often do include these sorts of statements (Forsyth 1983 and 1989 are exemplary), but when pottery classification and analysis is subsumed in larger studies or presented in shorter forms such as chapters or articles, these sorts of statements are often disconcertingly absent or vague. As Hill and Evans (1972: 236–37) note, this suggests that in at least some cases serious thought has not been given to the way in which research problems are linked to classificatory methods, resulting in the sense that taxa in given classifications are "real and immutable" rather than merely useful.

In terms of type-variety, it appears to me that ultimately there are two major ways of classifying Maya pottery: one that privileges paste and places it high in the hierarchy (above group, for example, to define wares or paste wares) and others that use it at the lowest level to define varieties or describe it modally in association with any hierarchical level (that is, ware, group, type, or variety). These approaches usually have to do with whether the analyst is interested in production or in consumption, as I note above. Disagreements—often heated ones—among archaeologists about the "correct" method of type-variety have been one of the most striking aspects of the production of this volume since the symposia that inspired it. Recognizing which strategy has been employed in a given study is generally easy, but a methodological statement about *why* a given strategy has been chosen would foreground these differences and eliminate the surprisingly common assumption that one method is correct or best. The challenge then becomes to make the classes (such as types) that result from these different strategies comparable.

The finer the distinctions we make about pottery, the more likely is disagreement. The logical conclusion is that lumping leads to more interanalyst consistency than does splitting. In type-variety, ceramic groups are one way to lump ceramics together, and a group-level classification combined with and a detailed documentation of modes provides a good basis for chronological assessment and stylistic comparison. In this volume and elsewhere (Aimers 2007a, 2009; Milbrath et al. 2008), I have also suggested systems assignments as a "lumpy" first step in classification, before samples are split into types, which tend to be accepted as fact rather than intermittently reassessed as hands-on comparison progresses and other data accumulate.

Conclusion

The many conversations and the correspondence I have shared with my colleagues about questions raised in this volume have made me acutely aware of the complexity of some of the issues involved in pottery classification, analysis, and interpretation, and how far we have to go in achieving consensus on many of them. At times, in reading through these chapters, I could practically see fists waving and hear cries of indignation about some of the points made, leading me to believe that years of animated discussions of similar issues with colleagues has led me to a kind of pottery-based post-traumatic stress disorder. Realistically, however, the disagreements I have witnessed about pottery study in Maya archaeology have almost always been good-natured and invariably representative of the passion that ultimately makes the study of pottery more intellectually and emotionally rewarding than many people realize. Maya pottery represents not simply one of the world's great artistic traditions but an almost inexhaustible source of data for interpretations about ancient Maya life. This volume barely scratches the surface of what can be derived from Maya pottery, but the chapters here will, I hope, stimulate more lively conversation.

Acknowledgments

I would like to thank E. Wyllys Andrews, Joseph Ball, Arlen Chase, Carol Gifford, and Prudence Rice for their insights into many of the issues raised in this chapter.

References

Adams, R.E.W.

1968 Implications of a Maya Elite-Class Funeral at Altar de Sacrificios, Guatemala. Paper presented at the 33rd Annual Meeting of the Society for American Archaeology, Santa Fe, N.Mex.

1971 *The Ceramics of Altar de Sacrificios.* Papers of the Peabody Museum of Archaeology and Ethnology, vol. 63, no. 1. Harvard University, Cambridge, Mass.

1977 Review of Prehistoric Pottery Analysis and the Ceramics of Barton Ramie in the Belize Valley. *American Anthropologist* 79 (4): 969–70.

2008 The Type: Variety-Mode System: Doomed to Success. *Latin American Antiquity* 19 (2): 222–23.

Adams, R.E.W., and A. Trik

1961 Temple 1 (Str 5-1): Post-constructional Activities. In *Tikal Reports No. 7*, edited by W. R. Coe, 97–156. University Monograph no. 20. University of Pennsylvania, Philadelphia.

Adams, R. W.

1953 Some Small Ceremonial Structures of Mayapan. In *Current Reports No. 9*, 144–64. Department of Archaeology, Carnegie Institution of Washington, Washington, D.C.

Adams, W. Y., and E. W. Adams

1991 *Archaeological Typology and Practical Reality: A Dialectical Approach to Artifact Classification and Sorting.* Cambridge University Press, Cambridge.

Aimers, J. J.

2004a *Cultural Change on a Temporal and Spatial Frontier: Ceramics of the Terminal Classic to Early Postclassic Transition in the Upper Belize River Valley.* BAR International Series 1325. British Archaeological Reports, Oxford.

2004b The Terminal Classic to Postclassic Transition in the Belize Valley. In *Archaeology of the Upper Belize Valley: Half a Century of Maya Research*, edited by J. F. Garber, 147–77. University of Florida Press, Gainesville.

2007a The Curse of the Ware: Using Ceramic Systems in Belize. *Research Reports in Belizean Archaeology* 4:101–10.

2007b The Impact of Fine Orange Ware on the Postclassic Ceramics of Lamanai, Belize. Paper presented at the 72nd Annual Meeting of the Society for American Archaeology, Austin, Texas.

2008 Snakes on Planes: Sinuous Motifs in the Art of Lamanai. *Research Reports in Belizean Archaeology* 5:115–23.

2009 Bring It On: Using Ceramic Systems at Lamanai. *Research Reports in Belizean Archaeology* 6:245–52.

2010 You Only Live Twice: The Agency of Ritual Ceramics at Lamanai. *Research Reports in Belizean Archaeology* 7:119–25.

2012 La Belle et La Bête: The Everyday Life of Ceramics at Lamanai, Belize. In *Proceedings of the 13th European Maya Conference, Paris, December 1–8, 2008, Acta Mesoamericana, Vol. 21*, edited by P. Nondédéo and A. Breton. Anton Saurwein, Germany. Forthcoming.

Alexander, R. T.

1998 Postclassic Settlement Pattern at Isla Cilvituk, Campeche, México. Paper presented at the 63rd Annual Meeting of the Society for American Archaeology, Seattle.

Andersen, P. K.

1998 Yula, Yucatán, Mexico: Terminal Classic Maya Ceramic Chronology for the Chichén Itzá Area. *Ancient Mesoamerica* 9 (1): 151–65.

Anderson, A. H., and H. J. Cook

1944 *Archaeological Finds near Douglas, British Honduras*. Notes on Middle American Archaeology and Ethnology no. 40. Carnegie Institute of Washington, Washington, D.C.

Andrews, A. P.

1984 The Political Geography of the 16th Century Yucatán Maya: Comments and Revisions. *Journal of Anthropological Research* 40:589–96.

Andrews, E. W., V

1990 Early Ceramic History of the Lowland Maya. In *Vision and Revision in Maya Studies*, edited by P. D. Harrison and F. S. Clancy, 1–19. University of New Mexico Press, Albuquerque.

Andrews, E. W., V, and N. Hammond

1990 Redefinition of the Swasey Phase at Cuello, Belize. *American Antiquity* 55 (3): 570–84.

Arnauld, C.

2001 La "Casa Larga": Evolucion de la Arquitectura del Poder del Clasico al Postclasico. In *Reconstruyendo la Ciudad Maya: El Urbanismo en las Sociedades Antiguas*, edited by A. Ciudad Ruiz, M. J. Iglesias Ponce de Leon, and M. del Carmen Martinez Martinez, 363–401. Sociedad Española de Estudios Mayas, Madrid.

Arnold, D. E.

1978 Ethnography of Pottery Making in the Valley of Guatemala. In *The Ceramics of Kaminaljuyú*, edited by R. K. Wetherington, 327–400. Pennsylvania State University Press, University Park.

1980 Localized Exchange: An Ethnoarchaeological Perspective. In *Models and Methods in Regional Exchange*, edited by R. E. Fry, 147–50. SAA Papers no. 1. Society for American Archaeology, Washington, D.C.

Arnold, D. E., H. Neff, and R. L. Bishop

1991 Compositional Analysis and "Sources" of Pottery: An Ethnoarcheological Approach. *American Anthropologist* 93 (1): 70–90.

Arnold, P. J.

2007 Ceramic Production at La Joya, Veracruz: Early Formative Techno Logics and Error Loads. In *Pottery Economies in Mesoamerica*, edited by C. A. Pool and G. J. Bey III, 86–113. University of Arizona Press, Tucson.

Awe, J. J.

1992 *Dawn in the Land between the Rivers: Formative Occupation at Cahal Pech, Belize, and Its Implications for Preclassic Development in the Maya Lowlands.* Unpublished Ph.D. thesis, Institute of Archaeology, University College London.

Awe, J. J., and C. Helmke

2007 Fighting the Inevitable: The Terminal Classic Maya of the Upper Roaring Creek Valley. *Research Reports in Belizean Archaeology* 4:29–42.

Ball, J. W.

1973 *Ceramic Sequence at Becán, Campeche, Mexico.* Unpublished Ph.D. dissertation, Department of Anthropology, University of Wisconsin, Madison.

1976 Ceramic Sphere Affiliations of the Barton Ramie Ceramic Complexes. In *Prehistoric Pottery Analysis and the Ceramics of Barton Ramie in the Belize Valley*, by J. C. Gifford, 323–30. Memoirs of the Peabody Museum of Archaeology and Ethnology, vol. 18. Harvard University, Cambridge, Mass.

1977a *The Archaeological Ceramics of Becan, Campeche, Mexico.* Middle American Research Institute Publication 43. Tulane University, New Orleans.

1977b Review of "Prehistoric Pottery Analysis and the Ceramics of Barton Ramie in the Belize Valley," by James C. Gifford. *American Antiquity* 42 (4): 661–64.

1979a Ceramics, Culture History, and the Puuc Tradition: Some Alternative Possibilities. In *The Puuc: New Perspectives*, edited by L. Mills, 18–35. Central College, Pella, Iowa.

1979b On Data, Methods, Results, and Reviews: A Reply to Michael E. Smith. *American Antiquity* 44 (4): 828–31.

1980 *The Archaeological Ceramics of Chinkultic, Chiapas, Mexico.* Papers of the New World Archaeological Foundation no. 43. Brigham Young University, Provo.

1986 Campeche, the Itzá, and the Postclassic: A Study in Ethnohistorical Archaeology. In *Late Lowland Maya Civilization: Classic to Postclassic*, edited by J. A. Sabloff and E. W. Andrews V, 379–408. School of American Research, University of New Mexico Press, Albuquerque.

1993 Pottery, Potters, Palaces, and Politics: Some Socioeconomic and Political Implications of Late Classic Maya Ceramic Industries. In *Lowland Maya Civilization in the Eighth Century*, edited by J. A. Sabloff and J. S. Henderson, 243–72. Dumbarton Oaks, Washington, D.C.

1994 Type:Variety Analysis and Masterworks of Classic Maya Polychrome Pottery. In *Painting the Maya Universe: Royal Ceramics of the Classic Period*, edited by D. Reents-Budet, 362–63. Duke University Press, Durham, N.C.

Ball, J. W., and J. T. Taschek

1989 Teotihuacán's Fall and the Rise of the Itzá: Realignments and Role Changes in the Terminal Classic Maya Lowlands. In *Mesoamerica after the Decline of Teotihuacán, A.D. 700–900*, edited by R. A. Diehl and J. C. Berlo, 187–200. Dumbarton Oaks, Washington, D.C.

1992 Economics and Economies in the Late Classic Maya Lowlands: A Trial Examination of Some Apparent Patterns and Implications. Paper presented at the 1992 Cleveland State University Wenner-Gren Foundation Symposium, "The Segmentary State and the Classic Lowland Maya: A 'New' Model for Ancient Political Organization," Cleveland.

2001 The Buenavista–Cahal Pech Court: A Multi-palace Royal Court from a Petty Lowland Maya Kingdom. In *Royal Courts of the Ancient Maya*, edited by Takeshi Inomata and Stephen Houston, 165–200. Westview Press, Boulder, Colo.

2003 Reconsidering the Belize Valley Preclassic: A Case for Multiethnic Interactions in the Development of a Regional Culture Tradition. *Ancient Mesoamerica* 14:179–217.

2004 Buena Vista del Cayo: A Short Outline of Occupational and Cultural History at an Upper Belize Valley Regal Ritual Center. In *The Ancient Maya of the Belize Valley: Half a Century of Archaeological Research*, edited by J. F. Garber, 149–67. University Press of Florida, Tallahassee.

2007a "Mixed Deposits," "Composite Complexes," or "Hybrid Assemblages": A Fresh Reexamination of Middle Preclassic (Formative) Ceramics and Ceramic Assemblages from the Northern Maya Lowlands. In *Archaeology, Art, and Ethnogenesis in Mesoamerican Prehistory: Papers in Honor of Gareth W. Lowe*, edited by M. E. Pye and L. Lowe, 173–91. Papers of the New World Archaeological Foundation no. 68. Brigham Young University, Provo.

2007b Sometimes a "Stove" Is "Just a Stove": A Context-Based Reconsideration of Three-Prong "Incense Burners" from the Western Belize Valley. *Latin American Antiquity* 18 (4): 451–70.

Barrera Rubio, A., T. W. Stanton, C. Peraza Lope, and L. Toscano Hernández

2003 Uso y Percepción de Estructuras Abandonadas, durante el Posclásico Tardío en el Noreste de Yucatán, Observadas en Kulubá, Xelhá, San Gervasio, Quintana Roo. *Temas Antropologicas* 25 (1–2): 47–175.

Bartlett, M. L.

2004 The Potter's Choice of Clays and Crafting Technologies. In *K'axob: Ritual, Work, and Family in an Ancient Maya Village*, edited by P. A. McAnany, 143–68. Cotsen Institute of Archaeology Monumenta Archaeologica 22. University of California, Los Angeles.

Beaudry, M.

1984 *Ceramic Production and Distribution in the Southeastern Maya Periphery: Late Classic Painted Serving Vessels*. BAR International Series 203. British Archaeological Reports, Oxford.

1987 Southeast Maya Polychrome Pottery: Production, Distribution, and Ceramic Style. In *Maya Ceramics: Papers from the 1985 Maya Ceramic Conference*, edited by P. M. Rice and R. J. Sharer, 503–24. BAR International Series 345 (1). British Archaeological Reports, Oxford.

Beaudry-Corbett, M., and J. S. Henderson

1993 Introduction. In *Pottery of Prehistoric Honduras: Regional Classification and Analysis*, edited by J. S. Henderson and M. Beaudry-Corbett, 1–2. Institute of Archaeology, University of California, Los Angeles.

Beck, C., and G. T. Jones

1989 Bias and Archaeological Classification. *American Antiquity* 54 (2): 244–61.

Becker, M. J.

1973 Archaeological Evidence for Occupational Specialization among the Classic Period Maya at Tikal, Guatemala. *American Antiquity* 38 (4): 396–406.

2003 A Classic Period Barrio Producing Fine Polychrome Ceramics at Tikal, Guatemala: Notes on Ancient Maya Firing Technology. *Ancient Mesoamerica* 14 (1): 95–112.

Benavides Castillo, A.

1981 *Cobá: Una Ciudad Prehispánica de Quintana Roo.* INAH Centro Regional del Sureste, Mexico City.

1997 *Edzná: Una Ciudad Prehispánica de Campeche.* Serie Arqueología de México. Instituto Nacional de Antropología e Historia, Mexico City.

Bill, C. R.

1997 *Patterns of Variation and Change in Dynastic Period Ceramics and Ceramic Production at Copán, Honduras.* Unpublished Ph.D. dissertation, Department of Anthropology, Tulane University.

2001 Tipología y Análisis Preliminar de la Cerámica de Cancuén. In *Proyecto Arqueológico Cancuén: Informe no. 2, Temporada 2000,* edited by A. A. Demarest and T. Barrientos, 170–255. Instituto de Antropología e Historia, Guatemala; Department of Anthropology, Vanderbilt University, Nashville.

2003 Preliminary Analysis of Ceramic Materials from Pusilha. In *Pusilha Archaeological Project: 2002 Annual Report,* by G. E. Braswell, C. R. Bill, S. Schwake, and C. Prager, 46–62. Preliminary report submitted to the Department of Archaeology, Belmopan, Belize.

2005a Chronological Patterns of Variation in the Late Classic Ceramics from Pusilhá, Belize. In *Pusilha Archaeological Project: 2004 Annual Report,* by G. E. Braswell, S. Schwake, and C. R. Bill, 38–64. Report submitted to the Department of Archaeology, Belmopan, Belize.

2005b A Preliminary Analysis and Comparison of Late Classic Ceramics from El Paraíso and El Cafetal. In *Proyecto Arqueológico Regional El Paraíso (PAREP), Informe Preliminar de la Temporada de 2005,* by M. A. Canuto and E. E. Bell, 68–89. Preliminary report submitted to the Instituto Hondureño de Antropología e Historia, Tegucigalpa, Honduras.

Binford, L. R.

1979 Organization and Formation Processes: Looking at Curated Technologies. *Journal of Anthropological Research* 35:255–73.

Bishop, Ronald L., Robert L. Rands, and George R. Holley

1982 Ceramic Compositional Analysis in Archaeological Perspective. In *Advances in Archaeological Method and Theory,* edited by Michael B. Schiffer, 275–330. Academic Press, New York.

Bishop, R. L., M. J. Blackman, E. L. Sears, W. J. Folan, and D. W. Forsyth

2006 Observaciones Iniciales sobre el Consume de la Ceramica de Champotón. *Los Investigadores de la Cultura Maya* 14 (1): 137–45.

Blanton, R. E., S. A. Kowaleski, G. M. Feinman, and J. Appell

1982 *Monte Albans Hinterland, Part I, Prehispanic Settlement Patterns of the Central and Southern Parts of the Valley of Oaxaca, Mexico*. Memoirs 15. Museum of Anthropology, University of Michigan, Ann Arbor.

Blashfield, R. K., and J. G. Draguns

1976 Toward a Taxonomy of Psychopathology: The Purpose of Psychiatric Classification. *British Journal of Psychiatry* 129:574–83.

Boone, E. H., and M. E. Smith

2003 Postclassic International Styles and Symbol Sets. In *The Postclassic Mesoamerican World*, edited by M. E. Smith and F. M. Berdan, 186–93. Salt Lake City, University of Utah Press.

Boot, E.

1997 Kan Ek', Last Ruler of the Itsá. *Yumtzilob* 9 (1): 5–22.

2005 *Continuity and Change in Text and Image at Chichén Itzá, Yucatán, Mexico: A Study of the Inscriptions, Iconography, and Architecture at a Late Classic to Early Postclassic Maya Site*. CNWS Publications, Leiden.

Boucher, S., and Y. Palomo

2000 Cerámica Ritual de Calakmul. *Arqueología Mexicana* 8 (42): 34–35.

2005 Dialogo con las Divinidades: Cosmos, Ritos, y Ofrendas entre los Antiguos Mayas. *I'Inaj: Revista de Divulagación del Patrimonio Cultural de Yucatan* 13:3–30.

Brady, J. E.

1989 *An Investigation of Maya Ritual Cave Use with Special Reference to Naj Tunich, Peten, Guatemala*. Unpublished Ph.D. dissertation, Department of Anthropology, University of California, Los Angeles.

1992 Function and Meaning of Lowland Maya Shoe-Pots. *Ceramica de Cultura Maya* 16:1–10.

Brady, J. E., J. W. Ball, R. L. Bishop, D. Pring, N. C. Hammond, and R. A. Housley

1998 The Lowland Maya "Protoclassic": A Reconsideration of Its Nature and Significance. *Ancient Mesoamerica* 9 (1):17–38.

Brady, J. E., A. Scott, A. Cobb, I. Rodas, J. Fogarty, and M. Urquizu Sanchez

1997 Glimpses of the Dark Side of the Petexbatun Project: The Petexbatun Regional Cave Survey. *Ancient Mesoamerica* 8 (2): 353–64.

Brainerd, George W.

1958 *The Archaeological Ceramics of Yucatan*. University of California Anthropological Records, vol. 19. University of California Press, Berkeley.

Brew, J. O.

1946 The Use and Abuse of Taxonomy. In *Archaeology of the Alkali Ridge, Southeastern Utah*, 44–66. Papers of the Peabody Museum of Archaeology and Ethnology, vol. 21. Harvard University, Cambridge, Mass.

Bricker, H. M., and V. R. Bricker

2011 *Astronomy in the Maya Codices*. American Philosophical Society, Philadelphia.

Brown, M. K.

2007 *Ritual Ceramic Use in the Early and Middle Preclassic at the Sites of Blackman Eddy and Cahal Pech, Belize.* Report submitted to the Foundation for the Advancement of Mesoamerican Studies, Inc. (FAMSI), Crystal River, Fla.

Brumfiel, E. M.

1989 Factional Competition in Complex Society. In *Domination and Resistance*, edited by D. Miller, M. Rowlands, and C. Tilley, 127–39. Unwin Hyman, London.

Bullard, William R.

1973 Postclassic Culture in Central Peten and Adjacent British Honduras. In *Classic Maya Collapse*, edited by T. Patrick Culbert, 221–41. University of New Mexico Press, Albuquerque.

Bullard, W. R., Jr.

1970 Topoxte: A Postclassic Maya Site in Petén, Guatemala. In *Monographs and Papers in Maya Archaeology*, edited by W. R. Bullard, 245–308. Papers of the Peabody Museum of Archaeology and Ethnology, vol. 61. Harvard University, Cambridge, Mass.

Callaghan, M. G.

2006 The Archaeological Ceramics of the Holmul Region, Guatemala. In *Proyecto Arqueologico Holmul: Informe Temporada 2005*, edited by F. Estrada-Belli, 200–303. Vanderbilt University, Nashville.

2008a Ceramica del Periodo Preclasico Terminal y "Tecnologia de Prestigio" en la Region de Holmul, Peten. In *XXI Simposio de Investigaciónes Arqueológicas en Guatemala*, edited by J. P. Laporte, B. Arroyo, and H. E. Mejía, 703–18. Museo Nacional de Arqueologia y Etnologia, Guatemala City.

2008b *Technologies of Power: Ritual Economy and Ceramic Production in the Terminal Preclassic Period Holmul Region, Guatemala.* Unpublished Ph.D. dissertation, Department of Anthropology, Vanderbilt University, Nashville.

Canuto, M. A., and E. E. Bell (editors)

2005 *Proyecto Arqueológico Regional El Paraíso (Parep), Informe Preliminar de la Temporada de 2005.* Preliminary report submitted to the Instituto Hondureño de Antropología e Historia, Tegucigalpa, Honduras.

Carmean, K., N. Dunning, and J. K. Kowalski

2004 High Times in the Hill Country: A Perspective from the Terminal Classic Puuc Region. In *The Terminal Classic in the Maya Lowlands: Collapse, Transition, and Transformation*, edited by A. Demarest, P. M. Rice, and D. S. Rice, 424–49. University Press of Colorado, Boulder.

Carrasco Vargas, R.

1989 Arquitectura Postclásica en Chicanná, Campeche. In *Memorias del Segundo Coloquio Internacional de Mayistas*, 449–68. Universidad Nacional Autónoma de México, Mexico City.

Castellanos, Jeanette, Cassandra R. Bill, Michael G. Callaghan, and Ronald L. Bishop

2003 Cancuen, Enclave de Intercambio entre las Tierras Bajas e Altas de Guatemala: La Evidencia Ceramica. In *XVI Simposio de Investigaciones Arqueológicas en Guatemala, 2002,* edited by Juan Pedro Laporte, Bárbara Arroyo, Héctor L.

Escobedo, and Héctor E. Mejía, 635–48. Museo Nacional de Arqueología y Etnología, Guatemala.

Cecil, L. G.

1997 Pilot Study for the Identification of a Topoxté Red Production Center in the Postclassic Period. Manuscript on file, Department of Social and Cultural Analysis, Stephen F. Austin State University, Nacogdoches, Texas.

2001a Developing Technological Styles of Petén Postclassic Slipped Pottery with Regard to Clay Mineralogy. In *Archaeology and Clays*, edited by I. Druc, 107–21. British Archaeological Reports, International Series 942, Oxford.

2001b *Technological Styles of Late Postclassic Pottery from the Central Petén Lakes Region, El Petén, Guatemala*. Unpublished Ph.D. dissertation, Department of Anthropology, Southern Illinois University, Carbondale.

2004 Inductively Coupled Plasma Emission Spectroscopy and Postclassic Petén Slipped Pottery: An Examination of Pottery Wares, Social Identity and Trade. *Archaeometry* 46 (3): 385–404.

2007 Postclassic Maya Ceramic Advances: Conjoining Stylistic, Technological, and Chemical Compositional Data. In *Developments in Ceramic Materials Research*, edited by D. Rosslere, 1–34. Nova Science Publishers, New York.

2009 Technological Styles of Slipped Pottery and Kowoj Identity. In *The Kowoj: Identity, Migration, and Geopolitics in Late Postclassic Petén, Guatemala*, edited by P. M. Rice and D. S. Rice, 221–37. University of Colorado Press, Boulder.

Cecil, L. G., and H. Neff

2006 Postclassic Maya Slips and Paints and Their Relationship to Socio-Political Groups in El Petén, Guatemala. *Journal of Archaeological Science* 33 (10): 1482–91.

Cecil, L. G., and T. W. Pugh

2004 Kowoj Symbolism and Technology at Late Postclassic Tipuj. Paper presented at the 69th Annual Society for American Archaeology Meeting, Montreal.

Chase, A. F.

1979 Regional Development in the Tayasal-Paxcaman Zone, El Peten, Guatemala: A Preliminary Statement. *Ceramica de Cultura Maya* 11:87–119.

1983 *A Contextual Analysis of the Tayasal-Paxcaman Zone*. Unpublished Ph.D. dissertation, Department of Anthropology, University of Pennsylvania, Philadelphia.

1994 A Contextual Approach to the Ceramics of Caracol, Belize. In *Studies in the Archaeology of Caracol, Belize*, edited by D. Z. Chase and A. F. Chase, 157–82. Pre-Columbian Art Research Institute Mongraph 7. San Francisco.

1998 Planeacion Civica e Integracion de Sitio en Caracol, Belize: Defiendo Una Economia Administrada del Periodo Clásico Maya. *Los Investigadores de al Cultura Maya* 6 (1): 26–44.

Chase, A. F., and D. Z. Chase

1987a *Investigations at the Classic Maya City of Caracol, Belize: 1985–1987*. Monograph 3. Pre-Columbian Art Research Institute, San Francisco.

1987b Putting Together the Pieces: Maya Pottery of Northern Belize and Central Petén, Guatemala. In *Maya Ceramics: Papers from the 1985 Maya Ceramic Confer-*

ence, edited by P. M. Rice and R. J. Sharer, 47–72. BAR International Series 345 (1). British Archaeological Reports, Oxford.

1994a Details in the Archaeology of Caracol, Belize: An Introduction. In *Studies in the Archaeology of Caracol, Belize*, edited by D. Z. Chase and A. F. Chase, 55–62. Pre-Columbian Art Research Institute, San Francisco.

1994b Maya Veneration of the Dead at Caracol, Belize. In *Seventh Palenque Round Table, 1989*, edited by M. Robertson and V. Fields, 55–62. Pre-Columbian Art Research Institute, San Francisco.

1996 A Mighty Maya Nation: How Caracol Built an Empire by Cultivating Its "Middle Class." *Archaeology* 49 (5): 66–72.

2000 Sixth Century Change and Variation in the Southern Maya Lowlands: Integration and Disbursement at Caracol, Belize. In *The Years without Summer: Tracing A.D. 536 and Its Aftermath*, edited by J. D. Gunn. BAR International Series 872. British Archaeological Reports, Oxford.

2004 Terminal Classic Status-Linked Ceramics and the Maya "Collapse": De Facto Refuse at Caracol, Belize. In *The Terminal Classic in the Maya Lowlands: Collapse, Transition, and Transformation*, edited by A. Demarest, P. M. Rice, and D. S. Rice, 342–66. University Press of Colorado, Boulder.

2005 Contextualizing the Collapse: Hegemony and Terminal Classic Ceramics from Caracol, Belize. In *Geographies of Power: Understanding the Nature of Terminal Classic Pottery in the Maya Lowlands*, edited by S. L. López Varela and A. E. Foias, 73–92. BAR International Series 1447. British Archaeological Reports, Oxford.

2007 This Is the End: Archaeological Transitions and the Terminal Classic Period at Caracol, Belize. *Research Reports in Belizean Archaeology* 4:13–27.

2008 Methodological Issues in the Archaeological Identification of the Terminal Classic and Postclassic Transition in the Maya Area. *Research Reports in Belizean Archaeology* 5:23–36.

2012 Belize Red Ceramics and Their Implications for Trade and Exchange in the Eastern Maya Lowlands. *Research Reports in Belizean Archaeology* 9: 3–14.

Chase, A. F., D. Z. Chase, E. Zorn, and W. Teeter

2007 Textiles and the Maya Archaeological Record: Gender, Power, and Status in Classic Period Caracol, Belize. *Ancient Mesoamerica* 19 (1): 127–42.

Chase, D. Z.

1982a The Ikilik Ceramic Complex at Nohmul, Northern Belize. *Cerámica de Cultura Maya* 12:71–81.

1982b *Spatial and Temporal Variability in Postclassic Northern Belize*. Unpublished Ph.D. dissertation, Department of Anthropology, University of Pennsylvania, Philadelphia.

1984 The Late Postclassic Pottery of Santa Rita Corozal, Belize: The Xabalxab Ceramic Complex. *Cerámica de Cultura Maya* 12:18–26.

1985a Between Earth and Sky: Idols, Images, and Postclassic Cosmology. In *Fifth Mesa Redonda de Palenque, Vol. 6*, edited by M. G. Robertson, 223–33. Pre-Columbian Art Research Institute, San Francisco.

1985b Ganned but Not Forgotten: Late Postclassic Archaeology and Ritual at Santa Rita Corozal, Belize. In *The Lowland Maya Postclassic*, edited by A. F. Chase and P. M. Rice, 104–25. University of Texas Press, Austin.

1986 Social and Political Organization in the Land of Cacao and Honey: Correlating the Archaeology and Ethnohistory of the Postclassic Maya. In *Late Lowland Maya Civilization: Classic to Postclassic*, edited by J. A. Sabloff and E. W. Andrews V, 347–77. School of American Research, University of New Mexico Press, Albuquerque.

1988 Caches and Censerwares: Meaning from Maya Pottery. In *A Pot for All Reasons: Ceramic Ecology Revisited*, edited by C. C. Kolb and L. M. Lackey, 81–104. Special Publication of *Cerámica de Cultura Maya*, Laboratory of Anthropology, Temple University, Philadelphia.

1998 Albergando a Los Muertos en Caracol, Belice. *Los Investigadores de la Cultura Maya* 6 (1): 9–25.

Chase, D. Z., and A. F. Chase

1982 Yucatec Influence in Terminal Classic Northern Belize. *American Antiquity* 47 (3): 597–613.

1988 *A Postclassic Perspective: Excavations at the Maya Site of Santa Rita Corozal, Belize*. Pre-Columbian Art Research Institute, San Francisco.

1994 *Studies in the Archaeology of Caracol, Belize*. Monograph 7. Pre-Columbian Art Research Institute, San Francisco.

1998 The Architectural Context of Caches, Burials, and Other Ritual Activities for the Classic Period Maya (as Reflected at Caracol, Belize). In *Function and Meaning in Classic Maya Architecture*, edited by S. D. Houston, 299–332. Dumbarton Oaks, Washington, D.C.

2000 Inferences about Abandonment: Maya Household Archaeology and Caracol, Belize. *Mayab* 13:66–77.

2008 Late Postclassic Ritual at Santa Rita Corozal, Belize: Understanding the Archaeology of a Maya Capital City. *Research Reports in Belizean Archaeology* 5:79–92.

Chase, P. G.

1985 Whole Vessels and Sherds: An Experimental Investigation of Their Quantitative Relationships. *Journal of Field Archaeology* 12:213–18.

Cheetham, D.

1998 *Interregional Interaction, Symbol Emulation, and the Emergence of Sociopolitical Inequality in the Central Maya Lowlands*. Unpublished master's thesis, Department of Anthropology, University of British Columbia, Vancouver.

Cheetham, D., and J. J. Awe

1996 *The Early Formative Cunil Ceramic Complex at Cahal Pech, Belize*. Paper presented at the 61st Annual Meeting of the Society for American Archaeology, New Orleans.

2002 *The Cunil Ceramic Complex, Cahal Pech, Belize*. Manuscript on file, Department of Anthropology, Trent University, Peterborough, Ont.

Chilton, E. S.

1999 One Size Fits All: Typology and Alternatives for Ceramic Research. In *Material Meanings: Critical Approaches to the Interpretation of Material Culture*, edited by E. S. Chilton, 44–60. University of Utah Press, Salt Lake City.

Chinchilla, O., R. L. Bishop, M. J. Blackman, E. L. Sears, J. V. Genovez, and R. Moraga
1997 Long-Distance Ceramic Exchange in Cotzumagualpa: Results of Neutron Activation Analysis. Electronic document, http://www.famsi.org/reports/03101/97oswaldo_bishop/97oswaldo_bishop.pdf, accessed August 10, 2009. Foundation for the Advancement of Mesoamerican Studies, Inc. (FAMSI), Crystal River, Fla.

Chuchiak, J. F.
2009 De Descriptio Idolorum: An Ethnohistorical Examination of the Production, Imagery, and Functions of Colonial Yucatec Maya Idols and Effigy Censers, 1540–1700. In *Maya World Views at Conquest*, edited by L. Cecil and T. W. Pugh, 135–58. University Press of Colorado, Boulder.

Clark, J., and D. Cheetham
2002 Mesoamerica's Tribal Foundations. In *The Archaeology of Tribal Societies*, edited by W. Parkinson, 278–339. International Monographs in Prehistory, Archaeological Series no. 15. Ann Arbor.

Clayton, S. C.
2005 Interregional Relationships in Mesoamerica: Interpreting Maya Ceramics at Teotihuacan. *Latin American Antiquity* 16 (4): 427–48.

Cobos, R.
1999 Fuentes Historicas y Arqueologia: Convergencias y Divergencias e la Reconstruccion del Periodo Clasico Terminal en Chichen Itza. *Mayab* 12:58–70.
2004 Chichén Itzá: Settlement and Hegemony during the Terminal Classic Period. In *The Terminal Classic in the Maya Lowlands: Collapse, Transition, and Transformation*, edited by A. Demarest, P. M. Rice, and D. S. Rice, 517–44. University Press of Colorado, Boulder.

Coe, M. D.
1978 Supernatural Patrons of Maya Scribes and Artists. In *Social Process in Maya Prehistory*, edited by N. Hammond, 327–47. Academic Press, London.

Coe, M. D., and J. Kerr
1998 *The Art of the Maya Scribe*. Abrams, New York.

Coe, W. R.
1990 *Excavations in the Great Plaza, North Terrace, and North Acropolis of Tikal*. Tikal Report 14, vol. 3. Monograph 61. University Museum, University of Pennsylvania, Philadelphia.

Coe, W. R., and W. A. Haviland
1982 *Introduction to the Archaeology of Tikal, Guatemala*. Tikal Report 12. Monograph 46. University Museum, University of Pennsylvania, Philadelphia.

Coggins, C.
1975 *Painting and Drawing Styles at Tikal: An Historical and Iconographic Reconstruction*. Unpublished Ph.D. dissertation, Department of Art History, Harvard University, Cambridge, Mass.

J. W. Cogswell, D. R. Abbott, E. J. Miksa, H. Neff, R. J. Speakman, and M. D. Glascock
2005 Compositional Analysis of Hohokam Schist-Tempered Pottery and Raw Materials from the Middle Gila River Valley, Arizona: Techniques and Prospects. In *Laser Ablation-ICP-MS in Archaeological Research*, edited by R. J. Speakman and H. Neff, 105–15. University of New Mexico Press, Albuquerque.

Cogswell, J. W., H. Neff, and M. D. Glascock

1988 Analysis of Shell-Tempered Pottery Replicates: Implications for Provenance Studies. *American Antiquity* 63 (1): 63–72.

Colton, H. S.

1943 The Principle of Analogous Pottery Types. *American Anthropologist* 45 (2): 316–20.

Colton, H. S., and L. L. Hargrave

1937 *Handbook of Northern Arizona Pottery Wares*. Bulletin 11. Museum of Northern Arizona, Flagstaff.

Conkey, M. W., and C. A. Hastorf

1990 Introduction. In *The Uses of Style in Archaeology*, edited by M. W. Conkey and C. A. Hastorf, 1–4. Cambridge University Press, Cambridge.

Cortés, H.

1976 *Cartas de Relación*. 9th ed. Editorial Porrua, Mexico City.

Cowgill, G. L.

1963 *Postclassic Period Culture in the Vicinity of Flores, Petén, Guatemala*. Unpublished Ph.D. dissertation, Department of Anthropology, Harvard University, Cambridge, Mass.

Cuevas García, M., and G. Bernal

2002 La Function Ritual de los Incesarios Compuestos del Grupo de Las Cruces de Palenque. *Estudios de Cultura Maya* 22:13–32.

Culbert, T. P.

1977 Early Maya Development at Tikal, Guatemala. In *The Origins of Maya Civilization*, edited by R.E.W. Adams, 27–43. University of New Mexico Press, Albuquerque.

1991 Maya Political History and Elite Interaction: A Summary View. In *Classic Maya Political History: Hieroglyphic and Archaeological Evidence*, edited by T. P. Culbert, 311–45. Cambridge University Press, Cambridge.

1993 *The Ceramics of Tikal: Vessels from the Burials, Caches, and Problematical Deposits*. Tikal Reports 25A. University Museum Monograph 81. University of Pennsylvania, Philadelphia.

n.d. Ceramic Analysis of Tikal Ceramics by Ceramic Complex. Unpublished manuscript on file in the American Section of the University Museum, University of Pennsylvania, Philadelphia.

Culbert, T. P., L. J. Kosakowsky, R. E. Fry, and W. A. Haviland

1990 The Population of Tikal, Guatemala. In *Precolumbian Population History in the Maya Lowlands*, edited by T. P. Culbert and D. S. Rice, 103–22. University of New Mexico Press, Albuquerque.

Culbert, T. P., and R. L. Rands

2007 Multiple Classifications: An Alternative Approach to the Investigation of Maya Ceramics. *Latin American Antiquity* 18 (2): 181–90.

Culbert, T. P., and D. S. Rice

1990 *Precolumbian Population History in the Maya Lowlands*. University of New Mexico Press, Albuquerque.

Daniels, S.G.H.

1972 Research Design Models. In *Models in Archaeology*, edited by D. L. Clarke, 201–29. Methuen, London.

Demarest, A. A.

2004 After the Maelstrom: Collapse of the Classic Maya Kingdoms and the Terminal Classic in Western Petén. In *The Terminal Classic in the Maya Lowlands: Collapse, Transition, and Transformation*, edited by A. Demarest, P. M. Rice, and D. S. Rice, 102–24. University Press of Colorado, Boulder.

Demarest, A. A., P. M. Rice, and D. S. Rice

2004 The Terminal Classic in the Maya Lowlands: Assessing Collapses, Terminations, and Aftermaths. In *The Terminal Classic in the Maya Lowlands: Collapse, Transition, and Transformation*, edited by A. Demarest, P. M. Rice, and D. S. Rice, 545–72. University Press of Colorado, Boulder.

Dibble, H.

2008 Non-anthropological Approaches to Understanding Lithic Artifact and Assemblage Variability. In *Archaeological Concepts for the Study of the Cultural Past*, edited by A. P. Sullivan III, 85–107. University of Utah Press, Salt Lake City.

Dietler, M., and I. Herbich

1989 Tich Matek: The Technology of Luo Pottery Production and the Definition of Ceramic Style. *World Archaeology* 21 (1): 148–64.

Dillon, B.

1977 *Salinas de Los Nueve Cerros Guatemala*. Studies in Mesoamerican Art, Archaeology, and Ethnohistory no. 2. Ballena Press, Socorro, N.Mex.

Dobres, M.-A., and C. R. Hoffman

1994 Social Agency and the Dynamics of Prehistoric Technology. *Journal of Archaeological Method and Theory* 1 (3): 211–58.

Dominguez Carrasco, M. d. R.

1994 *Calakmul, Campeche: Analisis de la Ceramica*. Universidad Autónoma de Campeche, Campeche, Mexico.

Drennan, R. D.

1984 Long-Distance Transport Costs in Pre-Hispanic Mesoamerica. *American Anthropologist* 86:105–12.

Dull, R. A., J. R. Southon, and P. Sheets

2001 Volcanism, Ecology, and Culture: A Reassessment of the Volcán Ilopango TBJ Eruption in the Southern Maya Realm. *Latin American Antiquity* 12 (1): 25–44.

Duncan, W. N.

2005 *The Bioarchaeology of Ritual Violence in Postclassic El Petén, Guatemala (A.D. 950–1524)*. Unpublished Ph.D. dissertation, Department of Anthropology, Southern Illinois University, Carbondale.

Dunnell, R. C.

1971a Sabloff and Smith's "The Importance of Both Analytic and Taxonomic Classification in the Type-Variety System." *American Antiquity* 36 (1): 115–18.

1971b *Systematics in Prehistory*. Free Press, London.

Dunning, N. P.

1992 *Lords of the Hills: Ancient Maya Settlement in the Puuc Region, Yucatan, Mexico.* Monographs in World Archaeology no. 15. Prehistory Press, Madison, Wis.

2005 Fine Paste Wares and the Terminal Classic in the Petexbatun and Pasión Regions, Petén, Guatemala. In *Geographies of Power: Understanding the Nature of Terminal Classic Pottery in the Maya Lowlands*, edited by S. L. López Varela and A. Foias, 23–40. BAR International Series 1447. British Archaeological Reports, Oxford.

Edmonson, M. S.

1986 *Heaven Born Merida and Its Destiny: The Book of Chilam Balam of Tizimin.* University of Texas Press, Austin.

Estrada-Belli, F., ed.

2003 *Archaeological Investigations in the Holmul Region, Peten: Results of the Fourth Season, 2003.* Vanderbilt University, Nashville.

Estrada-Belli, F.

2004 Cival, La Sufricaya, and Holmul: The Long History of Maya Political Power and Settlement in the Holmul Region. Paper presented at 2nd Belize Archaeology Symposium, Belize City, July 7, 2004.

2006 Las Épocas Tempranas en el Área de Holmul, Petén. *Las Investigadores de la Cultura Maya* 14 (2): 307–16. Universidad Autonoma de Campeche, Campeche, Mexico.

2010 *The First Maya Civilization: Ritual and Power before the Classic Period.* Routledge, London.

Fash, W. L., E. W. Andrews V, and T. K. Manahan

2004 Political Decentralization, Dynastic Collapse, and the Early Postclassic in the Urban Center of Copán Honduras. In *The Terminal Classic in the Maya Lowlands: Collapse, Transition, and Transformation*, edited by A. Demarest, P. M. Rice, and D. S. Rice, 260–87. University Press of Colorado, Boulder.

Feinman, G. M., S. A. Kowaleski, L. Finsten, R. E. Blanton, and L. M. Nicholas

1985 Long-Term Demographic Change: A Perspective from the Valley of Oaxaca. *Journal of Field Archaeology* 12 (3): 333–62.

Ferree, L.

1967 *The Censers of Tikal, Guatemala: A Preliminary Sequence of the Major Shape-Types.* Unpublished M.A. thesis, Department of Anthropology, University of Pennsylvania, Philadelphia.

Fields, V. M.

2006 *Lords of Creation: The Origins of Sacred Maya Kingship.* Scala Publishers, London.

Foias, A. E.

1996 Changing Ceramic Production and Exchange Systems and the Classic Maya Collapse in the Petexbatun Region. Unpublished Ph.D. dissertation, Department of Anthropology, Vanderbilt University, Nashville.

2002 At the Crossroads: The Economic Basis of Political Power in the Petexbatun Region. In *Ancient Maya Political Economies*, edited by M. A. Masson and D. Freidel, 223–48. Altamira Press, Walnut Creek, Calif.

2004 The Past and the Future of Maya Ceramic Studies. In *Continuities and Changes in Maya Archaeology: Perspectives at the Millennium*, edited by C. W. Golden and G. Borgstede, 143–75. Routledge, New York.

Foias, A. E., and R. L. Bishop

1997 Changing Ceramic Production and Exchange in the Petexbatun Region, Guatemala: Reconsidering the Classic Maya Collapse. *Ancient Mesoamerica* 8 (1):275–91.

2005 Fine Paste Wares and the Terminal Classic in the Petexbatun and Pasión Regions, Petén, Guatemala. In *Geographies of Power: Understanding the Nature of Terminal Classic Pottery in the Maya Lowlands*, edited by S. L. López Varela and A. Foias, 23–40. BAR International Series 1447. British Archaeological Reports, Oxford.

2007 Pots, Sherds, and Glyphs: Pottery Production and Exchange in the Petexbatun Polity, Petén, Guatemala. In *Pottery Economics in Mesoamerica*, edited by C. A. Pool and G. J. Bey III, 212–36. University of Arizona Press, Tucson.

Folan, W. J., A. Morales, R. González, J. Hernández, L. Florey, R. Domínguez, V. Tiesler, D. Bolles, R. Ruiz, and J. D. Gunn

2003 Champotón, Campeche: Su Presencia en el Desarrollo Cultural del Golfo de Mexico y Su Corredor Eco-Arqueológico. *Investigadores de la Cultura Maya* 11 (1): 65–71.

Ford, A.

1991 Economic Variation of Ancient Maya Residential Settlement in the Upper Belize River Area. *Ancient Mesoamerica* 2 (1): 35–46.

Ford, A., and F. Spera

2007 Fresh Volcanic Glass Shards in the Pottery Sherds of the Maya Lowlands. *Research Reports in Belizean Archaeology* 4:111–18.

Ford, J. A.

1952 *Measurements of Some Prehistoric Design Developments in the Southeastern States*. Anthropological Papers of the American Museum of Natural History, vol. 44, part 3. New York.

1954 The Type Concept Revisited. *American Anthropologist* 56 (1): 42–57.

Forsyth, D. W.

1983 *Investigations at Edzna, Campeche, Mexico*, vol. 2, *Ceramics*. Papers of the New World Archaeological Foundation no. 46. Brigham Young University, Provo, Utah.

1989 *The Ceramics of El Mirador, Peten, Guatemala*. El Mirador Series, Part 4. Papers of the New World Archaeological Foundation no. 63. Brigham Young University, Provo, Utah.

2004 Reflexiones sobre la Ocupación Postclásica en Champotón a Través de la Cerámica. *Los Investigadores de la Cultura Maya* 12 (1): 33–37.

Freidel, D. A.

1975 The Ix Chel Shrine and Other Temples of Talking Idols. In *Changing Pre-Columbian Commercial Systems: The 1972–1973 Seasons at Cozumel, Mexico*, edited by J. A. Sabloff and W. Rathje, 107–13. Monographs of the Peabody Museum no. 3. Harvard University, Cambridge, Mass.

1981 The Political Economics of Residential Dispersion among the Lowland Maya.

In *Lowland Maya Settlement Patterns*, edited by W. Ashmore, 371–82. University of New Mexico Press, Albuquerque.

Freidel, D., and R. A. Robertson (editors)

1986 *Archaeology at Cerros, Belize, Central America*. Vol. 1, *An Interim Report*. Southern Methodist University Press, Dallas.

Friedrich, M. H.

1970 Design Structure and Social Interaction: Archaeological Implications of an Ethnographic Analysis. *American Antiquity* 35 (3): 332–43.

Fry, R. E.

1969 *Ceramics and Settlement in the Peripheries of Tikal*. Unpublished Ph.D. dissertation, Department of Anthropology, University of Arizona, Tucson.

1973a The Archaeology of Southern Quintana Roo: Part 2, Ceramics. In *Proceedings of the 40th Annual Congress of Americanists, Vol. 1*, 487–93. Tilgher, Genoa.

1973b *Uaymil Project Ceramic Codebook*. Manuscript on file, Department of Anthropology, Purdue University, West Lafayette, Ind.

1974 Settlement Systems in Southern Quintana Roo. Paper presented at the 41st International Congress of Americanists, Mexico City.

1979 The Economics of Pottery at Tikal, Guatemala: Models of Exchange for Serving Vessels. *American Antiquity* 44 (3): 494–512.

1980 Models of Exchange for Major Shape Classes of Lowland Maya Pottery. In *Models and Methods in Regional Exchange*, edited by R. E. Fry, 3–18. SAA Papers no. 1. Society for American Archaeology, Washington, D.C.

1981 Pottery Production-Distribution Systems in the Southern Maya Lowlands. In *Production and Distribution: A Ceramic Viewpoint*, edited by H. Howard and E. L. Morris, 145–67. BAR International Series 120. British Archaeological Reports, Oxford.

1987 The Ceramic Sequence of South-Central Quintana Roo, Mexico. In *Maya Ceramics: Papers from the 1985 Maya Ceramic Conference*, edited by P. M. Rice and R. J. Sharer, 111–22. BAR International Series 345 (1). British Archaeological Reports, Oxford.

1989 Regional Ceramic Distributional Patterning in Northern Belize: The View from Pulltrouser Swamp. In *Prehistoric Maya Economies of Belize*, edited by P. A. McAnany and B. L. Issac, 91–111. Research in Economic Anthropology, Supplement 4. JAI Press, Greenwich, Conn.

1990 Disjunctive Growth in the Maya Lowlands. In *Precolumbian Population History in the Maya Lowlands*, edited by T. P. Culbert and D. S. Rice, 285–300. University of New Mexico Press, Albuquerque.

2003a The Peripheries of Tikal. In *Tikal: Dynasties, Foreigners, and Affairs of State*, edited by J. A. Sabloff, 143–70. School of American Research Press, Santa Fe, N.Mex.

2003b Social Dimensions in Ceramic Analysis: A Case Study from Peripheral Tikal. *Ancient Mesoamerica* 14 (1):85–93.

Fry, R. E., and S. C. Cox

1973 *Late Classic Pottery Manufacture and Distribution at Tikal, Guatemala*. Working Paper no. 70. Institute for the Study of Social Change, Purdue University, West Lafayette, Ind.

1974 The Structure of Ceramic Exchange at Tikal, Guatemala. *World Archaeology* 6 (2):209–25.

Gann, T. W.

1900 *Mounds in Northern Honduras*. In *Nineteenth Annual Report, 1897–1898, Bureau of American Ethnology, Part 2*, 661–92. Smithsonian Institution, Washington, D.C.

Gann, T., M. Gann, and A.J.E. Cave

1939 *Archaeological Investigations in the Corozal District of British Honduras*. Bureau of American Ethnology Bulletin 123. Washington, D.C.

Garber, J. F.

2009 A Terminal Early Formative Symbol System in the Maya Lowlands: The Iconography of the Cunil Phase (1100–900 B.C.) at Cahal Pech. *Research Reports in Belizean Archaeology* 6:151–60.

Garber, J. F., and J. J. Awe

2008a Ritual and Symbolism of the Early Maya of the Belize Valley. Paper presented at the 73rd Annual Meeting of the Society for American Archaeology, Vancouver.

2008b A Terminal Early Formative Symbol System in the Maya Lowlands: The Iconography of the Cunil Phase (1100–900 B.C.) at Cahal Pech. *Research Reports in Belizean Archaeology* 6:151–59.

Garber, J. F., M. K. Brown, J. J. Awe, and C. K. Hartman

2004 Middle Formative Prehistory of the Central Belize Valley: An Examination of Architecture, Material Culture, and Sociopolitical Change at Blackman Eddy. In *Archaeology of the Upper Belize Valley: Half a Century of Maya Research*, edited by J. F. Garber, 25–47. University Press of Florida, Gainesville.

Garber, J. F., J. L. Cochrane, and J. J. Awe

2005 Excavations in Plaza B at Cahal Pech: The 2004 Field Season. In *The Belize Valley Archaeology Project: Results of the 2004 Field Season*, edited by J. F. Garber, 4–41. Texas State University, San Marcos.

Garber, J. F., ed.

2004 *The Ancient Maya of the Belize Valley: Half a Century of Archaeological Research*. University Press of Florida, Gainesville.

Gell, A.

1998 *Art and Agency: An Anthropological Theory*. Oxford University Press, Oxford.

Gifford, C. A., and M. Kirkpatrick

1996 Pottery Types in the Cerámica Index of Nomenclature Listed by Type-Class. *Cerámica de Cultura Maya* 18:175–203.

Gifford, J. C.

1957 *Archaeological Explorations in Caves of the Point of Pines Region*. Unpublished M.A. thesis, Department of Anthropology, University of Arizona, Tucson.

1960 The Type-Variety Method of Ceramic Classification as an Indicator of Cultural Phenomena. *American Antiquity* 25 (3): 341–47.

1961 Place and Geographical Names in the Archaeological Nomenclature of the Maya Territory and Neighboring Regions (Part 1). *Ceramica de Cultura Maya* 1 (1): 3–25.

1963 *A Conceptual Approach to the Analysis of Prehistoric Pottery*. Unpublished Ph.D. dissertation, Department of Anthropology, Harvard University, Cambridge.

1976 *Prehistoric Pottery Analysis and the Ceramics of Barton Ramie in the Belize Valley.* Memoirs of the Peabody Museum of Archaeology and Ethnology, vol. 18. Harvard University, Cambridge, Mass.

Gladwin, W., and H. S. Gladwin

1930 *A Method for the Designation of Southwestern Pottery Types.* Medallion Papers no. 7. Globe, Ariz.

Glascock, M. D.

1992 Characterization of Archaeological Ceramics at Murr by Neutron Activation Analysis and Multivariate Statistics. In *Chemical Characterization of Ceramic Pastes in Archaeology*, edited by H. Neff, 11–26. Prehistory Press, Madison, Wis.

Goldstein, M. M.

1977 The Ceremonial Role of the Maya Flanged Censer. *Man* 12:405–20.

Gosselain, O. P.

1992 Technology and Style: Potters and Pottery among Bafia of Cameroon. *Man*, n.s., 27 (82): 559–86.

1998 Social and Technical Identity in a Clay Crystal Ball. In *The Archaeology of Social Boundaries*, edited by M. T. Stark, 78–106. Smithsonian Institution Press, Washington, D.C.

2000 Materializing Identities: An African Perspective. *Journal of Archaeological Method and Theory* 7 (3): 187–217.

Graff, D. H.

1997 Dating a Section of the Madrid Codex: Astronomical and Iconographic Evidence. In *Papers on the Madrid Codex*, edited by V. R. Bricker and G. Vail, 147–67. Middle American Research Institute Publication 64. Tulane University, New Orleans.

Graham, E.

1987 Terminal Classic to Early Historic Vessel Forms from Belize. In *Maya Ceramics: Papers from the 1985 Maya Ceramic Conference*, edited by P. M. Rice and R. J. Sharer, 73–98. BAR International Series 345 (1). British Archaeological Reports, Oxford.

1994 *The Highlands of the Lowlands: Environment and Archaeology in the Stann Creek District, Belize, Central America.* Monographs in World Prehistory no. 19. Prehistory Press, Madison, Wis.

2004 Lamanai Reloaded: Alive and Well in the Early Postclassic. *Research Reports in Belizean Archaeology* 1:223–41.

2008 Lamanai, Belize, from Collapse to Conquest—Radiocarbon Dates from Lamanai. Paper presented at the 106th Meeting of the American Anthropological Association, November 28–December 2, Washington, D.C.

Graham, E., and D. M. Pendergast

1989 Excavations at the Marco Gonzalez site, Ambergris Caye, Belize, 1986. *Journal of Field Archaeology* 16:1–16.

Graves, M. W.

1991 Pottery Production and Distribution among the Kalinga: A Study of Household and Regional Organization and Differentiation. In *Ceramic Ethnoarchaeology*, edited by W. A. Longacre, 112–43. University of Arizona Press, Tucson.

1994 Kalinga Social and Material Culture Boundaries: A Case of Spatial Convergence. In *Kalinga Ethnoarchaeology: Expanding Archaeological Method and Theory*, edited by W. A. Longacre and J. M. Skibo, 13–49. Smithsonian Institution Press, Washington, D.C.

Halperin, Christina T., and Antonia E. Foias

2010 Pottery Politics: Late Classic Maya Palace Production at Motul de San José, Petén, Guatemala. *Journal of Anthropological Archaeology* 29 (3): 392–411.

Hammer, Olga

1971 *Ancient Art of Veracruz*. Ethnic Arts Council of Los Angeles, Los Angeles.

Hammond, N.

1972 A Minor Criticism of the Type-Variety System of Ceramic Analysis. *American Antiquity* 37 (3): 450–52.

1974 Preclassic to Postclassic in Northern Belize. *Antiquity* 48:177–89.

1975 *Lubaantun: A Classic Maya Realm*. Monographs of the Peabody Museum of Archaeology and Ethnology no. 2. Harvard University, Cambridge, Mass.

1977 Ex Oriente Lux: A View from Belize. In *The Origins of Maya Civilization*, edited by R.E.W. Adams, 45–76. University of New Mexico Press, Albuquerque.

1984 Holmul and Nohmul: A Comparison and Assessment of Two Maya Lowland Protoclassic Sites. *Ceramica de Cultura Maya* 13:1–17.

Hammond, N., and G. Harbottle

1976 Neutron Activation and Statistical Analysis of Maya Ceramic Clays from Lubaantun, Belize. *Archaeometry* 18:147–68.

Hammond, N., D. Pring, R. Wilk, S. Donaghey, F. P. Saul, E. S. Wing, A. V. Miller, and L. H. Feldman

1979 The Earliest Lowland Maya? Definition of the Swasey Phase. *American Antiquity* 44 (1): 92–110.

Hargrave, L. L., and H. S. Colton

1935 What Do Potsherds Tell Us? *Museum Notes, Museum of Northern Arizona, Flagstaff* 7 (12): 49–51.

Haviland, W. A.

1966 *Maya Settlement Patterns: A Critical Review*. Middle American Research Institute Publication 26. Tulane University, New Orleans.

Haviland, W. A., M. J. Becker, A. Chowning, K. A. Dixon, and K. Heider

1985 *Excavations in Small Residential Groups of Tikal: Groups 4f-1 and 4f-2*. Tikal Report 19. University Museum Monograph 58. University of Pennsylvania, Philadelphia.

Hayden, B., and R. Gargett

1990 Big Man, Big Heart? A Mesoamerican View of the Emergence of Complex Society. *Ancient Mesoamerica* 1:3–20.

Healy, P. F., and J. J. Awe (editors)

1995 *Belize Valley Preclassic Maya Project: Report on the 1994 Field Season*. Trent University Department of Anthropology Occasional Papers no. 10. Peterborough, Ont.

1996 *Belize Valley Preclassic Maya Project: Report on the 1995 Field Season*. Trent University Department of Anthropology Occasional Papers no. 12. Peterborough, Ont.

Healy, P. F., D. Cheetham, T. G. Powis, and J. J. Awe

2004 Cahal Pech: The Middle Formative Period. In *The Ancient Maya of the Belize Valley: Half a Century of Archaeological Research*, edited by J. F. Garber, 103–24. University Press of Florida, Gainesville.

Hegmon, M.

1998 Technology, Style, and Social Practice: Archaeological Approaches. In *The Archaeology of Social Boundaries*, edited by M. T. Stark, 264–80. Smithsonian Institution Press, Washington, D.C.

Henderson, J. S., and R. F. Agurcia

1987 Ceramic Systems: Facilitating Comparison in Type-Variety Analysis. In *Maya Ceramics: Papers from the 1985 Maya Ceramic Conference*, edited by P. M. Rice and R. J. Sharer, 431–38. BAR International Series 345 (2). British Archaeological Reports, Oxford.

Henderson, J. S., and M. Beaudry-Corbett (editors)

1993 *Pottery of Prehistoric Honduras: Regional Classification and Analysis.* Monograph 35. Institute of Archaeology, University of California, Los Angeles.

Hermes, B., and R. Noriega

1997 El Período Postclásico en el Area de la Laguna Yaxhá: Una Vision desde Topoxté. In *XI Simposio de Investigaciones Arqueologicas en Guatemala*, edited by J. P. LaPorte and H. L. Escobedo, 878–902. Ministerio de Cultura de Desportes, Instituto de Antropología e Historia, Asociacion Tikal, Guatemala City.

Hester, T. R., H. J. Shafer, and J. D. Eaton

1982 *Archaeology at Colha, Belize: The 1981 Interim Report.* Center for Archaeological Research, University of Texas at San Antonio.

Hill, J. N., and R. K. Evans

1972 A Model for Classification and Typology. In *Models in Archaeology*, edited by D. L. Clarke, 231–73. Methuen, London.

Hirth, K. G.

1978 Interregional Exchange and the Formation of Prehistoric Gateway Cities. *American Antiquity* 43:35–45.

Holland, D., W. Lachicotte Jr., D. Skinner, and C. Cain

1998 *Identity and Agency in Cultural Worlds.* Cambridge University Press, Cambridge.

Houston, S. D.

1998 Classic Maya Depictions of the Built Environment. In *Function and Meaning in Classic Maya Architecture*, edited by S. D. Houston, 333–72. Dumbarton Oaks Research Library and Collection, Washington, D.C.

Howie, L. A.

2005 *Ceramic Production and Consumption in the Maya Lowlands during the Classic to Postclassic Transition: A Technological Study of Ceramics at Lamanai, Belize.* Unpublished Ph.D. thesis, Department of Archaeology, University of Sheffield.

Howie, Linda, J. Aimers, and E. Graham

2012 50 Left Feet: The Manufacture and Meaning of Effigy Censers from Lamanai, Belize. In *Selected Papers from the European Conference on Ancient Ceramics*, edited by M. Martinon-Torres and C. Cartwright. Archetype, London. Forthcoming.

Howie, L. A., P. M. Day, E. Graham, and V. Kilikoglou

2003 Ceramic Change during the Terminal Classic to Early Postclassic at Lamanai, Belize. Paper presented at the 68th Annual Meeting of the Society for American Archaeology, Milwaukee.

Ichon, A., and C. Arnauld

1985 *Le Protoclassique a La Lagunita, El Quiche, Guatemala*. Centre National de la Recherche Scientifique, Paris.

Inomata, T.

1997 The Last Day of a Fortified Classic Maya Center: Archaeological Investigations at Aguateca, Guatemala. *Ancient Mesoamerica* 8:337–51.

2001 The Power and Ideology of Artistic Creation. *Current Anthropology* 43 (3): 321–48.

Inomata, T., and D. Triadan

2000 Craft Production by Classic Maya Elites in Domestic Settings: Data from Rapidly Abandoned Structures at Aguateca, Guatemala. *Mayab* 11:2–39.

John, J. R.

2008 *Postclassic Iconography at Lamanai, Belize, Central America*. Unpublished Ph.D. dissertation, Institute of Archaeology, University College London.

Johnson, S. C.

1967 Hierarchical Cluster Schemes. *Psychometrika* 32:241–51.

Jones, C.

1991 Cycles of Growth at Tikal. In *Classic Maya Political History: Hieroglyphic and Archaeological Evidence*, edited by T. P. Culbert, 102–24. Cambridge University Press, Cambridge.

Jones, G. D.

1989 *Maya Resistance to Spanish Rule: Time and History on a Spanish Colonial Frontier*. University of New Mexico Press, Albuquerque.

1998 *The Conquest of the Last Maya Kingdom*. Stanford University Press, Stanford.

Jones, G. D., D. S. Rice, and P. M. Rice

1981 The Location of Tayasal: A Reconsideration in Light of Petén Maya Ethnohistory and Archaeology. *American Antiquity* 46 (3): 530–47.

Kerr, J.

1989 *Maya Vase Book: A Corpus of Rollout Photographs of Maya Vases, Vol. 1*. Kerr Associates, New York.

1990 *Maya Vase Book: A Corpus of Rollout Photographs of Maya Vases, Vol. 2*. Kerr Associates, New York.

1992 *Maya Vase Book: A Corpus of Rollout Photographs of Maya Vases, Vol. 3*. Kerr Associates, New York.

1994 *Maya Vase Book: A Corpus of Rollout Photographs of Maya Vases, Vol. 4*. Kerr Associates, New York.

1997 *Maya Vase Book: A Corpus of Rollout Photographs of Maya Vases, Vol. 5*. Kerr Associates, New York.

2000 *Maya Vase Book: A Corpus of Rollout Photographs of Maya Vases, Vol. 6*. Kerr Associates, New York.

Kidder, A. V.
1915 Pottery of the Pajarito Plateau and Some Adjacent Regions in New Mexico. *American Anthropological Association Memoir* 2:407–602.
1917 A Design Sequence from New Mexico. *National Academy of Sciences, Proceedings* 3:369–70.
1927 Southwestern Archaeological Conference. *Science* 66:489–91.
Kluckhohn, C.
1951 An Anthropological Approach to the Study of Values. *Bulletin of the American Academy of Arts and Sciences* 4 (6): 2–3.
1958 The Scientific Study of Values. In *University of Toronto Installation Lectures/1958*, 25–54. University of Toronto Press, Toronto.
1977 The Conceptual Structure in Middle American Studies. In *The Maya and Their Neighbors: Essays on Middle American Anthropology and Archaeology*, edited by C. L. Hay, R. L. Linton, S. K. Lothrop, H. L. Shapiro, and G. C. Vaillant, 41–51. Reprint, Dover, New York. Originally published 1940.
Kopytoff, I.
1988 The Cultural Biography of Things: Commoditization as Process. In *The Social Life of Things: Commodities in Cultural Perspective*, edited by A. Appadurai, 64–94. Cambridge University Press, Cambridge.
Kosakowsky, L. J.
1987 *Preclassic Maya Pottery at Cuello, Belize*. Anthropological Papers of the University of Arizona no. 47. University of Arizona Press, Tucson.
2003 Shaping Ceramic Research at the Maya Site of Cuello, Belize. *Ancient Mesoamerica* 14 (1):61–66.
Kosakowsky, L. J., and D. Pring
1998 The Ceramics of Cuello Belize: A New Evaluation. *Ancient Mesoamerica* 9 (1): 55–66.
Kovacevich, B.
2006 *Reconstructing Classic Maya Economic Systems: Lithic Production and Exchange at Cancuen, Guatemala*. Unpublished Ph.D. dissertation, Department of Anthropology, Vanderbilt University, Nashville.
2007 Ritual, Crafting, and Agency at the Classic Maya Kingdom of Cancuen. In *Mesoamerican Ritual Economy: Archaeological and Ethnological Perspectives*, edited by E. C. Wells and K. Davis-Salazar, 67–114. University Press of Colorado, Boulder.
Kowaleski, S. A., G. M. Feinman, L. Finsten, R. E. Blanton, and L. M. Nicholas
1989 *Monte Alban's Hinterland, Part II: Prehispanic Settlement Patterns in Tlacolula, Etla and Ocotlan, the Valley of Oaxaca, Mexico*. Memoirs no. 23. Museum of Anthropology, University of Michigan, Ann Arbor.
Kruskal, J. B., F. W. Young, and J. B. Seery
1972 *KYST: A Computer Program for Multidimensional Scaling and Unfolding*. Bell Telephone Labs, Murray Hill, N.J.
Laporte, J. P., and V. Fialko
1987 La Ceramica de Clasico Temprano desde Mundo Perdido, Tikal: Una Reevaluacion. In *Papers from the 1985 Maya Ceramic Conference*, edited by P. M. Rice

and R. J. Sharer, 123–81. BAR International Series 345 (1). British Archaeological Reports, Oxford.

1990 New Perspectives on Old Problems: Dynastic References for the Early Classic at Tikal. In *Vision and Revision in Maya Studies*, edited by F. J. Clancy and P. D. Harrison, 33–66. University of New Mexico Press, Albuquerque.

1995 Un Reencuentro con Mundo Perdido, Tikal, Guatemala. *Ancient Mesoamerica* 6 (1): 41–94.

Laporte, J. P., B. Hermes, L. de Zea, and M. J. Iglesias

1992 Nuevos Entierros y Escondites de Tikal, Subfases Manik 3a and 3b. *Ceramica de Cultura Maya* 16:30–101.

Lechtman, H.

1977 Style in Technology: Some Early Thoughts. In *Material Culture: Style, Organization, and Dynamics of Technology*, edited by H. Lechtman and R. S. Merrill, 3–20. West, New York.

1984 Andean Value Systems and the Development of Prehistoric Metallurgy. *Technology and Culture* 25 (1): 1–36.

1993 Technologies of Power: The Andean Case. In *Configurations of Power in Complex Societies*, edited by J. Henderson and P. Netherly, 244–80. Cornell University Press, Ithaca, N.Y.

Lechtman, H., and A. Steinberg

1979 The History of Technology: An Anthropological Point of View. In *The History and Philosophy of Technology*, edited by G. Bugliarello and D. B. Doner, 135–60. University of Chicago Press, Chicago.

LeCount, L. J.

1996 *Pottery and Power: Feasting, Gifting, and Displaying Wealth among the Late and Terminal Classic Lowland Maya*. Unpublished Ph.D. dissertation, Department of Anthropology, University of California, Los Angeles.

LeCount, L. J., J. Yaeger, R. M. Leventhal, and W. Ashmore

2002 Dating the Rise and Fall of Xunantunich, Belize: A Late and Terminal Classic Lowland Maya Regional Center. *Ancient Mesoamerica* 13 (1): 41–63.

Lemonicr, P.

1986 The Study of Material Culture Today: Towards an Anthropology of Technical Systems. *Journal of Anthropological Archaeology* 5:147–86.

Leventhal, R. M., A. A. Demarest, and G. R. Willey

1987 The Cultural and Social Components of Copan. In *Polities and Partitions: Human Boundaries and the Growth of Complex Societies*, edited by K. M. Trinkaus, 178–205. Arizona State University Anthropological Research Papers no. 37. Tempe.

Lincoln, C. E.

1985 Ceramics and Ceramic Chronology. In *A Consideration of the Early Classic Period in the Maya Lowlands*, edited by G. R. Willey and P. Matthews, 55–94. Mesoamerican Studies Publication 10. State University of New York, Albany.

1986 The Chronology of Chichén Itzá: A Review of the Literature. In *Late Lowland Maya Civilization: Classic to Postclassic*, edited by J. A. Sabloff and E. W. Andrews V, 141–96. School of American Research, University of New Mexico Press, Albuquerque.

Longacre, W. A.
1981 Kalinga Pottery: An Ethnoarchaeological Study. In *Patterns of the Past: Studies in Honour of David Clarke*, edited by I. Hodder, G. Isaac, and N. Hammond, 49–66. Cambridge University Press, Cambridge.
Longacre, William A., and Miriam T. Stark
1992 Ceramics, Kinship, and Space: A Kalinga Example. *Journal of Anthropological Archaeology* 11:125–36.
López Varela, S. L.
1989 *Análisis y Clasificación de la Cerámica de un Sitio Maya del Clásico: Yaxchilán, México*. BAR International Series 535. British Archaeological Reports, Oxford.
1996 *The K'axob Formative Ceramics: The Search for Regional Integration through a Reappraisal of Ceramic Analysis and Classification in Northern Belize*. Unpublished Ph.D. dissertation, Institute of Archaeology, University College London.
Loten, H. S.
1985 Lamanai Postclassic. In *The Lowland Maya Postclassic*, edited by A. F. Chase and P. M. Rice, 85–90. University of Texas Press, Austin.
Love, Bruce
1994 *The Paris Codex: Handbook for a Maya Priest*. University of Texas Press, Austin.
Lowe, G., and P. Agrinier
1960 *Mound 1, Chiapa de Corzo, Mexico*. Papers of the New World Archaeological Foundation no. 8. Provo, Utah.
Lyman, R. L., M. J. O'Brien, and R. C. Dunnell
1997 *The Rise and Fall of Culture History*. Plenum Press, New York.
Magurran, A. E.
2003 *Measuring Biological Diversity*. Wiley-Blackwell, Malden, Mass.
Malakoff, D.
2011 The Mesoamerican-Southwest Connection. *American Archaeology* 15:32–37.
Manahan, T. K.
2000 After the Fall: Examining the Nature of the Classic Maya Collapse of Copan. Electronic document, http://www.famsi.org/reports/98038/, accessed August 10, 2009. Foundation for the Advancement of Mesoamerican Studies, Inc. (FAMSI), Crystal River, Fla.
2004 The Way Things Fall Apart: Social Organization and the Classic Maya Collapse of Copán. *Ancient Mesoamerica* 15 (1): 107–25.
Mardia, K. V., J. T. Kent, and J. M. Bibby
1979 *Multivariate Analysis*. Academic Press, London.
Martos, L. A.
2002 La Costa Oriental de Quintana Roo. *Arqueología Mexicana* 9 (54): 26–33.
Masson, M. A.
2000 *In the Realm of Nachan Kan: Postclassic Maya Archaeology at Laguna de On, Belize*. University Press of Colorado, Boulder.
2002 Introduction. In *Ancient Maya Political Economies*, edited by M. A. Masson and D. Freidel, 1–30. Altamira Press, Walnut Creek, Calif.
2003 The Late Postclassic Symbol Set in the Maya Area. In *The Postclassic Mesoamerican World*, edited by M. E. Smith and F. M. Berdan, 194–200. University of Utah Press, Salt Lake City.

Masson, M. A., and C. Peraza Lope
2005 Nuevas Investigaciones en Tres Unidades Residenciales Fuera del Area Monumental de Mayapán. *Investigadores de Cultura Maya* 13:411–24.
2006 Figurines and Social Diversity at Mayapán. Paper presented at the International Congress of Americanists, Seville, Spain.
2010 Evidence for Maya-Mexican Interaction in the Archaeological Record of Mayapan. In *Astronomers, Scribes, and Priests: Intellectual Interchange between the Northern Maya Lowlands and Highland Mexico in the Late Postclassic Period*, edited by G. Vail and C. Hernandez, 77–114. Dumbarton Oaks, Washington, D.C.
2012 *Kukulkan's Realm: The Postclassic City of Mayapán*. University Press of Colorado, Boulder. Forthcoming.

Matheny, R. T.
1970 *The Ceramics of Aguacatal, Campeche, Mexico*. Publication no. 27. New World Archaeological Foundation, Provo, Utah.

Mathews, P.
1991 Classic Maya Emblem Glyphs. In *Classic Maya Political History*, edited by T. P. Culbert, 19–29. Cambridge University Press, Cambridge.

McAnany, P. A.
1998 Ancestors and the Classic Maya Built Environment. In *Function and Meaning in Classic Maya Architecture*, edited by S. D. Houston, 271–98. Dumbarton Oaks Research Library and Collection, Washington, D.C.

McCafferty, G. G.
2007 Altar Egos: Domestic Ritual and Social Identity in Postclassic Cholula. In *Commoner Ritual and Ideology in Ancient Mesoamerica*, edited by N. Gonlin and J. C. Lohse, 213–50. University Press of Colorado, Boulder.

McCullough, W. F.
1984 Sand-Gauge. Beltsville, Md.

McFarlane, W. J.
2005 *Power Strategies in a Changing World: Archaeological Investigations of Early Postclassic Remains at El Coyote, Santa Barbara, Honduras*. Unpublished Ph.D. dissertation, State University of New York, Buffalo.

McGee, R. J.
1998 The Lacandon Incense Burner Renewal Ceremony: Termination and Dedication Ritual among the Contemporary Maya. In *The Sowing and Dawning: Termination, Dedication, and Transformation in the Archaeological and Ethnographic Record of Mesoamerica*, edited by S. B. Mock, 41–52. University of New Mexico Press, Albuquerque.

Merwin, R. E., and G. C. Vaillant
1932 *The Ruins of Holmul, Guatemala*. Memoirs of the Peabody Museum, vol. 3, no. 2. Harvard University, Cambridge, Mass.

Milbrath, S.
1999 *Star Gods of the Maya: Astronomy in Art, Folklore, and Calendars*. University of Texas Press, Austin.
2005 The Last Great Capital of the Maya. *Archaeology* 58 (2): 26–29.

2007a Incensarios Efigie de Mayapán: Iconografía, Contexto y Relaciones Externas. Paper presented at VII Congreso Internacional de Mayistas, Mérida, Yucatán.

2007b Mayapan's Effigy Censers: Iconography, Context, and External Connections. Electronic document, http://www.famsi.org/reports/05025, accessed August 5, 2009. Final Report to the Foundation for Mesoamerican Studies, Inc. (FAMSI), Crystal River, Fla.

Milbrath, S., J. J. Aimers, C. Peraza Lope, and L. F. Folan

2008 Effigy Censers of the Chen Mul Modeled Ceramic System and Their Implications for Late Postclassic Maya Interregional Interaction. *Mexicon* 15 (5): 104–12.

Milbrath, S., and C. Peraza Lope

2003a Mayapán's Scribe: A Link with Classic Maya Artists. *Mexicon* 15 (5): 120–23.

2003b Revisiting Mayapán: Mexico's Last Maya Capital. *Ancient Mesoamerica* 14:1–46.

2009 Clash of Worldviews in Late Mayapán. In *Maya Worldviews at Conquest*, edited by L. Cecil and T. W. Pugh, 183–204. University Press of Colorado, Boulder.

Miller, A. G.

1982 *On the Edge of the Sea: Mural Painting at Tancah-Tulum, Mexico*. Dumbarton Oaks, Washington, D.C.

Millet Cámara, L.

1992 *Mirador Campechano*. Universidad Autónoma de Campeche, Campeche, Mexico.

Millon, R.

1973 The Teotihuacán Map, Part 1: Text. In *Urbanization at Teotihuacan, Mexico*, edited by R. Millon, B. Drewitt, and G. L. Cowgill, 1–154. University of Texas Press, Austin.

Mohr Chávez, K. L.

1992 The Organization of Production and Distribution of Traditional Pottery in South Highland Peru. In *Ceramic Production and Distribution: An Integrated Approach*, edited by G. J. Bey III and C. A. Pool, 49–92. Westview Press, Boulder, Colo.

Munsell Soil Charts

2000 Munsell Soil Color Charts. Revised washable edition. GretagMacbeth, New Windsor, N.Y.

Nalda, E.

2005 Kohunlich and Dzibanché: Parallel Histories. In *Quintana Roo Archaeology*, edited by J. M. Shaw and J. Matthews, 228–44. University of Arizona Press, Tucson.

Nalda, E., and J. López Camacho

1995 Investigaciones Arqueológicas en el Sur de Quintana Roo. *Arqueología Mexicana* 3 (14): 12–72.

Navarette, C., M.J.C. Uribe, and A. M. Muriel

1979 *Observaciones Arqueológicas en Coba, Quintana Roo*. Universidad Nacional Autonoma de Mexico, Mexico City.

Neff, H.

2001 Production and Distribution of Plumbate Pottery: Evidence from a Provenance Study of the Paste and Slip Clay Used in a Famous Mesoamerican Trade Ware. Electronic document, http://www.famsi.org/reports/98061/, accessed August

10, 2009. Foundation for the Advancement of Mesoamerican Studies, Inc. (FAMSI), Crystal River, Fla.

2003 Analysis of Mesoamerican Plumbate Pottery Surfaces by Laser Ablation–Inductively Coupled Plasma–Mass Spectrometry (La-Icp-Ms). *Journal of Archaeological Science* 30 (1): 21–35.

Neivens de Estrada, Nina

2010 Early Lowland Maya Ceramics: Material from Holmul, Peten, Guatemala. Paper presented at the 75th Annual Society for the American Archaeology Meetings, St. Louis, Mo.

Nichols, D. L., E. Brumfiel, H. Neff, M. Hodge, T. Charlton, and M. D. Glascock

2001 Neutrons, Markets, Cities, and Empires: A 1000-Year Perspective on Ceramic Production and Distribution in the Postclassic Basin of Mexico. *Journal of Anthropological Archaeology* 21:25–82.

Nielsen, J., and Bente Juhl Andersen

2004 Collecting in Corozal: Late Postclassic Maya Effigy Censers from Belize in the Danish National Museum (1860–1865). *Mayab* 17:84–98.

O'Brien, M. J., and R. L. Lyman

2003 *Cladistics and Archaeology*. University of Utah Press, Salt Lake City.

Ojeda Mas, H.

2007 Exploraciones Arqueológicas en el Sitio de Acanmul, Campeche. In *El Patrimonio Arqueológico Maya en Campeche: Novedades, Afectaciones y Soluciones*, edited by E. Vargas and A. Benavides, 23–46. Universidad Nacional Autónoma de México, Instituto de Investigaciones Filológicas/Centro de Estudios Maya, Mexico City.

Paxton, Merideth

2004 Tayasal Origin of the Madrid Codex: Further Consideration of the Theory. In *The Madrid Codex*, edited by Gabrielle Vail and Anthony F. Aveni, 89–127. University Press of Colorado, Boulder.

Pendergast, D. M.

1969 *The Prehistory of Actun Balam, British Honduras*. Occasional Paper 16. Art and Archaeology, Royal Ontario Museum, Toronto.

1971 *Excavations at Eduardo Quiroz Cave, British Honduras (Belize)*. Occasional Paper 21. Art and Archaeology, Royal Ontario Museum, Toronto.

1979 *Excavations at Altun Ha, Belize, 1964–1970, Vol. 1*. Royal Ontario Museum, Toronto.

1981 Lamanai, Belize: Summary of Excavation Results, 1974–1980. *Journal of Field Archaeology* 8 (1): 29–53.

1982 Lamanai, Belize, durante el Post-Clásico. *Estudios de Cultura Maya* 14:19–58.

1983/84 The Hunchback Tomb. *Rotunda* 16 (4): 5–11.

1985a Lamanai, Belize: An Updated View. In *The Lowland Maya Postclassic*, edited by A. F. Chase and P. M. Rice, 91–103. University of Texas Press, Austin.

1985b Stability through Change: Lamanai, Belize, from the Ninth to the Seventeenth Century. In *Late Lowland Maya Civilization: Classic to Postclassic*, edited by J. A. Sabloff and E. W. Andrews V, 223–49. School of American Research, University of New Mexico Press, Albuquerque.

1986 Under Spanish Rule: The Final Chapters in Lamanai's Maya History. *Belcast Journal of Belizean Affairs* 3 (1–2): 1–7.

1990 Up from the Dust: The Central Lowlands Postclassic as Seen from Lamanai and Marco Gonzalez, Belize. In *Vision and Revision in Maya Studies*, edited by P. D. Harrison and F. S. Clancy, 169–77. University of New Mexico Press, Albuquerque.

Peraza Lope, C., P. Delgado Kú, and B. Escamilla Ojeda

1997 Trabajos de Mantenimiento y Conservación Arquitectonica en Mayapán, Yucatán: Informe de la Cuarta Temporada, 1996. Centro INAH, Yucatán.

2003 Trabajos de Mantenimiento y Conservación Arquitectonica en Mayapán, Yucatán: Informe de la Cuarta Temporada, 1999–2000. Centro INAH, Yucatán.

Peraza Lope, C., J. Escarela Rodríguez, and P. Delgado Kú

2004 Trabajos de Mantenimiento y Conservación Arquitectonica en Mayapán, Yucatán: Informe de la Séptima Temporada, 2003. Centro INAH, Yucatán.

Peraza Lope, C., and M. A. Masson

2005 Patrones Espaciales del Uso de Efigies en Incensarios y Esculturals en Mayapán. Paper presented at Segundo Congreso Internacional de la Cultura Maya. Mérida, Yucatán.

Peraza Lope, C., M. Masson, T. H. Hare, and P. Delgado Kú

2006 The Chronology of Mayapan: New Radiocarbon Evidence. *Ancient Mesoamerica* 17 (2): 153–75.

Pérez Suárez, T., and M. Zabé

1999 Imágenes de Lost Mayas en San Ildefonso. Special issue, *Arqueología Mexicana* 3:8–75.

Phillips, P.

1958 Application of the Wheat-Gifford-Wasley Taxonomy to Eastern Ceramics. *American Antiquity* 24 (2): 117–25.

Plog, S., and S. Upham

1989 Productive Specialization, Archaeometry, and Interpretation. In *Pottery Technology: Ideas and Approaches*, edited by G. Bronitsky, 207–16. Westview Press, Boulder, Colo.

Pohl, J.

2007 *Sorcerers of the Fifth Heaven: Nahua Art and Ritual of Ancient Southern Mexico.* Princeton University Program in Latin American Studies, Cuadernos 9. Princeton, N.J.

Pollock, H.E.D.

1954 Excavations in Mayapan. *Carnegie Institution of Washington Yearbook* 53:277–79.

1980 *The Puuc: An Architectural Survey of the Hill Country of Yucatan and Northern Campeche, Mexico.* Memoirs of the Peabody Museum of Archaeology and Ethnology no. 19. Harvard University, Cambridge, Mass.

Pollock, H.E.D., R. L. Roys, T. Proskouriakoff, and A. L. Smith

1962 *Mayapán, Yucatán, Mexico.* Publication 619. Carnegie Institution of Washington, Washington, D.C.

Ponce de León, M.J.I.

2003 Problematical Deposits and the Problem of Interaction: The Material Culture of Tikal during the Early Classic Period. In *The Maya and Teotihuacan: Reinterpreting Early Classic Interaction*, edited by G. E. Braswell, 167–98. University of Texas Press, Austin.

Pool, C. A., and G. J. Bey III

2007 Conceptual Issues in Mesoamerican Pottery Economics. In *Pottery Economics in Mesoamerica*, edited by C. A. Pool and G. J. Bey III, 1–38. University of Arizona Press, Tucson.

Pring, D.

1977a Influence or Intrusion? The "Protoclassic" in the Maya Lowlands. In *Social Process in Maya Prehistory*, edited by N. Hammond, 135–65. Academic Press, London.

1977b *The Preclassic Ceramics of Northern Belize*. Unpublished Ph.D. dissertation, Institute of Archaeology, University College London.

2000 *The Protoclassic in the Maya Lowlands*. BAR International Series 908. British Archaeological Reports, Oxford.

Pring, D., and N. Hammond

1985 Investigation of a Possible River Port at Nohmul. In *Nohmul: A Prehistoric Maya Community in Belize*, edited by N. Hammond, 527–66. BAR International Series 205 (2). British Archaeological Reports, Oxford.

Proskouriakoff, T.

1962 Civic and Religious Structures of Mayapán. In *Mayapán Yucatán Mexico*, edited by H.E.D. Pollock, 87–164. Publication 619. Carnegie Institution of Washington, Washington, D.C.

Proskouriakoff, T., and C. R. Temple

1955 A Residential Quadrangle—Structures R-85 to R-90. *Carnegie Institution of Washington Current Reports* 29, 289–361.

Pugh, T. W.

1996 La Zona del Lago Salpetén-Zacpetén. In *Proyecto Maya-Colonial: Geografía Política del Siglo XVII en el Centro del Petén, Guatemala*, edited by D. S. Rice, P. M. Rice, R. S. Polo, and G. D. Jones, 206–21. Informe Preliminar al Instituto de Antropología e Historia de Guatemala sobre Investigaciones del Campo en los Años 1994 y 1995, Guatemala City.

2001a *Architecture, Ritual, and Social Identity at Late Postclassic Zacpetén, Petén, Guatemala: Identification of the Kowoj*. Unpublished Ph.D. dissertation, Department of Anthropology, Southern Illinois University, Carbondale.

2001b Flood Reptiles, Serpent Temples, and the Quadripartite Universe: The Imago Mundi of Late Postclassic Mayapán. *Ancient Mesoamerica* 12:247–58.

2002 Remembering Mayapán: Kowoj Domestic Architecture as Social Metaphor and Power. In *The Dynamics of Power*, edited by M. O'Donovan, 301–23. Southern Illinois University Occasional Paper no. 30. Carbondale.

2003 The Exemplary Center of the Late Postclassic Kowoj Maya. *Latin American Antiquity* 14 (4): 408–30.

2004 Maya Temples and Worldviews at Conquest. Paper presented at the 69th Annual Meeting of the Society for American Archaeology, Montreal.

Pyburn, A. K.

1990 Settlement Patterns at Nohmul: Preliminary Results of Four Excavation Seasons. In *Precolumbian Population History in the Maya Lowlands*, edited by T. P. Culbert and D. S. Rice, 183–97. University of New Mexico Press, Albuquerque.

Quintana Bello, N.

1927 Informe sobre la Localización de Un Montículo en Tixmucuy y la Necesidad de Poceder a la Limpieza de las Tuinas de Chenhuhá, Acanmul, y Dzibilnocac. Archivo Técnico de la Dirección de Monumentos Prehispánicos, Instituto Nacional de Antropología e Historia, Mexico City.

Rands, R. L.

1967 Ceramic Technology and Trade in the Palenque Region, Mexico. In *American Historical Anthropology*, edited by C. L. Riley and W. W. Taylor, 137–51. Southern Illinois University Press, Carbondale.

1979 Thematic and Compositional Variation in Palenque-Region Incensarios. In *Proceedings of the Tercera Mesa Redonda de Palenque, Vol. 4*, edited by M. G. Robertson and D. C. Jeffers, 19–30. Pre-Columbian Art Research Center, San Francisco.

Rands, R. L., and R. L. Bishop

1980 Resource Procurement Zones and Patterns of Ceramic Exchange in the Palenque Region, Mexico. In *Models and Methods in Regional Exchange*, edited by R. E. Fry, 19–46. SAA Papers no. 1. Society for American Archaeology, Washington, D.C.

Rathje, W. L.

1972 Praise the Gods and Pass the Metates: A Hypothesis of the Development of Lowland Rainforest Civilizations in Mesoamerica. In *Contemporary Archaeology: A Guide to Theory and Contributions*, edited by M. P. Leone, 405–54. Southern Illinois University Press, Carbondale.

Reents-Budet, D.

1994 *Painting the Maya Universe: Royal Ceramics of the Classic Period*. Duke University Press, Durham, N.C.

2000 Feasting among the Classic Maya: Evidence from the Pictorial Ceramics. In *The Maya Vase Book, Vol. 6*, edited by B. Kerr and J. Kerr, 1032–37. Kerr Associates, New York.

Reents-Budet, D., R. L. Bishop, and B. MacLeod

1994 Painting Styles, Workshop Locations, and Pottery Production. In *Painting the Maya Universe: Royal Ceramics of the Classic Period*, 164–233. Duke University Press, Durham, N.C.

Reents-Budet, D., R. L. Bishop, J. T. Taschek, and J. W. Ball

2000 Out of the Palace Dumps: Ceramic Production and Use at Buenavista del Cayo. *Ancient Mesoamerica* 11 (1): 99–121.

Reents-Budet, D., A. E. Foias, R. L. Bishop, M. J. Blackman, and S. Guenter

2007 Interacciones Políticas y Sitio Ik' (Motul de San José): Datos de la Céramica. In *XX Simposio de Investigaciones Arqueológicas en Guatemala, 2006*, edited by J.

P. Laporte, B. Arroyo, and H. Mejía, 1416–36. Museo Nacional de Arqueología y Etnología, Guatemala City.

Reese-Taylor, K., and D. Walker

2002 The Passage of the Late Preclassic in the Early Classic. In *Ancient Maya Political Economies*, edited by M. A. Masson and D. Freidel, 87–122. Altamira Press, Walnut Creek, Calif.

Reina, R. E., and R. M. Hill

1978 *The Traditional Pottery of Guatemala*. University of Texas Press, Austin.

Renfrew, C.

1975 Trade as Action at a Distance: Questions of Integration and Communication. In *Ancient Civilization and Trade*, edited by J. A. Sabloff and C. C. Lamberg-Karlovsky, 3–59. University of New Mexico Press, Albuquerque.

Rice, D. S.

1986 The Petén Postclassic: A Settlement Perspective. In *Late Lowland Maya Civilization: Classic to Postclassic*, edited by J. A. Sabloff and E. W. Andrews V, 301–45. School of American Research, University of New Mexico Press, Albuquerque.

Rice, D. S., and P. M. Rice

2004 History in the Future: Historical Data and Investigations in Lowland Maya Studies. In *Continuities and Changes in Maya Archaeology: Perspectives at the Millennium*, edited by C. W. Golden and G. Borgstede, 77–95. Routledge, New York.

Rice, D. S., P. M. Rice, R. Sánchez Polo, and G. D. Jones

1996 *Proyecto Maya-Colonial: Geografía Política del Siglo XVII en el Centro del Petén, Guatemala*. Informe Preliminar al Instituto de Antropología e Historia de Guatemala sobre Investigaciones del Campo en los Años 1994 y 1995. Guatemala City.

Rice, P. M.

1976 Rethinking the Ware Concept. *American Antiquity* 41 (4): 538–43.

1979 Ceramic and Nonceramic Artifacts of Lakes Yaxhá-Sacnab, El Petén, Guatemala, Part 1, The Ceramics; Section B, Postclassic Pottery from Topoxté. *Cerámica de Cultura Maya* 11:1–86.

1980 Petén Postclassic Pottery Production and Exchange: A View from Macanche. In *Models and Methods in Regional Exchange*, edited by R. E. Fry, 67–82. SAA Papers no. 1. Society for American Archaeology, Washington, D.C.

1981 Evolution of Specialized Pottery Production: A Trial Model. *Current Anthropology* 22 (3): 219–40.

1982 Pottery Production, Pottery Classification, and the Role of Physiochemical Analysis. In *Archaeological Ceramics*, edited by J. S. Olin and A. D. Franklin, 47–56. Smithsonian Institution Press, Washington, D.C.

1983 Serpents and Styles in Petén Postclassic Pottery. *American Anthropologist* 85:866–80.

1985 Reptilian Imagery and Vessel Function in Petén Postclassic Pottery: A Preliminary View. In *Fifth Palenque Round Table*, edited by M. G. Robertson and V. M. Fields, 115–22. Pre-Columbian Research Institute, San Francisco.

1987a Economic Change in the Lowland Maya Late Classic. In *Specialization, Ex-*

change, and Complex Societies, edited by E. M. Brumfiel and T. K. Earle, 76–85. Cambridge University Press, Cambridge.

1987b *Macanche Island, El Petén, Guatemala: Excavations, Pottery, and Artifacts*. University of Florida Press, Gainesville.

1987c *Pottery Analysis: A Sourcebook*. University of Chicago Press, Chicago.

1989 Reptiles and Rulership: A Stylistic Analysis of Petén Postclassic Pottery. In *Word and Image in Maya Culture*, edited by W. F. Hanks and D. S. Rice, 306–18. University of Utah Press, Salt Lake City.

1991 Specialization, Standardization, and Diversity: A Retrospective. In *The Ceramic Legacy of Anna O. Shepard*, edited by R. L. Bishop and F. W. Lange, 257–79. University Press of Colorado, Boulder.

1997 Tin-Enameled Ceramics of Moquegua, Peru. In *Approaches to the Historical Archaeology of Mexico, Central and South America*, edited by J. Gasco, G. C. Smith, and P. Fournier-García, 173–80. Institute of Archaeology Press, University of California, Los Angeles.

1999 Rethinking Classic Lowland Maya Pottery Censers. *Ancient Mesoamerica* 10:25–50.

Rice, P. M., and L. G. Cecil

2009 The Iconography and Decorative Programs of Kowoj Ceramics. In *The Kowoj: Identity, Migration, and Geopolitics in Late Postclassic Petén, Guatemala*, edited by P. M. Rice and D. S. Rice, 238–75. University of Colorado Press, Boulder.

Rice, P. M., and D. W. Forsyth

2004 Terminal Classic-Period Lowland Ceramics. In *The Terminal Classic in the Maya Lowlands: Collapse, Transition, and Transformation*, edited by A. Demarest, P. M. Rice, and D. S. Rice, 28–59. University Press of Colorado, Boulder.

Ringle, W. M., G. J. Bey III, T. B. Freeman, C. A. Hanson, C. W. Houck, and J. G. Smith

2004 The Decline in the East: The Classic to Postclassic Transition at Ek Balam, Yucatán. In *The Terminal Classic in the Maya Lowlands: Collapse, Transition, and Transformation*, edited by A. Demarest, P. M. Rice, and D. S. Rice, 485–516. University Press of Colorado, Boulder.

Robles Castellanos, F.

1986 Cronologia Ceramica de El Meco. In *Excavaciones Arqueológicas en El Meco, Quintana Roo*, edited by A. P. Andrews and F. R. Castellanos, 77–130. Colección Cientifica, Instituto Nacional de Antropología e Historia, Mexico City.

1990 *La Sequencia Cerámica de la Region de Cobá, Quintana Roo*. Coleccion Cientifica 184. Instituto Nacional de Antropología e Historia, Mexico City.

Rouse, I.

1939 *Prehistory in Haiti: A Study in Method*. Yale University Publications in Anthropology no. 21. New Haven, Conn.

1960 The Classification of Artifacts in Archaeology. *American Antiquity* 25 (3): 313–23.

Rovner, I.

1974 Implications of the Lithic Sequence at Becán. In *Preliminary Reports on Archaeological Investigations in the Rio Bec Area, Campeche, Mexico*, edited by R.E.W. Adams, 103–46. Middle American Research Institute Publication 31. Tulane University, New Orleans.

1975 Lithic Sequences from the Maya Lowlands. Unpublished Ph.D. dissertation, Department of Anthropology, University of Wisconsin, Madison.

Rovner, I., and S. M. Lewenstein

1997 *Maya Stone Tools of Dzibilchaltún, Yucatán, and Becán and Chicanná, Campeche.* Middle American Research Institute Publication 65. Tulane University, New Orleans.

Roys, R. L.

1933 *The Book of Chilam Balam of Chumayel.* Publication 438. Carnegie Institution of Washington, Washington, D.C.

1957 *The Political Geography of the Yucatán Maya.* Publication 613. Carnegie Institution of Washington, Washington, D.C.

1962 Literary Sources for the History of Mayapán. In *Mayapán, Yucatán, Mexico,* edited by H.E.D. Pollock, 25–86. Publication 619. Carnegie Institution of Washington, Washington, D.C.

Russell, B. W.

2000 *Postclassic Pottery Censers in the Maya Lowlands: A Study of Form, Function, and Symbolism.* Unpublished master's (MA) thesis, Department of Anthropology. State University of New York, Albany.

2007 *Postclassic Maya Settlement on the Rural-Urban Fringe of Mayapán, Yucatan, Mexico: Results of the Mayapán Periphery Project.* Unpublished Ph.D. dissertation, Department of Anthropology, State University of New York, Albany.

Sabloff, J. A.

1975 *Excavations at Seibal: Ceramics.* Memoirs of the Peabody Museum of Archaeology and Ethnology, vol. 13, no. 2. Harvard University, Cambridge, Mass.

2003 Preface to *Tikal: Dynasties, Foreigners, & Affairs of State,* edited by J. A. Sabloff, xvii–xxiii. School of American Research Press, Santa Fe, N.Mex.

2004 Looking Backward and Looking Forward: How Maya Studies of Yesterday Shape Today. In *Continuities and Changes in Maya Archaeology: Perspectives at the Millennium,* edited by C. W. Golden and G. Borgstede, 13–20. Routledge, New York.

Sabloff, J. A., and W. L. Rathje

1975 The Rise of a Maya Merchant Class. *Scientific American* 233:72–82.

Sabloff, J. A., W. L. Rathje, D. A. Freidel, J. C. Connor, and P.L.W. Sabloff

1974 Trade and Power in Postclassic Yucatán: Initial Observations. In *Mesoamerican Archaeology: New Approaches,* edited by N. Hammond, 396–416. University of Texas Press, Austin.

Sabloff, J. A., and R. E. Smith

1969 The Importance of Both Analytic and Taxonomic Classification in the Type-Variety System. *American Antiquity* 34 (3): 278–85.

Sachse, F. (editor)

2006 *Maya Ethnicity: The Construction of Ethnic Identity from Preclassic to Modern Times.* Acta Mesoamerica 19. Anton Saurwein, Markt Schwaben.

Sackett, J. R.

1990 Style and Ethnicity in Archaeology: The Case for Isochrestism. In *The Uses of Style in Archaeology,* edited by M. W. Conkey and C. A. Hastorf, 32–43. Cambridge University Press, Cambridge.

Schele, L., and N. Grube

1995 *The Proceedings of the Maya Hieroglyph Workshop: Late Classic and Terminal Classic Warfare, March 11–12, 1995*. Transcribed and edited by Phil Wanyerka. University of Texas, Austin.

Schele, L., N. Grube, and E. Boot

1995 *Some Suggestions on the Katun Prophecies in the Books of the Chilam Balam in Light of Classic Period History*. Texas Notes on Precolumbian Art, Writing and Culture no. 72. University of Texas Press, Austin.

Schele, L., and P. Mathews

1998 *The Code of Kings: The Language of Seven Sacred Maya Temples and Tombs*. Scribner, New York.

Schiffer, M. B.

1987 *Formation Processes of the Archaeological Record*. University of New Mexico Press, Albuquerque.

Schmidt, P. J.

1994 Chichén Itzá. *Arqueología Mexicana* 2 (10): 20–25.

2006 Nuevos Hallazgos en Chichén Itzá. *Arqueología Mexicana* 13 (76): 48–55.

Schortman, E. M.

1989 Interregional Interaction in Prehistory: The Need for a New Perspective. *American Antiquity* 54:52–65.

Sharer, R. J.

1978 *The Prehistory of Chalchuapa, Vol. 3*. University of Pennsylvania Press, Philadelphia.

2005 *The Ancient Maya*. 6th ed. Stanford University Press, Stanford.

Sharer, R. J., and A. F. Chase

1976 The New Town Ceramic Complex. In *Prehistoric Pottery Analysis and the Ceramics of Barton Ramie*, by J. C. Gifford, 288–315. Memoirs of the Peabody Museum of Archaeology and Ethnology, vol. 18. Harvard University, Cambridge, Mass.

Sharer, R. J., and J. C. Gifford

1970 Preclassic Ceramics from Chalchuapa, El Salvador, and Their Relationship with the Maya Lowlands. *American Antiquity* 35 (4): 441–62.

Sharer, R. J., and L. Traxler

2006 *The Ancient Maya*. 6th ed. Stanford University Press, Stanford.

Sheets, P.

1979a Environmental and Cultural Effects of the Ilopango Eruption in Central America. In *Volcanic Activity and Human Ecology*, edited by P. Sheets and D. Grayson, 525–64. Academic Press, New York.

1979b Maya Recovery from Volcanic Disasters Ilopango and Ceren. *Archaeology* 32:32–44.

Shepard, A. O.

1948 *Plumbate: A Mesoamerican Trade Ware*. Publication 573. Carnegie Institution of Washington, Washington, D.C.

1956 *Ceramics for the Archaeologist*. Publication 609. Carnegie Institution of Washington, Washington, D.C.

Shook, E. M., and W. N. Irving

1955 Colonnaded Buildings at Mayapan. *Current Reports no.* 22, 127–224. Department of Archaeology, Carnegie Institution of Washington, Washington, D.C.

Sidrys, R. W.

1983 *Archaeological Excavations in Northern Belize*. Institute of Archaeology, University of California, Los Angeles.

Sidrys, R. W., and C. Crowne

1983 The Aventura Double Mouth Jar. In *Archaeological Excavations in Northern Belize, Central America*, edited by R. V. Sidrys, 221–37. Mongraph 17. Institute of Archaeology, University of California.

Sierra Sosa, T. N.

1999 Xcambó: Codiciado Enclave Económico del Clásico Maya. *Arqueología Mexicana* 7 (37): 40–47.

2001 Xcambó. *Mexicon* 23 (2): 27.

Simmons, M. P.

1981 The Archaeological Ceramics of Dzibilchaltún, Yucatan, Mexico: The Ceramic Typology. Manuscript draft on file, Middle American Research Institute, Tulane University, New Orleans, and Centro Regional del Sureste, Instituto Nacional de Antropología e Historia, Merida.

Smith, C. A.

1976 Exchange Systems and the Spatial Distribution of Elites: The Organization of Stratification in Agrarian Societies. In *Regional Analysis, Vol.* 2, edited by C. A. Smith, 309–74. Academic Press, New York.

Smith, F. T.

1989 Earth, Vessels, and Harmony among the Gurensi. *African Arts* 22 (2): 94–200.

Smith, M. E.

1979 A Further Criticism of the Type-Variety System: The Data Can't Be Used. *American Antiquity* 44 (4): 822–26.

2003 Small Polities in Postclassic Mesoamerica. In *The Postclassic Mesoamerican World*, edited by M. E. Smith and F. M. Berdan, 35–39. University of Utah Press, Salt Lake City.

Smith, M. E., and F. Berdan

2000 The Postclassic Mesoamerican World System. *Current Anthropology* 41:283–86.

Smith, M. E., and F. F. Berdan

2003 Spatial Structure of the Mesoamerican World System. In *The Postclassic Mesoamerican World*, edited by M. E. Smith and F. F. Berdan, 21–31. University of Utah Press, Salt Lake City.

Smith, R. E.

1952 *Pottery from Chipoc, Alta Verapaz, Guatemala*. Contributions to American Anthropology and History no. 56. Carnegie Institution of Washington, Washington, D.C.

1955 *Ceramic Sequence at Uaxactun, Guatemala*. Middle American Research Institute Publication 20. Tulane University, New Orleans.

1971 *The Pottery of Mayapán*. Papers of the Peabody Museum of Archaeology and Ethnology, vol. 66. Harvard University, Cambridge, Mass.

Smith, R. E., and J. C. Gifford

1965 Pottery of the Maya Lowlands. In *Handbook of Middle American Indians, Vol. 2*, edited by R. Wauchope and G. R. Willey, 498–534. University of Texas Press, Austin.

1966 *Maya Ceramic Varieties, Types, and Wares at Uaxactun: Supplement to "Ceramic Sequence at Uaxactun, Guatemala."* Middle American Research Institute Publication 28. Tulane University, New Orleans.

Smith, R. E., G. R. Willey, and J. C. Gifford

1960 The Type-Variety Concept as a Basis for the Analysis of Maya Pottery. *American Antiquity* 25 (3): 330–40.

Smyth, M. P., and C. D. Dore

1992 Large-Site Archaeological Methods at Sayil, Yucatan, Mexico: Investigating Community Organization at a Prehispanic Maya Center. *Latin American Antiquity* 3:3–21.

Smyth, Michael P., Christopher D. Dore, Hector Neff, and Michael D. Glascock

1995 The Origin of Puuc Slate Ware: New Data from Sayil, Yucatan, Mexico. *Ancient Mesoamerica* 6 (2):119–34.

Spaulding, A. C.

1953 Statistical Techniques for the Discovery of Artifact Types. *American Antiquity* 18:305–13.

1974 Review of "Systematics in Prehistory" by Robert C. Dunnell. *American Antiquity* 39 (3): 513–16.

Speakman, R. J.

2005 *Laser Ablation-Icp-Ms in Archaeological Research*. University of New Mexico Press, Albuquerque.

Stanton, T. W., and T. Gallareta Negrón

2001 Warfare, Ceramic Economy, and the Itza. *Ancient Mesoamerica* 12:229–45.

Stark, B. L.

1992 Ceramic Production in Prehistoric La Mixtequilla, South Central Veracruz, Mexico. In *Ceramic Production and Distribution: An Integrated Approach*, edited by G. J. Bey III and C. A. Pool, 175–204. Westview Press, Boulder, Colo.

Stark, M. T.

1994 Pottery Exchange and the Regional System: A Dalupa Case Study. In *Kalinga Ethnoarchaeology: Expanding Archaeological Method and Theory*, edited by W. A. Longacre and J. M. Skibo, 169–67. Smithsonian Institution Press, Washington, D.C.

1998 *The Archaeology of Social Boundaries*. Smithsonian Institution Press, Washington, D.C.

1999 Social Dimensions of Technical Choice in Kalinga Ceramic Traditions. In *Material Meanings: Critical Approaches to the Interpretation of Material Culture*, edited by E. S. Chilton, 24–43. University of Utah Press, Salt Lake City.

Stark, M. T., R. L. Bishop, and E. Miksa

2000 Ceramic Technology and Social Boundaries: Cultural Practices in Kalinga Clay Selection and Use. *Journal of Archaeological Method and Theory* 7 (4): 295–331.

Sterner, J.

1989 Who Is Signaling Whom? Ceramic Style, Ethnicity, and Taphonomy among Sirak Bullahay. *Antiquity* 63:451–59.

Strelow, D., and L. LeCount

2001 Regional Interaction in the Formative Southern Maya Lowlands: Evidence of Olmecoid Stylistic Motifs in a Cunil Ceramic Assemblage from Xunantunich, Belize. Poster presented at the 66th Annual Meeting of the Society for American Archaeology, New Orleans.

Suhler, C. K., T. Ardren, D. Freidel, and D. Johnston

2004 The Rise and Fall of Terminal Classic Yaxuna, Yucatán, Mexico. In *The Terminal Classic in the Maya Lowlands: Collapse, Transition, and Transformation*, edited by A. Demarest, P. M. Rice, and D. S. Rice, 450–84. University Press of Colorado, Boulder.

Suhler, C. K., T. Ardren, and D. Johnston

1998 The Chronology of Yaxuna: Evidence from Excavations and Ceramics. *Ancient Mesoamerica* 9:167–82.

Sullivan, L. A.

2002 Dynamics of Regional Integration in Northwestern Belize. In *Ancient Maya Political Economies*, edited by M. A. Masson and D. Freidel, 197–222. Altamira Press, Walnut Creek, Calif.

2006 Cahal Pech Petrography: Results from the 2005 Season. In *The Belize Valley Archaeology Project: Results of the 2005 Field Season*, edited by J. F. Garber, 63–78. Report submitted to the Institute of Archaeology, National Institute of Culture and History, Belmopan, Belize.

Sullivan, L. A., J. J. Awe, and M. K. Brown

2008 Refining the Cunil Ceramic Complex. Paper presented at the 73rd Annual Meeting of the Society for American Archaeology. Vancouver.

Taube, K. A.

1989 Ritual Humor in Classic Maya Religion. In *Word and Image in Maya Culture*, edited by W. F. Hanks and D. S. Rice, 351–82. University of Utah Press, Salt Lake City.

1992 *The Major Gods of Ancient Yucatán*. Studies in Pre-Columbian Art and Archaeology no. 32. Dumbarton Oaks Research Library and Collection, Washington, D.C.

1998 The Jade Hearth: Centrality, Rulership, and the Classic Maya Temple. In *Function and Meaning in Classic Maya Architecture*, edited by S. D. Houston, 427–78. Dumbarton Oaks Research Library and Collection, Washington, D.C.

Taube, K. A., Z. Hruby, and L. Romero

2005 Jadeite Sources and Ancient Workshops: Archaeological Reconnaissance in the Upper Rio El Tamblor, Guatemala. Electronic document, http://www.famsi.org/reports/03023/index.html, accessed April 5, 2012.

Taylor, W. W.

1983 *A Study of Archaeology*. Center for Archaeological Investigations, Southern Illinois University, Carbondale. Originally published 1948.

Thomas, P. M., Jr.

1981 *Prehistoric Maya Settlement Patterns at Becán, Campeche, Mexico*. Middle American Research Institute Publication 45. Tulane University, New Orleans.

Thompson, J.E.S.

1931 *Archaeological Investigations in the Southern Cayo District, British Honduras*. Publication 301. Field Museum of Natural History, Chicago.

1939 *Excavations at San Jose, British Honduras*. Publication 506. Carnegie Institution of Washington, Washington, D.C.

1957 Deities Portrayed on Censers at Mayapán. *Current Report No. 40*, 599–632. Department of Archaeology, Carnegie Institute of Washington, Washington, D.C.

1970 *Maya History and Religion*. University of Oklahoma Press, Norman.

1972 *A Commentary on the Dresden Codex: A Maya Hieroglyphic Book*. American Philosophical Society, Philadelphia.

Thompson, R. H.

1958 *Modern Yucatecan Maya Pottery Making*. Society for American Archaeology Memoir 15. Salt Lake City.

Tozzer, A. M.

1941 *Landa's Relacion de Las Cosas de Yucatán*. Papers of the Peabody Museum of Archaeology and Ethnology, vol. 18. Harvard University, Cambridge, Mass.

Urban, P.

1993a Central Santa Barbara Region. In *Pottery of Prehistoric Honduras: Regional Classification and Analysis*, edited by J. S. Henderson and M. Beaudry-Corbett, 136–70. Institute of Archaeology, University of California, Los Angeles.

1993b Naco Valley. In *Pottery of Prehistoric Honduras: Regional Classification and Analysis*, edited by J. S. Henderson and M. Beaudry-Corbett, 30–63. Institute of Archaeology, University of California, Los Angeles.

Urban, P. A., and E. M. Schortman

1987 Copan and Its Neighbors: Patterns of Interaction Reflected in Classic Period Western Honduran Pottery. In *Maya Ceramics: Papers from the 1985 Maya Ceramic Conference*, edited by P. M. Rice and R. J. Sharer, 341–95. BAR International Series 345 (2). British Archaeological Reports, Oxford.

Vaillant, G. C.

1927 *The Chronological Significance of Maya Ceramics*. Unpublished Ph.D. dissertation, Department of Anthropology, Harvard University, Cambridge.

Valdez, F.

1987 *The Prehistoric Ceramics of Colha, Northern Belize*. Unpublished Ph.D. dissertation, Department of Anthropology, Harvard University, Cambridge.

Valdez, F., Jr., L. J. Kosakowsky, L. A. Sullivan, and D. Pring

2008 The Earliest Ceramics of Belize: A Comparative Analysis. Paper presented at the 73rd Annual Meeting of the Society for American Archaeology, Vancouver.

Vásquez, A. B.

1941 Sobre la Significación de Algunos Nobres de Signos del Calendario Maya. In *Los Antiguos Mayas*, 81–88. El Colegio de Mexico, Mexico City.

Villacorta C., J. A., and C. A. Villacorta

1976 *Códices Mayas*. Tipografía Nacional, Guatemala City.

Vogt, E. Z.

1994 *Fieldwork among the Maya: Reflections on the Harvard Chiapas Project.* University of New Mexico Press, Albuquerque.

Walker, D. S.

1990 *Cerros Revisited: Ceramic Indicators of Terminal Classic and Postclassic Settlement and Pilgrimage in Northern Belize.* Unpublished Ph.D. dissertation, Department of Anthropology, Southern Methodist University, Dallas.

Walker, D. S., K. Reese-Taylor, and P. Mathews

2006 Después de La Caída: Una Redefinición del Clásico Temprano Maya. In *XIX Simposio de Investigaciones Arqueológicas en Guatemala, 2005*, edited by J. P. Laporte, B. Arroyo, and H. E. Mejía, 659–71. Ministerio de Cultura y Deportes, IDAEH, Asociación Tikal, Fundación Arqueológica del Nuevo Mundo. Guatemala City.

Washburn, D. K., W. N. Washburn, and P. A. Shipkova

2011 The Prehistoric Drug Trade: Widespread Consumption of Cacao in Ancestral Pueblo and Hohokam Communities in the American Southwest. *Journal of Archaeological Science* 38:1634–40.

Webster, D. L., A. Freter, and R. Storey

2004 Dating Copán Culture-History: Implications for the Terminal Classic and the Collapse. In *The Terminal Classic in the Maya Lowlands: Collapse, Transition, and Transformation*, edited by A. Demarest, P. M. Rice, and D. S. Rice, 231–59. University Press of Colorado, Boulder.

Weigand, Phil C., Garman Harbottle, and Edward V. Sayre

1977 Turquoise Source and Source Analysis: Mesoamerica and the Southwestern U.S.A. In *Exchange Systems in Prehistory*, edited by Timothy K. Earle and Jonathan E. Ericson, 15–34. Academic Press, New York.

West, G.

2002 Ceramic Exchange in the Late Classic and Postclassic Maya Lowlands: A Diachronic Approach. In *Ancient Maya Political Economies*, edited by M. A. Masson and D. Freidel, 140–96. Altamira Press, Walnut Creek, Calif.

Wetherington, R. K. (editor)

1978a *The Ceramics of Kaminaljuyu, Guatemala.* Pennsylvania State University Press, University Park.

Wetherington, R. K.

1978b Ceramic Analysis: The Methodology of the Kaminaljuyu Project. In *The Ceramics of Kaminaljuyu, Guatemala*, edited by R. K. Wetherington, 3–50. Pennsylvania State University Press, University Park.

Wheat, J. B., J. C. Gifford, and W. W. Wasley

1958 Ceramic Variety, Type Cluster, and Ceramic System in Southwestern Pottery Analysis. *American Antiquity* 24 (1): 34–47.

Whittaker, J. C., D. Caulkins, and K. A. Kamp

1998 Evaluating Consistency in Typology and Classification. *Journal of Archaeological Method and Theory* 5 (2): 129–64.

Wiessner, P.

1990 Is There a Unity to Style? In *The Uses of Style in Archaeology*, edited by M. W. Conkey and C. A. Hastorf, 105–21. Cambridge University Press, Cambridge.

Wille, S. J.
2007 *Sociopolitics and Community-Building: The Entanglement of pre-Hispanic Maya Culture, Objects and Place at Chau Hiix, Belize.* Unpublished Ph.D. dissertation, Department of Anthropology, Indiana University.

Willey, G. R.
1945 Horizon Styles and Pottery Traditions in Peruvian Archaeology. *American Antiquity* 11 (1): 49–56.
1977 The Rise of Maya Civilization: A Summary View. In *The Origins of Maya Civilization*, edited by R.E.W. Adams, 383–423. University of New Mexico Press, Albuquerque.

Willey, G. R., W. R. Bullard Jr., J. C. Gifford, and J. B. Glass
1965 *Prehistoric Maya Settlements in the Belize Valley.* Papers of the Peabody Museum of Archaeology and Ethnology, vol. 54. Harvard University, Cambridge, Mass.

Willey, G. R., T. P. Culbert, and R.E.W. Adams
1967 Maya Lowland Ceramics: A Report from the 1965 Guatemala City Conference. *American Antiquity* 32:289–315.

Willey, G. R., and J. C. Gifford
1961 Pottery of the Holmul I Style from Barton Ramie, British Honduras. In *Essays in Pre-Columbian Art and Archaeology*, edited by S. K. Lothrop, 155–70. Oxford University Press, London.

Willey, G. R., R. M. Leventhal, A. Demarest, and W. L. Fash
1994 *Ceramics and Artifacts from Excavations in the Copan Residential Zone.* Papers of the Peabody Museum of Archaeology and Ethnology, vol. 80. Harvard University, Cambridge, Mass.

Willey, G. R., and J. A. Sabloff
1980 *A History of American Archaeology.* W. H. Freeman, San Francisco.

Williams-Beck, L. A.
1994 The Chenes Ceramic Sequence: Temporal, Typological, and Cultural Relations within a Regional Framework. In *Hidden among the Hills: Maya Archaeology of the Northwest Yucatan Peninsula*, edited by H. J. Prem, 133–63. Von Felmming, Möckmühl.
1999 *Tiempo en Trozos: Cerámica de la Región de Los Chenes, Campeche, México.* Universidad Autónoma de Campeche, Campeche.
2001 *Proyecto Territorio y Poder en la Provincia Ah Canul, Campeche: Historia Diacrónica Regional—Acanmul, El Cuyo y San Francisco de Campeche.* Informe de Investigación 2001; Propuesta de Investigación 2002. Centro de Investigaciones Históricas y Sociales, Universidad Autónoma de Campeche, Campeche.

Williams-Beck, L. A., and E. López de la Rosa
1999 Historía de Tres Ciudades: Ah Kin Pech, Acanmul, y San Francisco de Campeche. *Estudios de Cultura Maya* 20:93–116.

Willie, S. J.
2007 *Sociopolitics and Community-Building: The Entanglement of Pre-Hispanic Maya Culture, Objects and Place at Chau Hiix, Belize.* Unpublished Ph.D. dissertation, Department of Anthropology, Indiana University, Bloomington.

Winters, H. D.

1955 Excavation of a Colonnaded Hall at Mayapan. In *Current Reports no. 31*, 381–96. Department of Archaeology, Carnegie Institution of Washington, Washington, D.C.

Wobst, M. H.

1977 Stylistic Behavior and Information Exchange. In *For the Director: Research Essays in Honor of James B. Griffin*, edited by C. Clelland, 317–42. Anthropological Papers no. 61. University of Michigan, Museum of Anthropology, Ann Arbor.

Wonderley, A.

1981 *Late Postclassic Excavations at Naco, Honduras.* Latin American Studies Program Dissertation Series no. 86. Cornell University, Ithaca, N.Y.

Contributors

James John Aimers is associate professor of anthropology at the State University of New York (SUNY), Geneseo.

Marne T. Ausec directs the Center for Global Engagement at Kenyon College in Ohio.

Jaime J. Awe directs the Institute of Archaeology of the National Institute of Culture and History (NICH) in Belize.

Joseph Ball is Distinguished Professor of Anthropology at San Diego State University.

Cassandra R. Bill is faculty in the Anthropology Department at Capilano University in North Vancouver, British Columbia, and in the Latin American Studies program at Langara College in Vancouver, British Columbia.

Michael G. Callaghan is visiting assistant professor in the Department of Anthropology at Southern Methodist University.

Leslie G. Cecil is assistant professor of anthropology at Stephen F. Austin State University, Texas.

Arlen F. Chase is University Pegasus Professor and chair of the Department of Anthropology at the University of Central Florida.

Diane Z. Chase is University Pegasus Professor and executive vice provost for academic affairs at the University of Central Florida.

Francisco Estrada-Belli is visiting assistant professor in the Archaeology Department at Boston University.

Robert E. Fry is professor emeritus in the Department of Anthropology at Purdue University in West Lafayette, Indiana.

Elizabeth Graham is Professor of Mesoamerican Archaeology at the Institute of Archaeology, University College London.

Susan Milbrath is curator of Latin American art and archaeology at the Florida Museum of Natural History and affiliate professor of anthropology at the University of Florida.

Nina Neivens de Estrada is a doctoral candidate at Tulane University in New Orleans.

Carlos Peraza Lope is archaeologist and project director with INAH Yucatan (National Institute of Anthropology and History) in Mexico.

Prudence M. Rice recently retired from her position as Distinguished Professor of Anthropology and associate vice chancellor for research at Southern Illinois University Carbondale.

Edward M. Schortman is J. K. Smail Professor of Anthropology at Kenyon College in Ohio.

Lauren A. Sullivan is senior lecturer in anthropology at the University of Massachusetts, Boston.

Jennifer Taschek is adjunct professor of anthropology at San Diego State University.

Patricia A. Urban is J. K. Smail Professor of Anthropology at Kenyon College in Ohio.

Index

Maya Studies

Edited by Diane Z. Chase and Arlen F. Chase

The books in this series will focus on both the ancient and the contemporary Maya peoples of Belize, Mexico, Guatemala, Honduras, and El Salvador. The goal of the series is to provide an integrated outlet for scholarly works dealing with Maya archaeology, epigraphy, ethnography, and history. The series will particularly seek cutting-edge theoretical works, methodologically sound site-reports, and tightly organized edited volumes with broad appeal.

Salt: White Gold of the Ancient Maya, by Heather McKillop (2002)

Archaeology and Ethnohistory of Iximché, by C. Roger Nance, Stephen L. Whittington, and Barbara E. Borg (2003)

The Ancient Maya of the Belize Valley: Half a Century of Archaeological Research, edited by James F. Garber (2003; first paperback edition, 2011)

Unconquered Lacandon Maya: Ethnohistory and Archaeology of the Indigenous Culture Change, by Joel W. Palka (2005)

Chocolate in Mesoamerica: A Cultural History of Cacao, edited by Cameron L. McNeil (2006; first paperback printing, 2009)

Maya Christians and Their Churches in Sixteenth-Century Belize, by Elizabeth Graham (2011)

Chan: An Ancient Maya Farming Community, edited by Cynthia Robin (2012; first paperback edition, 2013)

Motul de San José: Politics, History, and Economy in a Maya Polity, edited by Antonia E. Foias and Kitty F. Emery (2012)

Ancient Maya Pottery: Classification, Analysis, and Interpretation, edited by James John Aimers (2013; first paperback edition, 2014)

Ancient Maya Political Dynamics, by Antonia E. Foias (2013; first paperback edition, 2014)

www.ingramcontent.com/pod-product-compliance
Lightning Source LLC
Chambersburg PA
CBHW020829270326
41928CB00006B/463
9780813060927